THE NEW POLITICS OF IMMIGRATION AND THE END OF SETTLER SOCIETIES

Over the past decade, a global convergence in migration policies has emerged, and with it a new, mean-spirited politics of immigration. It is now evident that the idea of a settler society, previously an important landmark in understanding migration, is a thing of the past. What are the consequences of this shift for how we imagine immigration? And for how we regulate it?

This book analyzes the dramatic shift away from the settler society paradigm in light of the crisis of asylum, the fear of Islamic fundamentalism, and the demise of multiculturalism. What emerges is a radically original take on the new global politics of immigration that can explain policy paralysis in the face of rising death tolls, failing human rights arguments, and persistent state desires to treat migration as an economic calculus.

Catherine Dauvergne is Dean of Law at the University of British Columbia. She has published six books, including *Making People Illegal* (2008). As part of her *pro bono* legal work in migration law, Professor Dauvergne has represented the Canadian Council for Refugees before the Supreme Court of Canada. In 2012, she was named a Fellow of the Pierre Elliot Trudeau Foundation in recognition of her contributions to public issues in Canada.

The New Politics of Immigration and the End of Settler Societies

CATHERINE DAUVERGNE

University of British Columbia

CAMBRIDGE
UNIVERSITY PRESS

32 Avenue of the Americas, New York, NY 10013–2473, USA

Cambridge University Press is part of the University of Cambridge.

It furthers the University's mission by disseminating knowledge in the pursuit of education, learning, and research at the highest international levels of excellence.

www.cambridge.org
Information on this title: www.cambridge.org/9781107631236

© Catherine Dauvergne 2016

First published 2016

Printed in the United States of America by Sheridan Books, Inc.

A catalog record for this publication is available from the British Library.

ISBN 978-1-107-05404-2 Hardback
ISBN 978-1-107-63123-6 Paperback

Contents

Acknowledgements   *page* vii

Preface   ix

1 **Introduction**   1

2 **Settler societies and the immigration imagination**   10

PART 1 THE END OF SETTLER SOCIETIES   35

3 The asylum crisis   39

4 Fear of fundamental Islam   62

5 The end of multiculturalism   90

PART 2 THE NEW POLITICS   115

6 Why economics and human rights are not enough   117

7 The loss of settlement and society   124

8 The close of the post-colonial   150

9 Contours and consequences of a new politics   174

10 Imagining immigration without a past – stories
    for the future   201

Appendices   215

Bibliography   259

Index   285

Acknowledgements

I would not have written this book without the support of the Trudeau Foundation. In June 2012, the Foundation awarded me a Fellowship and with it a challenge. The Fellowship offered me more time than I otherwise would have had to undertake a book-length project. The challenge was to deliver a book that would speak not only to migration scholars and policy makers, but also to the Trudeau community more broadly. I have returned to this idea regularly throughout my work on *The New Politics of Immigration*, and while it is for others to assess whether I have reached this goal, it was undeniably a significant influence on the tenor and the ambitions of the book.

I am especially grateful to the anonymous reviewers and to Cambridge University Press for engaging such thought-provoking individuals to offer comments. I have often felt myself to be in conversation with these people over the final months of writing. Their views have shaped this undertaking more than has been the case in much of my other work.

I have also benefitted from engagement with audiences at the Oxford Human Rights Hub, the Graduate Institute of International and Development Studies in Geneva, and the Big Thinking lecture series at Canada's Congress for the Humanities and Social Sciences. I am especially grateful to the migration group at the University of Manitoba Faculty of Law who listened to me, and asked hard questions, at a crucial point in puzzling through the book's conclusion. My colleagues at the Allard School of Law have listened to me talk about this project on formal and informal occasions and have offered comment, critique, and correction with generosity and good humour.

A phalanx of research assistants at the Allard School of Law have worked with me on this endeavour over the past two years. Fatima Cader, Hannah Lindy, Brendan Naef, and Catherine Repel have each devoted hundreds of hours to this project and to listening patiently to my questions and musings. In the final stages of this work, Asha Kaushal read the manuscript with incisive intelligence and her customary grace, long past her years of actually working as a researcher for me.

Throughout this project my family has sustained me. There is not much more to be said on an open page than this statement alone. I am very lucky to have a scholarly partner who is willing to talk and read, day or night, about twists of argument and turns of phrase, and to say the most difficult things very gently. For Peter, Hugh, Nina, and Duncan, my love and greatest thanks.

Catherine Dauvergne
October 2015

Preface

This book was published at an important time for Western states grappling with immigration matters. More important, even, than I had imagined when I set to work on it in earnest in 2013. But fortuitous timing, from an author's point of view at least, brings unique challenges.

I sent the finalized manuscript off to be copy-edited late in June, 2015. The following week, the United Nations High Commissioner for Refugees released its 2014 data showing that the number of displaced persons in the world was, in that year, higher than at any time since World War II. Throughout July and August of 2015, the number of people flowing out of Syria and attempting to seek refugee protection in Europe grew astronomically. This surge of need led, predictably, to a rising death toll from clandestine Mediterranean crossings, with the numbers rising rapidly, during some weeks, daily. In the final week of August, German Chancellor Angela Merkel announced that Germany would stop enforcing the Dublin regulations and instead welcome those who reached Germany and process their refugee claims. At that time, German authorities were estimating that as many as 800,000 asylum seekers would arrive in Germany by the end of 2015. The estimate was revised to a million by mid-September.

The German announcement triggered a series of border openings and closings in the European states that stand between Germany and the Mediterranean shores where most Syrians first set foot in the European Union, or in Europe more broadly. Images of Hungary's new border fence being erected transfixed the Western media. Desperate people were filmed lifting their children over the fencing separating Serbia from Croatia. People continued to die attempting to reach Lampedusa and Lesbos.

And then in the first week of September, someone photographed the body of three-year old Aylan Kurdi lying dead on a Turkish beach. This image had already acquired iconic status by October 2015. It is an image that seems to have seized the conscience of the Western world.

The question is: To what end?

Finally, the world is watching.

It has been a quarter of a century since the world paid attention like this to refugees. Over that period of time, the attitudes of Western publics and politicians have hardened markedly, and just about every indicator of the situation of refugees around the globe has worsened. Refugee camps have become a permanent feature of the global landscape, conflicts in distant corners of the world have displaced tens of millions, powerful regimes have continued to invent new and horrifying ways to infringe the human rights of their citizens, tens of thousands have lost their lives trying to reach safety. Refugee advocates have railed against all of this – but most often their calls have gone unheeded.

In this current terrible moment, then, there is something precious and unique. Every Western politician is now paying attention to refugees, every policy maker is engaged refugee advocates have an attentive audience for the first time in the adult lives of many now working in the advocacy trenches. It is vital that we use this attention to make some fundamental and lasting change. But are we capable of doing so?

There is an important intersection here with the arc of my analysis in *The New Politics of Immigration*. The events of the past two months fit my narrative, even though I wish that it were not so. Already the image of Aylan Kurdi that people could not stop talking about is fading into iconography, and the children who died making the same crossing this past weekend have gone unnamed in the global press, and did not even make headlines in Canada where I sit today. The way in which the asylum crisis has become perpetual, and the political consequence of this perpetuity, are clearer now than ever.

The challenges that migration, and especially asylum, bring to European cooperation and identity, are writ large in these events. At great political effort an agreement to share the burden of supporting this massive influx of people was reached in mid-September. If this agreement is honoured, it will affect about 10 percent of those who had already arrived by that time. In the new politics, Europe is continuing to lead in defining what immigration means. This is true even though the majority of the world's asylum seekers continue, of course, to be elsewhere. Even the majority of Syrian refugees are in Lebanon and Jordan, places that have rarely reached the front pages of the Western press in the crisis-filled Northern autumn of 2015.

Germany's response to the current wave of people is unprecedented and remarkable. It too reflects strands of the new politics that I have written about in this book. Commentators have repeatedly asserted that Germany's actions reflect its World War II collective guilt. Such an assertion is not amenable to empirics. Nor is much of the new politics. As I have argued in the conclusion to this book, the new politics of immigration is woven together in an intricate dance of remembering and forgetting the past. It is never solely a calculus of economics or human rights; it speaks instead to something much harder to name.

The stance that Germany has taken up to mid-October 2015 belongs with those glimmers of something new that I attempted to gather up in the final pages of the book. A tiny fragment of optimism that immigration could be reimagined, as a counter to the overwhelmingly negative thrust of the current mean-spirited politics. As in the conclusion, where I attempted to sketch both an optimistic and a pessimistic way forward, pessimism has a stronger hand to play. Just google "European border fence."

As of today, I do not know how this current story will end. But I do know that crises like that facing Europe in October 2015 will multiply in the coming years. Their contours will be oppressively familiar unless we summon, somehow, a new way of imagining immigration. It is to this end that I have written *The New Politics of Immigration*. I would dearly love to imagine that by the time this book is being read, the story it tells will belong to some sort of bad old days when the problems of global migration seemed intractable. I doubt this will be so.

But because there is something nearly unprecedented about this particular point in time, let me dare to go a bit further. Seizing this moment means thinking about game changing strategies at the same time as urgently saving lives. Here are three things the world could do in this moment that would make things different the next time around.

First, change international refugee law to include a requirement for resettlement. Right now, no state is obligated to take in refugees from afar, and few do. An obligation to resettle should be part of the international legal regime.

Second, require that all states party to international refugee law contribute a set and predictable amount to a global refugee support fund. States that host fewer refugees should pay more, those that host more would pay less, those who host the most would receive money from the fund.

Third, strengthen the right to seek asylum by making refugee deterrence mechanisms overseas illegal and eliminating legal barriers (like safe third country provisions) to asylum. All Western liberal democracies (except, just now, Germany) are presently engaged in making it harder and harder to seek asylum. These efforts lead directly to bodies on beaches.

Each of these ideas is so far from current refugee politics that they have become unsayable. Refugee advocates dare not whisper ideas like these, even though we know that the path to real change begin must begin by setting out in a new direction.

This book aims to be a compass in that search.

1

Introduction

We see all around us the evidence of a new politics of immigration. On any given day in the major newspapers and Twitter feeds of Western states, there is some story about immigration. These stories span people needing refugee protection, people being deported, people threatening our border, people dying in search of a new home, people in detention, international students, wealthy investors buying up real estate, communities welcoming newcomers, or dividing along previously invisible cultural cleavages. Immigration is big news. And even bigger politics. President Obama has an immigration agenda. Chancellor Merkel and Prime Ministers Cameron, Turnbull, and Trudeau are regularly involved, along with almost every leader of a Western democratic state. Immigration is an issue in every election in Europe, North America, and the antipodes. And while much of the new politics of immigration is Western driven, Western states are not its only location. When Indian Prime Minister Modi visited Canada in 2015, one of the key issues covered by the Canadian press was whether the visit would be a catalyst for allowing Canadians to participate in a preferential visa scheme. Kenya has called for closure of the world's largest refugee camp. Kiribati is calling for new laws to allow its citizens rights of entry elsewhere when their island nation sinks below sea level. South Africa is grappling with anti-immigrant violence.

The newness of this politics is found in its intensity, its urgency, and its legality. Never before have immigration issues been at the center of the political stage in so many places at the same time. Never before has the political attention to immigration drawn such a highly legalized response. Never before has hostility towards immigrants been quite so widespread, and quite so nasty. The politics of immigration has taken a sharp turn in the early years of the twenty-first century. This turn is decisive and irrevocable, and we are only just beginning to grapple with the how and why of it.

For some time now, analysts have been writing about the global convergence of immigration policy. This convergence is a vital clue to explaining the new politics. The explanation takes the multilayered dimensions of convergence as a starting point and looks behind them to see what has changed, and what the consequences will be for the future. This leads to the insight that the new politics of immigration arises because the era of settler societies has ended. There is no longer any basis, other than history, for saying that settler societies are different in regard to migration than other Western liberal democracies. Instead, a global convergence in migration policies has emerged, bringing with it a new, mean-spirited politics of immigration. This change is vitally important at a time when the global pace of migration is higher than ever, and migration aspirations even higher. It is now evident that the idea of a settler society, previously an important landmark in understanding migration, is a thing of the past. What are the consequences of this for how we imagine immigration? And, following from this, for how we regulate it? This book explores this dramatic shift, mapping the contours of the new politics of immigration.

With the close of the settler society era, the foundations for our global understandings of migration have vanished. We are left with an architecture that is no longer grounded; it has lost its supports. Like any structure with a weakened base, our vocabulary and theoretical framing of immigration can no longer bear the weight that they once did.

There are important consequences of this shifting foundation and chief among them is policy paralysis. The vocabulary with which immigration was first imagined as a global phenomenon, the terms with which we came to understand immigration politically, publicly, and legally, have been hollowed out. When we use this old vocabulary, it has less traction than it once did, less precision and less substance. This contributes to policy paralysis because we keep trying to talk about something that we cannot quite name. It also nurtures paralysis because the old vocabulary opens a gulf between our policy objectives and what is happening on the ground. In scientific terms, this is an instrument calibration problem: if we set out to determine whether something is a particle or a wave, but it is instead something else entirely, we will find that there are fewer waves and particles than that last time we took stock. But if our instrument can only look at those two things, it will not tell us what else is there. This can stifle innovation because it is easy enough to look at the policy terrain in this way and see simply that some good idea that we have already all agreed upon is simply not working. If we believe that our observation is accurate, a logical response is to work to tune up the way the idea is being implemented. But because our observations about migration policy are not accurate – they are reflecting back to us through a broken lens – this leads to repeated attempts to implement a policy that no longer fits the world we live in. It's like building a better mousetrap in an attempt to catch a butterfly.

Part of my endeavor in this book is to demonstrate how the old lens has cracked and to begin grinding a new one. A new way of thinking about immigration will emerge, but slowly. I want to hasten the process, because the old framework is harming people and frustrating states and fragmenting the law. The first half of the book examines why this has happened. The second half takes up the more challenging questions of how to describe the shift and what new frameworks for analysis are likely to work best in navigating the new politics of immigration.

LOCATING THE NEW POLITICS OF IMMIGRATION

The contemporary politics of immigration has global reach. This is not to say that it is the same everywhere. In contrast with many important policy areas in our post-globalization world, a great deal of migration regulation continues to be generated at the national level. Beyond this, there is also enormous variation in migration impacts on diverse states because of how states are situated geographically and economically. Despite a considerable array of variation, however, it makes sense to speak of a global politics of immigration for three reasons.

The first and most important of these reasons is that the prosperous industrialized states that are the most sought-after migration destinations in the world have enormous influence over the contours of migration policy worldwide. This influence is partially explained simply by the fact of being sought after. Prosperous states that people from around the world queue to enter are in a very strong position to set the terms of global migration. It is no coincidence that these states are global leaders economically and politically, and their hegemonic position adds to their capacity to enforce the immigration rules they design. State capacity is a closely related reason that the industrialized states set the tone for migration politics. In immigration matters, state capacity is visible in the capacity to control the border: to determine who gets in and who is put out. Here, geography strengthens the capacity of prosperous states. The principal contemporary migratory pressures arise in the global South. The principal location of prosperous industrialized states is the global North – distant, even when not literally North. The states that are setting the tone for global immigration politics are not – in the present or the recent past – anywhere near the places where millions of people flow over the borders in desperate need of assistance, and in circumstances where they cannot be sent home. And where exceptions to this rule arise they are well-known crisis points – the island of Lampedusa, the Rio Grande – that are highly policed and scrutinized and discussed, even though none of these crisis points see nearly the number of migrants annually as do the migration hot spots of the global South. The states of the global North have the power to determine what will be perceived as a crisis as well. These states normalize the aspiration to complete migration control, and set this as a goal for any state anywhere that believes it is sovereign.

The second reason to speak of a worldwide politics of immigration is that one feature of the contemporary landscape is that despite a surprising amount of national autonomy, immigration policies are converging. States watch each other closely, keen to copy or adapt ideas that seem to be working. As the older way of understanding immigration fades away, the goals of migration regulation have become the same for all states. This fosters both convergence and competition, as state objectives are now identical.

Finally, a vital underlying reason that it makes sense to speak of immigration politics globally is that the way immigration is conceptualized and the systems for regulating it are globally congruent. A central plank of this book's analysis is that this conceptualization has shifted. We can imagine the new politics of immigration as an eruption along a fault line created by the clash between an old vision of immigration and a new one. Part of my project here is to map out the contours of the new politics in order to foster understanding of this fault line, and to encourage a move away from it.

For this reason, settler societies are central to my analysis. There is no longer any logic in saying that settler societies are different in regard to migration than other Western liberal democracies. The global convergence in migration policies that has emerged has brought with it the new, mean-spirited, politics of immigration. This change is vitally important at a time when the global pace of migration is higher than ever, and migration aspirations even higher. It is now evident that the idea of a settler society, previously an important landmark in understanding migration, is a thing of the past. What are the consequences of this for how we imagine immigration? And, following from this, for how we regulate it? Answering these questions must begin with the idea of the settler society, because this is the paradigm in which global understandings of migration are anchored.

Settler societies, nations built through extensive migration, and which as a consequence led the world in developing migration regulation, are the settings that established our global understanding of migration. They are the crucible of our regulatory frameworks and of our immigration mythologies. Understanding the new politics of immigration requires that we understand that the settler society era is finished, and the paradigm has faded away. For this reason, the work of this book begins with examining what distinguished these societies and their particular embrace of immigration.

My settler society examples in this book are drawn primarily from the United States, Canada, Australia, and to a lesser extent, New Zealand. These paradigmatic settler societies have most fully embodied the immigration "ethos," and share broadly common trajectories – with comparable and instructive variations – in their immigration policies and politics. Part of their "success" as nations of immigration has been their capacity to almost fully erase the indigenous societies they displaced. This reality forms part of the backdrop to the new politics of immigration because it means that the paradigmatic settler states have not experienced a robust politics of decolonization. The politics of decolonization shaped migration patterns for a time between former colonies and former colonial masters. These contours do not have the same form in the paradigmatic settler states, which, when one considers an indigenous perspective, still carry many colonial markers and practices. Moving beyond both colonization and decolonization is part of what shapes the contours of the new politics of immigration.

POLITICS – LAW – POLITICS

It used to be the case that lawyers and legal scholars had a sideline role in migration analysis. This was certainly the case when I began working in this area twenty years ago – migration studies were firmly located with sociologists, geographers, political scientists, economists, historians, almost anywhere else really. Within the discipline of law, immigration and even refugee law were regarded as marginal areas of inquiry. This marginality was supported by the acute observation that law did very little to shape immigration policies and outcomes, and therefore, politics. From a domestic law point of view, migration was an area marked by broad swathes of discretion where executive power was often determinative of outcomes. From an international point of view, states were very minimally constrained in decisions about how to determine their membership rules, who to let in, and how and why. When I began teaching immigration law, there were very few decisions from final appellate courts on the syllabus. These days, those same courts make so many important pronouncements in migration law that it is challenging to keep a syllabus up to date.

One feature of the new politics of immigration is new roles for immigration regulation. At a very basic level, there is much more law than there was two decades ago, both the type produced by legislatures and the type produced by courts. But the more important part of the change is that what states are aiming to do with immigration law is subtly, and not so subtly, shifting. Some of this is due to the security turn in matters of migration, and some of it is due to increases in rights-based advocacy, while some of it reflects directly and indirectly state ambitions to speed the pace of change, and to get rid of previous frameworks. This change means that legal scholars who think about migration are increasingly involved in the rich interdisciplinary conversation about what migration means. It also means that the disciplinary tools of legal analysis are now integral to understanding the place of migration in our world.

The enhanced place of migration law has direct consequences for the new politics of immigration. With a higher pace of legal changes, and a greater role for courts, migration becomes more politically visible and a greater number of actors are perceived as potentially politically engaged. The politics becomes legalized as actors on all sides of migration debates turn increasingly to law as a tool. In a sense this transformation simplymirrors the broader trend in Western liberal democracies to perceive the law as the most vital social ordering mechanism. But the realm of migration has been slow to join this trend, and thus the effects of this change have yet to be absorbed. There is immense pressure on courts acting in this politicized atmosphere, the volume of cases reaching them is higher, and the political stakes of their rulings are intensified. The legalization of migration politics means that the law–politics dichotomy is often clouded and the distinction between the two is frequently unclear. And the legalization cannot help but work in reverse also, making the law highly politicized. This makes migration law vulnerable to charges of illegitimacy.

The increased importance of law in matters of migration also affects the rule of law. This consequence is more complicated, and it is only now beginning to unfold. The promise of the rule of law is simple enough at its core: that the government will conduct itself according to the law, that it will make law framing its actions, and that all in a society will be subject to the law, equally. A thin version of the rule of law requires little more than this. But it has persistently been the case that a thin version of the rule of law is difficult to maintain over time. A richer reading of rule of law values begins from the basic premises and finds within those premises robust ideas of fairness, substantive equality, and even human rights principles. In other words, rule of law in its richest form treats the law as a force of good in and of itself, rather than a mere modus operandi of governance. The tricky thing about the rule of law is that the shift between a thick and a thin version is not a governance choice. As law embeds itself in the systems it orders, the strength of the rule of law may wax and wane. With more law in the realm of migration, rule of law has more potential. In many migration areas, this is yet unrealized. But the increased importance of law in this area means the groundwork for tapping into this potential has been laid.

Much of what matters about the new politics of immigration can, indeed must, be expressed in legal terms. Following from this, explaining the new politics requires a firm grasp of the law, its limits, and its potential. The new politics of immigration is marked by the transformed place of law in this policy arena.

HOW DID WE GET HERE?

The central project of this book is to account for the current global trajectory of immigration regulation. This endeavor is motivated by a deep concern about the current policy paralysis in immigration regulation. This is not to say that no new policies are being developed, but rather that as prosperous Western states seek to alter their immigration regimes, and enhance their control, no new ideas are emerging. This is despite the fact that many actors – states and migrants – want something different from migration regulation at this point in time. States are not reaching their policy objectives; individuals are often unable to achieve their goals, or to adequately protect their basic rights. Something new is required, and yet we are completely stalled in considering where new ideas might come from. Most "new" policy rollouts in prosperous industrialized states at this point in time involve intensifying ideas that have been tried before, ratcheting up restrictions, heightening privileges for the most attractive migrants, and building bigger fences – literally and legally.

This book recounts the rapid end of the settler society era and the emergence of the new political framing for immigration, because this analysis explains the policy paralysis and provides the necessary groundwork for finding a way out of it. The comparatively rapid demise of settler societies has been brought about by three shifts. The first is the crisis of asylum, which began in the final decades of the twentieth century but has rapidly picked up speed since 2001. The second is the fear of Islamic fundamentalism, which has presented a profound challenge to liberal approaches to immigration and has ushered in a full-scale securitization of immigration questions. The third factor is the end of multiculturalism. While multiculturalism persists as a description of many societies, it has lost its ideological functions, and thus much of its political heft.

The new politics of immigration is marked by the end of both "settlement" and "society" as key values in migration. The shift away from Old World versus New World migration models has severed the linkages between migration and former colonial powers. Thus the new politics of migration belongs to a *post*-post-colonial era, and therefore, provides support for European citizenship and all it entails on the immigration front. Freed from settlement, society, and colonial linkages, the new politics of immigration is grounded in sharp distinctions between sought-after highly mobile individuals on the one hand, and illegal migrants on the other. This divide is the basis of the current policy convergence, and must be reinterpreted to successfully map the future. This book begins that process.

One of the book's central preoccupations is the place of economics, on the one hand, and human rights, on the other, within the new politics of migration. Contemporary policy adjustments are often cast in these terms: aiming to improve economic indicators concerning immigration or to improve human rights protections, or both. This makes sense, because there is much to be gained on either of these yardsticks. Economic outcomes are the logical domain of state policy across almost every sector. Human rights are the most powerful legal tools that migrant advocates can deploy. It would even be well worth doing sustained work on how economics and human rights could, within migration policy, develop a less antagonistic relationship. My argument, however, is that both economic and human rights discourses do not get to the root of the issue in terms of understanding the new politics of immigration. This insight has three consequences. First, these twinned discourses obscure features of the new politics, distracting us from the underlying currents that generate the present dilemmas. Second and closely related, these discourses as currently constructed contribute to policy paralysis, rather than providing avenues for innovation. Finally, neither economics nor human rights analyses have much predictive effect in matters of migration. This is essential for policy development, which is always about shaping what will happen in the future.

The new politics of immigration is characterized by legalization, rapid change, defiance of partisan expectations, a new worldwide "us" and "them" divide, existential fear, and an unprecedented place on the central political stage of all Western liberal democracies. Along with this runs a competitive convergence between states, and a persistent engagement with economic and human rights discourses. The level of hostility towards migrants is higher than ever before, and this hostility sweeps along with it a strident objection to asylum.

My analysis of this new politics draws on considering migration events and trends of the past decade or so, and considering what they have in common, and how each can be used to interpret the others. The book seeks to step back from isolated events or policy areas, and to look at the big picture that unites them. In this broad ambition, I build on the work of many others, and on the insights of teaching and supervising excellent research in this area for the past twenty years. The conclusion looks to the future, assessing what would be required for us to alter the new politics of immigration and where we will end up if we do not achieve this.

The book opens by outlining what the settler society paradigm has contributed to global, and national, mythologies of immigration. This outline is the foundation for my argument that something important has been lost since the opening of the twenty-first century, and for understanding why this loss is both permanent and deeply consequential. The trio of chapters that follows considers in turn, and in chronological order, the three factors that have brought the settler society era to a close: the asylum crisis, the fear of fundamental Islam, and the demise of multiculturalism. These three factors are anchored primarily in the settler society states, where the shifts they have brought are most profoundly felt. The second half of the book then turns to the new politics, exploring the loss of settlement and society as immigration values, as well as the concomitant shift in how immigration is understood in the so-called "Old World" nations that were the primary sending states for migrants to the New World. The conclusion attempts to unravel the consequences of the new politics – to consider what will happen if we ignore them and to raise the faint hope of finding new ways to imagine immigration futures.

2

Settler societies and the immigration imagination

Throughout the entire first century of global migration regulation, from the early 1900s to the present, a distinction between settler societies and others has informed and predicted patterns of migration and migration regulation. This distinction served as a guide to strategies of recruitment and reception, to global alliances around migration questions, to approaches to asylum, and to citizenship. This era has now come to a close. The work of this book is to demonstrate how and why this is so, and to outline what new predictors or patterns of migration and migration regulation may now be valuable. Global migration regulation first developed in the context of settler societies, and their demise contains key markers for the future. To understand why any of this matters, however, it is first crucial to understand how the concept of a settler society ordered global migration for more than a century. This chapter begins with unraveling this ordering, and then examines the legal architecture of migration in the settler society and considers the insights of critiques of the settler society concept.

Settler society is not a scientific category. It is an idea with a core of meaning, and considerable slippage around the edges. One is just as likely to see the term used by social commentators and politicians as by academics. This low-key omnipresence is part of its importance – it has slipped into everyday discourse. A rigorous definition is not helpful, as my purpose is not to stake out and police boundaries of a certain category. Indeed, some of the work of this book depends on a degree of wobbliness in the concept, on its ability to mean different things at different times or for different people. But it is important to set out the broad parameters of the idea. When a journalist, a politician, or a geographer talks about a settler society, we do know what they mean.[1]

A mythology of immigration is the core of the settler society. Settler societies were built from the ground up by people who left European nations and sought permanent homes in the New World. In an era of colonial empires, settler societies were a distinct chapter in the dominant colonizing narrative. While these were, of course, colonies of European empires, their ostensible "emptiness" distinguished them from colonies in Africa, Asia, and the Indian subcontinent. Settler societies were not simply colonized; they were populated by Europeans. So complete were these acts of population that the societies came to regard themselves as somehow European. For the settler society, immigration was a nation-building imperative.

One of the imprecisions in understanding settler societies turns on whether to draw a distinction between those places where European settlement came to completely dominate and define, and those places where resistance to settlement was more robust, and thus by the early twenty-first century they are no longer completely defined by their settlers. For this reason, Australia, Canada, the United States, and New Zealand are the paradigmatic settler societies. South Africa, Zimbabwe, Mexico, Peru, Israel, Algeria, and others fit more awkwardly into the box. One way to capture this distinction is to consider how the settler society emerges from colonial status. The processes bringing independence to settler societies do not belong to the late-twentieth-century story of decolonization. In the case of the United States, independence was staked out well before the first era of massive global migration. For the other three exemplars, independence was an incremental and amiable process. The ongoing struggles of decolonization are not part of the narrative in either case, and most of the rubric of the post-colonial is inapt.

The centrality of immigration mythology has several vital consequences. First among these is that the paradigmatic settler societies, Canada, Australia, New Zealand, and the United States, understand themselves as being nations built through migration. While this story plays out differently in each of these places, the variations do not disrupt a strong migration core to the story of national identity. In the United States the War of Independence and the Civil War are foundational moments but the founders themselves are from else-where. Canada cogitates on the French fact in Quebec, and Australia in its maturity embraces the convict stain. Possibly the greatest variation of the narrative is heard in New Zealand, where the indigenous Maori have been more persistent than original inhabitants in the other three, and thus the mythology of immigration as foundational has been more persistently disrupted. Perhaps this is why, of these four countries, only New Zealand does not have a major national immigration museum.[2] There is a certain irony here, of course, as the contemporary prominence of the Maori as compared to indigenous populations elsewhere is partially related to New Zealand's measured approach to immigration in the early settler colonial period. Aiming to build a "better Britain," New Zealand focused on migrant purity and thus reduced migrant numbers, and this is a contributing factor to somewhat less complete dominance over the indigenous population.[3]

Within this group, Canada, Australia, and New Zealand are often selected as the comparator group, and the United States is considered to be the outlier.[4] This grouping places the emphasis on colonial history. From my perspective, however, the United States fits squarely in the frame, as my focus is on the place of immigration in national institutions and the contemporary shape of immigration policies and politics. Excluding the United States from this picture amounts to excluding the most powerful example of all. The intertwining of migration and national identity is part of the settler ethos, and reaches all aspects of the national imagination. This is a key aspect of national identity in the United States, possibly more strongly embraced than anywhere else on Earth. In each state, this intertwining continues to shape migration policy and politics. The United States examples of the green card lottery and contemporary DREAM Act activism are among the most poignant examples.

Another distinguishing feature of the settler society is that the mythology of migration has been, throughout most of these nations' histories, translated into a contemporary commitment to ongoing migration. These countries were the predominant recipients of much of the great wave of global migration that took place between the late 1880s and early 1920s. David Held and his co-authors published an analysis comparing the intensity and effects of various phases of global migration and concluded that what they termed the "transatlantic surge of 1880 to 1920" was the most intense phase of global migration up to their 1999 publication date. Whether current conditions would exceed that surge on Held's measurement is unclear.[5] While widespread immigration restriction began in earnest in the early decades of the twentieth century, these states continued to welcome many categories of migrants. Rather than closing their doors completely, they sought to organize and control who would enter. And throughout the twentieth century, at varying points, each sought out particular groups of migrants as a remedy for some social or economic ill. Indeed, even into the second decade of the twenty-first century, Canada, Australia, and New Zealand are actively recruiting migrants in specified categories, and the United States continues to be home to more permanent *and* temporary migrants than any other nation on earth.[6] The commitment to migration in these states has been deep and ongoing.

The shared mythology of immigration also serves to mask the savage destruction of indigenous peoples and ways of life that is also shared across these nations. The very idea of "settlers" suggests that there was a wild land in need of taming, of settlement. And thus in each of these places the founding mythology has included the intrepid frontiersman battling the savagery of land and people to transform the place into a terrain of fences and measures. And law. The idea of Canada, Australia, or the United States being a nation of migration is such a profound and effective silencer of the trajectory of indigenous life that it is deeply challenging to bring indigenous peoples into a story of the immigrant nation. While contemporary social justice politics often sees allegiances between new migrants and indigenous peoples as those at the margins of these societies, the claims of these groups are not articulated in the same terms, and the allegiance rarely reaches the level of shared demands or joint manifestos. Indeed, it is the reality that these states *are* nations of immigrants that is the most damaging fact to be overcome in the struggle for indigenous justice and social inclusion.

Settler societies share this past and present trajectory. The idea that there can be such a thing as a "nation of immigration" has become commonplace. It structures the way we think about immigration, the way we regulate it, and the way we study it. Understanding how this is so is, therefore, key to seeing why the end of settler societies matters. This chapter now takes up each of these ideas in turn, situating the settler society in immigration thought, regulation, and critique.

THINKING IMMIGRATION: MELTING POTS, MOSAICS, REFUGE, AND RACE

The settler society commitment to immigrant identity is most succinctly expressed in the hyphenation of citizens: Italian-Americans, Chinese-Canadians, Greek-Australians, and so on. These monikers pair the Old World with the New; an identity embedded in national history and an idea of ethnicity (or an aspiration to national history, such as Kurdish-Australian or Palestinian-Canadian), with a New World citizenship that defies ethnic understanding. When I tell people that I identify myself on the Australian census as ethnically Canadian, they think I am joking, as they do when I refer to Canada as the Old Country. Settler society membership is expressed this way, as being often partial and never "ethnic." Even those of us who might be non-hyphenated citizens in everyday parlance in former settler states, are offered at census time the opportunity to identify ourselves as "coming from" somewhere else, having an ethnicity different from our citizenship.[7]

This is the commitment of the settler society: we are all immigrants. This is reinforced by the perpetual "hyphenation" of indigenous members. Indigenous peoples in settler societies are never signified by the mere omission of an adjectival modifier. The simple words Canadian or American postdate and erase indigeneity so completely that it must be *re*-signified in some other fashion with labels that vary over time and place – Indian, First Nations, Aborigine, Maori. For several years, when he was the Australian Minister of Immigration at the close of the twentieth century, Phillip Ruddock had a go at extending the "we are all immigrants" mantra to include the Australian Aborigines who had "migrated" to contemporary Australia some 50,000 years earlier during the last ice age when the sea crossing to Asia was considerably smaller. This conceit aimed to confront the emerging cracks in the settler society ethos brought about by the strengthening land rights claims of indigenous peoples in all settler societies at that time. But it was transparent political posturing. The effects of the first wave of British colonists on the Aboriginal population of the Australian continent are simply not comparable to the effect of subsequent waves of Europeans on the society established by those first settlers. To draw the comparison is beyond insult. We are not all immigrants, but the mythology of settler society eases our ignorance of this.

For many years, settler societies were contrasted with ethnic nations. In this analysis, settler societies were not true nations because they did not share a core of ethnic and historical identity. This analysis traveled particularly well in Canada where the "two nations" thesis was articulated to explain the roles of French and English settlers in Canadian history and politics, and where political heft was accorded to indigenous peoples by re-naming them as "First Nations."[8] Under this analysis, of course, a settler society cannot, by definition, be a nation. And much has been made of the search for national identity in settler societies. But this trend in scholarship and everyday political discourse has dissipated.

Benedict Anderson's 1983 seminal work *Imagined Communities*, arguing that all nations are both constructed and imagined and thus not ethnic and organic, is an important marker in this regard for scholars. It is certainly not a coincidence that Anderson drew the primary evidence for his argument from the "settler societies" of South America, demonstrating that the emergence of nationalism (and thus "nations") was tied to institutional structures and practices, rather than heredity. Anderson focused on Spanish America without using the term settler society, and this choice shows again that the settler society rubric is important to the extent that it is useful, but that no scholarly category can or ought ever to be more than that.

However influential Anderson's work has been, it cannot be the sole explanation for a shift in popular and political discourse over the past quarter century toward thinking more easily of Canada, Australia, and New Zealand as "nations." Furthermore, it would be unimaginable to suggest that the United States ever lacked a strong claim to the full cluster of related attributes:

nationhood, national identity, and nationalism. This is one reason that the United States is sometimes set outside the conversation about settler states: it has lacked this sense of national angst. But in many vital ways, the United States is a more complete settler state than any of the others. The path marked by the United States in emerging as "nation" is now being followed by Canada, Australia, and New Zealand. Immigrant identity and hyphenated memberships no longer have traction in suggesting that these settler societies are not properly considered nations. This can be seen, partially, as an ascendency of formalism, but it is also more than that. A shift away from uncertainty is linked with the move away from settler society status as an organizing category for immigration policy and politics.

Immigrant identity is key to understanding settler societies, but it is only the first ingredient. The contours of this identity are comparable at a finer level of detail as well. The first Europeans to come to these New World lands with an intent to remain (rather than discover and return) can be seen as successive waves of people for whom Europe was or had become an uncomfortable home. Major waves of migration, whether English, French, German, Italian, or other-speaking, included religious minorities and those who could not get enough to eat, or certainly not enough to get ahead. The sense of being a vast empty space in which Europe's "others" could find a new home was nowhere more evident than in Australia. There, convicts transported beyond the edge of the earth did the backbreaking labour of carving European-style settlement into sandstone cliffs, and were rewarded through this ritual purification with a place amongst the landed gentry of the New World.

The surveyors' markers for these paradigmatic settler societies were in place before migration regulation brought a sense of closure to the New World.[9] The early migrants arrived at a time when these societies were a place of promise for "huddled masses yearning to breathe free."[10] In this sense, settler societies were a place of refuge. But the story of openness and refuge introduces the darker notes of the narrative as well.

Settler societies have been predominantly white. The early European arrivals were from Northern Europe, and with the exception of what is now the Canadian province of Quebec, the early colonies of the paradigmatic settler states were British. Whiteness and the settler society paradigm go hand-in-hand, and many of those nations that fit less directly into the framework, Brazil, South Africa, or Mexico, for example, are decidedly less white. While Spanish America fits the definition of a settler society in most ways, its states rarely jump to mind as the first exemplars.

The story of how immigration hierarchy quickly became racialized hierarchy is well known. The Irish, who were the once the poor outsiders in the United States' immigration hierarchy, paled with the arrival of Greeks and Italians from Southern Europe. The first immigration restrictions in many settler societies were directed against East and South Asians. Each of the four paradigmatic nations has experienced significant social, political, and economic racialized divides. Each has been home to an ongoing conversation about the significance of race to immigration policy, a troubling undercurrent that persists well past the historic turn toward formal racial neutrality in the 1960s and 1970s. The narratives of settler societies have been shot through with racialization and exclusion for as long as there have been meaningful borders. Indeed these narratives are key to making borders meaningful.

The question of refuge is similarly fraught. The story of immigration as a nation-building project is intertwined with the idea of providing a safe haven for people in flight. In the first great wave of global migration beginning late in the nineteenth century, it was impossible and unnecessary to distinguish newcomers on the basis of their motive for flight. Migration to the New World was open to those who wanted to move, whether starving, persecuted, or adventuresome, or even all three. Since that time, however, the relationship between settler states and those seeking the shelter of a new home has been marked by the same exclusionary tensions seen in regard to all types of immigration. That is, while the United States, Canada, Australia, and, again to a lesser extent, New Zealand, have welcomed high numbers of refugees in (some) globally comparative terms, they have excluded even more. Canada and the United States, to their enduring shame, both turned away Jews fleeing the Nazi regime in the late 1930s. While these settler societies have been leaders in resettling refugees ever since World War II, it remains the case that only a tiny fraction, less than 1 percent, of refugees worldwide are resettled each year at the outset of the twenty-first century.[11] For most of the past century, refugee admissions have been viewed by these states as an immigration question, despite a carefully constructed international legal framework emphasizing that refugees are not immigrants. Here the mythology of immigration is stronger than the law: refugees *are* immigrants because they come and they stay. Our expectations of them are, in the end, no different than those of other newcomers. We align them to the nation-building enterprise, expecting them to settle, to make new lives, to become *us*, all the while providing a testimony by their mere presence to our enduring generosity and goodness.

The quiet backdrop of exclusion subtly serves to strengthen the mythology of immigrant identity in the settler society. Exclusion is one more barrier to overcome. The paradigmatic immigrant, whether starving, persecuted, or adventuresome, fits the society's story. Immigrants strive for a better life, successive waves of migrants sacrifice to put their children on an equal footing in a new homeland. Life is tough, and social exclusion is part of that toughness, but it is at any price better than the Old Country, and a secure and prosperous future for one's children brings the perseverance required to carry one through the punishing work in the field, sweatshop, or perpetually marginal corner store. This openness and meritocracy is also part of the story.

In my long-ago childhood we were taught that Canada was a cultural mosaic, in contrast to the American melting pot. But even as school children we could see that one metaphor was not necessarily better than the other; melting had a beautiful fluid freedom to it. Between the mosaic and the melting pot runs the gamut of immigrant identity. On the one hand is the pastiche of hyphenated citizens, each proudly transplanting their own cultures and customs from elsewhere and forming a new national home that is identifiable through its embrace of this cacophony of difference. On the other hand is the assimilationist vision of looking to the future based on shared values. Of course neither image tells us anything about lived experience. Rather, each expresses a vision of how individual immigrant experiences aggregate to national identity. What they share is the idea that such individual experiences do in fact aggregate to national identity. And this is a fulcrum point. For settler societies the belief that individual immigrant experiences accrete to national identity is foundational. National identity is what some "we" group shares when it cannot share race or religion or ethnicity or history. It is no wonder that fitting the traditional definition of "nation" onto these places has been such a squeeze. Conversely, it cannot surprise us that settler societies have been the birthplace of multiculturalism.

All of this, then, is the stock story of the settler society. Fractured identities, families spanning borders, progressive exclusions, racialized transformations, fledgling national identities. This collage is as familiar as a recurring dream to those of us who study migration. The four nations that became the paradigmatic settler societies embraced this story most fully. It is no coincidence that it is in the United States, Canada, Australia, and New Zealand, that the indigenous populations were almost completely destroyed. It is also no coincidence either that all four inherited British traditions and British law. The British imperial approach to immigration and the incredible adaptability of the common law are part of the story of settler societies. They also play a role in accounting for how these societies come to an end. But that story is not quite yet. This chapter turns now to the legal architecture of settler states.

LEGAL ARCHITECTURE OF THE SETTLER SOCIETY

Law is essential to the settler society story. The nation-building enterprise is structured by law: its constitutions and declarations; its rights and treaties. There is an occupational hazard, of course, for any legal scholar, to overstate the role of law. The law does not cause migration, nor does it determine policy choices. But it does create the conditions for building a settler society and provide much of the tool set for that construction. Importantly, at the close of settler societies, law is a central cause as well as a consequence. Thus the origin story is vital.

The story of how law clears the way for construction of the settler society is well known. It is most compellingly put in Australia, where the international legal doctrine of *terra nullius* has almost managed to slip into everyday speech. *Terra nullius* is the legal foundation for the idea of empty lands, available for Europe's overflow, without conquest or contract.[12] This doctrine is essential to making the indigenous population invisible, or at least irrelevant, because its relationship with the land did not "settle" the territory. *Terra nullius* appears in Australia's Macquarie Dictionary used in this sense; in the Oxford English Dictionary it does not appear. The doctrine of *terra nullius* plays a greater part in the Australian narrative than in any other, but key elements of the story are transportable. Everywhere that a settler society has been firmly established, the previous indigenous population has been legally displaced and confined, leaving vast tracts of land legally empty. Almost calling out for population. The nation-building ethic begins with this call: emptiness must be filled in order to be owned.

Beyond this foundational point, the legal architecture of settler societies provided three key nation-building tools; immigration regulation, citizenship as membership, and constitutional frameworks. These features, along with a particular trajectory toward independence and a minimal contribution from international law, make up the legal architecture of the settler society. I will address each of these in turn.

The largest foundation stone is an organized framework for immigration. For these states, immigration was not simply a social force that required a response, but a nation-building imperative. A legal framework grew up around this imperative. A shared desire to ensure that immigration remained a matter of domestic rather than international control was vital to the four paradigmatic settler societies in the early years of the twentieth century. This desire was central to the failure of the United States to join the League of Nations, and contributed significantly to the roles that Canada, Australia, and New Zealand played in the short-lived League. Moreover, underlying the impetus to preserve national control over immigration there was a shared commitment to exclude or strictly limit Asian immigration.[13] Regulation of immigration has at all times been closely tied to national values. Values have evolved over time, but have never been far from the text of the law.

In the early part of the twentieth century, race restrictions were a commonality of migration laws in each of these countries. The development of race-based restrictions on immigration was fundamental to the completion of worldwide migration regulation in the first decades of the twentieth century. These restrictions in favor of Europeans were a final piece in the progressive global closure of borders. The closure signaled an important shift in the development of settler societies, ushering in a new era of control. This control was tightly linked to the end of the first great wave of global migration, and the rise of a more directed nation-building project. Where previously the emptiness of these lands had made them fit for anyone who was willing to do the transformative work required, race-based restrictions articulated a vision of who would qualify for membership. These restrictions held the embryonic forms of much contemporary migration regulatory technique. Oddly structured continuous journey rules and nonsensical language testing were used alongside overtly racial restrictions. In the United States, the Chinese Exclusion Act of 1882 was the first major piece of federal immigration legislation.[14] In Canada, restrictions on Asian migration were an important part of defining the relationship between the national and the provincial governments.[15] In Australia, migrant-restricting legislation was the first act of the newly formed national Parliament, and a key impetus in the move toward national independence.[16] In New Zealand, migration regulation of the nineteenth century recognized only two categories: "Britons" and "non-Britons."[17] British citizens did not need entry permits for New Zealand until 1974.

In the second part of the century, following World War II and the global turn toward human rights and anti-discrimination norms, these states turned to a rationalized approach to immigrant admission, inventing "points systems" and "lotteries" to sort applicants on the basis of criteria that could be distanced from the racist past. National values, however, can still be read from these laws in a very straightforward manner. Immigration laws, for example, provide a rich source of definitions of "family," of marriage, of personal adaptability, and of economic value. While many Western states now have immigration laws that share similar features, the settler societies led the way in developing frameworks for attracting desirable permanent migrants who were not kin or co-ethnics, and for defining migrant desirability in a way that maps more closely onto the immigration mythology of the settler state. Rather than valuing a shared past or a religious commitment, what is valued is self-sufficiency, independence, and a rationally verifiable ability to assimilate. In other words, the hard-working immigrant of the earlier century is given rationalist-scientific form. This is one key example of how the logic of the settler society became embedded in its legal frameworks: as a new legal structure emerged in the mid-to-late twentieth century, the core value of the settler ethos became the singular anchoring feature of the regulatory structure.

The commitment to immigration as nation building also influences the structure of citizenship laws. The traditional distinction in citizenship regimes is between *jus sanguinis*, citizenship by descent, the model of the Old World, and *jus soli*, citizenship based on birth in the territory, the settler society's preference. Although *jus soli* did not originate with settler societies, its origins in Roman law and its long history in the British common law made a good fit for the new purpose: a unifying structure of legal membership designed to unite disparate groups and submerge distinctions; a law to build identity. Spanish American nations embraced *jus soli* despite their civil law tradition because it strengthened the independence of the colonies and distanced their populations from the metropole. The dividing line between these two models of citizenship law is now very close to collapse, and is a key symptom of the end of settler societies. Australia led the way on this score, abandoning birthright citizenship in 1986. New Zealand followed suit in 2006. A similar shift was squarely on the Canadian political agenda of the majority Conservative government from 2009 to 2015. In each case, the aim of the legal shift is to deny citizenship to children whose parents do not have a permanent right to reside in the state. As I will explore later, part of the reason for this collapse may well be that in the former settler states identity has now coalesced to the point that states are willing to relinquish the crude membership axiom of birth on the soil. It is also not coincidental that settler states initially led the way in developing an openness towards dual citizenship regimes. Thus legally reflecting hyphenated identities.[18]

The traditional linking of *jus soli* citizenship with the ethos of nations of immigrants points us in the direction of the constitutional space accorded to immigration in settler societies. In the United States, birthright citizenship has not disappeared because it is constitutionally entrenched. The Fourteenth Amendment's citizenship clause, introduced to ensure that former slaves would be guaranteed citizenship in the aftermath of the disastrous 1857 *Dred Scott* v. *Sandford* ruling, has immunized United States' citizenship from the erosion that is taking place elsewhere.[19] While it seems unlikely that constitutional amendment is on the horizon, the idea of an "anchor baby" has emerged as an American policy concern in the past decade. The concern is, of course, that a citizen child can open an immigration pathway for other family members, precisely the concern that animated the change in Australian law, and is on the near horizon in Canada. Constitutionalized birthright citizenship is uniquely American. In the other paradigmatic states, the constitutional space for immigration takes different forms.

In Australia, the desire to regulate immigration was an important motivator for the original constitution. In Canada, immigration and agriculture are twinned areas of shared responsibility for the national and provincial governments in the original 1867 British North America Act, singling them out as uniquely important. The legal skirmishes over efforts by the province of British Columbia to exclude Asian immigrants led to a ruling declaring national government paramountcy. These are not the only states where immigration is constitutional, but they do have particular markings. In the Israeli and German constitutions, immigration is tied to an already existing kinship community, which serves to frame immigration in a very different way. In the settler societies, immigration has a constitutional place tied to nation building. This place gives immigration as nation building an important legal anchor, reflecting its perpetual national importance on the political agenda.

In contrast, international law offers little in the realm of immigration regulation. Despite its inherent border-crossing character, immigration is almost absent from international law. Aside from a duty to admit their own citizens, states are free to admit or exclude whomever they choose. The only small and partial exception to this legal silence is the contemporary protection regime and its principle of *non-refoulement*. That is, the idea that some narrowly defined groups of people cannot be returned to places where they face a risk of certain types of serious harm. The *non-refoulement* principle is the centerpiece of international refugee law, and has more recently been recognized in the Convention Against Torture and, for European states, in the European Convention on Human Rights.[20] This international framing also forms part of the legal backdrop of settler societies. Indeed, as the settler society era ends, the international backdrop moves closer to the foreground, and with it comes a richer discourse of human rights that has an influence on migration policy and politics that is much debated by contemporary scholars.[21]

The 1951 Convention relating to the Status of Refugees and its 1967 Protocol define refugees and establishes states' obligations towards them. The core of the refugee definition is that a person is outside their home state and unable to safely return to it because they fear being persecuted for reasons related to their identity or beliefs. Refugees, therefore, are migrants. They move without much choice about doing so. In one sense, this fits them quintessentially into the mythology of immigration. But in another sense, they do not fit at all. They are not, first and foremost, seeking a better life or a new future. They are in flight from an immediate danger. Given this, it is striking that international refugee law does not provide a right for refugees to enter any country that is not their own. Refugee law stops short of a direct challenge to the right of states to admit or exclude at will. The result is, of course, an impasse. And it has largely been resolved by a series of interpretations finding that when a refugee reaches the border of a state that recognizes international refugee law, she must be admitted, at least until her status as a refugee has been considered.[22]

What refugee law does provide is a right not to be compelled to return to a place where a person faces the kind of danger that makes them a refugee in the first place. This *non-refoulement* principle, in combination with the rule that states are only compelled to admit their own citizens, translates in most cases into a right to remain in a country of refuge. A right to remain looks a lot like what is accorded to immigrants. Indeed in many Western migrant-receiving states, refugees are able to transform their international right to protection into a right of permanent residency. The stability that this creates allows refugees to settle and rebuild their lives. For many states this makes good policy sense. It is also humane.

It is no wonder, then, that states jealously guard their sovereign authority over their borders. The narrowest slip of exception to this authority on the face of the Refugee Convention has proven enough to transform refugees into permanent migrants.

The Convention Against Torture, which came into effect in 1987, does not have the same migratory flavor. It does not require that people cross an international border to come within its ambit, and it is not primarily focused on those outside their home states. It does, however, share refugee law's prohibition on return. Parties to the Convention must not return an individual to face torture. In many cases, the Torture Convention works as a subset of the Refugee Convention, because torture fits squarely within anyone's definition of persecution. On the other hand, the Torture Convention extends protection to anyone at risk of torture, and unlike the Refugee Convention does not require a linkage to identity or beliefs. At the border of a prosperous state, and seeking entry, a person claiming to be at risk of torture will likely be admitted because they are potentially a refugee. In the case of the European Convention on Human Rights, the principle of *non-refoulement* has grown through judicial interpretation of a right to protection from inhuman or degrading treatment; *non-refoulement* is not even mentioned in the text. Thus the Refugee Convention is what gets attention in migration analysis.

Beyond this, international law provides no border-crossing rights, and agreements about admissions or returns tend to be ad hoc and bilateral only. General human rights law declares a right to seek asylum, but not to obtain it. The sole international human rights instrument aimed specifically at immigrants, the Convention on the Protection of the Rights of All Migrant Workers and Members of their Families, has not been accepted by prosperous Western migrant-receiving states.[23] As far as formal legal architecture goes, the international law contributes remarkably little. This helps to account for how human rights commitments take shape in the post-settler state era.

This international picture, however, must be qualified in three ways. First, it is important to consider that it was the paradigmatic settler states that led the way, early in the twentieth century, in rejecting moves toward international regulation of migration.[24] This makes sense given the linkage between immigration and nation building. Second, the European Convention on Human Rights certainly belongs to the international plane, even though Europe is becoming ever more distinct, but it applies exclusively to a particular and privileged section of the globe. Third, international human rights arguments on behalf of migrants are sometimes useful, and their usefulness does not relate to the weakness of international human rights that are directed specifically at migrants.

The final element of the legal architecture of settler societies that has some resonance for the immigration narrative is to consider how these states emerged from colonial status without entering a politics of decolonization. There are three formal answers to this. In the case of the United States, there was, of course, a sharply violent politics of decolonization, but the War of Independence occurred so early on that it predated the peak of European colonial aspirations, and thus the protracted imperial angst that informs the post-colonial era. The second response is that Canada, Australia, and New Zealand emerged gradually into independent status over the first half of the twentieth century. Significant markers in the trajectory include participating in the post-World War I treaty process and the passage of the 1931 Statute of Westminster formalizing legislative independence from the British. Canadian citizenship began in 1947, Australian and New Zealand in 1949. It was not until the 1980s that formal constitutional independence from Britain was achieved for Canada and Australia, even though no one would argue that this final step was strictly required to achieve national independence.[25] This gradual trajectory skirted the politics of decolonization by its pace and its collaborative politics. The newly independent nations remained significantly "British" in national character at the time when independence was achieved, and many of their new citizens had ethnic origins somewhere in Britain. The third answer is that a number of the states that cluster in the penumbra of the settler society definition have been squarely involved in the maelstrom of decolonization. South Africa, Argentina, Zimbabwe, and Ireland come to mind. But in this final case, the question might be where on the continuum of colonial forms these states sit: their experience of decolonization moves them away from the settler society parameters. The political pressure point of decolonization derives always from the emerging re-independence of an indigenous population. In settler societies, such re-emergence seems impossible.

The role of the indigenous population points directly to the less legalistic response to the puzzle of settler societies averting a politics of decolonization. The United States, Canada, Australia, and New Zealand have simply not decolonized; they have become independent from their colonial masters without any return of power, sovereignty, or independence to the original inhabitants of these territories. This sheds light on the boundaries of the settler society paradigm. For the truest of settler societies, decolonization is impossible. The law has recognized this, and has confessed its impuissance. In the groundbreaking *Mabo* decision, Australia's Justice Brennan looked down into the legal precipice opened by indigenous claims to land and wrote that "this Court is not free to adopt rules that accord with contemporary notions of justice and human rights if their adoption would fracture the skeleton of principle which gives the body of our law its shape and internal consistency."[26] Less dramatically, but facing the same divide, Canada's Chief Justice Lamer wrote, "Let us face it, we are all here to stay."[27] Settler society has meant colonization so permanent that it can no longer be named as such. The legal architecture of the settler society depends upon being unable to articulate its origins.[28] Law at its origins is an act of faith. In the settler context, faith takes this specific form: a commitment to a mythology of immigration establishes the law.

SUNSET OF THE SETTLER SOCIETY

The idea of a settler society has shaped the way the Western world imagines immigration. And this in turn leads the global imagination because Western states have the political and economic heft to craft international rules and thus shape what will count as migration and what will be considered aberrant or illegal movement. Key strands of this imagination include the idea that immigration is permanent, that some countries are "senders" and others are "receivers," that migration and national identity are intertwined, that migration informs individual identity, but does not completely remake it. These ideas map out what scholars of migration investigate, what policymakers address, what historians trace. The influence of the settler society over the collective imaginary is predictable because these societies led the way in normalizing large-scale migration. This was especially the case of migration that was "volitional" rather than forced. Large-scale expulsions and flight from persecution aside, the pursuit of a better life as a potential *choice* of individuals and families was first imagined in the settler society context.

The opening decades of the twenty-first century can be considered an era of extensive migration, but it remains the case that most people live their lives in the countries where they were born. In 2013, the Population Division of the United Nations Department of Economic and Social Affairs (UN DESA) estimated that 232 million people were considered migrants.[29] This is a significant increase from the estimated 150 million migrants in the year 2000, but a very small increase (from 2.9 percent to 3.2 percent) in terms of proportion of the global population. Read inversely, these numbers tell us that nearly 97 percent of people in the world are living in the country of their birth. This way of presenting immigration statistics is an example of how the settler society picture of migration shapes all contemporary analysis. Migration is not travel, and it is not temporary – whether to work or to seek protection. Even framing the migration question as an international one serves to ignore one of the most numerically significant categories of contemporary immigration: that from rural to urban space. This is particularly important among the massive populations of China, India, and Indonesia, where more than 50 percent of the world's rural population lives. In the final two decades of the twentieth century, China experienced history's largest flow of rural to urban migration, with the urban population increasing by 222 million. This one country figure alone is nearly as large as the estimated number of global migrants in 2013.[30] But this migration is scarcely a topic of migration scholarship, and never comes to the regulatory attention of prosperous Western states.

The way we imagine immigration matters because we are at a point of complete failure of global policy innovation about migration. States around the globe, senders and receivers alike, look to each other for policy innovation, but convergence means that the range of options in migration policy is narrowing rather than broadening. The 2005 United Nations Ad Hoc Global Commission on International Migration, which worked for two years with a lavish budget and consultations with scholars around the globe, failed to embrace a single idea that had not been tried, or at least articulated, previously. This view is shared by a number of scholars who assessed the report shortly after its release in 2005.[31] Not surprisingly, the report generated little scholarly interest beyond that point in time, and did not significantly motivate regulatory innovation. At a time when more people around the world want to move than ever before, policy development is focused on keeping people in place, controlling borders, and, at the same time, intensifying competition for the best and the brightest of potential migrants. To truly enhance policy vision, we need, as a global community, to find new ways of imagining immigration. Loosening the grip of the settler society frame is vital to this project.

The settler society paradigm keeps our thinking about immigration locked in the past, and makes it hard to react to, and regulate, changes in migration trajectories. A good example of this is the preference of migrant-receiving states for highly skilled workers. Highly skilled workers fit the nation-building paradigm, whereas low-skilled workers represent risk: a risk that they will remain and become not only unremovable, but also unsuccessful and unintegrated. This trope does not link to the early patterns of settler society foundations, when most migrants would likely have fit into contemporary low-skilled categories. But it does draw directly on key ideas of the settler story: good migrants *remain*, good migrants *contribute*, good migrants *change themselves* to become a part of the new nation. Challenging the underlying structures of our immigration imagination would involve re-ordering some of these ideas. For example, casting the nation as aspiring to change; building policy from a global rather than a national perspective; building rules to fit our contemporary knowledge of circular migration, rather than using that knowledge to design regulations to halt those patterns. The subtle underlying persistence of the settler society paradigm is one factor blocking the flow of new information into the policy arena, contributing to a frustration many scholars have with immigration politics and policies that seem to evolve without attention to evidence about their effects and effectiveness.

The settler society concept is rarely an object of inquiry in contemporary immigration scholarship, but it remains an organizing structure for thinking about immigration. That is, it has become a part of the well-accepted backdrop. Christian Joppke embeds the concept in his 2005 analysis of the politics of ethnic immigration; Paul Sheffer's 2011 *Immigrant Nations* uses these states as a point of contrast. Harald Bauder's *Immigration Dialectic* relies on the contrast to settler societies and ethnic nations to structure his analysis. David Pearson uses it to define relevant comparators.[32]

There is also a well-developed critique of the acceptance of "settler society" as a benign descriptor. This scholarship focuses on the damage wrought by this paradigm of settlement and silencing, and the erasures that are required to keep the mythology intact. Much of this work aims at what Stasiulis and Yuval-Davis named "unsettling" settler societies. Disturbing the mythology. This scholarship, which directly tackles the settler society paradigm, has often originated with a focus other than migration, but in a terrain where, necessarily, migration is implicated because the work focuses on racialization or on social and legal patterns developing in the wake of the migrations that established settler societies.[33] This work makes a vital contribution to understanding the reach of settler society values far beyond the migration context. Its insights are, therefore, important in charting potential consequences of the demise of settler societies.

The end of settler societies, however, is not an assertion that this unsettling project has achieved its goals. The end of settler societies is not accompanied by a remedy for the exclusions and silencing of this mythology, but rather by an amnesia about what might be learned from this trajectory. In arriving at a point in time where there are no longer meaningful distinctions between the migration policies and aspirations of Old World and New World nations, immigration regulation has escaped its past.

In migration regulation, this insight reaches beyond the trope that neglecting the past ensures it will be repeated. The world has changed so much in the past century that we are at no risk of repeating immigration's past. Losing the past does of course rob us of its insights, which might recently have included better ideas about how to build temporary foreign worker programs or how to manage clandestine border crossings. Most importantly, however, amnesia about the past means not seeing that something *has* passed. My project here is to pick up this moment in time. In naming this shift as the end of settler societies my aim is to consider why the settler society era is over, and how this accounting contributes to our understanding of the present and our visions for the future.

The idea of a settler society formed our understanding of migration globally. It emerged at the time when the principal migration cleavages were between Old World ethnic nations and the vast empty imaginary of the New World. Migration was facilitated by the linkages of empire, and its value to the New World reached well beyond the logic of economics. Some nations needed immigrants and others did not. Some identities were fluid and diverse, others were fixed. The global closure of migration regulation developed as settler societies, as a group, were becoming independent and powerful global players. The resulting regulatory structures reflect those interests strongly. The settler society underpins the mythology of migration in former settler states, but also in the Old World nations of Europe, more accustomed to sending than receiving settlers. In its simplest iteration, the end of settler societies means that at this historical juncture, when more people want to move than ever before, there are no longer any places on earth that see this movement as ordinary, expected, and valued in and of itself. This realization is the starting point in exploring how the end of the settler society era sheds light on the new politics of immigration. This exploration is the project of the rest of this book.

The settler society paradigm has, of course, had its greatest influence on those societies that best fit the frame. For the paradigmatic states that have become the world's most successful "nations of immigration" the influence is profound. For other states on the settler society continuum, the work done by the central ideas of the settler society framework varies accordingly. Most compellingly, in the realm of immigration policy and politics the demise of the settler society is intertwined with the frequently observed convergence in immigration regulation. This convergence is part of the story I am pursuing here. The role of this paradigm in structuring global immigration rights and regulations helps us see how and why immigration policy convergence appears to emerge at this point in time. Looking beneath the surface of the settler society paradigm and grappling with the consequences of its demise lead to the conclusion that what masquerades as convergence is in fact a profound and permanent shift.

Notes

1. An open approach to the definition of settler societies, or a simple deployment of the term without any definitional attention, predominates in the scholarly literature. This is not, however, a unanimous position. Ronald Weitzer established a frequently cited definition in his 1990 book *Transforming Settler States: Communal Conflict and Internal Security in Northern Ireland and Zimbabwe* (Berkeley: University of California Press, 1990) at 24: "Settler societies are founded by migrant groups who assume a superordinate position vis-à-vis native inhabitants and build self-sustaining states that are de jure or de facto independent from the mother country and organized around the settlers' political domination over the indigenous population." Lorenzo Veracini offered a more contemporary definition in his 2010 book *Settler Colonialism: A Theoretical Overview* (New York: Palgrave MacMillan, 2010) at 12: "Settlers are founders of political orders and carry their sovereignty with them (on the contrary, migrants can be seen as appellants facing a political order that is already constituted)."
2. These include: Ellis Island Immigration Museum (1990); Canadian Museum of Immigration at Pier 21 (1999); Melbourne Immigration Museum (1998); Migration Museum (South Australia) (1986); NSW Migration Heritage Centre (1998).
3. See Nan Seuffert, *Jurisprudence of National Identity: Kaleidoscopes of Imperialism and Globalisation from Aotearoa New Zealand* (Aldershot,

UK: Ashgate, 2006); Patrick Ongley and David Pearson "Post-1945 International Migration: New Zealand, Australia and Canada Compared" (1995) 29:3 *Intl Migration Rev* 765.

4. David Pearson discusses the logic of this at some length in *The Politics of Ethnicity in Settler Societies: States of Unease* (New York: Palgrave, 2001) at 6–9. See also Davia Stasiulis and Nira Yuval-Davis, eds., *Unsettling Settler Societies: Articulations of Gender, Race, Ethnicity and Class* (London, UK: SAGE Publications, 1995) at 6–7.

5. David Held et al., *Global Transformations: Politics, Economics, and Culture* (Cambridge, UK: Polity, 1999) at 312. Held's assessment states that this finding was "a close call." See also, Stephen Castles and Mark Miller, *The Age of Migration: International Population Movements in the Modern World* (New York: Guilford Press, 2003).

6. Such a count excludes refugees, of course, as chapter 3 makes clear.

7. See Appendix 1 regarding census questions.

8. The most influential recent example of the ethnic understanding of nation is Anthony D. Smith's work, especially *The Ethnic Origins of Nations* (New York: Blackwell, 1986) and *National Identity* (Reno: University of Nevada Press, 1991). For an overview of the two founding nations or peoples thesis in the Canadian context, see Peter H. Russell, *Constitutional Odyssey* (Toronto: University of Toronto Press, 2004).

9. Scholars typically refer to the early twentieth century as the time when the world was brought fully within overlapping schemes of migration regulation. See Ann Dummett and Andrew Nicol, *Subjects, Citizens, Aliens and Others: Nationality and Immigration Law* (London, UK: Weidenfeld and Nicolson, 1990). See John Torpey, *The Invention of the Passport: Surveillance, Citizenship and the State* (Cambridge: Cambridge University Press, 2000), for a contrasting view.

10. Emma Lazarus, "The New Colossus," the poem engraved on the Statute of Liberty (monument dedicated in 1886, plaque mounted 1903).

11. See Appendix 2 "Refugee Resettlement."

12. This doctrine comes from Roman law, and was brought into international law by Francisco de Vitoria. See Randall Lesaffer, "Argument from Roman Law in Current International Law: Occupation and Acquisitive Prescription" (2005) 16:1 *Eur J Intl L* 25.

13. This paragraph draws on Sean Brawley's influential history of the international relations of Asian immigration restrictions. See Sean Brawley, *White Peril: Foreign Relations and Asian Immigration to Australasia and North America, 1919–1978* (Sydney: University of New South Wales Press, 1995), especially at 11–55. Brawley writes:

> In an age when the nations of the New World were discovering their national characteristics and their associated strengths, inflated by

notions of racial superiority, immigration exclusion had become "the cornerstone of the national edifice." (*ibid.* at 43)

14. *Chinese Exclusion Act* (An act to inaugurate certain treaty stipulations relating to Chinese), c 126, 22 Stat 58 (1882).

15. Bruce Ryder, "Racism and the Constitution: The Constitutional Fate of British Columbia Anti-Asian Immigration Legislation, 1884–1909" (1991) 29:3 *Osgoode Hall LJ* 619.

16. James Jupp, *From White Australia to Woomera: The Story of Australian Immigration* (Cambridge: Cambridge University Press, 2001).

17. Manying Ip, "Chinese Immigrants and Transnationals in New Zealand: A Fortress Opened" in Laurence J.C. Ma and Carolyn Cartier, eds., *The Chinese Diaspora: Space, Place, Mobility and Identity* (Lanham, MD: Rowman and Littlefield, 2003) 339 at 339.

18. Useful additional detail on citizenship history, and its linkages with immigration policy, is available in Patrick Weil, *The Sovereign Citizen: Denaturalization and the Origins of the American Republic* (Philadelphia: University of Pennsylvania Press, 2012); Graziella Bertocchi and Chiara Strozzi, "Citizenship Laws and International Migration in Historical Perspective" (2004) Centre for Economic Policy Research Discussion Paper No 4737. Regarding dual citizenship, see Kim Rubenstein, "Citizenship in a Borderless World" in Antony Anghie and Garry Sturgess, eds., *Legal Visions of the 21st Century: Essays in Honour of Judge Christopher Weeramantry* (The Hague: Kluwer Law International, 1998) 183; Kim Rubenstein and Daniel Adler, "International Citizenship: the Future of Nationality in a Globalized World" (2000) 7:2 *Ind J Global Leg Stud* 519.

19. *Dred Scott* v. *Sandford*, 60 US 393 (1857); US Const amend XIV. The first section of the Fourteenth Amendment reads:

> All persons born or naturalized in the United States, and subject to the jurisdiction thereof, are citizens of the United States and of the state wherein they reside. No state shall make or enforce any law which shall abridge the privileges or immunities of citizens of the United States; nor shall any state deprive any person of life, liberty, or property, without due process of law; nor deny to any person within its jurisdiction the equal protection of the laws.

20. *Convention relating to the Status of Refugees*, July 28, 1951, 189 UNTS 150 (entered into force April 22, 1954); *Protocol Relating to the Status of Refugees*, December 16, 1966, 606 UNTS 267 (entered into force October 4, 1967); *1984 Convention Against Torture and Other Cruel, Inhuman or Degrading Treatment or Punishment*, December 10, 1984, 1465 UNTS 85 (entered into force June 26, 1987); *European Convention for the Protection of Human Rights and Fundamental*

Freedoms, November 4, 1950, 213 UNTS 221 (entered into force September 3, 1953).

21. This debate intersects with the story of the new politics of immigration at several junctures and is discussed in Chapter 4 at 73–79 and Chapter 6 at 120–122.

22. James C. Hathaway reviews this development in *The Rights of Refugees Under International Law* (Cambridge: Cambridge University Press, 2005) at 156–85.

23. *International Convention on the Protection of the Rights of All Migrant Workers and Members of their Families*, December 18, 1990, 2220 UNTS 3 (entered into force July 1, 2003). There are thirty-eight signatories to the Convention (as of April 14, 2015). See detailed discussion in Chapter 9 at 190–193.

24. This point is one of the central arguments of Sean Brawley's *White Peril*, *supra* note 13.

25. *Australia Act 1986* (UK), 1986 c 2; *Canada Act 1982* (UK), 1982, c 11.

26. *Mabo and Others* v. *Queensland (No 2)*, [1992] HCA 23 at para 29; 175 CLR 1 [*Mabo*]. Sir (Francis) Gerard Brennan was the Chief Justice of Australia from 1995 to 1998.

27. *Delgamuukw* v. *British Columbia*, [1997] 3 SCR 1010 at para 186.

28. The point that origins of legal orders must frequently be forgotten or suppressed because of their unlawfulness is made most eloquently by Peter Fitzpatrick, *Modernism and the Grounds of Law* (Cambridge: Cambridge University Press, 2001).

29. United Nations Department of Economic and Social Affairs, Population Division, *International Migration Report 2013*, UNDESA, 2013, ST/ESA/SER.A/346. See also United Nations Department of Economic and Social Affairs, Population Division & Organization for Economic Cooperation and Development, *World Migration in Figures: A Joint Contribution to UN High-Level Dialogue on Migration and Development*, 3–4 October, 2013, online: www.oecd.org/els/mig/World-Migration-in-Figures.pdf. These data typically define migrants as people living outside of the country where they were born.

30. These data come from two sources: United Nations Department of Economic and Social Affairs, Population Division, *United Nations Expert Group Meeting on Population Distribution, Urbanization, Internal Migration and Development: New York, 21–23 January 2008*, UNDESA, 2008, ESA/P/WP.206 at 4; Kevin Honglin Zhang and Shunfeng Song, "Rural-Urban Migration and Urbanization in China: Evidence from Time-Series and Cross-section Analyses" (2003) 14:4 *China Economic Rev* 386 at 386–7. These numbers are comparable but with caution: while the Chinese data track twenty years of movement, the

UN DESA data take a snapshot of one point in time but do not reflect when the migrants actually moved.

31. For example, Howard Duncan wrote, "To their credit, the GCIM took a pragmatic and not an ideological tack to their task, and their report, overall, is characterized by pragmatism more than idealism ... In other words, the report appeals to existing common ground as a basis for progress." Howard Duncan, "The Pragmatism of the Global Commission on International Migration" (2009) 22:1 *Center for Migration Studies* Special Issue 36 at 37. Agustin Escobar Lapati put it slightly differently: "Controversial or new ideas are – almost by definition – excluded from such a report." Agustin Escobar Latapi, "The Economy, Development, and Work in the Final Report of the GCIM" (2006) 44:4 *Intl Migration* 15 at 15. Mary Kritz opined, "I wish the GCIM had incorporated more of the ideas found in the background papers into its Report." Mary M. Kritz, "Improving International Migration Governance" (2009) 2291 *Center for Migration Studies* Special Issue 56 at 65.

32. Christian Joppke's book, *Selecting by Origin: Ethnic Migration in the Liberal State* (Cambridge, MA: Harvard University Press, 2005), compares trajectories of ethnic migration in settler societies, post-colonial states, and diaspora patterns, examining the "justifications, mechanisms and pressures" surrounding ethnic migration (*ibid.* at 16) and concluding that the diverse patterns he identifies contribute explanatory values to current policies and controversies. Paul Scheffer's book, *Immigrant Nations*, translated by Liz Waters (Cambridge, UK: Polity Press, 2011), argues that immigration has profoundly changed European societies that had traditionally been perceived as ethnic nations comprised primarily of non-immigrants. Harald Bauder's comparison of Canada and Germany in *Immigration Dialectic: Imagining Community, Economy and Nation* (Toronto: University of Toronto Press, 2011), originated from his earlier comparative work in which he concluded that comparing the two nations in terms of immigration patterns alone was deeply challenging because of their divergent cultural and institutional settings. David Pearson's book, *The Politics of Ethnicity in Settler Societies: States of Unease, supra* note 4, focuses on Canada, Australia, and New Zealand, and sets the United States to the side as the "exception" among settler states because of its rapid movement to the "core" rather than the "periphery" of international relations. Pearson notes, however, that the United States is similar to his comparators in terms of its settler origins and subsequent immigrant and Aboriginal politics (at 7).

33. Davia Stasiulis and Nira Yuval-Davis's influential collection, *Unsettling Settler Societies: Articulations of Gender, Race, Ethnicity and Class, supra* note 4, stakes out the project of both reflecting a broader understanding of settler societies and arguing the constellations of power in these societies

are more complex than a focus on "settlers" and "others" permits. Other work that pursues this "unsettling" project includes Sherene H. Razack, ed., *Race, Space and the Law: Unmapping a White Settler Society* (Toronto: Between the Lines, 2002); Annie E. Coombes, ed., *Rethinking Settler Colonialism: History and Memory in Australia, Canada, New Zealand and South Africa* (Manchester: Manchester University Press, 2006); Paulette Regan, *Unsettling the Settler Within: Indian Residential Schools, Truth Telling, and Reconciliation in Canada* (Vancouver: UBC Press, 2010).

PART 1

THE END OF SETTLER SOCIETIES

The end of settler societies belongs to the twenty-first century. The transformations of the twentieth century brought increasing migration restrictions and a hardening of borders, but the ethos of the settler society largely survived this transformation. In contrast, the opening of the twenty-first century has seen a deep reorientation of immigration laws and politics that has pushed the settler society paradigm into the past.

The demise of settler societies has been brought about by three factors. The first is the crisis of asylum, which has rapidly picked up speed since 2001, and in mid-2015 is escalating exponentially. The second is a deep fear of Islamic fundamentalism, which challenges liberal approaches to immigration. The third factor is the end of ideological multiculturalism. While multiculturalism persists as a description of many societies, without its ideological functions it loses much of its political relevance.

These factors are presented chronologically, but also in order of increasing complexity and proximity to the core meaning of the settler society paradigm. The asylum crisis is the most straightforward. Given the way that international refugee law impinges on state sovereignty, it is clear why states develop an oppositional posture towards it, at least some of the time. Additionally, asylum flows truly do bring strangers to the door of the prosperous migrant-receiving states as most refugee-producing states are in the global South. The fear of fundamental Islam is more complex. It cannot be explained by legal formalism, and it embeds, even at a cursory level, a discomfiting line-drawing exercise: separating Islam from Islamic fundamentalism. It is closer to the core of our immigration politics than asylum questions because it presents core questions about the so-called neutrality and meritocracy that settler state migration policy has pursued for more than three decades now. The demise of multiculturalism is the most complicated of all. As multiculturalism has been central to the national identities of the paradigmatic settler states, a shift within it is both the most difficult to discern, and the most important for confirming the diagnosis of the end of settler societies. The demise of multiculturalism can be read in part as a response to the first two shifts; it goes to the heart of how these nations identify as nations.

The next three chapters describe these factors and show how they have intertwined to contribute to the close of settler societies. One thing these factors have in common is a relationship with human rights. Tracing these relationships is important because of the rise of human rights discourses in migration policy. There are well-marked positions in migration scholarship around the question of how human rights matter to immigrants. On the one hand, human rights arguments have led to some important victories for non-citizens, particularly those with permanent resident status. On the other hand, there is a case to be made that these same human rights decisions by national courts have become so significant that they constrain governments in their development of immigration policy. What separates these positions is an assessment of whether or not this is a positive development.

Evaluating the role of human rights cuts across my argument about the new politics of immigration. The new political climate is underpinned by a human rights structure, and resistance to it, which has developed in the closing decades of the settler society era. While rights arguments were foreign to early immigration regulation, they form an important backdrop to any regulatory structure that emerges moving forward. Analyzing the factors that brought an end to the former paradigm helps in grappling with the analysis of immigration and human rights. This work helps predict when rights arguments will work and when they will fail; when rights discourse will advance politics and when it will grind it to a halt.

Human rights analysis has traction in relation to each of the factors. The refugee law that underpins the asylum crisis emerged as part of the post-World War II human rights era. In the intervening decades, human rights have become increasingly important to asylum decisions, and to expanding the ways that refugee law limits sovereign action. Human rights arguments have also had center stage in Western reactions to the fear of Islamic fundamentalism. This fear has been woven into justifications for rights violations ranging from shifts in immigration screening to Guantanamo Bay detentions. Finally, multiculturalism has been a prominent backdrop to understanding what human rights mean in settler societies. The terrain of rights accommodations for multicultural societies has been a rich space of contestation, including skirmishes over Sunday closing laws, face coverings while voting, and laws condemning forced marriage. Tracing out the human rights story of the end of settler societies is central to these chapters as it establishes the ground work for understanding contemporary law and politics.

The following three chapters explore the forces that have ensured that the end of the settler society paradigm is a permanent transformation. The contours of these developments form the foundations for the new politics of immigration that have emerged in their wake. Attention to the role of human rights in this transformation helps explain how and why the new politics is more highly legalized than at any previous point in history, and opens the way to considering what the consequences of this must be.

3

The asylum crisis

The asylum crisis comes from the realization that Western states cannot effectively limit the number of asylum claims they will receive each year. By the mid-1980s the number of people claiming asylum in prosperous Western states was rising sharply. At that initial point Western states made a decision – implicitly or explicitly – that resulted in the rise in asylum numbers having long-term worldwide impacts. That decision, repeated over and over by diverse states, was that the appropriate response to a desire to curtail the number of asylum seekers would be to introduce measures directed at specific features of asylum flows, rather than to withdraw from or seek to alter the legal parameters of international refugee law. This approach has evolved into a profound commitment to international refugee law, which has altered the international framework of global migration. It has also ushered in a contentious and intransigent politics of asylum that was the first harbinger of a new politics of immigration.

International refugee law makes the asylum crisis possible. As I outlined in Chapter 2, the central commitment of refugee law is that people who are refugees must not be returned to countries where they face a risk of being persecuted. The law was negotiated in the immediate aftermath of World War II, and its objective was to resolve the problems of population displacement in Europe and to ensure that the "burden" of displaced populations would be shared between states. The specific contours of the Refugee Convention reflect its historic context in two important ways. First, the Convention does not aim to protect everyone: its protection is extended to individuals who are at risk because of their political views or identity. In this way, refugees as originally conceptualized resemble those who were most victimized and most valorized by the horrors of World War II and the onset of the Cold War: religious and racial and national minorities, dissidents, and resisters. Second, refugee law was initially limited to protecting only people in Europe and only those who were displaced prior to 1951. The Refugee Convention also set up a framework for limiting state responsibilities: decisions are made on an individual basis; states do not have any general responsibilities but, rather, are limited to caring for those who arrive on their territory; and a notion of "burden sharing" is written into the text of the Preamble. This backdrop helps us make sense of the internationally agreed definition of a refugee as:

> A person who owing to well founded fear of being persecuted for reasons of race, religion, nationality, membership of a particular social group or political opinion, is outside the country of his nationality and is unable or, owing to such fear, is unwilling to avail himself of the protection of that country; or who, not having a nationality and being outside the country of his former habitual residence as a result of such events, is unable or, owing to such fear, is unwilling to return to it.[1]

Contemporary refugee law has grown from this framework, and its growth is the basis for the asylum crisis. In 1967, states formally agreed to expand the reach of the Convention beyond Europe and past 1951 into the unbounded future. The most significant expansions, however, have come not from formal amendments but from interpretive expansions of key provisions. Crucially, the focal notion of "persecution" has never been defined. Thus decision makers around the world must decide over and over again whether particular types of harm are persecutory. They do this with one eye to the past, and the horrors of World War II, and, increasingly, one eye to international human rights. Other aspects of the refugee definition have also proven rich terrain for interpretation, and concepts such as "social group" and "political opinion" have similarly developed extensive jurisprudence. Together these features of refugee law mean that anyone in the world can enter a state that participates in the Refugee Convention and ask to remain there with refugee protection. This is what seeking asylum means. With 148 states formally signed up to the Refugee Convention or its Protocol, this commitment covers much of the globe. Furthermore, whether or not an individual fits within the refugee definition is in practice determined by a receiving state, and thus individuals do not know in advance if they will be accepted. These are the seeds of the asylum crisis.

It may well not be fair to attribute the current strength of refugee law to an actual "decision" by states not to withdraw from it. In hindsight, however, the incremental actions of Western states throughout the 1980s and early 1990s now look decisive, and have had the result of strengthening the Refugee Convention into a core piece of international law. While international law is often considered a space where "law" is voluntary and "un-law-like," refugee law has developed distinctive law-like characteristics that function as true constraints on states. In the 1980s, when asylum statistics first began to climb, much of the present trajectory was undoubtedly unforeseeable. Western states, which had very recently collaborated to expand the reach of the Refugee Convention, and settler societies that had recently dismantled racist provisions in their immigration laws, did not confront a domestic politics encouraging withdrawal from refugee law. In this political context other alternatives were preferable, whether or not an overt choice was made.

This chapter tells the story of how the asylum crisis contributed crucial elements of change to the immigration politics of prosperous Western states that frame global immigration politics. The first step is to sketch the elements of the asylum crisis, its twentieth-century past and its contemporary contours. I then turn to examining how this crisis is intertwined with the politics of immigration. This leads to a focus on the role that human rights play in the asylum crisis and in responses to it. Finally, I conclude by explaining how all of this contributes to the demise of the settler society paradigm, and lays the foundation for both fear of Islamic fundamentalism and the end of multiculturalism to flourish.[2]

ELEMENTS OF THE ASYLUM CRISIS

By 1980, seventy-nine states were formally participating in international refugee law. This number included North America and much of Western Europe, as well as Australia and New Zealand. The United States, which had treated the Refugee Convention with the cautious distancing it typically accords to international human rights instruments, had reached an awkward domestic compromise under which it ratified the Protocol in 1968 without becoming a state party to the Convention, but did not bring its domestic law into alignment with the internationally agreed refugee definition until 1980.[3] This widespread acceptance among states that are considered to be the most sought after immigration destinations set the stage for the asylum crisis and its immigration aftermath.

In 1985, the number of asylum seekers began to rise sharply. The annual average number of asylum seekers in the late 1970s and early 1980s had hovered around 100,000 people annually among industrialized states. In the mid-1980s, this number rose sharply and by the early-1990s, because of conflict in the Balkans, the annual averages hovered just under 1 million. In 2014, the United Nations High Commissioner for Refugees (UNHCR) reported a fourth consecutive rise in the annual number of asylum seekers in industrialized states, with a total of 866,000. This number is still shy of the 1990s peak, but strongly signals that the "new normal" for asylum has significantly shifted from the early 1980s. The most recent year is even higher. The figures for 2012 and 2013 were 488,000 and 596,600 respectively. There was a drop in the mid-1990s, and again in the middle of the 2000s, but even these drops did not come close to the level of the early 1980s. (See Appendix 3.) Furthermore, this shift in demand for asylum has persisted despite increased, and still increasing, state efforts to make it harder and harder for people to make asylum claims.

Two pieces of information put the asylum claim rate in context. First, asylum claim figures are related to the number of refugees in the world, but are tiny in comparison. The United Nations High Commissioner for Refugees historical refugee data show 8,454,937 refugees worldwide in 1980; 17,395,979 in 1990; and 16.7 million refugees out of a total of 51.2 million forcibly displaced in 2014.[4] Most people who are considered to be refugees never claim asylum, and the majority of these people remain in the regions of the world that they call home. While anyone classified as a refugee has crossed an international border, refugee camps are not a feature of the contemporary global North. This leads to the second important part of the context: asylum tends to be the way that the global North experiences refugee flows. Asylum is certainly not confined to the global North, indeed the state with the largest asylum numbers in most recent years is South Africa. Rather it is the case that asylum is the principal way that states (and citizens) in the global North encounter refugees. Furthermore, while some refugees are resettled to global North states, the numbers are small (about one-tenth) in comparison to the number of asylum claims.

Refugee resettlement has little to do with international refugee law, but it provides a powerful symbolic accompaniment to the asylum narrative. Resettlement occurs when a (usually Western) state brings refugees to its territory to remain permanently. Most resettled refugees come from camps near to the conflicts that displaced them from their homes. The number of people resettled annually is infinitesimally small in comparison to the number of refugees in the world, about 1 percent of that total. UNHCR government statistics for 2013 reveal the total number of resettled refugees admitted was 98,400. This level is fairly typical. Resettlement is remote from refugee law because it is not required by law. States are only required to assess the claims of people who reach their territory. They are not required to help people get there. But resettlement makes good politics and good advocacy as the images of mass exodus into squalid camps are mesmerizing. States are in control of resettlement; asylum is, by design, impossible to control.[5]

After a successful asylum claim an individual is, usually, permitted to remain in their state of refuge. But those whose claims are unsuccessful are usually required to return home. The global acceptance rate for asylum claims is very difficult to estimate, as each state has its own processes, avenues of appeal, and systems of complementary protection whereby individuals who are "not quite" refugees but in similarly vulnerable situations are allowed to stay. Among scholars in this area, it is often said that the global acceptance rate for asylum claims sifts out to be about 40 percent, taking into account various layers of review. It is similarly agreed that asylum acceptance rates are declining. In some places this is easy to demonstrate; for example, in 1989 when Canada's Immigration and Refugee Board first began adjudicating asylum claims, the acceptance rate was 89 percent. In the most recent year with complete data, 2013, the rate was 38 percent. What this means is that these days well over half of all those who claim asylum are expected to leave. Accordingly, asylum is part of the increasingly common "circular" migration pattern.

The roots of the asylum crisis are found in the 1980s rise in claim numbers. In response to that rise, prosperous states began to implement a variety of measures to reduce the number of asylum seekers. Tools used in the battle against asylum include carrier sanctions, visa requirements, extraterritorial migration enforcement, biometric screening, intensification of traditional border enforcement, and safe third country agreements, all of which aim at preventing asylum seekers from reaching particular countries. These provisions have been complemented by laws curtailing asylum rights and making the process of asserting a claim more miserable; for example, by reducing or eliminating welfare state entitlements during the claim period or by extending detention provisions for asylum seekers. While all prosperous Western states have eagerly participated in these efforts to make seeking asylum more difficult, and thus more dangerous, Australia has been the undisputed leader in this regard. Australia introduced mandatory detention for people who arrived in the country without authorization in 1992, and in 2001, following a highly publicized crisis involving a boat called the MV *Tampa*, began a series of legal maneuvers whereby most people arriving by boat are not allowed to remain in Australia for refugee status determination, but are instead transferred to other states, Nauru being one favoured example. At one point parts of the Australian mainland were nonsensically declared to be "not Australia" for the purposes of claiming asylum. The High Court of Australia struck down a 2011 agreement under which asylum seekers who reached Australia would be shipped to Malaysia in return for Australian acceptance of people who have been determined to be refugees by the UNHCR in Malaysia, which is not a state party to the Refugee Convention.[6]

Other states have similarly ratcheted up efforts to make their borders harder and less appealing for those in need of protection. In the past five years, Canada has introduced a list of countries designated as presumptively "safe," the European border security agency Frontex has increased its "enforcement" budget, and the United States has stepped up detention rates in an effort to deter asylum claims.[7] It is difficult at this point in time to imagine this trend abating; the desire to limit the number of asylum seekers is prominent on the political agenda of almost all Western states.

This intensive and expensive effort has had limited effectiveness. A typical pattern is demonstrated by the United States–Canada Safe Third Country Agreement. The Agreement provides that asylum seekers must seek protection in whichever of the two countries they reach first. As many asylum seekers travel to Canada via the United States, everyone anticipated that the Agreement would lead to a marked drop in asylum claims in Canada. This was certainly true in the first year of the agreement, 2005, when there was a sharp decline in numbers. However, within three years, the number of asylum claims in Canada had returned to pre-Agreement levels.[8]

Of course, it is possible that without these dramatic efforts by Western industrialized states asylum seeker numbers would be much higher than they are at present. How much higher is unknowable. And how people speculate about the answer to this question tends to reveal a great deal about where they position themselves on the spectrum of immigration politics. This occurs because the asylum crisis is intertwined with, and contributes to, important trends in migration politics more generally.

ASYLUM AND "ILLEGAL" MIGRATION

The most important of these trends is that a crackdown on asylum seeking is intertwined with a crackdown on migration flows generally, and extra-legal migration in particular. In 2015, it seems almost impossible to imagine a time when crossing a border without legal permission was considered to be a type of regulatory infringement, not a truly criminal act. Let alone to remember that for anyone who is an adult now, this shift has taken place within our lifetimes. It is difficult to separate the elements of the asylum crisis from the overall crackdown on extra-legal migration. In part this is because the technologies and policies deployed by states are the same in both cases: stopping people from crossing borders involves the same state apparatus regardless of the reason for seeking to cross. The asylum crisis began in the mid-1980s, and by the mid-1990s a full-scale global crackdown on extra-legal migration had been launched. The two trends are closely related, but are not the same politically or legally, and thus it is worth devoting some time to disentangling them.

The asylum crisis arises because there are many more people in the world entitled to asylum than Western industrialized states want to welcome as refugees. Once an asylum seeker reaches a Western country, that state is at least obligated to assess their status, may be obligated to allow them to remain, and might face considerable difficulties in compelling them to leave. These administrative, legal, and procedural realities mean that states are motivated to act "at a distance" in response to the crisis. The central strategy is to ensure that asylum seekers do not arrive in the first place, because once a person is on national territory, policy options dwindle. This underlies the "wet foot dry foot" approach to Cuban asylum seekers in the United States, and the stunningly illogical idea that Australia can be considered "not Australia" for the purposes of asylum only.

The motivations for a crackdown on extra-legal border crossing are different. States have sovereign rights to control which non-citizens enter and remain in their territory, and the right to remove those who lack permission to remain. In this arena, states are acting with the full authority of a power that is at the core of their identity as states. Acting against asylum seekers, on the other hand, can be read as acting against human rights, a much less solid terrain. The origins of the contemporary crackdown on extra-legal migration are murky. By the early 1990s, a number of Western states had considerable populations of temporary workers whose permission to remain had expired, but whom states were having difficulty "evicting," as it were. A number of former colonial powers were having trouble enforcing new legal regimes that cut off migration rights for nationals of former colonies. As these pressures mounted, states were increasingly confronted with the dilemmas of deportation, which often requires acts of coercion that liberal states have difficulty stomaching and that everyone has a hard time financing. The sharply rising asylum numbers were also part of the mix. In addition, by the 1990s the advance of globalizing forces was threatening states' capacity to assert themselves as autonomous actors in many policy realms. Population flows, however, remained an area of unbridled sovereign authority, and thus a key policy realm for states seeking to demonstrate their own continued relevance and power.

All of these factors contributed to the inception of the global crackdown on unwanted migration. Once ignited, the crackdown itself was efficiently self-perpetuating. Once states set out to "find" illegal migrants, they find more and more. The increased effort of "looking" generates, therefore, a steadily rising statistical trace: the more effort states put in to finding illegal migrants the more illegal migrants there are. Similarly, because "illegality" is produced by law, the more laws there are constraining migration, the more categories of people exist who are in breach of those laws. As the regulatory framework becomes more intricate, the number of lawbreakers rises, and thus more people are outside the law: illegal.

The idea of extra-legal migration is not new, but the moral panic surrounding it dates to the 1990s, and was the impetus for my work in writing *Making People Illegal*. Indeed, at the time the Refugee Convention was being negotiated, the drafters turned their mind to the conflict between migration control and refugee protection. The compromise struck is particularly apt in the contemporary political climate. The Refugee Convention does not grant anyone a right of entry to another country in order to seek asylum. It does, however, require that states not punish refugees for illegal entry to their country of refuge.[9] Under contemporary crackdown conditions, this provision is vital for refugees because it is not possible, anywhere in the world, to be granted a visa for the purpose of seeking asylum.[10] This means that refugees have limited – and bad – options: they can obtain a visa by misrepresenting their intentions, they can travel using falsified documents, or they can travel clandestinely. The protective effect of the Convention is to recognize how rotten this array of options is, and to excuse refugees from liability for their (constrained) choices. The catch, however, is that the Convention provides this protection to refugees, not to asylum seekers. Once a state has determined that a person is not a refugee, he or she can be punished like any other migration law evader. And although the UNHCR, and all good refugee lawyers, will tell you that refugee status is "declaratory" – that is, a formal decision does not make a person a refugee, it just confirms what was already true – formal decisions do most certainly determine when people are *not* refugees. Typically, if an asylum seeker can make it to the border of a prosperous Western state, she will be admitted on the basis of her asylum claim, but may well later be treated as an illegal migrant.

The main reason that asylum and illegal migration are intertwined is that a crackdown on extra-legal migration fuels the asylum crisis, and vice versa. The current suite of crackdown measures has made it harder and harder for people – especially poor or unskilled people – to cross borders. The Refugee Convention provides a way for people to cross borders, and has proven resiliently effective in constraining the sovereign power to close borders. Accordingly, people looking for border-crossing options look increasingly to the Refugee Convention as other options disappear. This puts more and more pressure on the Convention. This pressure is intensified by the complexity of refugee law, and the warm glow of humanitarianism. In the former case, it is difficult for people to know in advance whether they will be found to be refugees. In the latter, most Western states have at least some small reluctance to proclaim overtly their hostility to refugees – there is still some cachet, some value, in being seen to be humanitarian. In these ways the crackdown on extra-legal migration raises the stakes in the asylum crisis.

The reverse is also true. The sense of crisis about asylum, and the widespread goal of reducing numbers of asylum seekers, ratchets up the crackdown on extra-legal migration. Despite the protective provision of the Refugee Convention, states do not want asylum seekers arriving illegally, and states work to make it harder and harder for asylum seekers to arrive, all of which contributes to the crackdown apparatus.

The relationship between the asylum crisis and the crackdown on extra-legal migration is not causal or linear. Nor are the two simply mutually constituting phenomena. They are two closely related things, happening in the same policy terrain at the same time. They do not occupy the whole terrain, but their effects are found in every nook and cranny of the new politics of migration. What is clear is that these intertwined phenomena predate but contribute to the other two factors that combine with the asylum crisis to bring an end to the settler society era: fear of fundamental Islam and the demise of ideological multi-culturalism. In order to understand how the asylum crisis fits into the larger picture, it is important to consider why the asylum crisis has become "perpetual," how the asylum crisis links to human rights, and what the asylum crisis means for settler societies in particular.

THE POLITICS OF CRISIS

The asylum crisis has been in train for so long now that it is arguably unfair to continue to call it a "crisis" in the sense of an acute and short-term state that one might reasonably expect will be resolved. The asylum levels that provoked a crisis response in the mid-1980s have been transformed into the new normal, and an array of measures aimed at reducing asylum flows is now accepted as a routine part of refugee law. But the notion of crisis remains. It leaves an important imprint on Western responses to asylum and on immigration politics more broadly.

Refugee law has always been about crisis. The Convention was drafted with short-term goals and the ideal of imminent resolution. The doctrinal nuts and bolts of refugee decision making favour those whose circumstances fit most squarely into a "crisis" framework. Funding to the UNHCR is crisis driven, as is the structure of the organization and its mandate. Much of the ongoing reaction of prosperous states to asylum seekers is marked by a sense of crisis. Emma Haddad has even gone so far as to argue that the figure of the refugee represents a crisis point for the international state system, because the refugee is a person without a state in any effective sense.[11] Events that lead to large-scale refugee movements are always crises, whether the refugees are flowing into neighbouring states or arriving in scarcely seaworthy boats on wealthy shores.

The security turn following the terrorist attacks of 9/11 in the United States fits into the story of the asylum crisis, but is not its starting point. This distinction is one of the most frequently overlooked parts of this story. The tightening of borders against asylum seekers had already been in train for nearly a decade when the 9/11 attacks took place. The political shifts ushered in by those attacks, however, added a new and fearful element to the border-closing imperative. In the immediate aftermath of the attacks, asylum was singled out as a path for dangerous foreigners to enter prosperous states. This discourse persisted despite evidence that none of the attackers had entered the United States, or neighbouring Canada, as asylum seekers.

The security turn had the effect of dampening local opposition to asylum crackdown provisions, and making it politically easier for Western states to introduce enhanced security and suppression measures aimed at asylum seekers. One high-profile example of a shift of this nature was the Canada–United States Safe Third Country Agreement. This Agreement enacts a classic state tool of the asylum crisis – mirroring for this one border the requirement that the Dublin agreements impose throughout Europe. An agreement of this nature had been discussed intermittently from the outset of the crisis in the mid-1980s. Canada had been keen to pursue it, as the majority of asylum seekers enter Canada by crossing the border with the United States. For the same reason, interest in an agreement was lower on the American side. But following 9/11 the agreement offered the United States the opportunity to take procedural control of as many as 20,000 more asylum seekers annually. This control fit directly into the new security imperative. As well, the agreement was roughly coincident with other American measures that would reduce the overall numbers of refugees in the country, such as the introduction of a ban on claiming asylum after more than one year in the country, enhanced authority to detain, and a marked reduction in refugee resettlement.[12] Accordingly, the Agreement could be implemented without unleashing a significant rise in numbers.

The "bogus refugee" is a creature of the asylum crisis. Understanding the political positioning of this trope – most often encountered in the discourse of Western politicians – requires some understanding of the asylum crisis. This slur accuses people of purposely misusing the border-crossing exception that refugee law provides. Undeniably, some people do this. It is inevitable given the contours of the global crackdown on migration. And, similar to estimates of how many more asylum seekers there would be if states were not working so hard to stop them, estimates of how many "bogus" refugees exist reveal more about the political inclinations of the estimator than anything else. Determining whether someone fits within the refugee definition is often a complicated decision. In the best refugee determination systems, these decisions are made by people who understand at least some of the intricacies of refugee jurisprudence. Even experienced refugee lawyers are not able to fully predict which of their clients will be accepted as refugees with 100 percent certainty. It is, therefore, ordinary that people arrive in prosperous states thinking that they are refugees only to find out later, and officially, that they are not. In addition to this group, there will be another group of people who are desperate and destitute and want to improve their lives, who have no idea whether or not they are refugees, but who flee their homelands regardless and later make asylum claims. These people are not morally blameworthy, and some of them will have successful claims. Finally, there will be some people who know themselves *not* to be refugees who make asylum claims regardless. It is impossible to know with any accuracy the size of each of these groups. Those who use the "bogus refugee" discourse believe the latter group is large, possibly the largest. Those who work with refugee claimants on a day-to-day basis, however, tend to believe that this latter group is by far the smallest.

The "queue jumper" is a close relative of the "bogus refugee." This epithet accuses so-called "legitimate" refugees of seeking asylum on their own rather than waiting patiently in a camp somewhere to be resettled to a safe place. The idea that people can arrive in a refugee camp and join a queue is nonsense. The resettlement choices of those few countries that do resettle people are not based on queuing. For the overwhelming majority of refugees waiting in camps, resettlement will never happen. At the start of 2014, 11.3 million refugees were identified as being in what the UNHCR calls "protracted" situations – they have been in a camp for more than five years, along with a large group of at least 25,000 of their co-nationals.[13] If this were not enough, many asylum seekers flee from places without proximate refugee camps. Given all of this, the "queue jumper" slur is even more inaccurate than the "bogus" refugee. Rather than simply revealing the speaker's political stance regarding asylum, it also shows that the speaker does not have much basic information about refugees worldwide.

The commonplace of the "bogus refugee" and the "queue jumper" demonstrates that concerns about asylum have become a routine part of domestic politics in almost all prosperous Western countries by the outset of the present century. This is one of the most significant political results of the asylum crisis. Having a position in regard to asylum seekers is now *de rigueur* for political parties in Western liberal states. As this is a domestic political concern, it takes different forms, sometimes emphasizing the intertwining with extra-legal migration, sometimes leaning toward the security frame. Australia is possibly the extreme example in this regard, where the partisan conflict regarding asylum arrivals by boat has been a central issue in every national election this century. In Canada, the ministry responsible for immigration matters was seen as a "junior" cabinet position throughout most of the twentieth century. When the Conservative Party under Prime Minister Stephen Harper won a majority in 2011, his highly activist immigration minister was not promoted to a more high-profile post. Rather, the post itself was made more high profile and Immigration Minister Kenney was formally recognized as a leader within the Cabinet by being made the Chair of the Cabinet Committee on Operations. In the United States, immigration reform focused principally on extra-legal migration was a high priority for President Obama's second term.

A domestic politics concerning asylum is, almost of necessity, a politics of opposing asylum. It is unimaginable that a contemporary political party would build a campaign advocating for higher acceptance rates and more flexible borders for asylum seekers. The sole example that comes to mind is the 2007 election campaign in Australia, where the Labor party did signal an intent to dismantle some of the existing harsh policies (the harshest in any Western country at that time) toward asylum seekers. Following their election victory, the Labor government of Kevin Rudd acted on these promises. But within just three years, Rudd had been turfed out by his own party and Labor successor Julia Gillard had reintroduced some of the harshest provisions, and in some cases, extended punitive policies towards asylum seekers even further than those of the pre-2007 right-leaning government. The Gillard Labor government in Australia was fully engaged in what can be seen as the "normal" politics of asylum in the early twenty-first century: where domestic competitors seek to demonstrate that they are sufficiently tough-minded to be trusted with the question of asylum. In the 2013 national election, Gillard's government was defeated in a campaign where tough-on-asylum policies featured prominently.

Just as the asylum crisis itself is intertwined with immigration, the politics of the asylum crisis flow seamlessly into immigration politics more broadly. This linkage is what draws together the three chapters in this section: the fear of fundamental Islam and the demise of multi-culturalism both have antecedents in the asylum crisis, and each affects the ongoing contours of state responses to asylum. I turn to these key political effects in the chapters that follow. It is ironic that one effect of the enduring sense of crisis has been to achieve a greater degree of political separation between concerns related to immigration and those related to asylum flows. This separation is particularly important for settler societies, and I will elaborate this point below, but in all Western states an objective of refugee advocates in the 1980s and 1990s was to assert that refugees were not immigrants and ought not to be treated as immigrants in their selection, their support, or the expecta-tions upon them for integration and economic achievement. For those of us who are old enough to have been making that argument, it is astonishing that it has simply faded away. The point used to be that states had legal and moral obligations toward refugees and asylum seekers and needed to act accordingly, not simply treat refugees as additional economic and nation-building fodder. These days, however, the tables are turned, and advocates are more likely to assert that refugees do bring economic contributions and do become full members of society. One effect of the asylum crisis has been to shift the location of the desire to rhetorically merge refugees and immigrants. In part this is because some objectives of the earlier advocacy have been achieved; for example, both Canada and Australia have shifted their policies to prioritize resettling those who are particularly vulnerable.[14] But primar-ily, this is because asylum seekers are now more feared and reviled in public discourse than ever before.

The perpetuity of the asylum crisis brings with it crisis fatigue. There is a now-enduring sense that refugee flows will never end, that they are inevitable, or even a logical aspect of the international state system. This fatigue impairs our political will to respond in a "crisis" mode – the status quo is no longer perceived as something that if we paid close attention (and lots of money) for a short period of time we could end. Crisis fatigue also bolsters the political impetus to limit the exposure of prosperous Western states to asylum claims: if the number of people in the world who need refugee protection is endless, the question of where to draw the line becomes more arbitrary. Human rights principles stand against this logic. Understanding how human rights and asylum are woven together explains both how refugee law has become more law-like, and why Western states are so active in deterring asylum seekers.

ASYLUM CRISIS AND HUMAN RIGHTS

The Refugee Convention is not considered to be a core human rights instrument of the international system. There is probably an argument to be made that this traditional positioning is incorrect, but I want to put that aside for a moment, or perhaps more correctly, I want to approach it indirectly. In a sense, it does not matter how international refugee law is categorized, it matters what effects it has on the lives of individuals around the world.

The Refugee Convention engages with human rights in two very direct ways. The first is that international refugee law constrains state sovereignty. This is precisely what international human rights law is supposed to do, but where it so often fails in implementation. The great revolution of international law in the second half of the twentieth century was the presence of the individual. With the post-World War II rise of human rights, states were no longer the only subjects, and objects, of international law. Rather, runs the now shopworn narrative, individuals now appear in the texts of international law, and can through these appearances hold states to account. International law ceases to be a terrain for states alone. This revolution means that citizens whose rights are denied within their own states can reach beyond the border of the nation for legal vindication. The theory is sound. Much good work is being done to make it more realizable for individuals, but for most people meaningful rights vindication at the international level is a very remote possibility. The comparatively recent innovation of the European Court of Human Rights, and its increasing importance within the European Union, is the largest area of progress, but still remains inaccessible for most individuals.

The constraint that refugee law presents to state sovereignty is much more direct. Refugee law requires that when a person comes within its ambit, the state must protect that person in a very significant way, by allowing her, or him, to remain within its borders, to participate in the national community that it is otherwise free to wall off from the world. Because of this core commitment of refugee law, it has a "bite" that ordinary international human rights instruments do not. It is not a matter of degree, it is not available only to those with the legal and personal resources for a long fight, and it is not limited to high-profile test cases. Furthermore, national borders stake out clear bright lines: refugees are "in." This is part of the reason that refugee law is considered to be surrogate human rights protection; through this law the international community has made a commitment to protect people whose home states cannot or will not protect them. Asylum is the linchpin of the constraint on sovereignty. Refugee law is only triggered when an individual crosses a border. The legal constraint on sovereignty has a physical form, that of an individual standing on national soil.

The second way that refugee law intersects with human rights law is that over the now sixty years since refugee law came into being, international human rights have become the dominant interpretive source for understanding and applying refugee law principles. This is the other half of the explanation for considering refugee law to be surrogate human rights protection. The refugee definition ensures that the obligation is not to protect every vulnerable person from every kind of serious harm. It is only "persecution" from which people are sheltered, and even then only persecution on the basis of certain, discriminatory, reasons. As refugee law has developed, courts and governments around the world have accepted that the central concept of persecution ought to be interpreted in human rights terms and, similarly, that the accompanying idea of discrimination should be understood as having a central human rights meaning. Through these two principles, refugee law has drawn closer and closer to human rights law over time. The linkage between refugee law and human rights law has been the source of much of the important and principled expansion of refugee law.[15]

The human rights hermeneutic of refugee law has two consequences. The first is that growth in human rights law leads, although never seamlessly, to growth in refugee law. The evolution of refugee protection for lesbians and gay men provides a good example here. This is currently one of the most significant areas of jurisprudential growth within refugee law, following on a two-decade-long rights revolution in Western liberal democracies. The second consequence is that refugee status determinations are one of the main areas of day-to-day application of international human rights. More than half a million asylum decisions made every year for the last quarter of a century equates with many millions of decisions reflecting on, analyzing, and concluding about human rights arguments.

For these reasons, it does not matter whether the United Nations lists the Refugee Convention as a core human rights instrument. Its human rights effects are enormous.

I believe that the human rights core of refugee law is also vital to explaining both how and why refugee law has become more law-like in recent years. The most remarkable thing about the asylum crisis is that it has not triggered a massive withdrawal of states from the Refugee Convention. While states have pursued increasingly inventive measures to curtail access to asylum, and with it the meaningful constraint on sovereignty that adherence to refugee law brings, none has taken the relatively straightforward step of withdrawing from the Refugee Convention. Treaties only work – in both theory and practice – because states consent to be bound. Accounting for this is important for understanding the law, but also for understanding the new politics of immigration in which this law has a central role.

The human rights core of refugee law is one of the most persuasive explanations for its widespread legitimacy, and thus for the "law-like" aura that has grown up around it. That aura is hard to come by in international law, and it speaks to the emergence of rule of law values surrounding refugee law. It is plausible, even likely, that while prosperous Western states are politically comfortable acting to limit the reach of refugee law, they recoil from withdrawing from such a high-profile "almost core" human rights commitment. The tug, however, between the desire to limit the law's effects and the growth both politically and jurisprudentially of human rights, generates a hardening within refugee law. As states make the space within which refugee law operates progressively narrower by restricting asylum, the human rights backbone of the law is strengthening. Interpreting human rights is the bread and butter work of courts. While not all courts in prosperous democracies are taking strong human rights positions about refugee law rulings, many have done so, and continue to do so. This sets up strong contestation between courts and governments as a recurring feature of perpetual asylum crisis. Especially in common law systems, shared by the paradigmatic settler states, each clash in the courts develops more law. Each interpretive act of a leading appellate court expands space that refugee law occupies, and thereby reduces the discretion of states. The government–court tension here is a key ingredient for a polarized and intransigent politics.

The behaviour of the prosperous Western states who are the principal global actors in restricting asylum access demonstrates that these states believe refugee law to be a meaningful constraint on their sovereignty. In this regard, refugee law is unlike much of international human rights law, where it is always an open question whether a ruling from the UN's Torture Committee or Human Rights Committee will be followed. Some scholars and advocates are even suggesting that the *non-refoulement* principle, which ensures that refugees cannot be returned to face persecution, is emerging as a *jus cogens* norm of the international system – a norm so powerful that it binds even those states that have not formally consented to the treaty. My own view is that this is a stretch too far. But I am nonetheless impressed by the increased puissance of international refugee law that has developed over the past twenty years. A delicate intertwining of human rights and the rule of law explains this strength, along with the asylum crisis that provided the crucible in which this strength could be forged.

ASYLUM CRISIS AND THE ONSET OF A NEW POLITICS

The asylum crisis is the first step towards a new politics of immigration and the end of the settler society era. The overarching reason for this is that reconceiving asylum as crisis fractures its place in the mythology of settler societies. The subsidiary elements of this transformation comprise three factors: policy convergence throughout prosperous Western states, legalization, and an increasingly intransigent politics marked by a sharp South–North divide.

Turning first to policy convergence, the ratcheting up of measures designed to reduce access to asylum was the first time that settler societies and prosperous European states followed converging policies in the immigration terrain. Prior to the mid-1990s, immigration politics and patterns were still markedly different in the Old World and the New. However, once asylum numbers rose sharply, and states began to implement and innovate deterrence policies, borrowing across the Old World–New World divide quickly became commonplace. At least a decade before 2015, it was impossible to say that the basic approaches to restricting asylum showed any reflection of what had previously been quite divergent approaches to immigration issues.

Of course, immigration politics and asylum politics are not precisely the same, but the asylum crisis functioned to draw them closer together, and thus to increase the significance of the policy convergence. Cracking down on extra-legal migration meets its policy objective of reducing access to asylum, but it also serves to significantly increase pressure on the asylum systems worldwide. This pressure in turn means that asylum is now conceptualized as a migration option in a more significant way than ever before. Poor people have fewer options, and asylum remains one of them.

The asylum crisis also introduced a sharp uptick in legalization into an area that was previously marked by high levels of discretionary state action. Even the granting of asylum itself, which states party to the Refugee Convention are free to extend beyond the parameters of that Convention, is now considered almost everywhere in the world to be virtually synonymous with refugee status. In the 1970s, by contrast, Canada allowed thousands of Americans fleeing the Vietnam draft to remain permanently in the country. The United States based its pre-1980 asylum policy almost exclusively on Cold War politics. Until the mid-1980s refugee law served as a guidance policy for discretionary admissions to Australia. Thus even at this basic level, the asylum crisis brought a wave of legalization. This wave began first with asylum itself, but followed in two directions – increasing layers of restrictive provisions, and the hardening of the human rights core of refugee law. Because Western liberal democracies have never truly separated refugee and immigration law, the legalization that began with the asylum crisis led to a broader trend that is still notable in 2015, and will likely continue into the future.

The gradual replacement of discretion with law creates a greater and greater role for courts, a key feature of the increasingly intransigent politics introduced by the asylum crisis. The perpetuity of the asylum crisis has turned the anti-asylum posture of Western governments into a permanent part of the political landscape. The hostility that first emerged as focused on asylum is now focused on migrants of all ilk. Refugees were once the most sympathetic immigrant figures, now they are recast as asylum seekers and their bogus and queue-jumping co-conspirators. Within this new framing, it is impossible to truly cast one's mind back to a time when the linkage between "security" and refugee law was expressed in human security terms. In other words, people were refugees because security was what they lacked, not because they were a threat to our security in some way. At the time of the Indochinese boat crisis of the mid-1980s, Canada and Australia were at the forefront of providing protection for people made refugees by the political upheavals.[16] Faced with the extraordinary refugee production of the Syrian civil war that began in 2011, the Canadian government made a minimal commitment to accept 1300 people, and has been very slow to meet it. In August 2014, Australia committed to welcoming 2200 Syrian refugees under its quota for resettlement of the most vulnerable. These numbers are laughable in the face of the almost 4 million refugees who had fled this conflict by the end of 2014.[17] Additional commitments as the crisi mounted in 2015 were generally on the same scale.[18]

One of the most frustrating features of the contemporary political intransigence is a feature we can label "fact resistance." Refugee advocates are repeatedly at pains to interject factual information into public discourses about refugees. The easy example is the story of 9/11 recounted earlier. But this outdated instance is just the tip of the iceberg. Any scholar who regularly speaks on this topic with people outside their disciplinary enclave will be familiar with myriad questions about the criminal risks of refugee admissions, the security risks inherent in asylum, and the potential "illegality" of asylum seeking. The worldwide media coverage of the Mediterranean migrant disaster of the spring of 2015 repeated *ad nauseam* the condemnation of human trafficking.[19] Such labeling is just plain wrong. While the lines between human trafficking and human smuggling are hard to discern (and serve in public discourse mostly to apportion blame), those who help people fleeing their homelands to preserve their lives and physical integrity are smugglers at worst, humanitarians at best. This distinction also is difficult to untangle fully.

A further important feature of the political intransigence of the asylum crisis is that it enshrines a South–North global divide. The Balkan crisis, now two decades ago, was the last time that refugees from the so-called global North sought protection en masse. Part of the resistance to asylum comes from the fact that it is now principally a mechanism bringing those from the global South to the global North. This is a long way from the origins of refugee law as a mechanism to tidy up population displacement in Europe.

All of these effects of the asylum crisis contribute to the reconceptualization of asylum within settler states. The settler society mythology embraced the huddled masses. The immigration foundations of these states meant that they had a special place in their national stories for those in need of the kind of protection that only a new nation to call home could provide. The asylum crisis profoundly undermines this mythology. This matters because public and political discourses tap directly into our foundational understandings to make sense of our world. The asylum crisis is the starting point of a complete reorientation that leads to our new immigration politics. Although political and legal responses to the asylum crisis align throughout Western liberal states, the challenge this crisis brought to the relationship between immigration and national identity was far more significant in settler societies than in former sending states. When settler societies are no longer interested in the masses yearning to be free, a foundation stone in their mythic origin has eroded.

The asylum crisis marks a direct path toward the next two factors bringing the settler society era to a close. With its human rights turn and its transformation towards a South–North dynamic, asylum has brought increasing numbers of Muslims to the prosperous West. Asylum is not the principal avenue for the rise in Muslim migration, not by a long shot, but its constraint on sovereignty makes it a flashpoint in what has become a now quite open Islamophobia. Similarly, the asylum crisis lays some of the ground work for the demise of multiculturalism, as it provides an avenue for migration in defiance of any nation-building aspiration. The next chapters outline these two trajectories. The overarching lesson of the asylum crisis, however, is that it has introduced a new and powerful intransigence and has established a pattern of entrenched political wrangling – a stand-off if you will – between those who support asylum and those who oppose it. With each skirmish, the battle lines are more deeply drawn.

Notes

1. *Convention relating to the Status of Refugees*, 28 July 1951, 189 UNTS 150 art 1(A)(2) (entered into force 22 April 1954) [*Refugee Convention*]. The 148 count was correct in October 2015.
2. The analysis in this chapter is the most directly touched by the events beginning in July 2015. To address this, I have added a Preface to the book.
3. Deborah E. Anker and Michael H. Posner, "The Forty Year Crisis: A Legislative History of the Refugee Act of 1980" (1981) 19:1 San Diego L Rev 9; *Refugee Act of 1980*, Pub L No 96–212, 94 Stat 104 (codified as amended at 8 USC §§ 1157–1159 [1980]).
4. Historical refugee data is available at UNHCR, *UNHCR Historical Refugee Data*, online: data.unhcr.org/dataviz/. The UNHCR statistical yearbooks, which compare refugee populations and total populations of concern to the Agency, are available as far back at 1994. See also Appendices 2 and 3.
5. UNHCR, *Global Trends 2013: War's Human Cost* (Geneva: UNHCR, 2014). See Appendix 2 for additional resettlement statistics. See also Shauna Labman, "Resettlement's Renaissance: A Cautionary Advocacy" (2007) 24:2 *Refuge* 35.
6. For a discussion of the early parts of this trajectory in Australia, see Catherine Dauvergne, *Humanitarianism, Identity and Nation: Migration Laws in Canada and Australia* (Vancouver: UBC Press, 2005). For discussion of the developments of the past decade, see Sharon Pickering, *Women, Borders and Violence: Current Issues in Asylum, Forced Migration, and Trafficking* (New York: Springer, 2010); Michelle Foster, "The Implications of the Failed 'Malaysia Solution': The Australian High Court and Refugee Responsibility Sharing at International Law" (2012) 12:1 *Melbourne J Intl L* 395; Jane McAdam and Fiona Chong, *Why Seeking Asylum is Legal and Australia's Policies Are Not* (Sydney: University of New South Wales Press, 2014). The High Court case was handed down in August 2011: *Plaintiff M70/2011* v. *Minister for Immigration and Citizenship*, [2011] HCA 32, 280 ALR 18.
7. See *Balanced Refugee Reform Act*, SC 2010, c 8; Frontex, "Budget 2015", online: frontex.europa.eu/assets/About_Frontex/Governance_documents/Budget/Budget_2015.pdf, with the largest share going toward joint operations at sea borders. The Obama administration policy was successfully challenged in Federal Court. See *R I L-R, et al.* v. *Jeh Charles Johnson, et al.*, Memorandum Opinion, Civil Action No 15–11 (JEB) (DC Cir 2015); Mollie Reilly, "Judge Blocks Obama Administration from Detaining Asylum-Seekers as Immigration Deterrent," *Huffington*

Post (2 February 2015), online: www.huffingtonpost.com/2015/02/20/immi
gration-detention-injunction_n_6724662.html. I consider the European
experience at greater length in Chapter 8.

8. Efrat Arbel and Alletta Brenner, *Bordering on Failure: Canada-U.S.
Border Policy and the Politics of Refugee Exclusion* (Cambridge, MA:
Harvard Immigration and Refugee Clinical Law Program, 2013). See
also Efrat Arbel, "Gendered Border Crossings" in Efrat Arbel et al.,
eds., *Gender in Refugee Law: From the Margins to the Centre* (London,
UK: Routledge, 2014).

9. This is provided for in art 31(1) of the *Refugee Convention, supra* note 1,
which states:

> The Contracting States shall not impose penalties, on account of their
> illegal entry or presence, on refugees who, coming directly from a
> territory where their life or freedom was threatened in the sense of
> article 1, enter or are present in their territory without authorization,
> provided they present themselves without delay to the authorities and
> show good cause for their illegal entry or presence.

The *Universal Declaration of Human Rights*, GA Res 217A (III),
UNGAOR, 3rd Sess, Supp No 13, UN Doc A/810 (1948), contains in art.
14 a right to seek asylum. The Declaration does not specify how this right
can be realized, nor is the Declaration regarded as enforceable.

10. Until September 2012, Switzerland offered the option to apply for asylum
at its embassies. Legislative repeal of this option was confirmed in
referendum in 2013.

11. Emma Haddad, *The Refugee in International Society: Between Sovereigns*
(Cambridge: Cambridge University Press, 2008). I have made the
argument about the role of crisis in refugee law at greater length in
Catherine Dauvergne, "Refugee Law as Perpetual Crisis" in Satvinder
Singh Juss and Colin Harvey, eds., *Contemporary Issues in Refugee Law*
(Cheltenham, UK: Edward Elgar, 2013)[Dauvergne, "Perpetual Crisis"].

12. Eleanor Acer, "Refuge in an Insecure Time: Seeking Asylum in the Post
9/11 United States" (2004) 28:5 *Fordham Intl L J* 1361.

13. Cameron Thibos and Sara Bonfanti, "Worldwide Protracted Refugee and
IDP Populations" (December 10, 2014), online: Migration Policy Centre
www.migrationpolicycentre.eu/worldwide-protracted-refugee-idp-popu
lations/. Until 2009, the UNHCR definition of a protracted refugee
situation included that at least 25,000 people of the same nationality
had been internationally displaced for at least five years. In 2009, the
25,000 minimum threshold was removed. See "Conclusion on Protracted
Refugee Situations" in *Report of the Extraordinary Meeting of 8 December
2009 of the Sixty-First Session of the Executive Committee of the*

Programme of the United Nations High Commissioner for Refugees, UNGAOR, 2009, UN Doc A/AC.96/1080, 3.

14. In Canada some priority is now given to resettling particularly vulnerable refugees, including women at risk and gay and lesbian refugees. See Citizenship & Immigration Canada, "Urgent Protection Program (UPP)" (January 2, 2015), online: www.cic.gc.ca/english/refugees/out side/resettle-gov.asp; Citizenship & Immigration Canada, News Release, "Government of Canada to help gay and lesbian refugees fleeing persecution" (March 24, 2011). In Australia, see Department of Immigration and Border Protection, Special Humanitarian Program, online: www.immi.gov.au/visas/humanitarian/offshore/shp.htm, which reserves 4000 places in its resettlement program for those most in need of resettlement.

15. Regarding the relationship between refugee law and human rights, see James C. Hathaway and Michelle Foster, *The Law of Refugee Status,* 2nd edn. (Cambridge: Cambridge University Press, 2014) at 1–12; James C. Hathaway, *The Rights of Refugees under International Law* (Cambridge: Cambridge University Press, 2005); Guy S. Goodwin-Gill and Jane McAdams, *The Refugee in International Law,* 3rd edn. (Oxford: Oxford University Press, 2007); Dauvergne, "Perpetual Crisis," *supra* note 11.

16. Between July 1979 and July 1982, more than 20 countries – led by the United States, Australia, France, and Canada – together resettled 623,800 Indochinese refugees. W. Courtland Robinson, *Terms of Refuge: The Indochinese Exodus and the International Response* (London, UK: Zed Books, 1998).

17. Citizenship and Immigration Canada, News Release, "Canada to Resettle 1,300 Syrian Refugees by end of 2014" (3 July 2013), online: news.gc.ca/web/ article-en.do?crtr.sj1D=&crtr.mnthndVl=12&mthd=advSrch&crtr.dpt1D= 6664&nid=754739&crtr.lc1D=&crtr.tp1D=1&crtr.yrStrtVl=2002&crtr.kw= &crtr.dyStrtVl=1&crtr.aud1D=&crtr.mnthStrtVl=1&crtr.page=4&crtr.yrnd Vl=2013&crtr.dyndVl=31. By mid-2014, it was revealed that far fewer than this number had actually made it to Canada. See Peter Goodspeed, "Canada Slow to Respond to Syrian Refugee Crisis," *Toronto Star* (September 19, 2014), online: www.thestar.com/news/atkinsonseries/2014/09/22/ canada_slow_to_respond_to_syrian_refugee_crisis.html; Laura Lynch, "457 Syrian Refugees Resettled in Canada, but Pledge Was for 1,300," *CBC News* (December 4, 2014), online: www.cbc.ca/news/politics/ 457-syrian-refugees-resettled-in-canada-but-pledge-was-for-1-300-1.2860 721; Stephanie Levitz, "Canada Finally Fills 2013 Syrian Refugee Promise, Says Work Is Underway on Next One," *The Globe and Mail* (March 26, 2015), online: www.theglobeandmail.com/news/politics/canada-finally-fills-2013-syrian-refugee-promise-says-work-underway-on-next-one/arti cle23628469/. In 2014, Canada extended its commitment to 10,000.

See Susana Mas, "Canada to Resettle 10,000 More Syrian Refugees over 3 Years," *CBC News* (January 7, 2015), online: www.cbc.ca/news/politics/canada-to-resettle-10-000-more-syrian-refugees-over-3-years-1.2892652. Regarding Australia, see "Australia to Take 4,400 Refugees From Syria and Iraq, Scott Morrison Says," *ABC News* (August 17, 2014), online: www.abc .net.au/news/2014-08-17/stopping-boats-frees-up-places-for-iraq-syria-refu gees-morrison/5676608. UNHCR counts more than 3.9 million registered refugees from syria as of May 2015. See UNHCR, "Syria Emergency: Operational Data Portal" (last updated May 7, 2015), online: data.unhcr .org/syrianrefugees/regional.php#_ga=1.12899249.745513563.1429299991.

18. By late 2015, as this book went to print there were some small signs of greater assistance by prosperous western states. But a great deal of uncertainty remained. The Preface has more to say about this.

19. Nick Squires, "Migrants Severely Burned in Latest Human Trafficking Horror," *The Telegraph* (April 17, 2015), online: www.telegraph.co.uk/news/worldnews/europe/italy/11546105/Migrants-severely-burned-in-latest -human-trafficking-horror.html; Eric Reguly, "EU Tables Plan to Fight Human Traffickers as Tragedies Mount," *The Globe and Mail* (April 20, 2015), online: www.theglobeandmail.com/news/world/eu-rallies-to-combat -migrant-crisis-as-more-die-in-mediterranean/article24025901/; James Politi et al., "Italy Arrests Trafficking Suspects after Hundreds Drown off Libya," *Financial Times* (April 21, 2015), online: www.ft.com/cms/s/0/2e61fc44-e761- 11e4-a01c-00144feab7de.html#slideo; Horand Knaup et al., "Risky Deterrence: Europe Prepares Plan to Fight Human Traffickers," *Spiegel Online International* (May 12, 2015), online: www.spiegel.de/interna tional/europe/eu-plans-military-action-to-stem-tide-of-illegal-migrants- a-1033388.html; "Mediterranean Migrants: Hundreds Feared Dead after Boat Capsizes," *BBC News* (April 19, 2015), online: www.bbc.com/news/ world-europe-32371348.

4

Fear of fundamental Islam

The terrorist attacks of 2001 unleashed a fear of Islamic fundamentalism in Western societies. This fear has freed Western politics from the uncomfortable constraints of cultural relativism, and has made it permissible – really – to prefer some cultures to others. There is some irony in the fact that liberalism itself allows, or even fosters, this preference, on the grounds that some cultures espouse "illiberal" values. This in turn leads to the loss of the liberal dream of immigration, which had served as a core underpinning of the settler society ethos. The true-or-not realization that some newcomers will not bend to the liberal values that are required or expected of immigrant communities is a long step from a focus on fundamentalism. But the two are often presented as inextricably linked. This ostensible linkage is at the heart of how the fear of Islamic fundamentalism becomes the second factor contributing to the end of settler societies. This chapter explores how this fear has both affected immigration regulation, and flowed outwards in all directions into a troubling Western acceptance of Islamic "culture" as unintelligible to liberalism.

The starting point in this analysis is to consider how "Islamophobia" has come to be understood as an artefact of mainstream Western popular and political culture. Following this, the chapter turns to an examination of two recent developments in immigration law which each relate – in distinct ways – to the fear of fundamental Islam. These developments are the security turn in immigration regulation and the immigration response to the practice of forced marriage. Comparing these two features of contemporary immigration law illustrates the distinction between fear of fundamentalism on the one hand, and consternation about illiberalism and unintelligibility on the other. These ideas merge in the final section, which demonstrates how the liberal underpinnings of settler societies have been deeply shaken by this recent cultural and political shift, in ways that make a return to the status quo ante impossible.

GROUND ZERO

The difference that the fear of fundamental Islam makes lies in the elision between this fear and what has been termed in Western popular culture, "Islamophobia." Most liberal-minded, educated, human rights-respecting citizens of Western democracies are well aware that the percentage of the world's Muslim population that politically supports terrorist actions is minute, and that the number actually engaged in such acts in some way is even smaller. But the decade following the terror attacks of 9/11 has demonstrated that this knowledge does not translate well into either politics or policy. Understanding what this means for settler societies requires unpacking the elision between a rational fear and the broader phenomenon.

Islamophobia is not new to Western cultures. Contemporary Islamophobia's antecedents can be traced as far back as the Crusades, to a time when Western culture was emergent. Islamic culture and religious tradition were part of the backdrop against which it became possible to understand Western civilization as a coherent entity.[1] This lineage is important. Understanding its long-term contours makes it possible to see both how and why the terrorist attacks of September 11, 2001, mark a turning point.

Despite the enduring character of Islamophobia, the decade following the 9/11 terror attacks brought an enormous cultural production of both anti-Islamic thought and inchoate fear, along with anxiety about both that almost perversely serves to fuel the divide. Samuel Huntington's *The Clash of Civilizations and the Remaking of World Order*, published in 1996, experienced a revival and was regarded as prescient. The War on Terror was launched, first by the United States, then by various partner nations scrambling (or not) to occupy the ground on their own terms. For Western populations, the War on Terror merged into the wars in Iraq and Afghanistan, intertwined with the idea that this is about saving someone else as much as it is about saving ourselves. Films ranging from the award-winning *The Hurt Locker*, to the much-criticized *Saving Jessica Lynch* or the blockbuster *Body of Lies* contributed to the cultural production of Islam and its crisis. Locations such as Abu-Ghraib and Guantanamo Bay became firmly anchored in the minds of Westerners. Five years after 9/11, most educated citizens of the United States, Britain, or Australia probably knew more about conditions in these prisons than in the penitentiaries and immigration detention centers within their own states. Western universities scrambled to recruit scholars with knowledge of Islamic anything: history, religion, law, politics, sociology. And many of these scholars in turn led the critique of the Islamophobia phenomenon.

However enduring some form of "othering" from Islam may have been in Western culture, 9/11 brought Islamophobia to the center of Western cultures. Whether reviled as ignorant and racist or embraced as ordinary and finally out-in-the-open, the relationship between Islam and the West has taken up a central space in popular and political discourses for now more than a decade. The generation of young people for whom this phenomenon occupies their entire socially and politically conscious life-span is now entering our university classrooms. This is the new twist in the long story of the West's relationship with Islam. It is likely not since the Crusades themselves that Islam has occupied such a central space in the Western imagination.

Imagination is the key word. Despite all of the attention to Islam, not nearly enough detailed and nuanced knowledge has followed. We in the West are coming to know Islam as a Western cultural production. Even as we duly note the perils of this trajectory, we travel along it. This is a vital piece in understanding how we move from a fear of fundamentalism to a pervasive Islamophobia that changes the way we think about immigration. Most of us lack the knowledge to meaningfully enact what we tell ourselves in polite circles: Islamic culture, or even religion, is not the problem; the threat comes from a few fringe fundamentalists. This sounds perfectly innocuous and maybe even correct while sipping Chardonnay in Balmain or Chelsea or Georgetown. But what does it possibly mean? Very few of us have any idea at all how to differentiate Islam from Islamic fundamentalism, in even a rudimentary way.

At this point, then, we bump up against the problem of unintelligibility. We are confronted with the juncture of what we do not know and what we cannot understand. True cultural difference is about just this: difference that does not submit itself to coherent analysis through the lens of the other. Despite all of the attention to Islam over the past decade, few Westerners could, for example, name the most important Muslim sects, recount a basic history of the religion, tell you when Mohammad lived, or explain the now pervasive concept of "radicalization." This is the knowledge problem. The deeper and more truly "cultural" problem is that there is much about Islamic culture that is so different it does not make sense to us. Learning about it, therefore, does not address the problem. It remains "other." I will return to this unintelligibility in a moment when I get to women. But for the moment it is enough to say that both lack of knowledge and unintelligibility contribute to the elision between fear of fundamentalism and Islamophobia. Even when we know these two things are different, we do not know nearly enough to draw a line between them.

The 9/11 terrorist attacks made it permissible, even logical and rational, to be afraid. A fear of religiously motivated terrorists is grounded in plenty of clear evidence that such people do exist, and will pursue violent aims at any and all cost to themselves. This fear has had the effect of rendering Western populations almost instantly accepting of greater security measures. There has been a remarkable acceptance of full-body scanners, biometric passports, closed-circuit televising of public spaces, and the packaging of gels and liquids into zip-lock bags for scrutiny at the now endless airport security queues. Acceptance of these measures, and more, comes from the belief that they will make us safer; that they are the price of safety for all of us in our less brave new world. A small grain of fear that no one can prove is irrational can support a vast and growing security apparatus because it is only logical that vigilance must be by definition overbroad.

Evidence that such measures might not be working does appear, but it scarcely breaks the surface of our more-security-conscious-than-ever populations. In Canada, such evidence includes at one end of the spectrum, the news in January 2014 that a young man found with a pipe bomb in his luggage was still permitted to board a plane. And at the other end, the errors reach to the government's role in the rendition of Canadian citizen Mahar Arar to imprisonment and torture in Syria. But against these "mistakes" we also learn of the security success stories. The successful capture of the would-be shoe bomber, or the aversion of a major attack on a border-crossing passenger train.[2]

The security turn in Western policies and politics has not, of course, been met with seamless acceptance. Following closely on the heels of a stunning array of security superlatives there has been a questioning about how much is too much, how much is useful, and, most importantly, how much security scrutiny can a liberal society tolerate before it loses its liberal character. But even within this critique, few argue that a return to the status quo ante is possible, or even desirable. The challenge is often how to deliver better security without breaching human rights or how to contest the meaning of security. There is rarely an argument that security ought not to be prioritized, valorized, and generally increased.[3]

The security turn, its critique, and its political normalization relate directly to fear of Islamic fundamentalism and fuel the broader Islamophobia. While the new measures have been employed liberally, it is no secret which people we most imagine will be caught in the net or put on the "no-fly" list. The image of our fear is a young Arab-looking man. Recent research about racial profiling shows that this stereotype has not dissipated in the years since 9/11. The familiar processes of racism are being deployed in this setting with banal predictability. The tiny grain of "rational" fear, combined with the understanding that overreach is essential to the logic of security, leads to an acceptance of heightened scrutiny focused especially on those who look dangerous, and willingness to be more tolerant of racial-profiling practices than in years past.[4]

The cultural production of Islamophobia and the welcoming of new security measures directly affect matters of immigration: Islamophobia because immigration policy is always a matter of national aspirations and national self-image, and security because so many of the new security measures are located at the border. As with other aspects of this terrain, the immigration linkages are often light on facts.

The Western cultural production of Islam occurs against the backdrop of a growing Muslim population globally. The Pew Research Center projects that the global Muslim population will grow by 35 percent over the twenty years from 2010 to 2030, an increase twice the rate of the overall global population. This sounds like a huge jump, but in overall terms it will move the proportion of the global population from 23.4 percent to 26.4 percent, hardly an enormous leap. Furthermore, this projection represents a slower growth rate than in the twenty-year period from 1990 to 2010. In the Western liberal democracies, most of the growth of the Muslim population will come from immigration. There is certainly an empirical basis for the intertwining of Islamophobia and migration, but in the overall scheme of things, the number of Muslim migrants to Western states is lower than many would expect. Indeed, estimating Muslim migration is a fraught endeavor and relies on a number of assumptions that can be challenged in various ways. Foremost among these is the assumption that migrants who are nationals of Muslim-majority countries are Muslim. Despite this problem, the importance of this question makes the attempt worth it. In the 2010 to 2030 projection time frame for the Pew Research Center study, the Muslim population of Europe, most of which is in Eastern Europe, will increase by nearly a third, rising from 6 percent overall to 8 percent. In terms of the paradigmatic settler states, the United States has the largest Muslim population, which is expected to double to 1.7 percent of the population. In Canada, the number of Muslims is expected to triple, to 6.6 percent of the population. Both Australia and New Zealand are projected to see very high percentage increases (79 percent and 147 percent respectively), but given the low numbers at present, the total population numbers will remain low, with a projected 101,000 Muslims in New Zealand by 2030 and 714,000 in Australia. Just like the overall rate of population growth, the rate of migration from Muslim-majority countries to Western industrialized states is projected to fall over this time frame, after steadily increasing from the 1990s onwards.[5]

Migration law shifts in the past decade reflect diverse aspects of the Western cultural production of Islamophobia. The fear of fundamental Islam has opened a space in which it is possible to move away from some core commitments of liberalism, in the name of liberalism itself, and migration regulation provides some rich examples of this paradox. Understanding how this shift is taking place tells part of the story of the end of settler societies. Furthermore, because this terrain is predominantly legal, studying this shift also yields insights into when and how human rights arguments work. I now turn to exploring two examples that I have chosen because they reverberate well beyond the migration setting, and because they are telling instances for human rights analysis. The first example is the use of immigration law for preventative security detention. The second example is the use (or not) of immigration law as a way to regulate forced marriage.

IMMIGRATION LAW'S ILLIBERAL POWER

The terrorist attacks of 2001 are a curious marker in the evolution of migration regulation in Western liberal democracies. The security turn in migration laws did not begin in 2001, but for those advocating a tightening of the immigration–security nexus, 9/11 had a macabre convenience. Throughout the 1990s, in many Western states, there had been a political contestation over the ratcheting up of migration restrictions. This was partially, but not entirely, spurred on by the asylum crisis. In the aftermath of 9/11, political opposition to the restrictive agenda was swept away. It became impossible *not* to advocate at least some new security measures, at least some of the time; impossible to assert that migration was not a security issue. All migration law scholars became security scholars in the early years of the twenty-first century. There was no other way to remain engaged with public and political discourses about migration.

In the security climate following 9/11, detention of suspected terrorists was the most high-profile use of immigration law in Western states. In the United Kingdom, Canada, and New Zealand, cases reached the highest courts seeking clarity about the limits of immigration law's capacity to function in this manner. These rulings became the site for core statements about national identity, security, the limits of human rights, and the value of citizenship. In each case, the people detained were Muslim men. In the United States, the issue played out somewhat differently as the political parallel came in the form of the Guantanamo Bay-related cases, but it was still the case that "[i]mmigration policy rapidly became the most visible domestic tool in the war on terror."[6]

Immigration law became an important location for terrorism concerns for three reasons. The first is straightforward: following the September 11 attacks, Western concerns about terrorism were concerns about "elsewhere" – the threat was outside, so closing borders was a conceivable response to it. Indeed, in the immediate aftermath of the attacks, the United States closed its airports and placed land borders on the highest level of alert, causing border crossings to come to a virtual standstill. The second reason is that within liberal immigration law, it had long been established that deportation is not a punishment. At first blush this seems odd. In ancient times, banishment had certainly been used in many societies as a punishment, so to rule that deportation does not fit this framework is somewhat incongruous, more so when one considers the potentially draconian use of force which, in extreme cases, is required to effect deportation. The idea that deportation is not a punishment is a legal fiction supported by the contemporary view that states have ultimate control over who enters and leaves, and that this control will trump any rights claim to enter or remain, save that of a citizen or a refugee. The third reason that immigration law became a focus of terrorism scrutiny is that immigration detention is considered to be "administrative" detention. That is, it is detention to facilitate legitimate state purposes, such as deportation or confirming one's identity.

These last two factors ("deportation is not a punishment" and "immigration detention is administrative") mean that people can be detained under immigration law without attracting the procedural protections of the criminal law. In immigration matters, the central rights are those of the state: to control who enters and who must leave; to detain in order to facilitate administration. These central rights are in direct contrast with the aspirational core of the criminal law, where one can speak of the rights of the accused whose liberty is at risk and who is an unequal adversary in his contest with the state. Combined with a terror fear that was firmly located among non-citizens, immigration law looked like an ideal tool for combatting terrorism.

In the United Kingdom, Canada, and New Zealand, the story played out in broadly similar ways: the government used provisions of the immigration law to achieve effectively indefinite detention of Muslim men suspected of terrorist links and the result was a major confrontation in the courts. Once in the courts, the response varied, reflecting levels of engagement with international human rights commitments.

The first of these rulings was handed down by the Supreme Court of New Zealand in November 2004 in the case of Ahmed Zaoui.[7] Zaoui, an Algerian citizen, had been elected in 1991 to Algeria's National People's Assembly as a member of the Islamic Salvation Front. The army canceled the elections after the first round signaled victory for the fundamentalist Islamic Salvation Front party and dissolved the National People's Assembly. His party was later denounced as a terrorist organization. He was convicted of terrorism-related charges in Algeria, Belgium, and France. Zaoui came to New Zealand in 2002, and was found to be a refugee in 2003. In 2002 he was detained under New Zealand's immigration legislation on provisions that allowed detention because of impending deportation on security grounds that were not publicly disclosed. Zaoui challenged the deportation order, in part on the basis that he would face torture or death if returned to Algeria. This challenge resulted in Zaoui being detained for a seemingly indefinite period. By the time of the November 2004 ruling, he had been in detention for two years.

The New Zealand Supreme Court ruled that courts were empowered to release security detainees such as Mr. Zaoui on bail, despite legislative attempts to limit this traditional power of the courts. In coming to this vital conclusion, the Supreme Court spent considerable time analyzing the Refugee Convention, and considering New Zealand's human rights obligations towards refugees. These obligations included, in the Court's view, that refugees could only be detained to an extent "necessary." Following a substantive hearing about bail details, the Supreme Court released Mr. Zaoui in December 2004. Several months later the same Court determined that Zaoui could not be deported to face a risk of torture. The security certificate against Zaoui was eventually lifted in 2007. In May 2014, he became a New Zealand citizen.

In the United Kingdom, the case in question was decided by the House of Lords late in 2004, handed down one week after the Supreme Court of New Zealand released Mr. Zaoui.[8] The case involved nine Muslim men, all of whom were not British citizens and who had been detained because of suspected involvement with international terrorism. The legal challenge was directed at provisions of British immigration legislation that had been introduced in the months following the 9/11 attacks and that allowed for indefinite detention of non-citizen terror suspects when they could not be deported because of provisions of international treaties (i.e., the Convention Against Torture) or for "practical reasons" (i.e., no other state would take them). In enacting this legislation, the British government had also stated that it was derogating from the European Convention on Human Rights because of a "public emergency threatening the life of the nation."

It is a measure of the politics of the time that the Court wrote directly of the terrorist attacks of 2001 in introducing its reasoning, and linked those attacks directly to the United Kingdom:

On 11 September 2001 terrorists launched concerted attacks in New York, Washington DC and Pennsylvania. The main facts surrounding those attacks are too well known to call for recapitulation here. It is enough to record that they were atrocities on an unprecedented scale, causing many deaths and destroying property of immense value. They were intended to disable the governmental and commercial power of the United States. The attacks were the product of detailed planning. They were committed by terrorists fired by ideological hatred of the United States and willing to sacrifice their own lives in order to injure the leading nation of the western world. The mounting of such attacks against such targets in such a country inevitably caused acute concerns about their own security in other western countries, particularly those which, like the United Kingdom, were particularly prominent in their support for the United States and its military response to Al-Qaeda, the organisation quickly identified as responsible for the attacks. Before and after 11 September Usama bin Laden, the moving spirit of Al-Qaeda, made threats specifically directed against the United Kingdom and its people.[9]

A decade on from this decision, this language is almost shocking. This shock comes not from the fact that we have moved beyond these security politics, but rather that these security politics have become so "normalized" that the sense of outrage in this passage seems odd and out of place for the staid language of the law.

The Court in *Belmarsh* was explicit about two things. The first was that the nub of the discrimination was that foreigners were being treated in a way that citizens could not be. The second was that this discrimination is prohibited by the European Convention on Human Rights. In other words, within British law alone, it is possible that the indefinite detention of these men could have continued, but because of Britain's participation in broader human rights standards, the law was struck down. There is some question about how fully "international" the European Convention on Human Rights actually is, but there is no doubt that it effectively calls at least some states to account to human rights standards that they otherwise may well choose to ignore. In the end, the United Kingdom government's declaration of departure from the European Convention did not matter, as the government had not sought to derogate from the anti-discrimination provision.

In Canada, the key ruling came a few years later, in February 2007, in a case known as *Charkaoui*.[10] This case was a challenge to the "security certificate" provisions of Canada's *Immigration and Refugee Protection Act*. By the time it reached the Supreme Court of Canada, three security detainees were involved, all of them Muslim men who were suspected of terrorist links. In each case, the details of the suspicions were unclear because the procedure allowed key aspects of the evidence to be kept secret on the grounds of national security concerns. Charkaoui himself had permanent resident status in Canada; his co-litigants Harkat and Almrei were refugees. By the time of the Supreme Court ruling, they had been detained without charge for up to six years. As was the case in New Zealand and the United Kingdom, long-term detention came about because the state wanted to deport these men but there was persuasive evidence that if they returned home they would face torture or death.

Unlike the results in New Zealand and the United Kingdom, the Canadian court did not plainly reject this use of immigration law. While the Court did find fault with some aspects of the process, on the key issue of indefinite detention it ruled that because of the system of periodic review of the grounds of this detention, it could not reasonably be found to be "indefinite" and detention remained meaningfully linked to the state's intention to deport these individuals. This decision makes a stark contrast with the outcomes in both *Zaoui* and *Belmarsh*, where the periods of detention had been less than half as long. The court ruled that is was impermissible to distinguish between permanent residents and other non-citizens, and that the procedures surrounding secret evidence ought to be modified. The comparison with citizens that the British court focused on did not arise, nor was refugee law a feature of the Court's analysis.

While both the New Zealand case and the British case relied heavily on international statements of human rights (the European Convention, the Refugee Convention), the Canadian court kept its reasoning within the parameters of Canada's own constitutional *Charter of Rights and Freedoms*. This choice as a source of rights was undoubtedly important to the outcome. The *Charter of Rights and Freedoms* has not been a strong source of protections for non-citizens in Canada, and as the *Charkaoui* ruling demonstrates, its interpretation has not kept pace with international developments in some key areas.[11]

These cases are a telling instance in the story of immigration law and the fear of fundamental Islam. The underlying facts are remarkably similar – immigration provisions, including secret evidence, used to detain people who cannot be deported and, presumptively, would not be convicted if brought to trial. (Because otherwise, surely these people would have been tried.) In each case, the legal battle was protracted. Not only did the cases reach the highest appellate court, but they returned to that pinnacle repeatedly. The *Belmarsh* appellants were twice before the House of Lords and reached the European Court of Human Rights in 2009. Mr. Zaoui was thrice before the New Zealand Supreme Court. Mr. Charkaoui went twice to the

Supreme Court of Canada, and one of his co-litigants, Mohamed Harkat, was back in that court as I was writing this book, seven years on from the first ruling and almost eleven years from when he was first detained, challenging aspects of the detention procedure that were reformed in response to the first ruling.

The cases bring us face to face with immigration law's illiberal power. Immigration law has a constitutive relationship with liberal states. This is true in a metaphoric sense for settler societies, but in a mundane and literal sense for all Western liberal states. The parameters of immigration law determine who will be part of the community, and set the terms and conditions for membership, including the terms on which new members can join. Within the enclosure drawn by this law, liberal norms may govern, but the circle itself is necessarily illiberal. The more-or-less arbitrary power to exclude non-citizens at the border cannot be squared with liberalism, unless a strong dose of communitarianism is added to the mix. This has several important consequences, all of which are sharpened by the security politics unleashed after 9/11. The first is that immigration law is the obvious place to turn when seeking a legal context with reduced rights protections. Detention is much easier to effect in the immigration context than the criminal one. Indeed, one reason that the Canadian constitutional rights yielded a different outcome in *Charkaoui* than the other courts reached was that the Court began by defining a "security" context in which to interpret those rights. The second is that the provisions of "ordinary" human rights are impoverished in immigration law. Not one of these cases relied on the core texts of the international human rights regime. Both refugee law and the European Convention are specialized, and thus they provide important indicators of when international human rights law will gain some traction: that is, when it is articulated as something "less" than international and aimed at a group more specific than "humans." And, finally, that a commitment to liberal values within immigration law is always and ever partial and in pursuit of some state objectives.

It is impossible for immigration law to fully embrace a liberal paradigm because of its role in constituting the border. This imperfect commitment to liberalism means that immigration law contains, always, the possibility of moving away from its liberal moorings; a possibility well illustrated by the terrorism cases of the first decade of the twenty-first century. It is not a coincidence that these draconian immigration law provisions were deployed solely against Muslim men – these laws are the strongest tool for exclusion and "othering" in the legal arsenal of Western liberal states.

The security cases demonstrate immigration law responses to the fear of Islamic fundamentalism. The use of secrecy – a direct challenge to the ideal of transparent justice – illustrates how unknowability is to be managed in a security setting. But in this setting the issue is unknowability rather than unintelligibility. In the security context we assume we actually *do* understand the threat, and that not exposing the details makes us more secure. Unintelligibility, to which I turn next, is different from this, but related. That relationship draws together the fear of fundamental Islam with pervasive Islamophobia.

These cases are not, of course, confined to settler societies. It is, however, the case that immigration law has a special place in settler societies, and the consequences of using it in this way, which expose its necessarily illiberal powers, are different. Return to this point shortly.

WOMEN, HUMAN RIGHTS, AND THE LIMITS OF INTELLIGIBILITY

Security detention forces us to come to terms with the illiberal power of our immigration law, and to ask ourselves how far away from our commitments to personal liberty and privacy we will allow our fear to push us. The story of these cases, therefore, tells us something about our fear, about our law, and about human rights, but it does not require us to come to terms with the unintelligibility that is at the vexing core of Islamophobia. Shifting focus to examine how forced marriage has emerged as an immigration-linked concern in Western states, by contrast, moves the conversation directly into that terrain. In thinking of forced marriage, we confront the limits of immigration law's liberalism at the other end of the spectrum where it bleeds into a rigid openness rather than illiberalism. Here we must consider how the fear of fundamentalist Islam has altered the encounter between liberalism and unintelligibility.

By 2014, most Western states had expressed official concern about forced marriage. Forced marriage is illegal (because all marriage requires consent of both parties) and it is a human rights breach contravening no fewer than four binding international human rights treaties, as well as the Universal Declaration of Human Rights.[12] The first frissons of public concern about forced marriage in Western states began in Europe in the 1990s. Two high-profile stories of young girls abducted and forced into marriages by their families made headlines in 1992 and 1997, respectively. In 1998, Rushkana Naz was killed by her mother and brother in Britain after seeking to leave a marriage her family had forced upon her.[13] European communities and states responded to these actions with a range of new laws and policies, ranging from new immigration provisions raising the age at which a spouse could be sponsored and introducing stricter scrutiny of marriage sponsorships in a variety of ways (Denmark, Norway), new criminal provisions (Norway,

Germany, Belgium), and new civil laws (France, Britain). The most creative and extensive efforts were those in Britain where a "Forced Marriage Unit" was established, initially within the Foreign and Commonwealth Office and now jointly shared with the Home Office. The British trajectory was distinguished by strong involvement from grassroots feminist organizations, and a considered rejection of both immigration law reform and criminalization options. Instead, innovative civil law reform included extending the reach of British law to provide for legal remedies for citizens and even permanent residents who are out of the country at the time that they are forced into marriage. Britain introduced criminal provisions specifically targeting forced marriage only in 2014.[14]

Public concern about forced marriages has been slower to develop in the paradigmatic settler states. Australia was the early leader in this group, with the national government releasing a discussion paper on "Forced and Servile Marriage" in 2010. Also in 2010, an Australian court intervened to prevent a family taking their daughter abroad to be forcibly married. In 2013, legislation criminalizing forced marriage was passed.[15] In New Zealand, a petition calling for legislative action was presented to Parliament in 2009. This led to hearings before a Parliamentary Committee and a significant data-gathering exercise by NGOs. In 2011 the government responded to the Committee report by saying that further legislation would not be helpful and that it would emphasize "building relationships of trust with migrant and other groups." In 2012 a private member's bill aimed at requiring court consent in order for minors to marry was introduced, but was still on the order paper early in 2015.[16] Canada's Department of Justice commissioned a research paper on forced marriage in 2008.[17] In 2010 the South Asian Legal Clinic of Ontario founded a network for NGOs in Canada dealing with forced marriage, and in 2013 the group published a survey of the incidence of forced marriage in Canada.[18] The Canadian government's first foray into this area was to publish advice for travelers on its foreign affairs webpage.[19] In 2015, the government passed legislation criminalizing forced marriage, with a title that left no question about how the new law fits under the Islamophobia umbrella: the "Zero Tolerance for Barbaric Cultural Practices Act."[20] In the United States, where the issue of forced marriage has been politically and rhetorically overshadowed by the issue of child marriage abroad, comparatively less action has been taken. The Tahirih Justice Center surveyed service agencies in 2011 and reported on the prevalence of forced marriage "in Immigrant Communities in the United States."[21]

The trajectory of Western concern about forced marriage is intertwined with immigration and with Islamophobia in intricate ways. While a minority of states have made immigration law reform part of the official response to forced marriage, immigration is intertwined with the narrative everywhere. This intertwining begins at the definitional stage, as analysts often set out to demarcate a clear line between forced marriage and arranged marriage.[22] With some variation, arranged marriage is an acceptable practice in some cultures where the marriage partners do ultimately consent to the union, and forced marriage is a breach of human rights in which there may be no consent at all, or where consent might be obtained by violence or coercion. This distinction is instructive, and emphasizes the extent to which *both* practices are distinctly foreign to the Western model of marriage as a contract between two autonomous and romantically attracted individuals. The need for such care in the line-drawing exercise demonstrates the foreign-ness of the terrain.

The linkages with immigration are developed in several ways. The high-profile news cases have all involved communities within Western states with strong ties to "elsewhere." The exemplar instructive cases in public education material often warn about young people who are taken to another country on the pretext of a vacation or a visit to relatives, only to find they are to be married while away, or about vulnerable young people who are forced into a marriage to facilitate an immigration sponsorship. The statistics portray a story of forced marriage linkages to communities with various markers of minority status in Western states.

This intertwining leads to three troublesome points. First, while arranged marriage is "cultural" (and by contrast, romantic marriage is cast as "culture-free") and forced marriage is a heinous human rights breach, official and unofficial accounts carefully skirt the issue of forced marriage being something done by "others." The effort to separate forced marriage from arranged marriage is emphatic that these are not practices that exist on a continuum. Indeed, it is often the case that in Western states governments and non-governmental organizations emphasize that forced marriage happens everywhere and can happen to anyone, regardless of gender, sexual identity, race, religion, citizenship, or country of origin. The Ontario, Canada, group that completed Canada's first survey of forced marriage by canvassing service providers put it this way:

> Men and women of all ages, from varied cultural religious and socio-economic backgrounds experience FM. . . . FM victims come from varied backgrounds, communities, cultures, ages, religions, etc.[23]

This presentation is strategic, emphasizing that this is a problem that we (Australians, Canadians, Americans, . . .) must confront in our own communities. Despite this strategy, data in every Western state currently producing it show that those forced into marriage are more frequently young Muslim women than any other group. In the United Kingdom, which has the most sophisticated governmental statistics in this area, 82 percent of victims in 2012 and 2013 were female, and approximately 70 percent of victims in each of those years came from India, Pakistan, and Bangladesh, all states with large Muslim populations.[24] The Ontario report found 92 percent of women among 219 cases, of whom 47 percent were Muslim (the next largest group was Hindu, followed by Sikh). The United States report also emphasized that "individuals facing forced marriage in the United States are from very diverse national, ethnic and religious backgrounds"; however, a majority were female and more than half were Muslim.[25] There are advantages, disadvantages, and incredible complexities to "de-gendering" the discourse surrounding a highly gendered harm. While the politics of inclusion is certainly vital, it risks obscuring the vulnerability of being young and female and living within a newcomer community inside a prosperous Western state. Those complexities are multiplied by presenting the practice as both de-gendered and de-linked to immigration.

A second difficulty with the linkage between forced marriage and immigration draws us back to considering the asylum crisis. Because forced marriage is well recognized as a serious human rights breach, those facing a risk of being forcibly married, or of returning to a forced marriage that has already taken place, ought to be easily considered to fit within the "being persecuted" standard that is central to the refugee definition. Despite this, it is often the case that these risks are considered not to constitute "being persecuted" by refugee decision makers in the very states that are working on other fronts to combat forced marriage.[26] The reasons for this are not uniform, of course, but include ideas that "consent" may be culturally determined (i.e., that things that look coercive to us are not, really, or that educated or older women cannot actually be coerced), and that forced marriage and arranged marriage are not well distinguished. There may also be a shadow of a floodgates concern in the asylum context, as Western attention to forced marriage means that we are now beginning to understand the broad global extent of this practice in those "elsewhere" corners of the world. A 2012 UN study estimated that 400 million girls are forced into marriage worldwide. Child marriage is a subset of forced marriage.[27] In this instance of the intertwining, forced marriage would become a reason that Western states would be compelled to admit people if they chose to seek asylum, and thus it is resisted.

The third problem with the intertwining of forced marriage and immigration is the uncomfortable specter that immigration may itself increase the risk of forced marriage. There is persistent anecdotal evidence now arising in a wide range of Western states that forced marriage is sometimes used by families against young people who have strayed too far from the traditional values of the "old country" wherever it is, or, worse, who show evidence of transgressive sexuality (the Forced Marriage Unit in the United Kingdom has gathered evidence that there are heightened risks of forced marriage for LGBTI youth). This linkage with immigration is less straightforward than the immigration sponsorship connection, and therefore is thornier to unravel.

Against all these complicating layers, then, what can be said about Islamophobia, unintelligibility, and settler societies in particular? Just like the security turn in immigration law, concerns about forced marriage did not begin with the terrorist attacks of 9/11. Instead, there has been a sharp increase in interest, attention, and possibly occurrences since that time, which has had the effect of altering a trajectory that had commenced in Western states shortly before 9/11. In thinking through how we understand the question of forced marriage, we are confronted sharply with a standoff between unintelligibility and human rights. It unfolds as follows. A firm line is drawn between arranged marriage and forced marriage to render "culture" intelligible via the tool of human rights. In other words, while some practices, or traditions, particularly those involving women and sexuality, may be foreign to Western states and especially to Western law, once they cross over the line into human rights abuse, we are no longer concerned about their cultural origins. This kind of analysis underpins the entire notion of human rights: that they are held in common by everyone, and the distinctions that make us particular and individual as human beings do not alter our entitlements. Human rights, therefore, offer a solution to the problem of unintelligibility. Once a practice can be understood as a human rights abuse, we are free to ignore the aspects of it that we cannot understand – it is firmly located and contained in a universe of liberal values and commitments.

At this juncture it is worth noting that forced marriage is an easy case for the analysis of unintelligibility. Fitting this analysis around laws banning Muslim women from wearing various forms of headscarves in a variety of settings is more complicated because it is not (always) clear that such women are "oppressed", even within their own "cultures", by that practice. The headscarf controversy has now played out across Western (e.g., France), non-Western (e.g., Turkey), settler (e.g., Canada), and non-settler states.[28] Its challenge to Western analysis is profound and points directly to unintelligibility. The incomplete resolutions to this conflict are as varied as the form of the veil itself. It can be no coincidence that culture, unintelligibility, and women fit neatly together like a set of nested dolls. The forced marriage context ties these questions directly to immigration and its regulation.

There is nothing wrong, and much that is laudable, in the strong commitment to human rights values that the battle against forced marriage
demonstrates. But it is interesting and important that this struggle has ramped
up at this point in time, and that settler states have been slower to develop both
a grassroots consciousness about it and official state responses to it. This timing
is linked to the renewal of Islamophobia, and with it a freeing from the cultural
relativism that plagued human rights debates in the last quarter of the twentieth century. It is now permissible, at least in those places that fully embrace
human rights, to prefer some cultures to others. There is a subtle irony in this
preference in that its basis is liberal. A liberal commitment to rights,
autonomy, and culture balks at a culture where liberalism itself is not
protected. The argument is like a dog chasing its tail. It is also the case that
human rights discourse, itself a creation of the mid-twentieth century, is
maturing and is therefore stronger than it was two or three decades ago. This
strengthening is part of the story, but it is equally important to understand how
Islamophobia has contributed to this maturation.

The timing of concerns about forced marriage in settler societies is also
curiously instructive. It seems implausible given immigration patterns, and
the strong intertwining of forced marriage and immigration, that forced
marriage was simply more prevalent, earlier, in the Old World Western liberal
democracies. While the Muslims made up a higher percentage of the population in the United Kingdom, France, and Germany in 2010 than in any of the
four settler states, by raw numbers the population of Muslims was similar in
the United States (2,595,000) to in the United Kingdom (2,869,000). Similarly,
despite very low numbers comparable to those of Australia and New Zealand,
the European moral panic surrounding forced marriage was ignited in
Norway and Denmark. One explanation for the later emergence of concern
in the settler states is that concern about forced marriage cuts against many
core ideas of the settler society, making the concern harder to articulate and
thus harder for it to be socially visible. A good example of this is the insistence,
stronger in settler society discourses, that forced marriage can happen to
anyone, anywhere. That is, that newcomers and existing members must be
on an equal footing. It remains to be seen whether this analysis of forced
marriage will be equally effective to those approaches that located forced
marriage more overtly as an immigration problem, but it is certainly plausible
that countries that have worked to create a greater space for multiculturalism
and "retention" of immigrant cultures, would be slower to separate forced
marriage from the unintelligible core of "culture."

Whether or not a state chooses immigration law as a tool for battling forced
marriage, key immigration law provisions of all Western states are adaptable to

this purpose. Law reform is not required to achieve this end; it can be pursued by additional scrutiny of rules about marriage sponsorship, family reunification, and the like. More difficult to achieve would be deploying these tools in a "neutral" way without attention to profiling markers such as race, religion, age, and country of origin. Unlike redeploying immigration law for security purposes, however, in this instance liberalism and human rights line up on the same side of the issue. It is much more politically palatable to use immigration law to protect human rights and liberal values, and thus it is more complicated to bring scrutiny to these usages of the law. Here liberalism is what leads to a discourse in which forced marriage is not gendered or linked to immigration: it can happen to anyone anywhere. The British engagement with forced marriage, which initially introduced "crack-down" immigration measures, has managed to achieve remarkable subtlety in its approaches to forced marriage, with strong engagement with feminist, immigrant, and feminist immigrant communities. But even in Britain, battling forced marriage has proven scarcely possible without reifying the "us" and "them" divide at the core of immigration law.[29] Settler societies are less well positioned to achieve this subtlety because of their ideological embrace of immigration. It is not coincidental that attention to forced marriage is surfacing later in these states, emerging as the settler society paradigm fades.

In a sense the battle against forced marriage fits directly into the fear of fundamentalist Islam. Like the security concern, it justifies our condemnation. The fight against forced marriage can be read as a liberal response to "otherness" that attempts to use legal tools (human rights) to identify within a sea of unknowability particular ideas that can be isolated, known, and sanctioned. There is nothing to suggest that forced marriage is linked to fundamentalism, and no reason to think that it is more likely to occur in more deeply religious communities or families. But we are on firm ground when we disdain it, and it adds to our perception of a cultural abyss. It is this abyss that makes all the difference for the settler society paradigm. Prior to 9/11 it was vital to ignore this, to pretend it did not exist, and to work (in settler societies in any case) to overcome it. Now the reverse is true. Thoughtful analysis of Western responses to forced marriage brings us face to face with the problem of unintelligibility. The "how" of forced marriage becomes known through human rights work, but the "why" of the practice escapes us. This escape is a glimmer of the passage from a fear of fundamental Islam to a pervasive Islamophobia.

ASSIMILATION AND THE LIBERAL DREAM OF IMMIGRATION

One way to think about what the fear of Islamic fundamentalism contributes to the end of settler societies is that it has repositioned the liberal response to unintelligibility. There used to be an openness and a presumption of tolerance for that which we could not understand. Now, that which we cannot understand is suspect. Rather than an object of respect, it is an object to be feared. What is unintelligible must be scanned, x-rayed, patted down. We do not know quite what it is, but we fear what it might be.

This shift is a body blow to the settler society because the idea of assimilation was a foundational concept. The abiding presumption was that people could move from anywhere on the Earth and become, truly, citizens of the New World. Assimilation was a presumptive difference between immigrating to a settler society and immigrating to the Old World. In a settler society, the status of "immigrant" was a passage. After a generation, maybe two, it disappeared. This progression was not by design. The settler societies were as keen on racial (and other) exclusions as any other state, but over the two-hundred-year trajectory of the paradigmatic settler societies, the shifting boundaries of this exclusion have become part of the mythology. The story of assimilation is one that served to comfort both members and newcomers: look at the Irish, the Greeks, the Ukrainians, the Chinese – they have all become part of the included group, why would these newcomers be any different? It is this mythology of assimilation that Doug Saunders evokes in *The Myth of the Muslim Tide* when he talks of those earlier waves of immigrants wearing funny scarves and worshiping incomprehensibly who were the Irish Catholics.[30]

Assimilation is important to the settler society paradigm because of its mythic dimensions. Assimilation was never presumed or required to be literal. Canadian state-sanctioned mythology contrasting the northern cultural mosaic with the American melting pot where newcomers were required to give up their distinctiveness and "become American" was always an inadequate and triumphalist account. Anyone who spent any time in the United States was surprised to find that the ostensible distinction between mosaic and melting pot was hard to discern. What is more, it was always clear that it was "Canadian culture" that was a mosaic; the culture itself still aspired to a holistic identity as culture. Accordingly, even if assimilation was considered a bad word of sorts, it remained a vital part of what an ethos that "we are all immigrants" represented. Assimilation was also a promise – a promise that in the settler society divergent origins could, and would, be overcome.

This idea is deeply liberal. It enshrines equality, openness, and tolerance. It commits to elevating individuals over groups because there is no alternative if one is going to transform group affiliation so fluidly. And it maps nicely on to the liberal egalitarian logic of the settler society.

With the rise of the fear of fundamental Islam, however, we can see how this liberalism can, indeed must, cut both ways. The new positioning of unintelligibility disrupts this liberal mythology in the name of liberalism itself. When the unknown is a physical threat to liberal society (security), or a threat to human rights (forced marriage), it cannot be tolerated. To tolerate it would be un-liberal. And once we become comfortable with this un-liberalism, and defend it in liberal terms, two things are true. First, we have to admit that assimilation was all along quite important. Second, we must articulate limits to our tolerance, and thus our liberalism.

This challenges the idea of the settler society in crucial ways. It is no longer true that anyone can come from anywhere and emerge as "one of us" within a generation or two. Now there are formal conditions. We can now say openly that acceptance in and of the settler society depends upon commitments to its liberal core. This idea is, of course, not new. But its open acceptance, as well as an open labeling of some groups as "un-liberal" and therefore "un-assimilable" and "intolerable" is new. The foundational idea of the settler society was profoundly liberal and thus profoundly assimilationist: it depended on a belief that a core set of liberal values could and would be broadly shared as the basic compact of the new nation. Nowhere is this more basely transparent than in the much-debated "Quebec Charter of Values" proposed in 2013, which sought to prohibit public sector employees in the province from wearing "overt" religious symbols or clothing. The proposed prohibition on "conspicuous" religious displays would have banned headscarves and turbans while still permitting "smaller" displays such as crosses or stars of David displayed as necklaces or earrings. This Charter is the Western world's most recent (and most bizarre) twist on the headscarf controversy.

Now more than a decade after 9/11 we have become accustomed to a less liberal world. Its most overt face is our own image on the CCTV screen, but it reaches much deeper. This shift is the deeper consequence of the surface skirmishes that the fear of fundamental Islam unleashed. Our failure to see these skirmishes for what they were meant that most of us never did engage in the true battle. Lord Hoffmann tried to tell us this in the *Belmarsh* decision. Writing on the question of whether the post-9/11 security climate in the United Kingdom constituted a "threat to the nation," which could justify suspending key human rights principles, he said:

> This is a nation which has been tested in adversity, which has survived physical destruction and catastrophic loss of life. I do not underestimate the ability of fanatical groups of terrorists to kill and destroy, but they do not threaten the life of the nation. Whether we would survive Hitler hung in the

balance, but there is no doubt that we shall survive Al-Qaeda. The Spanish people have not said that what happened in Madrid, hideous crime as it was, threatened the life of their nation. Their legendary pride would not allow it. Terrorist violence, serious as it is, does not threaten our institutions of government or our existence as a civil community.

... Others of your Lordships who are also in favour of allowing the appeal would do so, not because there is no emergency threatening the life of the nation, but on the ground that a power of detention confined to foreigners is irrational and discriminatory. I would prefer not to express a view on this point. I said that the power of detention is at present confined to foreigners and I would not like to give the impression that all that was necessary was to extend the power to United Kingdom citizens as well. In my opinion, such a power in any form is not compatible with our constitution. The real threat to the life of the nation, in the sense of a people living in accordance with its traditional laws and political values, comes not from terrorism but from laws such as these. That is the true measure of what terrorism may achieve. It is for Parliament to decide whether to give the terrorists such a victory.[31]

He was a lone voice on the Court on that day. His call may have already been too late.

The shift away from unbounded liberal commitments is important for all Western democracies. It forces a coming to terms with the limits of the British common law commitments and the French liberty-equality-fraternity triumvirate. This shift is shared with the Western democracies that are also settler societies. And for those settler societies, its consequences are more far-reaching. The loss of these liberal commitments brings with it the end of the liberal vision of immigration. This vision was at the heart of settler society mythos. Without this mythology, settler societies cease to differ from the Old World nations they once defined themselves by opposing. This, as we shall see in the second half of this book, reframes what immigration can mean.

Relinquishing the commitment to tacit or overt assimilation provides some predictive value about which human rights arguments will resonate in the new politics. The fear of fundamental Islam presents a sharp challenge to the framework of human rights, challenging the capacity of that paradigm to span the border between the liberal and the illiberal. The spanning capacity is instructively uneven, as illustrated by immigration security cases, and the immigration response to forced marriage. Human rights are by definition both universalistic and Western. When the interests they protect fit comfortably within a Western cultural frame, their appeal is amplified. This is what happens in the case of forced marriage. Human rights form a powerful discourse in this setting because they sever the unintelligible from its "otherness" and assimilate it into a familiar cultural frame. On the other hand, in the security setting human rights arguments have encountered more resistance. In that setting the rights arguments run straight into the fear itself. In this setting there is no question of unintelligibility: there is instead a presumption that we know what the risk is, and therefore must counter it. The difference between the unknowable and the unintelligible helps make this clear.

The fear of Islamic fundamentalism challenges the settler society paradigm more deeply than does the asylum crisis. The asylum crisis is about numbers and control. The notion of asylum itself is not the problem, and the asylum crisis itself would not have ushered in a paradigm shift. In the case of Islamic fundamentalism, however, the challenge is no longer at the border, so to speak, but rather within the settler society framework. The fear of Islamic fundamentalism disrupts the tacit assumption of the benign inevitability of assimilation. This assumption is central to the idea of nation building itself, for how can a nation be built but of assimilated pieces. Relinquishing the liberal dream of immigration tells us something about culture, and how culture is imagined in the settler society framework, but does not yet tell us about how culture and multiculturalism became intertwined. That relationship is even closer to the core of the immigration imagination of the settler society. The lessons of the fear of Islamic fundamentalism point us in this direction.

Notes

1. Hilal Elver, "Racializing Islam Before and After 9/11: From Melting Pot to Islamophobia" (2012) 21:2 *Transnat'l L & Contemp Probs* 119; Chris Allen, *Islamophobia* (Surrey, UK: Ashgate, 2010); Peter Morey and Amina Yaquin, eds., *Framing Muslims: Stereotyping and Representation After 9/11* (Cambridge, MA: Harvard University Press, 2011); Junaid Rana, 'The Story of Islamophobia" (2007) 9:2 *Souls: Critical J Black Politics, Culture, & Society* 148; Muhammed Safeer Awan, "Global Terror and the Rise of Xenophobia/Islamophobia: An Analysis of American Cultural Production since September 11" (2010) 49:4 *Islamic Studies* 521; Deborah A Ramirez, Jennifer Hoopes, and Tara Lai Quinlan, "Defining Racial Profiling in a Post- September 11 World" (2003) 40:3 *Am Crim L Rev* 1195.

2. Regarding the luggage pipe bomb, see "Man Who Brought Pipe Bomb to Edmonton Airport Blasted by Judge," *Toronto Star* (January 16, 2014), online: www.thestar.com/news/canada/2014/01/16/edmonton_airport_staff_let_go_teen_found_with_explosive.html. Regarding Mahar Arar, see Commission of Inquiry into the Actions of Canadian Officials in

Relation to Maher Arar, *Report of the Events Relating to Maher Arar* (Ottawa: Public Works and Government Services Canada, 2006). Regarding the trial of two men arrested while preparing to blow up a passenger train in southern Ontario, see Christie Blatchford, "So-Called Via Rail Pair Left Little Doubt They Were a Public Menace," *The National Post* (March 20, 2015), online: news .nationalpost.com/full-comment/christie-blatchford-so-called-via-rail-pair-left-little-doubt-they-were-a-public-menace. The man now well known as the "shoe bomber" was the first well-publicized would-be terrorist to be successfully apprehended prior to doing any harm post 9/11. Richard Reid was arrested in December 2001 after attempting to set off explosives hidden in his shoes on a flight from Paris to Miami.

3. Some scholarship in the security critique area includes: David Cole and Jules Lobel, *Less Safe, Less Free: Why America is Losing the War on Terror* (New York: New Press, 2007); David Cole, *Enemy Aliens: Double Standards and Constitutional Freedoms in the War on Terror* (New York: New Press, 2003); Didier Bigo and Anastassia Tsoukala, eds., *Terror, Insecurity and Liberty: Illiberal Practices of Liberal Regimes after 9/11* (New York: Routledge, 2008); Kent Roach, *The 9/11 Effect: Comparative Counter Terrorism* (Cambridge: Cambridge University Press, 2011).

4. Colin J. Bennett, "Unsafe at Any Altitude: The Comparative Politics of No-Fly Lists in the United States and Canada" in Mark B. Salter, ed., *Politics at the Airport* (Minneapolis: University of Minnesota Press, 2008); Peter H. Schuck, Karin D. Martin, and Jack Glaser, "Racial Profiling" in Judith Gans, Elaine M. Replogle, and Daniel J. Tichenor, eds., *Debates on U.S. Immigration* (Thousand Oaks, CA: SAGE Publications, 2012) 491; BC Civil Liberties Association, *Racial Profiling: A Special BCCLA Report on Racial Profiling in Canada* (Vancouver: BC Civil Liberties Association, 2010).

5. These data are drawn from Pew Forum on Religion & Public Life, *The Future of the Global Muslim Population: Projections for 2010–2030* (Washington, DC: Pew Research Center, 2011), online: www.pewforum .org/files/2011/01/FutureGlobalMuslimPopulation-WebPDF-Feb10.pdf. I have also consulted the Pew Forum on Religion & Public Life, *Mapping the Global Muslim Population: A Report on the Size and Distribution of the World's Muslim Population* (Washington, DC: Pew Research Center, 2009), online: www.pewforum.org/files/2009/10/Muslimpopulation.pdf, as well as OECD and United Nations migration data. Appendix 4 summarizes some of this information in chart form. The Pew Research Center's 2012 report is detailed, thoughtful, and explicit in its methodology and its shortcomings, and definitely of interest to anyone curious about the limitations and challenges of these data.

6. Donald Kerwin, "Counterterrorism and Immigrant Rights Two Years Later" (October 13, 2013) 80:39 *Interpreter Releases* 1401 at 1401, cited in Kevin B. Johnson, "Racial Profiling After September 11: The Department of Justice's 2003 Guidelines" (2004) 50:1 *Loy L Rev* 67 at 68. In Australia, immigration detention used as a security tactic did not attract the same judicial scrutiny. One reason for this absence is that Australia's administrative detention regime for non-citizens was already by 2001 more rigid than any other detention regime in the world. In 2004, prior to the rulings in the other states, the Australian High Court approved indefinite detention for non-citizens who were not terror risks and who could not be deported. Having taken this position, the question that arose in the other jurisdictions (whether terror suspects can be indefinitely detained on the basis of a deportation that will never happen) simply disappears. See *Al-Kateb* v. *Godwin*, [2004] HCA 37.

7. *Zaoui* v. *Attorney-General*, [2005] 1 NZLR 577 (CA), comprising Judgment No 1 (November 25, 2004), establishing that it was possible for a New Zealand court to release Mr. Zaoui on bail, and Judgment No 2 (December 9, 2004), deciding the substance of his bail application that resulted in his release from detention.

8. *A (FC) and others (FC) (Appellants)* v. *Secretary of State for the Home Department (Respondent)*; *X (FC) and another (FC) (Appellants)* v. *Secretary of State for the Home Department (Respondent)*, [2004] UKHL 56 [*Belmarsh*]. This case is referred to as the *Belmarsh* ruling, after the prison where the litigants were being held.

9. *Ibid.* at para 6.

10. *Charkaoui* v. *Canada (Citizenship and Immigration)*, [2007] 1 SCR 350.

11. I have studied the effect of the *Charter* on non-citizens' claims before the Supreme Court of Canada over a thirty-year period and have published the results in Catherine Dauvergne, "How the *Charter* Has Failed Non-citizens in Canada: Reviewing Thirty Years of Supreme Court of Canada Jurisprudence" (2013) 58:3 *McGill LJ* 663.

12. *Universal Declaration of Human Rights*, GA Res 217A (III), UNGAOR, 3rd Sess, Supp No 13, UN Doc A/810 (1948) art 16(2); *International Covenant on Civil and Political Rights*, 19 December 1966, 999 UNTS 171 art 23(3) (entered into force March 23, 1976); *Convention on Consent to Marriage, Minimum Age for Marriage and Registration of Marriages*, 7 November 1962, 521 UNTS 231 art 1 (entered into force December 9, 1964); *International Covenant on Economic, Social and Cultural Rights*, 16 December 1966, 993 UNTS 3 art 10(1) (entered into force January 3, 1976); *Convention on the Elimination of All Forms of Discrimination Against Women*, 18 December 1979, 1249 UNTS 13 art 16 (entered into force September 3, 1981).

13. Hannana Siddiqui, "There Is No 'Honour' in Domestic Violence, Only Shame!: Women's Struggles Against 'Honour' Crimes in the UK" in Lynn Welchman and Sara Hossain, eds., *"Honour": Crimes, Paradigms and Violence Against Women* (London, UK: Zed Books, 2005) 263.

14. *Anti-social Behaviour, Crime and Policing Act* 2014 (UK), c 12. The United Kingdom had introduced legislation criminalizing forced marriage in 2006 but it was not passed.

15. *Crimes Legislation Amendment (Slavery, Slavery-like Conditions and People Trafficking) Act* 2013 (Cth), amending *Criminal Code Act* 1995 (Cth). See Australia, Attorney-General's Department, Criminal Justice Division, *Discussion Paper: Forced and Servile Marriage* (Barton, ACT: Attorney-General's Department, 2010); Frances Simmons and Jennifer Burn, "Without Consent: Forced Marriage in Australia" (2013) 36:3 *Melbourne UL Rev* 970.

16. Priyanca Radhakrishnan, *Unholy Matrimony: Forced Marriage in New Zealand* (MA Thesis, Victoria University of Wellington, 2012) [unpublished] at 7. See also the New Zealand *Marriage (Court Consent to Marriage of Minors) Amendment Bill.*

17. Canada, Department of Justice, *Report on the Practice of Forced Marriage in Canada: Interviews with Frontline Workers*, by Naïma Bendriss (Ottawa: Department of Justice, 2008).

18. Maryum Anis, Shalini Konanur, and Deepa Mattoo, *Who – If – When to Marry: The Incidence of Forced Marriage in Ontario* (Toronto: South Asian Legal Clinic of Ontario, 2013) [*SALCO Report*].

19. Foreign Affairs, Trade & Development Canada, *Forced Marriage* (May 1, 2015), online: travel.gc.ca/assistance/emergency-info/forced-marriage. The contents of this advice certainly leave something to be desired, for example:

    > If you are forced to travel abroad, you may wish to provide the following information to someone you trust in Canada:
    > - your contact information abroad
    > - a photocopy of your passport photo page and birth certificate
    > - a recent photograph of yourself
    > - your itinerary (anticipated travel details, flight information, return date).

20. Bill S-7, *Zero Tolerance for Barbaric Cultural Practices Act*, 2nd Sess, 41st Parl, 2015 (second reading March 23, 2015).

21. Heather Heiman and Jeanne Smoot, *Forced Marriage in Immigrant Communities in the United States: 2011 National Survey Results* (Falls Church, VA: Tahirih Justice Center, 2011), online: www.tahirih.org [*Tahirih Report*]. Regarding the politics of child marriage versus forced marriage, see Jenni Millbank and Catherine Dauvergne, "Forced

Marriage and the Exoticization of Gendered Harms in United States Asylum Laws" (2011) 19:3 *Colum J Gender & L* 898 [Millbank and Dauvergne, "Exoticization of Gendered Harms"]; USAID, *Fact Sheet: Child, Early, and Forced Marriage: United States Government's Response* (Washington, DC: USAID, 2014), online: www.usaid.gov/news-information/fact-sheets/child-early-and-forced-mar riage-usg-response.

22. See, for example, The *SALCO Report, supra* note 18 at 4, which states:

> Forced/non-consensual marriage is a form of domestic violence and a global human rights issue. FM is characterized by coercion, where individuals are forced to marry against their will, under duress and/or without full, free and informed consent from both parties. Men and women of all ages, from varied cultural religious and socio-economic backgrounds experience FM. FM and arranged marriage are often mistakenly conflated. While arranged marriage has full, free, and informed consent of both parties who are getting married, FM does not – Lack of consent is the critical distinguishing factor in a forced marriage.

The *Tahirih Report, supra* note 21 at 2, which states:

> An arranged marriage is not the same as a forced marriage. A forced marriage, in which an individual feels she has no ultimate right to choose her partner and/or no meaningful way to say no to the marriage, is distinguishable from an arranged marriage, in which the families of both parties (or religious leaders or others) take the lead but ultimately, the choice remains with the individual.

The UK Forced Marriage Unit's *The Right to Choose: Multi-agency Statutory Guidance for Dealing with Forced Marriage* (London: HM Government, 2014) at 1, online: www.gov.uk/government/uploads/system/uploads/attachment_data/file/322310/HMG_Statutory_Guidance_publication_180614_Final.pdf, which states:

> There is a clear distinction between a forced marriage and an arranged marriage. In arranged marriages, the families of both spouses take a leading role in arranging the marriage, but the choice of whether or not to accept the arrangement still remains with the prospective spouses. However, in forced marriage, one or both spouses do not consent to the marriage but are coerced into it. Duress can include physical, psychological, financial, sexual and emotional pressure. In the cases of some vulnerable adults who lack the capacity to consent, coercion is not required for a marriage to be forced.

23. *SALCO Report, supra* note 18 at 4.

24. UK stats are available online: www.gov.uk/forced-marriage. The next countries on the two lists are also Muslim majority: Afghanistan, Somalia, Turkey, Iraq, Nigeria, Saudia Arabia, and Yemen each accounted for 1 percent or more of victims in either 2012 or 2013.

25. *Tahirih Report, supra* note 21 at 8. This study had even lower numbers than the Ontario study, with a total of 150 individuals listed as having a religious affiliation (at footnote ix).

26. Jenni Millbank and I have done research on forced marriage in refugee decision making in Canada, Australia, the United Kingdom, and the United States. See Catherine Dauvergne and Jenni Millbank, "Forced Marriage as a Harm in Domestic and International Law" (2010) 73:1 *Mod L Rev* 57; Jenni Millbank and Catherine Dauvergne, "Exoticization of Gendered Harms," *supra* note 21.

27. UNICEF, *Committing to Child Survival: A Promise Renewed* (New York: UNICEF Division of Policy and Strategy, 2012), online: www.unicef.org/ethiopia/APR_Progress_Report_2012_final.pdf.

28. See Joan Wallach Scott, *The Politics of the Veil* (Princeton, NJ: Princeton University Press, 2007); Nicky Jones, "Religious Freedom in a Secular Society: The Case of the Islamic Headscarf in France" in Paul Babie and Neville Rochow, eds., *Freedom of Religion under Bills of Rights* (Adelaide: University of Adelaide Press, 2012) 216; Adriana Piatti-Crocker and Laman Tasch, "Unveiling the Veil Ban Dilemma: Turkey and Beyond" (2012) 13:3 *J Intl Women's Studies* 17.

29. A compelling example of this is the idea that the British government, as part of its forced marriage work, will sometimes undertake "rescue missions" overseas. The first of these to gain widespread attention involved a thirty-two-year-old Bangladeshi woman who had been living in the United Kingdom where she had studied medicine and was working as a trainee doctor. In August 2008, she was tricked by her family into returning to Bangladesh where they locked her up in order to force her into a marriage she had previously rejected. The High Court of England and Wales issued a protection order on her behalf, and with the assistance of diplomatic officials, she was eventually brought before a court, placed in police protection, and then returned to England. She was neither a British citizen nor a dual national. See Owen Bowcott and Jenny Percival, "Bangladeshi 'Forced Marriage' GP Due Back in Britain Tomorrow," *The Guardian* (December 15, 2008), online: www.theguardian.com/uk/2008/dec/15/gp-bangladesh-forced-marriage; Peter Walker, "NHS Doctor Saved from Forced Marriage Gets Court Safeguards," *The Guardian*

(December 19, 2008), online: www.theguardian.com/world/2008/dec/19/humayra-abedin-forced-marriage; "Statement from Humayra Abedin," *The Guardian* (December 19, 2009), online: www.theguardian.com/world/2008/dec/19/statement-nhs-doctor-abedin-forced-marriage.

30. Doug Saunders, *The Myth of the Muslim Tide* (Toronto: Knopf Canada, 2012).

31. *Belmarsh, supra* note 8 at paras 96, 97.

5

The end of multiculturalism

The third factor contributing to the end of settler societies is the demise of multiculturalism. This statement invites objections from everyone who hears it. On the one hand, people point to the evident diversity in most Western democracies these days and raise an empirical objection to the idea of demise. On the other hand, the objection comes from those who assert that as a scholarly argument the end of multiculturalism has already been proclaimed, and thus it is not a claim worth making. Finally, there are those who argue that multiculturalism as a social and political idea is as vital as ever, and thus not in decline at all. The objections cover a range of variations on these themes, and a significant part of the work of this chapter is to issue responses.

Multiculturalism is a national project. It is a commitment to a vision of nation-building through immigration, where people from around the world join together as one nation, but bring with them and continue to embrace their own "cultures" from elsewhere. The multicultural nation is not simply a pastiche, however. It requires some core commitments from its citizens, often articulated as tolerance, respect for diversity, and an embrace of freedoms of speech and association that guarantee a space for culture. A commitment to democracy is often included on this list but because multiculturalism empha-sizes groups, democracy is not always a straightforward fit. Majoritarian ver-sions of democracy clash with multiculturalism because protection for minorities is one of its central tenets. All of these things, because they are shared by all members of the nation, are by necessity considered to be some-thing other than "culture."

At this point another objection arises, coming from anyone with some training in a discipline such as anthropology that has devoted serious time and effort to defining culture. It is absolutely true that my definition does not engage with that serious scholarly effort to understand culture. And neither does multiculturalism. Indeed, multiculturalism relies on an impoverished understanding of culture, and this is a central factor in explaining its demise.

Multiculturalism is the end phase of the settler society. Or at least it is the end phase for those most successful settler societies that form the paragon examples. Recalling Chapter 2, the settler society begins as a blank canvas, onto which settlers bring their own (European) identities. Pre-existing indigenous cultures are quickly politically marginalized using an intricate and varied combination of disease, conquest, unconscionable bargain, and the all-powerful capacity to simply define "nationhood" through European law, as if the indigenes had never been there at all. In the early phases, the notion of culture was tied up with the desire to import the culture of the Old Country, wherever that may have been. As successive waves of immigrants followed the same pattern, cultural tensions developed between groups of European immigrants who had arrived more and less recently. This is the stock story of the settler society. And with it come the origins of the multiculturalism narrative. The experience of Australians, Americans, Canadians, and to a lesser extent New Zealanders, about eventually embracing the Irish, Greek, Ukrainians, and others was later drawn upon as newcomers began to arrive from further afield in cultural, racial, and religious terms. Of course, because this is a stock story, it oversimplifies things. For example, sharp racist exclusions directed at Asian migrants formed part of the story almost from the outset, but despite this people from China and Japan lived their lives in these countries long before the word multiculturalism was coined, at a time when the idea of a national culture was predominantly about being "more British" (or, in Quebec, "more French").

From the outset, the narrative of these societies included both assimilation and identity preservation. The transition that turned assimilation into a bad word and made multiculturalism the order of the day did not arise simply over time or in response to a more diverse migration mix. The whole trajectory of the twentieth century is intertwined with this shift: the rise of human rights, the progress of decolonization, the horrors of World War II, the "invention" of genocide, the shift of economic power away from Europe. Beginning in the 1970s, the settler societies moved toward an official embrace of multiculturalism as a core political and social value. The idea of multiculturalism is immensely powerful for these societies, making sense of their past, their present, and their futures. It is this logic, this "sense," which comes to an end with the end of the settler society era.

The end of multiculturalism is the most complex of the three factors that bring settler societies to a close. Both the asylum crisis and the fear of Islamic fundamentalism contribute to the end of multiculturalism, and may even

have been necessary to reach this point. The end of the settler society paradigm, however, could not have happened without a rejection of multiculturalism. This fact points in two directions. First, it points to multiculturalism's
ideological identity. Second, it directs us to the very-nearly-contemporary
recency of this shift. These two factors are the starting points for this chapter.
Exploring ideological multiculturalism and its current decline in settler
societies together go a long way to addressing the central assertion of this
chapter. Following these explorations, I turn to the rise of "monoculturalism"
and to the reasons why multiculturalism should be understood in the same
ways across Western liberal democracies.

IDEOLOGICAL MULTICULTURALISM

When people object to my assertion about the end of multiculturalism on the
basis of the diversity they see all around them, it is tempting to make a
scholarly line-drawing retort. In other words, to address this critique by saying
what I am talking about is ideological multiculturalism, not empirical multiculturalism. Indeed, I have done this on several occasions as I have spoken
publicly about working on this book. But the answer has never really satisfied
me. And as it comes time to commit to the book itself rather than to talk about
the idea of the book, I know why. Partly, it is because this kind of line-drawing
academic-y response sounds like weaseling out of something. But mostly it is
because multiculturalism makes the most sense when we understand it as fully
and plainly ideological. Ideological, period.

Multiculturalism is a commitment to a set of ideas about how different
groups should live together in a state. In particular, it is a set of ideas about
groups that end up living together because of immigration, so it includes some
specific views about immigration. Will Kymlicka, probably the best-known
multiculturalism theorist (at least from a settler society perspective), makes a
foundational distinction in his account of multiculturalism between cultural
groups that found a nation and those that arrive later. This distinction ensures
that his theory is a good fit for Canada, as it provides a basis for treating the
French differently from the Italians, Ukrainians, Vietnamese, and so on.
Ghassan Hage demonstrates how what he terms "White multiculturalism"
works to ensure white dominance and manage difference. Hage is writing
about Australia, but his argument is broadly transportable. Tariq Modood
argues that multiculturalism provides a roadmap for managing the religious
division that has become a European focus in the post-9/11 years. Arthur
Schlesinger argues that multiculturalism is destroying American unity and
identity. Multiculturalism is ideological because of its strong "idea" content

and its clear directionality. Regardless of whether one is stressing its inherent liberalism (Kymlicka, Taylor), arguing about its political hegemony (Hage, Schlesinger), or asserting the need for its resurrection, it has a political directionality and expresses an "ought" (even if in an "ought not" form).[1] So describing a nation as empirically multicultural leaves out a key component of what multiculturalism *always* means.

Ideology can be an off-putting term, and because it has a pedigree much longer, deeper, and wider than that of multiculturalism, some caveat is useful. I certainly am not claiming that multiculturalism is an opiate of the masses or that it is a false consciousness, although those ideas could be usefully provocative. I use the term ideology as Purvis and Hunt do, to call attention to the "directionality" of an idea, to its capacity to "favour some and disadvantage others" and its concomitant ability to make that distinction appear neutral and inevitable, thereby disguising the power and politics that underlie it.[2] Most importantly, ideology need not be a negative value. To say that multiculturalism is ideological is not to say that it is bad or false in any way. Indeed, there is much to lament about the demise of multiculturalism, specifically because of its ideological power to direct political and social energies toward forms of inclusion. The politics of racial diversity is uglier without the veneer of multiculturalism, and I think this is something about which both Ghassan Hage and Tariq Modood would agree, despite their marked disagreement about what the ideological heft of multiculturalism is; and despite their possible disagreement about the political value of this new ugliness.

To say that multiculturalism is ideological is not to say that everyone agrees about what it means. This is most assuredly not so. The intellectual terrain of multiculturalism is pitted and uneven, and its political terrain is no smoother. But nowhere in these terrains is multiculturalism functioning as a bland demographic descriptor.

One example of this is the way that multiculturalism causes us to think about culture: at least those of us who are not anthropologists or other varieties of culture sophisticates. Multiculturalism requires us to think about culture in a narrow, or shallow, way in part because of its role as a national project. That is, multiculturalism loses its meaning when it loses its tie to some kind of territory because it contains within it an idea of shared space.[3] Accordingly, multiculturalism demands a commitment to openness and sharing about that territory, and the fact of that demand reduces what can be considered as culture, because any value that *must* be held in common is *not culture*, but some other ingredient of the sharing formula. This starting point is the thin edge of the wedge that can transform multiculturalism into an appreciation for ethnic food and traditional costumes. It does not require this shallowness, but it opens the door to it. A discourse of "accommodation," which has been more and more common in multiculturalism's end phase, has a similar effect. It draws a line between what is an "acceptable" difference (and, thus, "culture") and what is not. This is a shallow account of culture in several ways: culture is not something "we" share, it is something over which we agree to differ; culture does not delimit politics, liberal commitments do; culture is largely an aspect of private, not public, life, in that it is something we can keep at home where it will not get in anyone's way, bringing it out only when invited. Multiculturalism also offers a narrow account of the background or dominant culture of the nation – the culture against which everyone else becomes "ethnic." In this turn, culture comes from elsewhere and is more interesting than the bland and mixed "culture" or "ethnicity" of being Australian, American, or Canadian. Multiculturalism turns culture into a decorative piece for a nation that would otherwise be unremarkable. This effect of multiculturalism redounds onto the treatment of indigenous cultures, and assists in rendering their challenge to the settler state manageable by transforming it into a tourism product.

The ideological nature of multiculturalism and its impoverished account of culture are linked. Whether we embrace multiculturalism, disdain it, or believe that is has come to an end, it is more a social or political account of relations between difference than it is an account of culture. This is the nature of ideology: it masks something important and causes us to focus on things other than the underlying commitments of the concept. One reason why multiculturalism is coming to an end is that this mask is wearing thin because people's lived experience of culture is deeper than the account that multiculturalism offers.

But before turning to this point, there is one more ideology question to address. Multiculturalism is undeniably intertwined with liberalism. There is a rich conversation among scholars about the extent to which liberalism requires a commitment to multiculturalism.[4] The core commitments that multiculturalism pushes toward are of liberal pedigree, but by the same token the strong emphasis on group identity and group definition does bridle against the individualism of some versions of liberalism. Multiculturalism is difficult to square with a communitarian version of liberalism, because it cannot rely on just one vision of community, and cannot tolerate that vision eventuating in closed borders. Multiculturalism could not have emerged without the ideas of liberalism, including some valuing of human rights. But it is also true that liberalism has such broad hegemonic reach these days that many accounts of liberalism would not require multiculturalism as a necessary commitment. This is another element of its demise.

ARE WE THERE YET?

Every year my university hosts an annual lecture celebrating multiculturalism. University advertising proclaims it to be "Canada's premier lecture on multiculturalism," and this is certainly plausible. In 2014 the speaker was the world-renowned environmentalist Dr. David Suzuki. Suzuki is a compelling speaker, and certainly worth listening to on almost any subject. One could look at this choice and conclude that multiculturalism is so important that even environmental scientists are engaged in its key debates. But this is not the case. Suzuki is a master, and his talk was certainly engaging for the traditional audience of this lecture, but his starting point was not multiculturalism as migration scholars and government policy makers think of it. Creatively, Suzuki offered a different story:

> But over the past five centuries, a wave of immigrants to new lands came with a radically different sense of the land from the indigenous people. Land to them was opportunity, a commodity to be exploited, developed and sold.
>
> Over the past century, we have had the remarkable confluence of population growth, technological innovation, hyper-consumption and a globalized economy. This is the Anthropocene Epoch. Humans are now the dominant factor shaping the planet, but in the process, we are undermining the very life-support systems of air, water, soil, photosynthesis and biodiversity.
>
> In such uncertain times, we must look to biology to find a strategy for survival. The key is **diversity** at the genetic, species and ecosystem levels. Canada is an experiment in diversity through its program of multiculturalism. I believe that, as in biological diversity, our diverse backgrounds provide a rich resource of perspectives, experience and ideas that will be important in an increasingly uncertain world.[5]

There is a lot to be said for pressing the idea of multiculturalism into service in this way. But note that the focus is on diversity rather than multiculturalism itself, and the migration narrative is the true long game – a 500-year view that would consequently include a number of indigenous population movements and thus put indigenous people on the same footing as "other" migrants, from European colonizers to the current exodus from the global South. Treating multiculturalism as diversity is a vital shift. It moves us from ideology to demographic. This shift is important to the end of settler societies and I return to it presently.

The end of multiculturalism is the third factor drawing the settler society era to a close because it is the most recent. It follows closely on the heels of the transformations wrought by the fear of fundamental Islam, and it is yet unfolding in the paradigmatic settler states. In the vast scholarly literature on multiculturalism, the question of its death is currently the most widely debated. This is a conversation that politicians and policy makers are also engaged in, with figures ranging from British Prime Minister David Cameron, to Pauline Marois, one-time leader of Canada's Parti Québécois, to German Chancellor Angela Merkel to former Australian Prime Minister Julia Gillard, having a voice.[6] The pronouncement of its death is firmly anchored in Europe, where Tariq Modood is an important exception. Those asserting longevity are more likely to be elsewhere; for example, Will Kymlicka in Canada and Julia Gillard in Australia, both supporters of the concept, or Schlesinger in the United States, asserting its nefarious effects.

Modood's 2013 argument that multiculturalism is, and ought to be, a continuing factor and social/political resource for Europe relies on distinguishing European multiculturalism from what goes on in the United States or, by logical extension and a few passing references, Canada, Australia, and to a much lesser extent, New Zealand. This distinction is instructive. It is absolutely the case that the trajectory of multiculturalism has been different in Old World and New World nations, but this does not mean that the thing itself is different. Modood himself does not make this claim in any detail; he suggests that it is possible but beyond his purview.[7] But in a narrative of settler societies, it is not possible to set aside such a large chunk of the world as "Europe" – the origin of those who gave sense to the term "settlers." The difference in the multiculturalism narrative between the Old World and the New points to the fact that multiculturalism is more fully intertwined with the logic of the New World. Despite Modood's assertion of a distinctly European multiculturalism, his argument about its political value finds direct parallels in the United States, where Irene Bloemraad argues for the value of multiculturalism for incorporating immigrants into the political process and Ronald Takaki argues for a multicultural reading of American history.[8]

Multiculturalism has a special relationship with settler societies. It was in Canada and Australia that multiculturalism was first asserted as a policy objective, and in the United States that it has achieved an organic vibrancy. Canada is the global leader in the legalization of multiculturalism, with its constitutional commitment and its *Multiculturalism Act*.[9] The multiculturalism that has had a place in European consciousness over the past two decades bears many linkages with this settler society origin, and emerged as a political and discursive response to diversity after having been tested, and found resilient, in those places which had immigration embedded in their very identity. It is logical that multiculturalism would decline first in European societies: its roots there are much less strong. Multiculturalism is so closely intertwined with the logic of the settler society that it cannot truly be dead until it is proclaimed so in these places. This point is approaching.

David Suzuki's "multiculturalism" lecture is hardly an empirical data point, but it is symptomatic of a shift. In its cradle states of Canada and Australia, multiculturalism is officially on the defensive. Australia's most recent official government statement on multiculturalism takes a decidedly defensive posture. The opening principle of the Gillard government's 2011 "new" multiculturalism policy stated that, "[T]he Australian Government celebrates and values the benefits of cultural diversity for all Australians, within the broader aims of national unity, community harmony and maintenance of our democratic values."[10] This opening statement makes plain that multiculturalism in Australia is still official policy, but the celebration is somewhat muted. As the Chair of Australia's Multiculturalism Council stated in marking the 2014 version of Harmony Day, "Harmony Day is a day for all Australians to celebrate our cultural diversity and the benefits that cultural diversity brings. It is also a day for Australians to affirm our commitment to combating racism and discrimination." The portrait of multicultural Australia engaged in battle could not be clearer – the word was not mentioned.

In a 2013 cabinet shuffle, the Canadian government removed the title "multiculturalism" from any government ministry for the first time since 1973. Official responsibility for multiculturalism in the Canadian cabinet has typically been paired with another responsibility such as "immigration" or "citizenship" from which some indication of governmental priorities can be read. Several months after the term was dropped, it re-emerged as the then-Minister of Employment and Social Development was given the secondary title of Minister of Multiculturalism, but the title was not applied to a government department. Admittedly, this shift was ushered in by a majority right-wing government, and the truer test may come with the next regime. But no one predicts a return to the status quo ante. In 2015, Minister Jason Kenney was Minister of Defense and Multiculturalism, the first time this particular pairing had been used.

In the United States, multiculturalism has followed a different trajectory. It has never been a center piece of governmental policy, but it has taken root in a more organic way, growing from civil society upwards. It is for this reason that the United States has not scored nearly as strongly as Canada and Australia on Banting and Kymlicka's "Multiculturalism Policy Index," which monitors the evolution of multiculturalism policies in twenty-one Western democracies. Both Schlesinger and Takaki, from diametrically opposite positions, associate American multiculturalism with a 1990s rise in advocacy for educational reforms to direct curriculum innovation toward cultural diversity.

Multiculturalism in the United States became enmeshed with identity politics, which placed it alongside causes and movements. It is perhaps for this reason that David Hollinger calls multiculturalism in America a "movement". Critique of multiculturalism takes a different form when it is directed toward a social movement or trend in political discourse, rather than toward government policy. The most obvious reason for the divergent location of multiculturalism in the United States is that much of the political contestation focused on multiculturalism in Canada, Australia, and European nations is, in the United States, focused directly on the question of race. This lens emerges, of course, because of the importance and impossibility of national recovery from the history of slavery. Regardless of this difference, the United States has shared many aspects of multiculturalism with Canada and Australia, but race has been its more politically charged terminology. The retreat from multiculturalism in the United States has, accordingly, been less dramatic and probably, as I discuss later in this chapter, less effective.[11]

As in the United States, in New Zealand, the discourse of multiculturalism has had to share space with a more pressing integration issue: in this case the political, social, and economic integration of the Maori, who have a much more prominent presence than indigenous peoples in the three other paradigmatic settler societies. New Zealand has also had lower levels of immigrant diversity until very recently. For both these reasons, "official" multiculturalism has not been prominent and, as a result, New Zealand scores similarly to the United States on the Multiculturalism Policy Index (with a "moderate" rating). More recently, there has been some discussion of making multiculturalism more "official" in New Zealand, but this conversation seems to have come too late in multiculturalism's political trajectory to be implemented.[12]

In the settler societies, the sense that multiculturalism as a social and political objective is ending is both more and less than a response to the fear of fundamental Islam. The fear of fundamental Islam brought two important confrontations to multiculturalism. First, it threatens the narrow account of culture. The unintelligibility at the center of Islamophobia cannot be squared with a decorative account of culture. Second, it opened the door for preferring some cultures to others. Both these factors contribute to the current state of affairs, but alone neither would have been enough to bring ideological multiculturalism to a close in settler states.

The challenges of unintelligibility and the new security politics hasten the end of multiculturalism, but there is an array of other factors at play as well. One of these is a general fatigue with the search for national identity, which had marked Canadian and to a lesser extent Australian political discourse for half a century. Multiculturalism's shallow account of culture was never able to fill this gap. The fear of Islamic fundamentalism has pushed along the acceptance of the idea that these nations *do* have some cultural core that is not simply either a sum of their parts or a borrowing from former colonial powers. This brings Canadian, Australian, and New Zealand identity politics closer to those of the United States. The time lag in this evolution mirrors the time lag in political independence, and in doing so provides clues about multiculturalism's diverse trajectories.

In addition, the former settler states have sought most recently to alter their relationship with immigration. A leading example is the rise of temporary labor migration programs, particularly those aimed at ostensibly "low-skilled" workers. This policy preference, which I analyze in Chapter 7, transforms "people" into "labour," with culture as one of the key attributes lost in the shift. There has also been a re-imagining of how permanent immigration to settler states should be managed. This is taking place differently in each of the settler societies, as I discuss in Chapter 7, but overall these changes point to a collective desire to depart from the half-century-long trajectory that brought multiculturalism to the fore: a trajectory that marked an important phase in the nation-building enterprise.

It is for all these reasons that the demise of multiculturalism was visible first in Europe and is as yet becoming visible in the settler societies. Where the logic of multiculturalism was less deeply embedded, less about defining the nation itself, the fear of fundamentalism is a more thoroughgoing challenge. For the nations of the Old World that have only recently become nations of immigration – and for which that label is less about foundational identity than about contemporary change – a transformation in the way immigration is linked to the national project is an antecedent to multiculturalism, rather than the inverse. Tariq Modood's call for multicultural logic as a solution to manage the challenges of Islamophobia fits into this backdrop. Modood argues for adopting a politics of inclusion that uses multiculturalism as a model to embrace religious difference. In defense of his assertion against the death of multiculturalism in Europe, he argues that the only areas exhibiting policy changes departing from multicultural values are immigration and citizenship rules. This stance makes some sense in a European context, but for settler societies it fails to ring true. The linked policy terrains of immigration and citizenship are the core of multiculturalism. They are the prime nation-building tools of settler states and the building-blocks of multiculturalism itself. A multiculturalism that has turned away from immigration and citizenship has lost its mooring. Multiculturalism must have an ongoing connection to the core ways that the community is constituted or it will be cut off from its lifeblood.

The clearest answer to the question of whether we are yet at the end of multiculturalism in settler societies comes from the domain of citizenship, to which I turn next. The broader answer to what follows the demise of an ideology of multiculturalism is the new politics of immigration, to which the second half of the book is devoted.

MUSCULAR CITIZENSHIP AND MONOCULTURE

Over the past decade, many Western liberal democracies have altered their citizenship laws to strengthen the relationship between national identity and legal text, to infuse value statements into the law, or to enhance the exclusionary reach of these laws. The settler states are no exception to this trend. However, in the settler states citizenship regimes had formerly been distinct from those of the Old World liberal democracies. The shifts in citizenship regimes for settler states are trebly significant: they alter what had been a cornerstone of the legal architecture of the settler state; they provide powerful evidence of the demise of multiculturalism; and they are a part of the story of policy convergence because, in these states, citizenship rules have long been an aspect of immigration policy.

Citizenship testing has attracted significant scholarly attention recently and it is a good place to begin because its rise, and partial fall, provides insights on all three of these points.[13] The idea of a citizenship test is simple enough: for those becoming citizens through some other means than birth (whether on the territory or by heredity), there ought to be some proof that they understand what their new citizenship means. It sounds straightforward and blandly unobjectionable, but the symbolic weight of citizenship ensures that any analysis of "what citizenship means" sparks debate. All the recent citizenship test changes have aimed at ensuring that the tests are sufficiently stringent, and that they convey the essential values of the nation in question. Thus the citizenship test becomes not simply a way of ensuring that new citizens understand what this particular citizenship means, but also a way of communicating the essential qualities of this citizenship generally.

The recent rise of citizenship testing began in major European immigrant-receiving countries including Britain, Germany, the Netherlands, Denmark, and Austria, most of which had not previously had citizenship tests in a formal sense. This European "innovation" has generally been interpreted as a response to anti-immigrant sentiment, and to a concern that newcomers do not share established values of the society. Accordingly, goes this logic, newcomers ought to be required to demonstrate an understanding of core values and national identity prior to being allowed full membership. This vision of the role of citizenship testing evinces a concern about multiculturalism, and also confirms the shallow understanding of culture that is at the heart of multiculturalism.

The substance of citizenship tests varies both in the nation-specific details, and in the approach to the enterprise. Christian Joppke recounts the Dutch test as the outlier because of its stringency. The Dutch test was introduced in 2003 and devotes 20 percent of its questions to what Joppke terms "public morality" or "social norms." The test is four hours in duration and the government does not produce a study guide or publicize the questions in advance. Because of this, Joppke concluded that "the Dutch citizenship process stand[s] out as a nationalistic anomaly among the citizenship tests now practiced in Western states."[14] But aside from the Dutch example, Joppke concludes that the substance of the European citizenship tests does not match the popular and political discourse about their contents. They are generally much more focused on queries about liberal political values than about culture in any guise.

The starting point for the citizenship test story in the settler states is to note that the recent round of changes followed the developments in Europe and the controversy they generated. Australia introduced a formal citizenship test in 2007, during the final months of Prime Minister John Howard's right-wing coalition government. The test replaced the previous practice of requiring applicants to answer questions about the rights and responsibilities of Australian citizenship in a brief oral interview that simultaneously assessed English language skill. The 2007 test included questions about liberal political values, as well as about Anglo-Australian culture. The test sparked controversy, and was reformed in 2009 by the Labor government, which came to power late in 2007. Despite the rhetoric that surrounded it, however, even the 2007 version of the test was not onerous. The test comprised twenty multiple-choice questions based on the material provided in the government's citizenship booklet. The passing grade was twelve questions out of twenty, and the pass rate during the almost two years the test was in place was 97 percent. In 2009, the Labor government chose to continue with formal citizenship testing. The 2009 changes removed the cultural content questions, and raised the pass mark to fifteen questions. In 2013, the conservative coalition was returned to power and, as yet, the test has not been further altered.[15] Initial attention to this test has faded, and it seems to have become an accepted part of the naturalization process.

In Canada, the already-existing citizenship test was strengthened in 2010. As was the case in Australia, this change was initiated by a conservative government, and was introduced with strong statements about appropriately valuing

Canadian citizenship. Public commentary was focused on the new version of the citizenship booklet (as the test itself was not new), which included condemnation of "barbaric cultural practices that tolerate spousal abuse, 'honour killings,' female genital mutilation, forced marriage or other gender-based violence" and a new commitment to Canadian military history.[16] The new booklet was strongly criticized for failing to make any comment about the rights of gay men and lesbians when it was first released in draft form, and several months later it was re-issued with statements about Canada's protections for same-sex marriage. With the introduction of the new test, the failure rate rose from 4 percent to 30 percent. This failure level was a point of concern for the government, which then adjusted the test to create a passing rate of 80–85 percent.[17] Like the Australian test, the Canadian test is a multiple-choice online affair, with ample opportunities to practice.

The United States introduced a new test in 2008, following five years of consultation and rumination. As in Australia and Canada, the impetus for the new test came from the political right, concerned that the existing test was not hard enough, nor sufficiently focused on core values. Noah Pickus describes the shift as moving to "concepts related to the rights and responsibilities of citizenship rather than memorization of what many regarded as relatively unimportant trivia."[18] This phrasing nicely captures both the nub of the change and the politics of the situation, which is that any test question that someone judges as not reflecting an important value can quickly be assigned the "unimportant trivia" label. In Pickus' assessment, the new United States test is easier than those in use elsewhere. Having attempted the American, Australian, and Canadian online practice tests myself, I found them to be broadly similar. Not surprisingly, the American test was harder for me as I hold Australian and Canadian citizenship and have taught constitutional law in both places. But I still scored 100 percent on the fifty practice questions for the United States' test. I certainly agree with Pickus that the test is not hard.

What each of these settler states have in common is a reasonably high degree of public attention to citizenship testing, some controversy, and ultimately an easy test focused on liberal political values that states generally want people to pass. It is tempting to conclude on these bases that this round of change was not particularly meaningful.[19] But on reflection, there are several important indicators that come from the citizenship test saga of the past few years. The first is that ruminations arose on the political right and, in every case, things actually changed. The second is that the symbolic power of citizenship tests was important enough to fight about. In each country, the intensity of the public and political discourses surrounding the tests belies the eventual formula agreed upon. The third is that in each case something has become more stringent, even if not nearly as stringent as the hype surrounding any particular test would lead us to believe. The conclusion that citizenship requirements are becoming tougher in settler societies is significant because for the half century preceding this recent round of changes, the incremental shifting of citizenship rules in these states was in the opposite direction, toward liberalization.

The small shift at this pinpoint in time will prove to be the tide turn. Its importance is underlined by two factors: the striking parallel with European states, and the singular way in which citizenship testing intersects with ideological multiculturalism. The European connection is significant because settler society immigration policy (of which naturalization rules are one example) has rarely emulated the Old World. The twentieth-century history of migration regulation has been a tale of New World policy examples gradually adopted (or emphatically rejected) by the Old World states, which have come only lately to understand themselves as nations of migration. In terms of multiculturalism, citizenship *testing* is a distinct pressure point. The conversation around citizenship testing has been all about how multiculturalism has gone too far; how despite everything multiculturalism stands for and however much we embrace it, there is still something unique, coherent, and worth protecting that is Canadian, Australian, or American identity, which is somehow threatened when new members join the polity without understanding it. Never mind that we might not know, exactly, what "it" is. Indeed this is part of the allure and importance of citizenship testing, a belief that we do know what "it" is, even if it escapes easy definition or reduction to a series of multiple-choice answers. At some level, the deep challenge of providing a definition propels us to the conclusion that this is, after all, "culture." And once settler societies are assured of a full and mature culture of their own, multiculturalism is not as integral to national identity, and can be more comfortably consigned to window dressing.

What is more, citizenship testing is only part of the story. In recent years, each of these once-settler states has bolstered other aspects of its citizenship rules. New Zealand, by far the smallest of these states, has not introduced a citizenship test at all and has continued to rely on asking a few questions orally, as Australia did prior to 2007. But in 2005, New Zealand eliminated birthright citizenship as one part of a comprehensive new citizenship law. The United States initiated a massive global citizen-tracking exercise through changes to its tax-filing regime. Canada's citizenship law changes are the most far-reaching. In 2009 a significant reform act made a number of shifts, the most significant of which was to eliminate the possibility of citizenship for second-generation born-abroad children. This change is enormously far-reaching and will render an unknown and increasing number of people stateless over the coming decades if it is not undone. In 2014 the Canadian government lengthened the residency requirement prior to naturalization and eliminated any citizenship credit for time spent as a temporary resident. This shift primarily affected international students and temporary workers, two groups that the Canadian government has been actively courting over the past five years. As these two groups have not posed any particular problems in the naturalization queue, the only possible explanation for this shift is that it responds to a desire to make a politically symbolic gesture. The new legislation also gave the Canadian government the power to strip dual citizens implicated in particular crimes (terrorism and organized crime are the main targets) of Canadian citizenship.[20]

All of these changes add up to an assertion of a more muscular version of citizenship in the former settler societies and a desire to express a "monocultural" account of the nation rather than a multicultural one. For Australia, Canada, and New Zealand, the present era marks the strongest moment yet for their citizenship laws, as their citizenship regimes postdate their emergence as independent states. In these states, the trajectory of the past sixty to eighty years has been a progressive emergence of a coherent and value-laden citizenship emerging from the ashes of British subject status. It is for this reason that each recent round of Canadian citizenship law reform has included provisions to rescue so-called "lost Canadians." The Lost Canadian movement is a very successful lobby on behalf of individuals who thought that they were Canadian but whose formal identification as such slipped through the cracks of the legal progression from British subjecthood to Canadian citizenship in various ways. Their "rescue" has made for a very successful politicking around the reforms of 2009 and 2014, which in all other ways reduced citizenship entitlements.

In contrast to the other three countries, the United States has a longer history of citizenship rules, as well as a much deeper tradition of independent identity. The distinction between the United States and the other exemplars is reflected at many junctures in a comparative reflection on settler societies, but is particularly acute in matters of multiculturalism and citizenship. It is logical that this distinction stands out in these two areas, because they are integrally linked. Multiculturalism has never been a matter of central government policy in the United States. Rather, it has been a more subtle and dispersed influence. The American version of multiculturalism, however, retains ideological features even in the absence of official statements about the values and preferred mode of accommodating cultural diversity. The strength of these commitments is partially reflected in the arc of the citizenship testing debate.

In the United States, the current round of changes was marked by some of the sharpest debate, and yet the resultant changes were the smallest, in comparison to shifts in both Canada and Australia. Pickus concludes from his analysis of American changes that there is a pervasive view that the state need not involve itself in assisting immigrants to assimilate and acquire cultural knowledge; an understanding of civic values and liberal principles is sufficient. This is a classic multiculturalist stance. The United States is the hardest case to fit into the story of the demise of multiculturalism. There is a subtle irony in the fact that American multiculturalism was not led primarily by governmental commitment, and thus is harder to unwind. Like all of the most successful ideologies, it is deeply embedded in public values, and its unwinding comes slowly.

The recent changes to citizenship rules across all four of the paradigmatic settler states cleave in the same direction: toward using citizenship as a symbolic vehicle to express a vision of cultural and value coherence, while at the same time failing to achieve that goal. This paradox reveals a frayed and vulnerable multiculturalism, an ideology in demise. Shifts in citizenship rules are a key part of the Western convergence of migration policy. The combined effects of changes in the New and Old World nations mean that Western liberal democracies now generally have citizenship laws that combine elements of *jus sanguinis* and *jus soli* rules. In order to achieve this convergence, the settler societies have moved further than the European states. This is significant because *jus soli* citizenship laws had formerly been a cornerstone of the legal architecture of settler states.

COMPLEXITY, FINALITY, AND WHY IT'S ALL THE SAME

Not only is the demise of multiculturalism the newest factor bringing the settler society era to a close, it is also the most complicated. The earlier factors – the asylum crisis and the fear of fundamental Islam – fuel the demise of multiculturalism, but its implications reach beyond the changes that either of those shifts introduced. The asylum crisis heightened the control impulses of Western liberal democracies, and the fear of fundamental Islam ushered in a new security imperative. The demise of multiculturalism grows out of both of these concerns, as well as from the concomitant notion that cultural unintelligibility is a threat to liberal practices. It is this final factor that is even now in the process of decisively turning the settler societies away from their traditional view of immigration as a nation-building enterprise to instead an understanding of migration that does not differ from that of the Old World nations that were "source" immigration countries when settler societies were first established. The effects of the demise of multiculturalism in the former settler states stretch in several directions and contribute significantly to the distinctive new politics of immigration. This very new development is still in train, but it is already possible to see that multiculturalism is no longer a policy objective that is central to current agendas in these states, nor is this unique to the settler society context.

The assertion of a more muscular citizenship as a crucial marker of something truly different happening defies turn-of-the-century predictions about the future of citizenship rights. For a time, many scholars were arguing that citizenship rights were being eclipsed by human rights. Mostly in a good way. The thrust of the argument was that given the rise of human rights protections globally, citizenship could no longer be considered essential to full rights protection for immigrants. Some people went so far as to suggest that courts in liberal democracies were using the human rights of migrants to thwart governmental policy initiatives. The argument, of course, pertained to legal residents, mainly legal permanent residents. People for whom there was scarcely any gap between what citizenship offered them and what protection permanent residency could provide. And that gap was getting smaller at every turn.[21]

This is no longer true. Each move toward toughening citizenship rules has the effect of widening the gap in entitlements between permanent residents and citizens. Indeed, as I explore in Chapters 7 and 9, even the "permanence" of permanent residency is waning. The idea that citizenship rights might be fading in importance has disappeared over the past five years or so. While part of the settler society ethos had been to promote a fast track toward naturalization, and thus full membership in the polity, each of these states has now made naturalization more difficult. It is harder to become a citizen, even as it is more important now to be one. This shift reflects directly the demise of multiculturalism, which developed as the end phase of the nation-building project that was the settler state. Citizenship law changes have been undertaken in the name of promoting a stronger vision of national identity, but they reverberate well beyond this symbolic function. It is axiomatic that citizenship functions to exclude as well as include, and strengthening it serves to bolster its exclusionary power.

The demise of multiculturalism is absolutely not the end of diversity. Rather, it is at least partially a response to the achievement of diversity. This demise has been triggered by public and political sentiment that the lived experience of diversity has passed its potential for nation-building and has moved to a phase where it is diversity itself that threatens, at an existential level, the national project. Comparing the four paradigmatic settler states on crude numeric assessments of population diversity yields little insight into the relationship between diversity, multiculturalism's development, and its demise. The United States has had the highest number of immigrants over the past fifty years, and at a policy level its commitment to multiculturalism has been the weakest. Australia and Canada are similarly situated on this score and have both celebrated multiculturalism and then explicitly rejected it. New Zealand, with its small and comparatively homogeneous population, has been very differently situated in this regard.[22] It is almost surprising given New Zealand's distinct desire to attract more migrants that it has nonetheless participated in the turn toward a more rigid citizenship regime (and conversely, not at all surprising that it has not instituted or ratcheted up a citizenship test).

One way to express the current state of affairs would be to say that these former settler societies remain empirically multicultural, but are no longer ideologically so. This formulation might work for those who are skeptical about my claim that multiculturalism is necessarily ideological. But I advance it here only to pursue that claim a bit further. The governments of settler societies are in the process of abandoning a policy preference for multiculturalism and are, instead, replacing their former stance with a posture of rights-based protections for diversity and pursuit of a vision of national "culture" that is sufficiently robust to be considered "culture" despite having a history much shorter than the ethnic nations of the Old World. The project of imagining Canadian-ness, Australian-ness, or (more easily) American-ness as being an "ethnic-like" equivalent to being German or French or Italian has been aided immensely by the idea of multiculturalism, and the narrow account of culture that it has offered to settler societies. If culture is only that deep, surely we all have some by now. Empirical multiculturalism, what might be left if we stripped the ideological elements out, is not anything more than diversity. Especially as human rights protections for diversity are becoming increasingly important as the mechanism for binding a nation.

Rights work in two ways to fill in the picture of contemporary diversity in post-settler societies. The rise of rights-based politics everywhere brings with it an individual focus. This is inherent in the nature of rights, which have both Western and political origins. While rights arguments and discourses have begun to evolve to encompass group claims, this evolution is slow and is not outstripping multiculturalism's demise. The most powerful example of this is provided by Canada's constitutional rights statement regarding multiculturalism. Section 27 of the *Charter of Rights and Freedoms* provides that "[t]his Charter shall be interpreted in a manner consistent with the preservation and enhancement of the multicultural heritage of Canadians." Accordingly, this is an interpretive principle rather than some sort of "right to multiculturalism." The *Charter* was introduced in 1982, but section 27 has received detailed attention from courts less than twenty times, and most of these cases were in the 1980s and 1990s. Only four cases with a robust discussion of section 27 have been issued by the Supreme Court of Canada since 2000.[23] The rise of rights politics is also linked to the continuing importance of citizenship rights. It is foreseeable that an enhanced commitment to rights in legal and political landscapes would eventually re-enliven citizenship rights that were the paradigm from which human rights were born.

The demise of multiculturalism is not simply the result of a political shift to the right that we can expect to be "corrected" after the next series of changes in government. There is more to it than that, although right-wing governments have certainly hastened these developments. Both John Howard's government in Australia (1996–2007) and Stephen Harper's government in Canada (2006 to 2015) expunged multiculturalism from much official state vocabulary. But in both cases, the changes they introduced were part of the broader zeitgeist and were so far-reaching that it is impossible now to expect a return to the multiculturalism of the past. Australian Prime Minister Julia Gillard's multi-culturalism-on-the-defensive was good evidence of this, during her brief tenure from 2010 to 2013. In addition, the coincidence of the turn away from multiculturalism in Europe provides important ballast against a return to any earlier formation.

A vital piece of the puzzle here is that multiculturalism is the same idea across Western liberal democracies Old and New. Wherever multiculturalism has been pursued as an overt state policy, it has had the same core content, aimed at including post-immigration groups into a national polity on respect-ful terms. It is infused with specific liberal and democratic commitments, and with an acknowledgement of group identity that tempers both democratic majoritarianism and rigid communitarianism. Multiculturalism's narrow ren-dering of culture means that the unintelligibility problem at the heart of Islamophobia cannot be easily addressed within its parameters. But the allure of multiculturalism as a way of uniting difference remains compelling. This is the heart of the case that Tariq Modood makes for extending multiculturalism to the challenge of integrating Muslim immigrants in Europe. This is a noble aspiration. But it will not succeed, at least for the present. Understanding this more fully is the work of the second half of this book. At this juncture what is crucial is that the multiculturalism that has been pronounced dead in many European states is materially the same as the multiculturalism that is dying in the settler societies. It is an idea borrowed from the New World to meet the challenges of the Old World nations as they transformed into nations of migration. And in that borrowing, the weaknesses of multiculturalism as an idea were fatally exposed.

It remains possible that multiculturalism will become one of those terms that means something different every time it is uttered. This is the lesson of the David Suzuki lecture. But we are not yet in a place where multiculturalism is unhinged from its history in this way. Suzuki's use of the term as a biological metaphor remains playful and provocative. It shocks us. And it also serves to mark multiculturalism's demise that there is not someone whom the University of British Columbia would rather invite in 2014 to celebrate multi-culturalism's influence on Canadian society. It is for this reason that it is unpersuasive for Modood to set aside the settler societies when assessing the health of multiculturalism. It is for this reason that we can meaningfully talk about multiculturalism in the United States, in the absence of any official policy of that name. Multiculturalism resonates with meaning. And in the very places where this meaning was first created in response to the logic of the nation-building spirit, multiculturalism is in decline.

This decline is the final step in bringing the settler society era to a close. The way that settler societies structured our global understanding of migra-tion is shifting, and this shift ushers in a new politics of immigration reflecting, in all Western liberal states, the after effects of the asylum crisis, the fear of fundamental Islam, and the failures of multiculturalism. This new politics of immigration provides more lessons for charting immigration futures than the old distinctions between the Old World and the New, and it finds its foundations in the ways of thinking that settler societies have left in their wake.

Notes

1. There is a vast academic literature on multiculturalism. Leading works presenting the views discussed in this paragraph include: Will Kymlicka, *Multicultural Citizenship: A Liberal Theory of Minority Rights* (Oxford: Oxford University Press, 1995) [Kymlicka, *Multicultural Citizenship*]; Will Kymlicka, *Multicultural Odysseys: Navigating the New International Politics of Diversity* (Oxford: Oxford University Press, 2007) [Kymlicka, *Multicultural Odysseys*]; Will Kymlicka, "Multicultural Citizenship Within Multination States" (2011) 11:3 *Ethnicities* 281; Ghassan Hage, *White Nation: Fantasies of White Supremacy in a Multicultural Society* (New York: Routledge, 2000); Tariq Modood, *Multiculturalism: A Civic Idea*, 2nd edn. (Cambridge, UK: Polity Press, 2013) [Modood, *Multiculturalism*]; Tariq Modood, *Multicultural Politics: Race, Ethnicity,*

and Muslims in Britain (Minneapolis: University of Minnesota Press, 2005); Arthur M. Schlesinger, *The Disuniting of America: Reflections on a Multicultural Society*, revised edn. (New York: WW Norton & Company, 1998); Charles Taylor, "Multiculturalism: Examining the Politics of Recognition" in Amy Gutmann, ed., *Multiculturalism* (Princeton, NJ: Princeton University Press: 1994). Other influential accounts of multiculturalism that provide further evidence of the ideological point I am making include: Ayelet Shachar, *Multicultural Jurisdictions: Cultural Differences and Women's Rights* (Cambridge: Cambridge University Press, 2001); Sneja Gunew, *Haunted Nations: The Colonial Dimensions of Multiculturalisms* (London, UK: Routledge, 2004); Bhikhu Parekh, *Rethinking Multiculturalism: Cultural Diversity and Political Theory*, 2nd edn. (Basingstoke, UK: Palgrave Macmillan, 2006); Ronald Takaki, *A Different Mirror: A History of Multicultural America* (Boston: Little, Brown & Company, 2008).

2. Trevor Purvis and Alan Hunt, "Discourse, Ideology, Discourse, Ideology, Discourse, Ideology. . ." (1993) 44:3 *British J Sociology* 473 at 478. As Purvis and Hunt elaborate:

> [T]he critical project of a theory of ideology is concerned to explain how the forms of consciousness generated by the lived experience of subordinate classes and social groups facilitate the reproduction of existing social relations and thus impede such classes and groups from developing forms of consciousness that reveal the nature of their subordination. In its simplest and most pervasive form ideology presents the existing social relations as both natural and inevitable; particular interests come to be disassociated from their specific location and come to appear as universal and neutral.

3. Ghassan Hage writes of multiculturalism as a "nationalist practice" that loses meaning without a national territory in which to be applied: Hage, *supra* note 1 at 28–32.

4. Kymlicka and Taylor find this commitment within liberalism. Young, Modood, and Parekh are more skeptical, but do argue for an extension of liberalism's tenets to reach multicultural commitments. Hage analyzes multiculturalism as a hegemonic discourse that justifies exclusionary practices in liberal terms. See Kymlicka, *Multicultural Citizenship*, *supra* note 1; Kymlicka, *Multicultural Odysseys*, *supra* note 1; Taylor, *supra* note 1; Iris Marion Young, *Justice and the Politics of Difference* (Princeton, NJ: Princeton University Press, 1990); Modood, *Multiculturalism*, *supra* note 1; Hage, *supra* note 1; Parekh, *supra* note 1.

5. This excerpt was reprinted on the talk's advertisement page: Dr. David Suzuki, *The Global Eco-Crisis: Diversity, Resilience and Adaptability* (2014 Milton K Wong Lecture delivered at the University of British

Columbia, May 14, 2014), online: www.alumni.ubc.ca/2014/events/2014-milton-k-wong-lecture/ [emphasis in original].

6. Some examples of this discourse include Angela Merkel's 2010 declaration that multiculturalism has failed. See "Merkel Says German Multicultural Society Has Failed," *BBC News* (October 17, 2010), online: www.bbc.com/news/world-europe-11559451; Matthew Weaver, "Angela Merkel: German Multiculturalism Has 'Utterly Failed,'" *The Guardian* (October 17, 2010), online: www.theguardian.com/world/2010/oct/17/angela-merkel-german-multiculturalism-failed; David Cameron's statement that multiculturalism has failed to promote a sense of common values among Britons: John F. Burns, "Cameron Criticizes 'Multiculturalism' in Britain," *The New York Times* (February 5, 2011), online: www.nytimes.com/2011/02/06/world/europe/06britain.html?_r=0; Matt Falloon, "Multiculturalism Has Failed in Britain, PM Cameron Says," *The Globe and Mail* (February 5, 2011), online: www.theglobeandmail.com/news/world/multiculturalism-has-failed-in-britain-pm-cameron-says/article565157/; Nicholas Sarkozy's contemporaneous echo of this sentiment: "Nicholas Sarkozy Declares Multiculturalism Had Failed," *The Telegraph* (February 11, 2011), online: www.telegraph.co.uk/news/worldnews/europe/france/8317497/Nicolas-Sarkozy-declares-multiculturalism-had-failed.html; "Sarkozy Calls Multiculturalism a 'Failure,'" *Maclean's* (February 11, 2011), online: www.macleans.ca/general/sarkozy-calls-multiculturalism-a-failure/. In Quebec, the value of multiculturalism became a partisan issue in 2013: Daniel Leblanc, "Marois Blasts Multiculturalism in Defence of 'Values' Charter," *The Globe and Mail* (September 6, 2013), online: www.theglobeandmail.com/news/politics/marois-blasts-multiculturalism-promises-gradual-phase-in-of-quebec-secular-values-charter/article14158590/. Julia Gillard defending multiculturalism as an Australian value stands in contrast: Phillip Coorey, "Gillard, Lowy Defend Multiculturalism," *The Sydney Morning Herald* (September 20, 2012), online: www.smh.com.au/federal-politics/political-news/gillard-lowy-defend-multiculturalism-20120919-26710.html. In the United States, the Tea Party called multiculturalism a dangerous cult: Kevin Hechtkopf, "Tom Tancredo Tea Party Speech Slams 'Cult of Multiculturalism,'" *CBS News* (February 5, 2010), online: www.cbsnews.com/news/tom-tancredo-tea-party-speech-slams-cult-of-multiculturalism/.

7. This holds insofar as his seminal analysis in Modood, *Multiculturalism*, *supra* note 1. Modood has published hundreds of papers and thirty books; he may develop further analysis elsewhere.

8. Irene Bloemraad, *Becoming a Citizen: Incorporating Immigrants and Refugees in the United States and Canada* (Berkeley: University of California Press, 2006); Irene Bloemraad, "Unity in Diversity: Bridging

Models of Multiculturalism and Immigrant Integration" (2007) 4:2 *Du Bois Rev* 317; Takaki, *supra* note 1.

9. *Canadian Charter of Rights and Freedoms*, Part I of the *Constitution Act, 1982*, being Schedule B to the Canada Act 1982 (UK), 1982, c 11, s 27; *Canadian Multiculturalism Act*, RSC 1985, c 24 (4th Supp).

10. Australia, Department of Immigration and Citizenship, *The People of Australia: Australia's Multiculturalism Policy* (Belconnen, ACT: Department of Immigration and Citizenship, 2011) at 5.

11. See Queen's University, *Multiculturalism Policy Index*, online: www.queen su.ca/mcp/index.html; Schlesinger, *supra* note 1; Takaki, *supra* note 1; David Hollinger, *Postethnic America: Beyond Multiculturalism*, 2nd edn. (New York: Basic Books, 2000).

12. See Mervin Singham, "Multiculturalism in New Zealand – the Need for a New Paradigm" (2006) 1:1 *Aotearoa Ethnic Network J* 33; Michael Field, "Ethnic Rights Advice Stuns Communities," *Sunday Star Times* (February 12, 2012), online: www.stuff.co.nz/national/6403952 /Ethnic-rights-advice-stuns-communities.

13. See Rainer Bauböck and Christian Joppke, eds., "How Liberal Are Citizenship Tests" (2010) European University Institute Working Paper No RSCAS/2010/41; Rainer Bauböck, *Migration and Citizenship* (Amsterdam: Amsterdam University Press, 2007); Christian Joppke, "Through the European Looking Glass: Citizenship Tests in the USA, Australia and Canada" (2013) 17:1 *Citizenship Studies* 1; Geoffrey Brahm Levey, "Liberal Nationalism and the Australian Citizenship Tests" (2014) 18:2 *Citizenship Studies* 175; Noah Pickus, "Laissez-faire and Its Discontents: US Naturalization and Integration Policy in Comparative Perspective" (2014) 18:2 *Citizenship Studies* 160; Randall A Hansen, "A New Citizenship Bargain for an Age of Mobility: Citizenship Requirements in Europe and North America" (Washington, DC: Migration Policy Institute, 2008); Ines Michalowski, "Required to Assimilate? The Content of Citizenship Tests in Five Countries" (2011) 15:6–7 *Citizenship Studies* 749.

14. Joppke, *supra* note 13.

15. For details about this test, see Levey, *supra* note 13; Joppke, *supra* note 13; Sarah-Jane Bennett and Meghan Tait, "The Australian Citizenship Test" (2008) 1:2 *Queensland L Student Rev* 75.

16. Citizenship and Immigration Canada, *Discover Canada: The Rights and Responsibilities of Citizenship* (Ottawa: CIC, 2012) at 9, online: www.cic .gc.ca/english/pdf/pub/discover.pdf.

17. Regarding the initial test, see Dean Beeby, "Massive Failure Rates Follow New, Tougher Canadian Citizenship Tests," *The Toronto Star* (November 29, 2010), online: www.thestar.com/news/canada/2010/11/29/ massive_failure_rates_follow_new_tougher_canadian_citizenship_tests

.html. Three years later, the pass rate had risen by 10–15 percent. See Tobi Cohen, "New Rules Will Allow Free Do Over for Applicants Who Fail Canadian Citizenship Test," *The National Post* (June 2, 2013), online: news.nationalpost.com/news/canada/canadian-politics/new-rul es-will-allow-free-do-over-for-applicants-who-fail-canadian-citizenship-test#__federated=1.

18. Pickus, *supra* note 13 at 162.

19. Indeed, this is the conclusion drawn by Joppke and Pickus.

20. David Jolly, "For Americans Abroad, Taxes Just Got More Complicated," *The New York Times* (April 15, 2012), online: www.nytimes.com/2012/04/ 16/business/global/for-americans-abroad-taxes-just-got-more-complica ted.html?_r=0; Araminta Wordsworth, "American Expats Feeling Less Free As Draconian Tax Law Kicks In," *The National Post* (September 27, 2013), online: fullcomment.nationalpost.com/2013/09/27/american-expats-feeling-less-free-as-draconian-tax-law-kicks-in/; Louise Humpage, "Talking About Citizenship in New Zealand" (2008) 3 *Kōtuitui* 121; Melissa Hackell, "Taxpayer Citizenship and Neoliberal Hegemony in New Zealand" (2013) *J Political Ideologies* 129; *An Act to amend the Citizenship Act*, SC 2008, c 14 (some portions of this Act had not yet been brought into force as this book went to press); *An Act to amend the Citizenship Act and make consequential amendments to other Acts*, SC 2014, c 22; *Australian Citizenship Act 2007* (Cth).

21. This point is discussed further in Chapter 6 at 119–121.

22. See Appendix 5 regarding immigrant proportions of the population and naturalization rates.

23. This count is tricky because the Court generally does not analyze section 27, but instead uses it as a hortatory value, or an offset to a claim of freedom of religion. The following cases do contain some detailed discussion: *Multani* v. *Commission scolaire Marguerite-Bourgeoys*, [2006] 1 SCR 256; *Bruker* v. *Marcovitz*, [2007] 3 SCR 407; *R* v. *NS*, [2012] 3 SCR 726 (concurring reasons); *Mouvement laique quebecois* v. *Saguenay (City)*, 2015 SCC 16. Canada's *Multiculturalism Act*, *supra* note 9, is not a rights document. It is a short document (nine sections) that is directed to requiring government to implement multiculturalism as a policy and to report to Parliament on its activities pursuing this goal. The *Multiculturalism Act* has not been interpreted by a Canadian court.

PART 2

THE NEW POLITICS

6

Why economics and human rights are not enough

Before turning from the past toward the future, it is crucial to say something about economics and human rights. The new politics of immigration is permeated by economic discourse, but economic factors cannot account for its emergence. Migrant advocates cast many of their arguments in human rights terms, but human rights, like economics, do not account for the shape of the policy terrain that is presently emerging. Economics and human rights predominate in calls for migration law and policy reform. My argument, however, is that both economics and human rights fail to account for contemporary immigration politics. Indeed the fact that these discourses are often twinned in migration policy arguments contributes to policy gridlock. The end of settler society analysis aims to loosen this gridlock. And to that end, before turning to the new politics of immigration, I will highlight how these two factors fit into the picture.

In other words, I want to explain why one of factors hastening the arrival of a new politics is *not* the global financial crisis that began in 2009 and is still reverberating powerfully. And I need to explain why human rights, which have been a transformational idea in many areas, have made so few inroads into immigration politics.

Turning first to economics. Economic trends are obviously important to immigration policy making and immigration politics. They are also vitally important to the hundreds of thousands of individual decisions about moving or not moving that undergird both "immigration" as a statistical phenomenon and most of our presumptions and theoretical propositions about migration (push factors, pull factors, circular migration, family migration, etc.). Indeed, economic factors are best understood as a constant feature of immigration decision making. As a constant, economics does not explain the current significant change that is taking place in how the world imagines immigration.

There are two important corollaries to this proposition. The first is that economics is a hegemonic discourse in twenty-first century politics of all types. There is an (often enormous) gulf between how sophisticated immigration economists talk about immigration and how politicians talk about immigration. Because of this it is fair to say that immigration policy development is presently dominated by economic discourse, which is not always the same as being dominated by economic analysis. It is commonplace for politicians to assert that particular economic trends can be addressed through adjusting immigration policy. The most common example, worldwide, is the idea that temporary migrants can be quickly "imported" to fill labor market shortages. Chapter 7 looks at this dynamic more closely. For the moment it suffices to say that political rhetoric frequently endorses this idea, whereas economists specializing in immigration are less certain that this can be achieved.[1] This would be so even assuming that perfect labor market data exist in order to make the filling proposition possible. The 2014 mini-scandal about the paucity of Canadian labor market data gave the public a rare glimpse into how difficult it is to aggregate employment statistics for this purpose. The broad point here is that economic discourse is a constant of immigration policy development, even when *actual* economic analysis may not be.

The second corollary to my assertion that economics is a constant in immigration policy is the idea that as settler society ethos is stripped away, economics is often left as the only evident explanatory factor remaining. It is crucial to grapple with what this means for policy making and politics. And it is equally vital to understand that conceptualizing immigration in this way is new. But its newness is obscured by the hegemony of economic discourse in politics generally, and by the previous intertwining of settler society values and economic discourses. There are myriad problems with this newness, which I tackle in the chapters that follow. The most obvious problem is that immigration policies that reduce human beings to economic inputs have been demonstrated to fail, repeatedly and inevitably. It is also problematic that this narrow understanding of immigration is not rich enough to provide explanations of the politics of immigration, and it is within this political domain that policy is generated.

In other words, economics is part of the picture, as it has always been. There is nothing new about this, and therefore it does not explain the contemporary political shift and cannot show any way forward. Immigrant numbers rise when economies are stronger and decline when they are weaker. This is true of both legal and extra-legal migration. The idea that immigrants can meet the economic needs of settler societies is as old as the foundation of these societies themselves. Over the past two hundred years, Canada, Australia, and the

United States have all operated "economic objective only" temporary migration schemes alongside "regular" nation-building migration programs. Pacific Islanders harvesting sugar cane in Queensland, Chinese laying rail track across the Canadian prairie, and the more recent Braceros working in the rural United States, have all been welcomed for narrowly defined economic objectives but explicitly not invited to be part of the nation-building project. Regardless of the fact that many of these individuals did end up staying and becoming part of the nation, they were not originally imagined as "immigrants," and were explicitly excluded from the legal framework of immigration, with its attendant rights and incentives.

Asylum figures do not tend to track economic cycles, which is an indication – for skeptics and economists – that asylum is about human rights protection, rather than being a principal route for deceptive and low-skilled economic migration. Asylum policy is a terrain where economic discourses and human rights discourses intersect. Refugee advocates emphasize that asylum policy ought not to be driven by the concerns that drive immigration policy. I am committed to this view. But I also believe that asylum deeply shapes state perspectives on immigration. Furthermore, there are some ways that refugees and immigrants raise the same concerns from a state perspective, even if their reasons for entry to the country are not comparable. Both groups have families, have ties in foreign countries, need work, and need the kinds of services that are typically state services, such as healthcare and education. One of the clearest indicators that refugees cannot be treated as immigrants is that in regard to refugees, human rights arguments are strong and economic arguments are often at odds with legal responsibilities.

Human rights are, like economics, a factor that often arises in the immigration policy conversation – typically, but not exclusively, on the advocacy side rather than the state side. As a legal scholar, I am particularly attuned to how human rights discourses function, and as an immigrant advocate I want human rights arguments to be successful. But often they are not. One of the broad goals of this book is to demonstrate when and why human rights arguments succeed or fail. At this juncture, I want to emphasize how human rights share some terrain with economic discourse. Over recent years, human rights talk has become a persistent feature of the immigration policy conversation. However, just like economics, human rights cannot explain contemporary immigration politics and thus do not have much predictive value as we look to immigration futures.

This is a dramatically different position from the way that many migration analysts conceptualized human rights ten or fifteen years ago, at the outset of the twenty-first century. As I noted in considering the emergence of a more muscular citizenship discourse in Chapter 5, a body of scholarship was developing that argued that human rights were becoming increasingly important for immigrants and non-citizens. Analysts had opposing reactions to this observation. Some, such as Saskia Sassen and David Jacobson, argued that this was a good thing because, as domestic courts (particularly in the United States) paid more and more attention to the human rights of immigrants, the exclusionary role of citizenship entitlements was diminishing. Others, like Christian Joppke and Gary Freeman, argued that as courts took increasing notice of the human rights of non-citizens, Western governments were robbed of their policy-making powers in matters of immigration. Instead, the courts were (over-) determining policy outcomes.[2] Whether one thought the rise of human rights in the domain of immigration was a good thing or a bad thing, it was clearly a "thing" and it was clearly "legal." Indeed, it was a compelling example of the legal thwarting the political on a number of fronts.

There are primarily two factors that have pushed the human rights argument to the wayside in migration analysis. The first is the rise of illegal migration and the second is the securitization of this policy terrain. I have written about both of these factors before, and each is closely interwoven with the building-blocks of the first half of this book: the asylum crisis, Islamophobia, and the end of multiculturalism. My argument here in part builds on what I have argued before. But it also moves beyond my earlier assertion to situate the demise of a once very small but very promising advance of human rights in the realm of migration within an overall account of the new politics of immigration.

I like human rights arguments, and I want them to work for migrants at least as well as they do for a lot of other folks, and I want these arguments to become more and more successful over time. But in order for human rights to achieve any traction at all for migrants, we have to truly grapple with why the trajectory of forward movement stopped, why the backsliding happened so quickly, and where the pockets of resistance are located.

By the time scholars got around to arguing that human rights were overtaking citizenship rights, clouds were visible on the horizon. The first international human rights document directed specifically toward the rights of migrants, which had been opened for ratifications in 1990, had taken twelve years to reach the modest ratification threshold of 25 states.[3] The *Convention on the Protection of the Rights of All Migrant Workers and Members of their Families* had fallen victim to changing political winds, no doubt in part because of its attempt, however impuissant, to accord at least some basic rights to migrant workers without legal status. This harbingered the faltering of human rights for non-citizens, which has now seeped in to affect even how domestic constitutional rights claims on behalf of non-citizens have been addressed in Canada and the United States, two paradigmatic former settler societies with strong constitutional human rights statements. Its struggle for importance is a consequence of the new politics of immigration, which Chapter 9 considers in more detail.

The human rights aspects of the factors bringing settler societies to an end are illuminating to consider together. In the asylum crisis the growing strength of human rights analysis within all aspects of refugee law contributes both to making asylum stronger and to wrestling it into "hard law" form a stark exception to the sovereign power and discretionary decision making, which are the strongest markers of state decision making in the immigration realm. But this strength also contributes prominently to state resistance to asylum. In the terrain of Islamophobia, human rights arguments act as a salve to unintelligibility. In this role, human rights provide no answers to the consternation of indefinite detention and provide a one-size-fits-all response to forced marriage. This response uses human rights discourse to impose intelligibility. In the demise of multiculturalism, the resurgence of citizen rights over human rights is made explicit, and the inescapable individual focus of Western, liberal human rights proves inadequate to the task of group recognition and accommodation. The turn toward rights politics subtly tugs against multiculturalism.

Thus in the demise of settler societies, human rights are a marker but not an explanation. It is in this regard that they occupy the same space as economics. Furthermore, because I believe that human rights are an important advocacy tool, I pay particular attention to situating them within the new politics of immigration in the hopes of mapping their optimal uses. This is the argument yet to come.

A final point to be made at this juncture, however, is that I want to be careful not to overstate my view that economics and human rights are on the same terrain here. By this I mean that each of these important ideas, functioning as both discourses and disciplines, are frequently present in discussions of immigration. But neither one can sustain the weight that is far too often placed upon them in those conversations. Understanding the new politics of immigration, and navigating a way forward in it, requires recourse to much more than either economics or human rights, and to much more than can be gleaned from a sophisticated pairing of the two. I am not attempting to say anything at all at this juncture about the potentially fruitful intertwining of economics and human rights. Many people have noted the dissonance between economics and human rights and are working to address it.[4] This work, however, is not informing immigration policy nor immigration politics.

On the terrain I am mapping here, economics and human rights appear in opposing positions. Their opposition is often, furthermore, not a full-on clash with sparks and scars. Rather they are ships passing in the night. And immigration policy is the worse for it.

Turning from the end of settler societies to analysis of the contents of the new politics, economics and human rights occupy a vital position. It is within economics and human rights terms that immigration policy aspirations are most often cast. It is, therefore, against these standards that immigration policy is most often seen to fail. It fails because it does not deliver in economic or human rights terms. This defeat is all the more stark because the old settler society immigration values – nation building, cultural diversity, permanence, integration, identity – are no longer measures of immigration achievements. I turn now to consider the new politics of immigration. This politics is marked by the contours of what preceded it. In highlighting how economics and human rights analyses fit into the story of the new, we can begin to see why these discourses are hegemonic and how to shift that position of prominence in order to achieve policy innovation.

Notes

1. See, for example, George J. Borjas, *Immigration Economics* (Cambridge, MA: Harvard University Press, 2014); David A. Green and Christopher Worswick, "Immigrant Earnings Profiles in the Presence of Human Capital Investment: Measuring Cohort and Macro Effects" (2012) 19:2 *Labour Economics* 241; Michael Trebilcock, "The Law and Economics of Immigration Policy" (2003) 5:2 *Am L & Econ Rev* 271; Arthur Sweetman, "Spotlight on the Economic Effects of Immigration: A North American Perspective" in Christiane Kuptsch, ed., *The Internationalization of Labour Markets* (Geneva: International Institute for Labour Studies, 2010) 15.

2. The contours of this debate range from arguments, such as those of Saskia Sassen and David Jacobson, applauding the notion that human rights have become almost as meaningful as citizenship rights for those with permanent residency (Saskia Sassen, *Losing Control? Sovereignty in an Age of Globalization* (New York: Columbia University Press, 1996); David Jacobson, *Rights Across Borders: Immigration and the Decline of Citizenship* (Baltimore: Johns Hopkins University Press, 1996); David Jacobson and Galya Benarieh Ruffer, "Courts Across Borders: The Implications of Judicial Agency for Human Rights and Democracy" (2003) 25:1 *Hum Rts Q* 74) to the views of Gary Freeman and Christian Joppke lamenting that international human rights have robbed national

governments of policy autonomy in the migration realm (Christian Joppke, *Citizenship and Immigration* (Cambridge, UK: Polity Press, 2010); Gary Freeman, "The Decline of Sovereignty" in Christian Joppke, ed., *Challenge to the Nation-State: Immigration in Western Europe and the United States* (Oxford: Oxford University Press, 1998); Gary Freeman, "Can Liberal States Control Unwanted Migration?" (1994) 534:1 *Annals American Academy Political & Social Sciences* 17).

3. *International Convention on the Protection of the Rights of All Migrant Workers and Members of their Families*, December 18, 1990, 2220 UNTS 3 (entered into force July 1, 2003). For further history and analysis, see Chapter 9 at 191–193.

4. See, for example, Manuel Court Branco, *Economics Versus Human Rights* (New York: Routledge, 2009); Marion Fourcade, *Economists and Societies: Discipline and Profession in the United States, Britain and France* (Princeton, NJ: Princeton University Press, 2009); Galit A Sarfaty, *Values in Translation: Human Rights and the Culture of the World Bank* (Stanford: Stanford University Press, 2012).

7

The loss of settlement and society

Immigration is no longer about "settlement" or "society." It is because these two ideas have disappeared as immigration values that the demise of the settler society paradigm is a vital explanatory metaphor for contemporary migration. Under the logic of the settler society an organized immigration program was concerned with inviting people to settle – to stay permanently in a new place – and to build a society – at some level to assimilate, or at least adapt, to a wholly new culture or a wholly new transplant. To say that these two values have disappeared means that permanent settlement and the creation and adaptation of a new culture are no longer goals of migration policy. To the extent that these objectives persist, they are weakened and incidental. This chapter documents this shift and interrogates its consequences.

On the settlement side of the coin, the shift is visible in the slippage away from categories of "permanent" and "temporary" migration, toward a recognition that "circular," "cyclical," or "chain" migration are better descriptors of the dominant trends. From the state perspective, the shift away from settlement is expressed in a marked rise in preferences for temporary migration programs – involving primarily workers, but with consideration also of students – and a concomitant decrease in "permanent" migration numbers. This same shift away from permanence as a core immigration value is also seeping into those spaces where asylum and immigration converge.

On the society side of the coin, the demise of multiculturalism as an ideological force leaves in its wake a diversity-dotted landscape. Without the ideological promise of multiculturalism, a key part of the glue that makes many cultures into one "society" is gone. Diversity allows a space for incommensurability and neither expects nor demands assimilation. We see this shift most evidently in the rise in prevalence of ethnic enclaves within settler societies, a most recent shift that has preoccupied politicians, policy makers, and migration scholars. The same shift is visible in reduced funding for a variety of settlement services and also in the increased xenophobia that the fear of fundamental Islam has made socially and politically acceptable.

Settlement and society were true markers of the place of immigration in the settler society. These values have never been paramount in immigration programs of European states, even as those states have transformed themselves into nations of immigration over the most recent decades. The policy objectives of expanding formal immigration to Germany or the United Kingdom or Sweden have never been a nation-building agenda – an agenda that requires both settlement and society. The backdrop assumption of European immigration has instead been that the nation, in its robust cultural identity sense, will endure any number of new arrivals essentially culturally unchanged. The diminution of the settler society values of settlement and society was, therefore, a prerequisite for the policy convergence that is now so prominent among Western liberal democracies, as Chapter 9 makes plain.

Before getting there, however, it is pivotal to understand the shifting terrain in both the former settler societies and the Old World nations. These shifts are intertwined with the new politics of immigration: they reflect its priorities and foster its continuation. I begin here, examining first the loss of settlement and then the more complex loss of society. The chapter concludes by assessing the effects and political fallout of these two trends.

LOSS OF "SETTLEMENT"

The movement away from settlement as a core immigration value has been in train for some time now. In part, this idea emerges from the maelstrom of globalization. It is now easier for people to imagine moving around the world than at any other point in history. Travel is cheaper, easier, and faster than ever before, and every technology of communication facilitates an understanding of what it might be like to live on the other side of the world. Technology also reduces the personal risks of immigration because remaining part of a community thousands of miles away has never been easier. It is possible, even, to envision communities constituted by people in different countries and different parts of the world.[1] But despite all of this, place remains tangible. We live our lives locally, even daily contact with friends or family on the other side of the world cannot mitigate this fact.

Globalization, that amorphous shape shifter, has brought with it three migration effects that are relevant here.[2] The first of these is an increasing rate of migration and, for some people, an easing of restrictions. As global competition for the best and the brightest minds in the world intensifies, those who are highly skilled and highly educated have more options about where to live their lives than ever before. A second globalization effect is that as states lose control over other aspects of policy at a national level, migration is transformed into sovereignty's last bastion. This shift contributes powerfully to the rise in both the prevalence and the policy importance of illegal migration. An enormous Western state apparatus is now devoted to controlling who can cross borders. Finally, globalization itself strengthens the hegemony of economic discourse, and contributes to transforming people into "labor." Even some immigration advocates speak in these terms, arguing that "labor" ought to be free to cross borders in the same way that capital now does. Each of these factors erodes the value of settlement in the migration context: the highly skilled have myriad opportunities to move and move again; those who live outside the law live insecure lives, where truly settling is impossible because their very status is precarious; and the conceptualization of people as "labor" renders the idea of settlement meaningless, particularly in a narrative that argues for increased and increasing mobility at all stages. Globalization is an important part of this story, but it is not the whole story. In the vast and clamoring narrative of globalization, immigration is often treated as one unified phenomenon. It is too complicated for that treatment.

The end of settlement as an immigration value emerges in several ways. For some time now, migration scholars have remarked that the labels "temporary" and "permanent" are no longer good descriptors of migration outcomes.[3] Many people who arrive as "permanent" immigrants do not, in fact, remain permanently. There is sometimes a tendency to consider these people as "failed migrants." But this can only be understood as a failure from a state perspective. Of course *some* of these "failed migrants" may well have come to Australia (or Canada or New Zealand . . .), lived for a time, and then decided that Australia was not for them and thus returned home. But it is equally possible (maybe even more possible) that some people had planned all along to live in Australia for a time, but not forever, or that some people who leave Australia do not return home, but instead move to a new destination. Consider this illustrative example. Among people permanently departing from Australia, Australian citizens rank second only to foreign students. Among these citizens, more than a third are foreign born – that is, they are "former migrants" in the words of the Australian government. Furthermore, the principal destination countries of those permanently leaving Australia are the United Kingdom, the United States, Canada, and New Zealand.[4]

There has been a similar erosion of the "temporary" label. Much effort has been devoted to ensuring that people with temporary permission to remain in a prosperous Western country return home when their permission lapses. This phenomenon is considered a major challenge in designing temporary foreign work programs, and was once considered a principal reason for states to use such programs sparingly.

The labels "permanent" and "temporary" do persist, but rather than reflecting results – what migrants actually do – they instead reflect outcomes desired by states. That is, states would prefer if certain people remained permanently and others stayed only for a limited time, and would very much prefer to decide in advance who is in which category. The labels remain meaningful in this way: they describe how migration rights are accorded and, through this apportioning, reflect state desires. A further erosion of "permanence" is found in the fact that all states are eroding the value of permanent residency by making "permanence" itself more vulnerable to loss through bad behavior. The lowering of the threshold at which criminal activity leads to stripping of residency rights has advanced rapidly in the past ten years. This change is intertwined with the rise of deportation enforcement, part of the policy convergence landscape examined in Chapter 9.

The fact that many individuals with a permanent right to remain choose not to do so does contribute to eroding the idea of settlement; but even more important to weakening the value of settlement is a recent shift in state preferences. Over the past decade, the paradigmatic settler states have, mostly, shifted toward prioritizing temporary migration over permanent arrivals. This twenty-first century shift is significant for two reasons. The first is because 2014 is still the beginning of this trend. And the second is that temporary foreign worker programs had a previous popularity in the 1980s and 1990s and were well documented as a policy failure, primarily because it proved very difficult to actually get workers to leave at the required time.

Temporary foreign worker programs all operate with the same basic parameters: workers are invited in for a limited time and are required to leave when that time ends. Often their right to work is tied to a specific employer or a designated sector, but sometimes the only limit is time. The two greatest problems with these programs, which several decades ago were widely known as guest worker programs, have been ensuring that workers depart at the end of their term, and adequately protecting worker rights. Reform efforts have focused on either heightening regulatory incentives to ensure departure (especially through penalties to both workers and employers) or improving rights entitlements. Or very occasionally both. But a seesawing debate between how many workers to bring in and how to protect their rights has not succeeded in addressing either problem adequately.[5] This is because temporary foreign worker programs are inherently problematic.

The human rights side of the problem is intractable because temporary workers are temporary. The goal of any temporary worker program is to make available a pool of workers who have fewer rights, different skills, and greater needs than resident or citizen workers and who are, therefore, willing to work in jobs that are not being filled by members of the national labor pool. Without a permanent right to remain, temporary foreign workers cannot be put on an equal footing with resident workers. Without this equal footing, they are always vulnerable within the labor market. This is precisely the point: to have workers who do not have an entitlement or expectation of employment within a national economy and who will never be added to national unemployment statistics. There are better and worse ways to bundle up rights for temporary workers. For example, people whose permission to be in the country is tied to one employer and one particular job and who have limited avenues for effective complaint and who face conditions about where they live, or who can be paid less than national workers, are at the low end of the rights scale. At the top end of the rights scale are those who are highly skilled and thus their labor is sought after in many countries of the world. Their bargaining position means they can command good wages and conditions of work. Most importantly, the fact that they do not have a right to remain is of little consequence – other forms of privilege outweigh it.

This spectrum provides a keen insight into human rights arguments. No matter how lavishly the rights entitlements within temporary foreign worker programs are designed, they cannot deliver equality to temporary foreign workers. This does not mean that rights arguments are not worth making. In almost every case, temporary foreign workers' lives could be improved by improving rights entitlements. Furthermore, there is ample evidence that – for good reasons – temporary workers very often do not attempt to utilize the rights that they do have, for fear of losing their jobs, or because they cannot remain in the country to see a complaint through. Advocating to improve the rights of temporary foreign workers is useful and important, but cannot make them equal to those with a permanent right to remain.

The other point about rights arguments that is illustrated by migrant workers is that rights are not the only form of privilege in the world. Indeed, rights protections are often most dearly sought, and most meaningful, for those who are disadvantaged. For people who benefit from multiple forms of privilege, rights are sometimes no more than an icing on a very rich cake. Rights-based advocacy for highly skilled workers from the global North is not nearly as pressing as for low-skilled workers from the global South. The highly skilled are protected by their attractiveness in many economies and by their citizenship in a wealthy home state.

The other persistent problem is ensuring that temporary foreign workers leave when their work is done and their permission to remain ends. This problem is intractable because workers are human beings. Not only do they work, they also make friends, fall in love, belong to communities, have children, become ill, change their minds, and many other very human things. Within any foreign worker program there are always some people who embark on the journey hoping to stay permanently, and others who make that decision part-way through. And there are also, because temporary workers are human beings, reasons why most states, at least some of the time, let some temporary workers remain. That is, state resolve to require people to depart weakens. The state sometimes relents, when the person has become part of a citizen family or has become especially economically valuable, or has learned new skills. Or sometimes even, when the person has become so vulnerable that the liberal state cannot countenance expelling her.

It is also the case that once a person has remained on a temporary basis for an increasingly long time, she begins to develop a sense of belonging. And it becomes harder and harder to understand what it is that keeps "them" from being one of "us." These days, legal frameworks are pretty clear about this. But the morality behind these frameworks is shaky. Why would someone who has worked hard, paid taxes, sent their children to school, made ties in a community, volunteered in their extra time, and not caused any kind of trouble at all, not be allowed to stay? At some level, have they not earned membership? This question was the basis of much scholarly analysis of the late-twentieth-century wave of temporary foreign worker programs, which were popular mostly in European states. The moral challenge to settler states is even more pronounced: how are such newcomers any different from the foundational folk who built the nation in the first place? The recent desire to insist upon this difference, and to maintain a distinction between "us" and "them" in this way, is a marker of the new politics of immigration. It demarcates settler societies as turning sharply away from their former logic and insisting that "settlement" not occur. That the new wave of temporary foreign work programs is more able to ensure an end date than ever before distinguishes it from programs like Chinese labor on Canadian railroads or Australian cane fields, or Mexican labor in American harvests, where the ending was often not "successful" in policy enforcement terms.

Each paradigmatic settler state is participating in preferring temporariness in slightly different ways.[6] The shift is most overt in Canada. In 2006, for the first time ever, Canada admitted more temporary foreign workers than permanent economic migrants. This trend has continued in every year since, with a slight dip in 2009 following a rise in domestic unemployment scarcely shifting the trajectory. Two specialized temporary worker programs, for agricultural workers and for in-home caregivers, also expanded dramatically over these years. The policy objective of this shift was trumpeted as a solution to labor shortages in a variety of industries. The government has been steadfast in its commitment to temporary foreign work as a migration panacea, and to the underlying view that temporary foreign work makes better, and faster, economic sense than permanent migration, even permanent migration of highly skilled individuals. Despite a widespread promulgation of this view, public reactions to the temporary foreign worker influx have been mixed at best. Over the past three years, eruptions of discontent have surrounded an influx of Mandarin-speaking mining workers; systematic underpayment of the restaurant sector; and employment of temporary foreign workers on Indian reserves with a high rate of Aboriginal unemployment.[7] There seems to be a new headline controversy every month or so. As this book goes to press, in 2015, the most recent flurry of criticism surrounded errors in the government's labor and employment statistics that undermine a foundational premise of the program. In 2014, the government announced changes to the program, including heightened enforcement of the overall framework and closing the program to workers in the restaurant industry, where most foreign workers had been "low skilled." This shift was accompanied by a renewed "Canadians first" rhetoric.

The shift in numbers in New Zealand has followed a similar pattern.[8] In the fiscal year 2002–03, the number of permanent resident admissions was just shy of 50,000 and the number of approved work visas was higher, at just under 70,000. In the decade that followed, the levels shifted dramatically, mirroring the Canadian pattern (although from a different starting point). By 2012–13, the number of permanent admissions had dropped by approximately 20 percent to near 40,000 and the total number of approved temporary workers was over 138,000. As in Canada, the most recent few years have been marked by a decline in skilled temporary worker admissions, which has been more than compensated for by the admission of working holidaymakers and agricultural workers who are classified as "unskilled." Unlike Canada, however, the discussion of temporary foreign workers reflected in the mainstream press is less hostile to the workers, and includes considerable coverage of worker exploitation. Early in 2014, a new bill aimed at providing significant new powers to curtail abuses of migrant workers was introduced.[9]

In Australia, the embrace of temporary foreign workers has been less overt. There is some evidence of a rise in temporary foreign work visas being issued from 2006 onwards, but it is much less pronounced than in Canada, and the Labor government in power until 2013 did publicly speak against increasing migrant workers.[10] But the story of foreigners entering Australia for temporary work is more complex. A high number of foreign students have entered the

Australian labor force. This trend is so pronounced that large numbers of people were rumored not to be genuine students at all. This issue attracted such attention that it led to a national inquiry in 2011.[11] Beyond student entry, Australia also has a very sizeable working holiday program, which admits foreigners to work temporarily, and which has expanded greatly in the early years of the twenty-first century. Finally, in 2009, Australia introduced a temporary foreign work pilot program for seasonal agricultural workers from nearby Pacific island nations. This program took very seriously the twinned concerns of adequately protecting worker rights and ensuring that temporary workers depart at the conclusion of their contract. It was designed with stronger rights protections than any comparable program in the world, and with considerable commitment to enforcement. Ironically, the program was not nearly as attractive to employers as the government had anticipated, and in the first few years, the quota of foreign workers went unfilled. In total, only 1623 people were admitted under the program in four years, with almost 70 percent of those admissions in the final year. The pilot program was replaced with a permanent version in mid-2012, data for which are not yet available as I write.[12] Given all of this, it is evident that while statistics about temporary foreign workers in Australia are being kept lower than in Canada, in a variety of more hidden ways Australia is hosting a marked increase in migrant workers with no right to remain.

The United States presents the most complex picture of shifting temporary work patterns in the paradigmatic settler states. Temporary entry has long outstripped permanent entry to the United States, and thus it differs from Canada and Australia in that it is not possible to say that there is a "new" preference for temporary workers. But there have been two shifts that show the United States is moving in the same direction as the others. The first is that the number of low-skilled temporary workers has increased sharply – a trend that is also evident in Canada and New Zealand, and that can be discerned from Australia's reliance on young foreigners who are not skill screened, but are instead holidaymakers and students. The second is a massive increase in the illegal or undocumented population of the United States from the mid-1990s onward.

The well-established pattern underpinning the massive American temporary work force is the idea that for the most successful temporary workers, permanence may become an option. In other words, the United States' immigration system has for some time had a complicated way for those arriving temporarily to gain a permanent right to remain, mostly on the basis of skills and economic success. This formalizes the notion of "earning membership," and also reduces the idea of membership to economic value.

Accompanying the shift to higher numbers of temporary workers, Canada has explicitly emulated this idea by introducing in 2008 a preferential access to permanence scheme for people who have succeeded as foreign workers and international students. New Zealand is pursuing a similar route, under an existing legal provision. In both the United States and Canada, this pathway is for those who have successfully integrated into the skilled labor force, and is not available for low-skilled workers.[13]

The rise in so-called "illegal" migration, which is massively more pronounced in the United States than in the other paradigmatic settler societies, ensures that there is an available pool of labor with even fewer rights than temporary foreign workers. This clandestine labor force fits into the economic equation in much the same way as temporary workers: people who will work with reduced rights or poor conditions and who will simply "disappear" when their labor is no longer needed. An informal workforce is more easily accessible to employers than temporary workers who must be recruited via state apparatus. While "illegal" workers do have rights, they have even fewer rights than those at the lowest rung of the rights scale for temporary workers, and they are even less likely to access any of those rights. Understanding the landscape of illegal migration is deeply complicated, but one aspect of it is certainly as an alternative to temporary foreign labor.[14]

Of all the ways in which "settlement" has been lost as an immigration value in settler societies, the rise in temporary foreign labor is the most important symbolically and practically. Temporary workers have had a place in settler societies from the outset, as there have long been some categories of workers who were *not* invited to join the nation-building project, often on the explicit basis of race in the early days. What is different now, however, is that the growth of temporary worker admissions is outstripping permanent admissions, and the embrace of the idea that temporary workers are preferred economic actors. Temporary foreign workers are a better fit with a post-globalization vision of the idea of a national economy than permanent immigrants who are admitted on an economic basis. One reason that the United States example varies from the other three in the contours of temporariness is that the United States had never formalized a preference for economic migrants over family migrants, something that had taken place in Canada and Australia in the 1990s. Rather than shifting away from family reunification at that time, the United States turned, a decade ahead of the others, to temporary migration as its economic solution. This shift reflects two things: first, it allows the formal immigration program to retain its symbolic function conforming to the mythological role of immigration in a settler society; second, it demonstrates that the size of the American economy, as well as American global hegemony, draw migrants from around the globe and give the United States an advantage in all competitive migration endeavors, a point that I turn to in Chapter 9.

Temporary foreign worker programs are a special dark corner of policy paralysis. Sarah Marsden and I have described the ideology of temporary labor migration as the key reason for this. In policy conversations about temporary migrant labor, the concepts of temporariness, human rights, and labor markets are always present. They function ideologically. By this we mean that they conceal a great deal about the power dynamics that anchor their meaning, and thus they serve to make things that are disparate look like equality. Until the inequality is better examined, it is almost impossible to shift the discourse in a way that can truly mitigate against the disadvantages it perpetuates.[15]

The recent rise in popularity of temporary labor, including temporary low-skilled migrant labor, has dramatically increased options for women from the global South to become migrant workers. In the settler society phase, permanent economic migration was dominated by men and family migration was dominated by women.[16] The feminization of labor migration has become possible because prosperous states have turned to categories of migration where people have fewer rights, and thus women (sadly, predictably) fit more easily into them. It is a simple equation: the more poor people are admitted to do tough work in bad conditions, the more women are admitted. Despite this, it is precarious to argue that these avenues should be closed for this reason. To make such an argument limits the options available to women, if viewed from a global perspective. And it is paternalistic. The feminization of labor migration under these conditions reflects the global disadvantage of women as economic actors, and also reflects women's agency. Shutting down these programs would not "benefit" women in a global sense, but it would distance the exploitation of women from Western eyes – removing this uncomfortable contradiction from our playgrounds and neighborhood shops. Women make the choice to move to work, even when they are aware of the rotten conditions they may encounter. That people make this choice reflects the range of choices available to them. To attempt to solve the problem by removing what many women see as their best possible option amounts only to removing this inequality from the Western gaze. It does nothing to remedy it. To the extent that women are the traditional bearers of culture and family, feminizing temporary migration cuts directly into settlement as a core value. The settlement aspect of nation building has always relied on a (hidden) gendered aspect: people stay in a new place because women build families and put down roots.

The preference for temporary foreign work is central to the loss of settlement as an immigration value, and illustrates its contours well. There are a number of currents that run alongside it. Cutbacks in funding services for newcomers that are bundled together under the heading "settlement services" (things like language classes, help adapting to the employment market, assistance with registering for state entitlements) are another marker. A significant rise in recruitment of international students creates another category of migrants who remain temporarily. Finally, under a number of the world's new "free trade" agreements, people who move to do certain types of work are brought within the agreement and thus no longer appear as "migrants." This is a linchpin of migration in the European Union, which Chapter 8 addresses. But it happens increasingly around the world. For example, under the North American Free Trade Agreement, NAFTA, which is as old as 1994, service sector workers are not migrants. When migration is defined away as a term of trade, settlement is irrelevant. Some of this trend can be sheeted home to the economic forces of globalization, but the settler society backdrop against which it occurs determines the meanings that we can read in this trend. Furthermore, the precipitating factors of asylum crisis, Islamophobia, and the demise of multiculturalism provide a more nuanced picture of what globalization might mean in this context, and can even be understood in its absence.

LOSS OF SOCIETY

The loss of settlement as a value brings with it the loss of society. In some ways, the relationship is causal: when fewer people are encouraged to "settle" and when another group of people *could* settle but chooses not to, there are fewer people available overall to adapt or assimilate to the culture of the new place where they now live. But the loss of society is too complicated to understand it as solely an effect of diminished settlement value, or as some kind of dependent variable. The loss of society also occurs at the same time as the devaluing of settlement, and, additionally, finds expression in the decline of multiculturalism. The loss of the "society" aspect of the settler society dyad is sometimes what fosters a turn away from the settlement ethos. The two losses are deeply intertwined, sometimes it is simply a question of which thread one pulls at first in the overall unraveling project of changing what immigration means. Over the past decade, two phenomena that signal the loss of "society" as an immigration value have been on the rise: ethnic enclaves and illegal migration.

What ethnic enclaves and illegal migration have in common is that each phenomenon operates to exclude from within; in other words, to separate people from the national "group" and from a full sense of membership or belonging, even though they are within the territory of the nation. In recent years, both illegal migration and ethnic enclaves have been reinterpreted within the migration policy conversation. Each is now viewed as more threatening than at earlier points in time. And both have drawn attention from policy makers and scholars because of this. Both phenomena are symptomatic of the end of settler societies, and thus they are interpreted differently in these states than in Western nations of the Old World, where they are also on the rise.

I turn first to illegal migration, which is the easier occurrence to analyze because Western states have reacted to it in very similar ways, making it appear more straightforward than ethnic enclaves. Around the world, beginning in the final years of the twentieth century, rates of illegal migration have risen sharply. There are many reasons for this; for example, the complex relationship between extra-legal migration and the asylum crisis that Chapter 3 examined. Two of these reasons are especially important for understanding the migration law response to this phenomenon. The first is that as states seek to "crack down" on migration outside the law, a primary weapon deployed in this battle is law itself. That is, Western states have responded to a rise in rates of illegal migration by making more, and more stringent, laws. With each increase in the number of laws, there is a rise in the number of ways in which a person can transgress the law, and thus the number of transgressors rises. The second reason is closely related to this; it is enforcement activity. Clandestine migration is by its nature difficult to measure. Increased efforts to prevent it mean more people paying attention to it more often and in more places. These efforts mean that more illegal migration is detectable, and this also causes numbers to rise.

Illegal migration is a product of migration law. Without legal prohibition, there is no illegality. The social movement styling itself *No One Is Illegal* takes this as its fundamental point of departure: ending migration law would end illegal migration. I use the term illegal migration (but never "illegals") not because I believe "illegal" is a good way to describe people, but because my focus is on the law and the responsibility it bears.

From our position in the middle of the second decade of the twenty-first century, it is almost impossible to imagine that in the very recent past, the 1990s, migration law transgressions were scarcely criminalized. Unauthorized border crossing was widely regarded in Western states as a type of regulatory infringement – against the law in a technical way, but not truly criminal. The term "illegal" was not used regularly as a noun to describe unauthorized migrants until the final two decades of the twentieth century, and became widespread even more recently.

The state-fostered moral panic surrounding illegal migration is one marker of the end of "society" because it operates to exclude a group of people who have lived in a state for a considerable time. The idea that some people have no "status" or place in our society serves a powerful ordering function, and has an enormously detrimental effect on rights-based forms of social inclusion. That is, people with no migration status also become excluded from a wide range of state services, such as education, health care, welfare support, and the protections of labor law. This exclusion is meaningful, whether or not it is "legal". By this I mean that while in almost every Western liberal democracy, some rights do in fact extend to people with no migration status, those without the security of migration status are often reluctant to attempt to exercise those rights, for any number of very good reasons. The label "illegal" serves to prevent them from earning a form of moral inclusion on the basis of long-time residence and community contribution. In this way it acts as a perverse solution to the late-twentieth-century problem of guest workers earning membership and thus becoming exceptionally difficult to eject. If one is "illegal" rather than a "guest," moral blameworthiness attaches: the policy problem of (over-) settlement by long-term residents that states do not want to accept is solved by undermining the attachment to society through moral condemnation.

DREAM Act activism in the United States maps this dynamic in all its complexity.[17] The Development, Relief, and Education for Alien Minors (DREAM) legislation is designed to provide a pathway to social membership for some people who are non-status migrants. The Act is focused on a group of people who can be characterized as morally blameless in their own illegality. The proposed law would regularize the status of young people who were brought to the United States as young children and who are excluded from an "ordinary" progression to adulthood, especially access to higher education, by their illegal migration status. The prototypical DREAM Act beneficiary only learns of her migration status at the point when it becomes impossible for her to get a driver's license, take a part-time job after school, or apply for college admission. Often her younger siblings face a different life path, having been born after their parents' clandestine entry to the United States, they are citizens. Amongst the massive illegal migrant population of the United States, these young people are the most morally appealing, and the most comprehensively excluded from the American Dream. A dream that itself follows an immigrant script of transformation within a generation and rescuing oneself through hard work and dedication. Many of these young people have put themselves at considerable risk by advocating for the Act, publicly "outing" themselves as non-status migrants, telling their stories, and risking expulsion.

It is almost surprising that the DREAM Act has not become law.[18] Of all the options on the Obama regime's immigration reform menu, it has to be one of the most broadly appealing. Indeed, those who could benefit from the DREAM Act would do so on the basis that they are already ideal immigrants: they speak the language, are fully socially integrated, have spotless records of good behavior, have been fully visible to the state throughout their lives, and are on their way to either a college education or military service for the country. In short, they qualify because they need nothing from the state and they have a lot to offer. There are an estimated 1.9 million so-called DREAMers in the United States who might be eligible to apply for the reprieve contemplated by the DREAM Act.[19] They also make up a reasonably small proportion of the illegal population. Resistance to their inclusion despite strong social support, moral blamelessness, economic rationality, and good human rights arguments reveals the power of "illegality" as a barrier to membership and a sustained incapacity to think differently about immigration policy questions.

Indeed, the political difficulties faced by the DREAM Act, which has languished after being rejected by the Senate in 2010, are emblematic of a hardening of attitudes to migration law transgressions. In the latter half of the twentieth century, episodes of extra-legal migration were punctuated by periodic amnesty programs that granted migration status to large numbers of "deserving" people. The idea that illegal migrants can *ever* "deserve" membership in the polity is now much more contested.

The United States has progressed further than my other exemplar states down the road of grappling with the meanings of illegality as a form of exclusion applied to those within its borders. This is indubitably because of the size of the population, and because of its long duration, which means that "illegal" children are now becoming adults. This sustained grappling has produced two effects: hardening and softening. Hardening in the form of deportations from hospitals, minutemen as border vigilantes, and a spate of horrific legislation in Arizona. Softening in the form of pockets of social inclusion for people without status, such as access to public education, provision of driver's licenses in some states, and recognition by some unions that including illegal migrants in their membership and their cause may be a way forward.

Thus far, hardening is winning. And this is because of law – its basic characteristics and its inflexible binary nature. Human rights arguments have been remarkably hard to deploy in the service of those without migration status. Hannah Arendt's aphorism about the right to have rights has become truer and truer in the long decades since she wrote it. Without membership, a basic right of belonging, it is very difficult to make other legal entitlements stick in any way, even when there is nothing formally barring the application of the law. The problems of illegal migration are problems created by the law; the simple application of more law is not providing a solution.

The rise of ethnic enclaves is considerably more complex. In settler states in the contemporary era, this is happening without the law, and without the state, and yet marks an erosion of precisely the logic that once propelled the nation-building enterprise of settler societies. An ethnic enclave is a neighborhood or geographic area where people of the same "ethnic" background form a dominant part of the population. As one example, the Canadian government defines ethnic enclaves as census tracts in which at least 30 percent of the population belong to a minority group.[20] The old story of ethnic enclaves within the settler society is that they break down within a generation or so. In other words, when new immigrants first arrive they choose to live near others from the same cultural background, but as they adapt to the new society, this desire wanes and prosperity grows and thus geographic population patterns become more mixed, a measure of integration and adaptation.

But most recent census data in Canada and Australia show that this pattern is no longer holding. Between the 1981 census and the 2006 census the number of "ethnic enclaves" in Canada rose from 6 to more than 260.[21] In Australia, the trend is visible, but somewhat less stark. In New Zealand, the 2006 census did reveal increased ethnic diversity, but the starting point in comparison with both Canada and Australia was a much higher degree of ethnic homogeneity, and the shift is occurring, therefore, at a much smaller scale. In the United States, the question of ethnic enclaves has been perpetually overshadowed by the related issue of communities dominated by African-American population: typically labeled ghettoization rather than enclaves. In some American analyses the question is treated as primarily economic, focusing on types of employment and assimilation. But a shift in academic attention to ethnic enclaves is nonetheless observable. It is in the United States, after all, that Wei Li's term "ethnoburb" was coined and first gained traction.

Some scholars have floated the idea that the rise in ethnic enclaves is a straightforward result of more racially mixed immigrant flows from the 1970s onwards. But the timeline does not fit this explanation well, especially in Canada and Australia, where the trend is most visible. It is far more plausible that something else is going on here, part of which is reflected in the "ethnoburb" idea.

The notion of the ethnoburb is a direct challenge to the old story of gradual assimilation, accompanied by moving out of the inner city and into the suburbs. Rather, the ethnoburb is affluent – a group of people with myriad options about where to live, who choose nonetheless to "stick together" in the same neighborhood, and to move directly to the suburbs rather than beginning life in the new country in inner-city neighborhoods. In coining the term "ethnoburb" Wei Li sought to distinguish this phenomenon, which she located primarily in major immigrant-receiving cities of the Pacific Rim, from the idea of an ethnic "enclave" or "ghetto."[22] Li's analysis points to factors that mere demographic data cannot reveal, as she focuses on the global interconnections of migrants in the "ethnoburb" that render settler society-style connectedness to the national culture irrelevant. Whether or not it is possible to identify among the burgeoning enclave statistics which would meet Li's ethnoburb criteria, it is clear from the attention that Li's work has gotten that something new is happening here. The way that ethnic enclaves fit within settler societies geographically, culturally, and symbolically is shifting.

In Canada in particular, the marked increase in ethnic enclaves has generated a flurry of concern in scholarly and policy circles.[23] At the core of this concern is the loss of "society" as an immigration outcome. Immigrants who come to a new state but who actively reject integrating into the new society are threatening to the idea of immigration that the settler state model fostered. The old story that immigrants may start out in an enclave (or even a ghetto) but that over time and generations this pattern will (naturally) break down was woven into the nation-building enterprise. This well-known account, first examined by the Chicago school of sociologists in the 1920s, is now a firmly anchored aspect of settler society beliefs about how immigrants conduct themselves. The rise of ethnic enclaves is, therefore, a direct confrontation to the idea of what immigrants do, especially in settler societies. Population dispersion appears to be waning, at least for some immigrant groups, which challenges the idea that such dispersion was *ever* "natural." Indeed, this new population trend may well be understood as a "result" or at least a "coincident" of Islamophobia and the demise of multiculturalism. These shifts postdate the original "ethnoburb" analysis, and move the analysis well beyond it. It is certainly one way that the new politics of immigration is requiring us to think anew about what immigration means; in this case, to think anew about what immigrants *do*, from which new political formations will necessarily follow.

The law has a confusing relationship with ethnic enclaves.[24] In liberal democracies, with their individual-rights focus, there are few points of contact between the enclave and the law. People are free to live in any neighborhood that they can afford. (We never think of groups of poor people, or rich people, living together as raising the same types of concerns as ethnic enclaves, even though these patterns are strongly prevalent.) In Vancouver, Canada, where one of the ethnoburbs Wei Li considered in her 2009 book is located, neighbors have attempted to deploy legal tools, on both sides, in establishing enclaves. For example, zoning laws have been used to discourage housing design preferences that were widespread among Chinese migrants; and rules at the same local level have ensured bilingual English-Mandarin signage in some areas. Inevitably, the case for such rules must be articulated in liberal terms – it is difficult or impossible to use "liberal" law to either foster or thwart ethnic enclave aspirations. Ethnic enclaves that also have a religious identity have been more successful in using rights arguments; for example, Montreal's Orthodox Jewish community has won legal protection for its use of the Sabbath "eruv". This result fits with the traditional liberal rights context: freedom of religion is sacrosanct. Freedom of ethnicity, or culture, is nearly unheard of.

Together, the rise of illegal migration and of ethnic enclaves are revealing about the power of law. Law does some things well – like create prohibitions, and does other things poorly – like enforce cultural assimilation. This insight at one level fits directly onto the earlier point about rights and privilege. Once people are wealthy enough, rights matter less. This is the story of the ethnoburb: when migrant communities are wealthy, integration is merely a choice. It cannot be understood as a result of increasing prosperity when the newcomers are prosperous from the outset. At another level, this insight tells us a great deal about rights: rights do little for those without migration status, and do little for groups. There will, of course, be counter examples on both of these scores, but none with the strength to defeat the point overall. Rights have some limitations tied to their liberal individualist pedigree, and these limits frame how rights fit into the new politics of immigration. The liberal society cannot use legal tools to disperse migrant concentrations both because the idea of dispersal is contrary to individual rights and because the groups in question are simply invisible to the law. In an earlier iteration of this dilemma before enclaves became the concern, many states would have preferred newcomers to become more evenly geographically distributed (to rural areas, to take the most common example) but have been completely unsuccessful in achieving this outcome. This is because liberal law cannot organize this result. The vague threat that prosperous enclaves, or even ethnoburbs, represent comes from its deep challenge to our idea of what immigrants "naturally do" and of our inability to alter it with legal tools. Ironically, this is a predictable result of a selection preference for economically successful immigrants: communities that are themselves "privatized" and do not need to integrate into the national economy because they are made up of global economic actors, and the poorer folk who do their dry cleaning.

The idea of "society" was integral to settler societies. The society part of the descriptor signaled the creation of a social identity that was newly created, and at least partially coherent. It also marked out the "new" element as something other than a colonial outpost, and something more than a mere economy. The increase in importance of both illegal migration and the contemporary form of ethnic enclaves threaten all of these values, imprinting new meanings on immigration. The vision of a New World where all newcomers are on an equal footing, and where origins are submerged or forgotten, cannot dominate our understanding of immigration under these conditions.

AFTER SETTLEMENT AND SOCIETY

At the end of settler societies, both settlement and society are lost. These losses transform the logic of immigration, and thus of the politics that surround it. One way to analyze these shifts may be to conceptualize this transition as a "maturing" of the settler society. In other words, to look back at two hundred years of historical trajectory and to conclude that the seeds of this ending were there all along. Now that these paradigmatic settler societies have moved beyond their nation-building phase, and have matured in their political identities, they have no need for immigration as either a source of population or of identity. This translates into a different understanding of immigration, and thus a different politics surrounding it.

As settler societies shift their orientation toward immigration, its value becomes more narrowly economically focused. Political discourses surrounding economic immigration come to predominate. While the immigration conversation has always had this element, in contemporary politics it is stripped bare. The older conversations about cultural composition, family reunification, or even humanitarianism have faded into the background. Not all of this shift is negative from an immigrant advocate's perspective, but much of it is. For example, most advocates would assess positively the end of overt racial and cultural discrimination in immigrant selection. The early years of the nation-building phase were marked by strong preferences for cultural kin of the first wave of European settlers. The fading of this bias was accomplished gradually, but is now firmly in place. Points systems, the original innovation that led this change, have become more and more closely tied to presumed economic success indicators. Even within immigration streams that are labeled "family" or "humanitarian," economic values are at the forefront of contemporary innovation. In Australia, the idea of private sponsorship has become entrenched in refugee resettlement – relieving the state of the "burden" of supporting the world's most needy newcomers. In Canada, the economic demands of family sponsorship have been ratcheted up and a long backlog of grandparent sponsorships has been addressed through a "supervisa" program available to those who can finance their own top-tier health insurance.[25] The US Congress recently considered reducing its family-based immigration policy and increasing employment-based admissions. It would accomplish this by eliminating two kinship categories (siblings and adult children of US citizens). This proposal was initially floated in 1997 and then re-emerged in 2013 in the Senate comprehensive immigration reform proposal.[26]

Immigration policy in liberal states has always responded to national need or desire, however defined. In a nation-building mode, a variety of needs were inscribed on migration texts. Family, family reunification, population expansion, culture, and community were all part of the discourse. Even humanitarian migration met a national need to be perceived as benevolent and prosperous. In contemporary politics, however, the needs of the nation have narrowed. Concerns about family have been privatized; multiculturalism – a group concept no matter how one assesses it – has given way to diversity; humanitarian discourses have faded (ironically) in the face of security concerns. In the former settler states, where immigration laws have been structured to quickly accommodate shifts in national priorities, the shift to a singular economic priority has been quickly accomplished. There have, by and large, been no major national debates about this transformation; rather political leaders claim to be acting in pursuit of public opinion. But it is also evident that political leaders are working to shape this opinion. And it is not at all clear which comes first.

Despite this discursive shift, and the policy and law transformations that follow from it, our conceptualization of what immigration means has not altered to nearly the same extent. Part of contemporary consternation about immigration comes from the persistence of an immigration mythology that is no longer embedded in our legal and political orientation toward migrants. The stereotypical vision of the hard-working immigrant who will come to a new country, work at backbreaking labor in order to make a better life for the children, and who will eventually join the same community groups, clubs, and even political parties as the long-established population, is still intact. Those who live in enclaves, fail to learn the language, earn their income partially or primarily in "the old country," and do not let their children attend the local public school, are somehow suspect. Their lives are at odds with the image of an immigrant that we are comfortable with: the image that was forged through the experience of settler societies. Never mind that these newcomers are the ones who now qualify for admission under contemporary immigration law.

Even in the policy universe dominated by economic discourse, economics fails to be a solid predictor of future policies and fails to explain social and political discourses about immigration. Economic analysis cannot deliver this information because it is inevitably too uncertain, the policy time lags are too long, and even those immigrants recruited solely (if this is even possible) on economic criteria, remain human. Doctors continue to be willing to drive taxis. Aboriginal unemployment continues to be more complicated than just providing more low-skilled work in Aboriginal "enclaves." And in matters of social and political discourse, the shift to economic priorities has not stopped the "background" populations from wanting the new newcomers to behave like the old newcomers. The mean-spirited new hostility to migrants is fueled by their failure to conform to the stereotypes that make up the settler society. Even as we withdraw settlement services through persistent underfunding, and privatize all measures related to integration (if not assimilation), we want settlement and integration at some deep-seated level.

The loss of settlement and society as core immigration values impoverishes human rights analysis and rhetoric. Human rights are poorly tooled to confront the trends of privatization and temporariness, as both of these factors make rights arguments harder to deploy. Regarding privatization, this is because human rights are better at binding states than at controlling private actors; regarding temporariness, the problem is not having a secure enough underpinning to make a rights argument stick in either practical or substantive terms. Human rights are also a poor tool for protecting ethnic enclaves or people without migration status: in the first case because of the dilemma of "group-ness" and the absence of a history of legal recognition of ethnicity; in the second because the law is better at constructing illegality than remedying it.

Asylum is deeply affected by this shift as well. In both positive and negative ways, refugees used to be welcomed in the former settler societies on terms that were similar to the implicit immigration contract. Both those who made it to settler society borders on their own, and those who were assisted by governments to "resettle" from distant, violent places, were encouraged to remain permanently in these countries. On the positive side, refugees were welcomed on a smooth path toward citizenship, and were treated to an array of "settlement services" fostering cultural integration (or possibly even assimilation). On the negative side, immigration-like criteria were applied to refugees seeking resettlement, as states sought to ensure that refugees would be able to both "settle" and join "society" easily. The demise of settlement and society values has been accompanied by a rise in hostility toward refugees, and a variety of policy shifts aiming to both reduce their numbers and their permanence, which were discussed in Chapter 3. Both Canada and Australia, which had traditionally allowed refugees to remain permanently, have introduced categories of refugees who, as a punitive measure tied to their method of arrival (boat arrivals in particular), are allowed to remain only temporarily. This change fits in with the broader shift to temporariness, even though it undercuts the permanence that actually allows refugees to rebuild their lives and that is reflected in the Refugee Convention's requirement that pathways to naturalization be open.

One important result of this series of changes is that immigration in the New World is now similarly situated to immigration in the European countries that were the source countries for the original settlers of the settler society era. It is no coincidence that temporary foreign worker programs that were the focus of much European migration policy in the 1980s are now central to the policy aims of former settler societies. The shift away from settlement and society values is an ingredient of immigration policy convergence. In order to understand fully the new politics of immigration, however, it is essential also to assess how European states have shifted their own perspectives in order to reach the current state of global immigration politics. The next chapter examines the trends in immigration policy and politics in European states that have accompanied the much-touted transformation of many former source countries into "countries of immigration." The new politics of immigration, and the policy convergence that emerges from it, involve not only the end of settler societies, but also a transformation of the global picture of migration, in which European states, and Europe as a whole, are major players.

Notes

1. The role of migration in constituting transnational or trans-border communities is explored by Jennifer Hyndman and Margaret Walton-Roberts, "Interrogating Borders: A Transnational Approach to Refugee Research in Vancouver" (2000) 44:3 *Canadian Geographer* 244; Linda Basch, Nina Glick Schiller, and Cristina Szanton Blanc, *Nations Unbound: Transnational Projects, Postcolonial Predicaments, and Deterritorialized Nation-States* (Langhorne, PA: Gordon and Breach, 1994).
2. It is a bit of a risk to launch into a discussion of globalization without engaging in an exercise of developing definitions and drawing borders.

My defense to this accusation is that I have written at length about globalization and migration, most completely in *Making People Illegal: What Globalization Means for Migration and Law* (Cambridge: Cambridge University Press, 2008). Here I will say simply that I regard globalization as a force with a centuries-long history, which has undergone both qualitative and quantitative shifts in the final decades of the twentieth century.

3. David Ley, *Millionaire Migrants: Trans-Pacific Life Lines* (Malden, MA: Wiley-Blackwell, 2010); Transatlantic Council on Migration, *Talent, Competitiveness and Migration*, ed. by Bertelsmann Stiftung (Gütersloh, Germany: Bertelsmann Stiftung, 2010); Steven Vertovec, "Is Circular Migration the Way Forward in Global Policy?" (2006) International Migration Institute Working Paper; Pew Research Center, *Changing Patterns of Global Migration and Remittances: More Migrants in U.S. and Other Wealthy Countries; More Money to Middle-Income Countries* (Washington, DC: Pew Research Center, 2013), online: www.pewsocialtrends.org/files/2013/12/global-migration-final_12–2013.pdf; Phillip Connor, D'Vera Cohn, and Ana Gonzalez-Barrera, *Changing Patterns of Global Migration and Remittances* (Washington, DC: Pew Research Center, 2013).

4. Australia is an easy country to highlight here as publicly available data on this point is particularly transparent. See Australia, Department of Immigration and Citizenship, *Australia's Migration Trends 2011–12* (Belconnen, ACT: Department of Immigration and Citizenship, 2013) ch. 6.

5. An excellent example of attempts to reform these programs is the work of the Global Commission on International Migration, which has a chapter on migrant workers that reads as a catalogue of tried and true reform efforts. See United Nations Global Commission on International Migration, *Migration in an Interconnected World: New Directions for Action* (Geneva: Global Commission on International Migration, 2005), online: www.refworld.org/publisher,GCIM,,,435f81814,0.html. Useful commentaries, which approach the issues from various points on the political spectrum include, for example, Stuart Rosewarne, "Globalisation and the Commodification of Labour: Temporary Labour Migration" (2010) 20:2 *Economic & Labour Relations Rev* 99; Stephen Castles, "Guestworkers in Europe: A Resurrection?" (2006) 40:4 *Intl Migration Rev* 741; Joseph Carens, *Immigrants and the Right to Stay* (Cambridge, MA: MIT Press, 2010); Philip Martin, Manolo Abella, and Christiane Kuptsch, *Managing Labor Migration in the Twenty-First Century* (New Haven, CT: Yale University Press, 2006); my own work with Sarah Marsden, "The Ideology of Temporary Labour Migration in the Post-Global Era" (2014) 18:2 *Citizenship Studies* 224 [Dauvergne and Marsden, "Ideology"].

6. See Appendix 6 for details of these trends. In work with Sarah Marsden, I have analyzed this trend in detail: see Dauvergne and Marsden, "Ideology", *supra* note 5; Catherine Dauvergne and Sarah Marsden, "Beyond Numbers Versus Rights: Shifting the Parameters of Debate on Temporary Labour Migration" (2014) 15:3 *J Intl Migration & Integration* 525.

7. Peter O'Neil, "BC Coal Mine's Temporary Workers Will Be Here for Years, Maybe Decades," *The Vancouver Sun* (January 7, 2013), online: www.vancouversun.com/coal+mine+temporary+workers+from+China+w ill+here+years+maybe+decades/7388916/story.html; "Temporary Foreign Worker Program Misuse Sanctioned by Harper Government, Union Says," *CBC News* (August 15, 2014) online: www.cbc.ca/news/canada/ca lgary/temporary-foreign-worker-program-misuse-sanctioned-by-harper-government-union-says-1.2737422; Renata D'Aliesio and Joe Friesen, "Temporary Foreign Workers Hired in Area with High Aboriginal Unemployment," *The Globe and Mail* (October 14, 2014), online: www .theglobeandmail.com/news/national/first-nations-coming-second-to-te mporary-foreign-workers/article21084696/.

8. All data regarding New Zealand comes from successive years of the government's *Migration Trends and Outlook* reports. For details, see Appendix 6.

9. Isaac Davidson, "Migrant Worker Abuse Crackdown," *The New Zealand Herald* (February 25, 2014), online: www.nzherald.co.nz/nz/news/article .cfm?c_id=1&objectid=11209212; Bill 156–2, *Immigration Amendment Bill No. 2*, (NZ), 2013, 50–51 Parl (In Committee 31 as of March 2015).

10. The stated aim was to reduce the number of temporary work permits by 50 percent by 2012 through "deregulation and simplification": Australia, Department of Immigration and Citizenship, *Simpler Visas: Implementing a Simpler Framework for Temporary Residence Work Visas* (Belconnen, ACT: Department of Immigration and Citizenship, 2010). Following the change of government, the proposal has been updated: Australia, Department of Immigration and Border Protection, *Proposal Paper: Simplification of the Skilled Migration and Temporary Activity Visa Programmes* (Belconnen, ACT: Department of Immigration and Border Protection, 2014).

11. Australia, *Strategic Review of the Student Visa Program 2011* (June 30, 2011) (Hon Michael Knight).

12. Therese MacDermott and Brian Opeskin, "Regulating Pacific Seasonal Labour in Australia" (2010) 83:2 *Pacific Affairs* 283; Australia, Department of Employment, *Pacific Seasonal Worker Pilot Scheme*, online: employ ment.gov.au/pacific-seasonal-worker-pilot-scheme; Australia, Department of Employment, *Seasonal Worker Program*, online: employment.gov.au/ seasonal-worker-program.

13. The one important exception to this in the United States is the idiosyncratic "green card lottery." A comparatively small number of permanent residency places are made available each year on a lottery basis, with "winners" spread out around the globe. Some level of education is needed to even enter the lottery, and it has been critiqued as aiming explicitly at reducing Mexican immigration, but it is undeniable that it does distribute residency by chance. It is a powerful reflection of the settler society ethos, with its vision of a land of opportunity and a chance of a new future. See US, Department of Homeland Security, United States Citizenship and Immigration Services, *Green Card Through the Diversity Immigrant Visa Program*, online: www.uscis.gov/green-card/other-ways-get-green-card/green-card-through-diversity-immigration-visa-program/green-card-through-diversity-immigrant-visa-program; Anna O. Law, "The Diversity Visa Lottery: A Cycle of Unintended Consequences in United States Immigration Policy" (2002) 21:4 *J American Ethnic History* 3.

14. See Appendix 7 for information about so-called "illegal" migration. This is one aspect of my earlier argument in *Making People Illegal: What Globalization Means for Migration and Law, supra* note 2.

15. Dauvergne and Marsden, "Ideology," *supra* note 5.

16. Catherine Dauvergne, "Globalizing Fragmentation – New Pressures on the Women Caught in the Immigration Law – Citizenship Law Dichotomy" in Seyla Benhabib and Judith Resnick, eds., *Migration and Mobilities: Citizenship, Borders and Gender* (New York: New York University Press, 2009) 333; Catherine Dauvergne, "Citizenship, Migration Laws and Women: Gendering Permanent Residency Statistics" (2000) 24:2 *Melbourne UL Rev* 280.

17. For discussion of the DREAM Act, see Elisha Barron, "The Development, Relief and Education for Alien Minors (DREAM) Act" (2011) 48:2 *Harv J on Legis* 623; Michael A. Olivas, "The Political Economy of the DREAM Act and the Legislative Process: A Case Study of Comprehensive Immigration Reform" (2009) 55:4 *Wayne L Rev* 1757.

18. Despite this fact, some of the spirit of the law has been implemented using executive authority. In June 2012, President Obama announced that he was using executive authority to protect a group of DREAM Act eligible youth from deportation. This is the DACA directive (Deferred Action for Childhood Arrivals). It lets them apply for temporary protection from deportation and work authorization and grants them deferred action for two years. See Memorandum from Janet Napolitano, Secretary, Department of Homeland Security, to David V. Aguilar, Acting Commissioner, US Customs and Border Protection, et al. (June 15, 2012) re Exercising Prosecutorial Discretion with Respect to Individuals Who Came to the United States as Children ("Napolitano

Directive"), online: www.dhs.gov/xlibrary/assets/s1-exercising-prosecutor ial-discretion-individuals-who-came-to-us-as-children.pdf.

19. Migration Policy Institute, *MPI Updates National and State-Level Estimates of Potential DREAM Act Beneficiaries* (December 2010), cited in *We Cannot Afford Not to Pass the DREAM Act: A Plea from America's Scholars*, online: www.immigrationpolicy.org/sites/default/files/docs/Scholar%20Sign-on%20 DREAM.pdf.

20. Statistics Canada, *Recent Immigration and the Formation of Visible Minority Neighbourhoods in Canada's Large Cities*, by Feng Hou (Ottawa: Statistics Canada, Business and Labour Market Analysis Division, 2004).

21. Statistics Canada does not track "ethnic enclaves" directly, it produces numbers based on census tracts, to which a definition of "ethnic enclave" can then be applied by others.

22. Wei Li, *Ethnoburb: The New Ethnic Community in Urban America* (Honolulu: University of Hawai'i Press, 2009); Wei Li, ed., *From Urban Enclave to Ethnic Suburb: New Asian Communities in Pacific Rim Countries* (Honolulu: University of Hawai'i Press, 2006). In this second book Li defines ethnoburb at 12:

> An ethnoburb is the spatial expression of a unique set of ethnic relations; it appears to be characterized by a unique spatial form and internal socioeconomic structure and involves interethnic group and intraethnic class differences and tensions. An ethnoburb is a suburban ethnic cluster of residential areas and business districts in a large metropolitan area. It is a multiracial, multiethnic, and multicultural community in which one ethnic minority group has a significant concentration but does not necessarily comprise a majority of the total population.

23. Citizenship and Immigration Canada, *Exploring Minority Enclave Areas in Montréal, Toronto, and Vancouver*, by Daniel Hiebert (Ottawa: Citizenship and Immigration Canada, 2009), online: www.cic.gc.ca/english/resources/ research/minority-enclave.asp; R. Alan Walks and Larry S. Bourne, "Ghettos in Canada's Cities? Racial Segregation, Ethnic Enclaves and Poverty Concentration in Canadian Urban Areas" (2006) 50:3 *Canadian Geographer* 273; Mohammad Qadeer and Sandeep Kumar, "Ethnic Enclaves and Social Cohesion" (2006) 15:2 *Canadian J Urban Research* 1; David P. Varady, ed., *Desegregating the City: Ghettos, Enclaves, and Inequality* (Albany, NY: State University of New York Press, 2005).

24. I am grateful to the insights into this issue that Asha Kaushal analyzed in her 2013 doctoral thesis: *The Jurisdiction of Difference: Groups and the Law* (PhD Thesis, University of British Columbia Faculty of Law, 2013) [unpublished], and for our many conversations about her groundbreaking analysis of jurisdiction and group identity.

25. In Australia, this is reflected in the priorities issued under the "special humanitarian (offshore)" program. For details about the Canadian supervisa, see Minister of Citizenship and Immigration Canada & Minister of Public Safety, *Ministerial Instruction regarding the Parent and Grandparent* Super Visa (November 30, 2011), online: www.cic.gc.ca/english/department/mi/supervisa.asp.

26. US, Bill S 744, *Border Security, Economic Opportunity, and Immigration Modernization Act*, 113th Congress, 2013 (Committee on the Judiciary December 10, 2014). The Senate passed this bill but the House of Representatives did not.

8

The close of the post-colonial

The end of settler societies also reverberates through the European nations that were the source of the original settlers, and of the cultures, laws, and governance systems that were foundational in the settler nations. The new politics of immigration is as prevalent in European states as in the former settler societies themselves. Indeed one of the markers of this politics is its commonality throughout the prosperous Western liberal democracies. The shifting political winds that usher in this new politics arise from changes in both the former settler societies and the former colonial masters. One baseline marker is the transformation of many European states into nations of immigration, in at least a statistical sense. But this alteration is no more than a starting point for understanding the deeper societal and political transformation.

One far-reaching consequence of the end of settler societies is that post-colonial linkages are obscured. This happens in settler states, in colonial masters, and in non-settler former colonies. In the settler states, this obscuring took place when the post-colonial moment was elided and the new nations emerged as fully independent. A final marker of this severing of colonial ties is the end of special immigration and citizenship linkages between the former European powers and the settler societies, the final pieces of which ended as late as the 1990s. The gradual and possibly ineffectual end of the colonial era in the settler societies, discussed in Chapter 2, is not the site of post-colonial politics. Rather, these politics are firmly located in the global South, where European colonization and conquest was never as "effective" as in the settler societies. European colonization of these global South states left a powerful immigration trace, as colonial subjects typically benefited from preferential access to states of their colonial masters. This immigration – for example, of Indians to England, Moroccans to France, and Congolese to Belgium – fueled post-colonialism in myriad ways.

By the early twenty-first century, however, European countries had largely ended their special migration relationships with former colonies and are now moving to shed the overhang of liberal guilt that was embedded in those affiliations. This is a vital step in moving toward a pan-European approach to asylum and to migration. These shifts follow from the "invention" of European citizenship and give tactile meaning to this ideal. Freeing itself from post-colonial ties allows Europe to forge an identity as a whole, as "Europe." Much of this identity project, its successes and its strains, is an immigration project.

Accordingly, for the countries of Europe, the former colonial powers, the end of settler societies coincides with the end of an overt politics of colonial guilt, and thus the opening of a *post*-post-colonial era.[1] The idea of "One Europe" provides a means of assuaging the post-colonial guilt because this merged new Europe has distanced itself from its colonial past. New Europe is not post-colonial but, more immediately, post-national. Immigration politics and immigration regulation are no longer marked by preferences for former colonials. Indeed, this would be impossible given the Schengen accord, the harmonization of asylum, and the ever-enlarging European Union. What is more, by rebranding themselves as "Europe," the former colonial powers are once again part of an "empire."

This chapter considers the European transformations that have accompanied the end of settler societies, laying the foundation for the global convergence that grounds the new politics of immigration. The first step is to interrogate the logic and immigration consequences of European citizenship and to follow these through to the partially harmonized asylum and immigration regimes. The next step is to consider the example of the recurring Lampedusa crisis and the challenge it has presented to this new Europe. Finally, these insights lead to an assessment of how immigration regulation is integral to re-inventing Europe as a new empire for the twenty-first century.

PAN-EUROPEAN IMMIGRATION LAW

European immigration law at the outset of the twenty-first century is even further from its 1970s configuration than is its settler society parallel. The new configuration is both a foundation for the new politics of immigration and a key marker of potential future directions. There are three notable shifts that contribute to the particular way in which European states have become nations of immigration, and hence of immigration politics. These are the invention of European citizenship, the end of colony-linked migration patterns, and the emergence of an almost harmonized asylum system, and a partially harmonized immigration system.

European citizenship has the clearest parameters of these three factors. It came into being with the Maastricht Treaty of 1992. The idea of European citizenship is powerfully symbolic and it draws on the deeply emotive ideas that have long been associated with citizenship generally. Combining its symbolic pedigree and its legal structure, European citizenship serves to vault immigration into both a symbolic function and a vital feature of European identity. This proposition requires elaboration in two directions.

First, European citizenship is primarily an immigration category. The main reason for this is that it is a derivative status – one becomes an EU citizen by being a citizen of one of the member states. It is not possible to hold EU citizenship on its own, neither is it possible *not* to hold EU citizenship if one is a national of one of the member states. EU citizenship does bring with it a cluster of rights, but these rights reside predominantly in the realm of immigration. The most important entitlement is free movement within the Union. In typical immigration regulation form, however, the right of free movement has been tied to being a worker or a work-seeker, or a family member of such an economic actor. In other words, it is linked to fulfilling a defined and highly valued immigration role. The principal right belonging to EU citizens that is not directly linked to migration is the right to vote in local elections. This is truly innovative, but does still fit with a well-developed understanding of immigration and immigrant settlement as being especially transformative within urban areas.

Second, despite its legal formulation as an immigration status, European citizenship operates symbolically. European citizenship operates symbolically because citizenship everywhere does so. What this boils down to is the idea that the emotional "value" of European citizenship outstrips the value of the bare legal status. Over the past fifty years, since the rise of the welfare state, citizenship has been a powerful tool in rhetorical calls for inclusion. Citizenship has come to mean full participation in a society, and full recognition of membership. Without this accrued meaning of "citizenship-as-social inclusion" the political heft of "second-class citizenship" would lose meaning. European citizenship is no different: it provides a slim list of rights beyond those of the underlying nationality, but it communicates powerfully the notions of both inclusion in a wider project, and identity as European. It is these values, more than the right to vote locally, that make European citizenship appear to be more than an immigration status.

The legal and symbolic functions of European citizenship combine, perversely, to present an impoverished understanding of citizenship. Whilst the trajectory of citizenship in the latter half of the twentieth century, power-fully analyzed by T.H. Marshall, was toward an ever more robust vision of inclusion, the recent trajectory of European citizenship has been about insuring that citizens can be excluded.[2] In other words, about breaking the bond between citizenship and inclusion. European citizenship has done enormous work in recent years to normalize the idea of "second-class" citizen-ship and thus reduce the emotive power of citizenship itself. In this shift, an impoverished understanding of citizenship emerges that is tied to economic values. This clever shell game performs the reverse function of that described by Saskia Sassen and David Jacobson in the closing years of the twentieth century. Rather than human rights growing to eclipse citizenship rights, in the case of European citizenship, citizen rights are shrinking rather than human rights expanding. The result is that full citizens may need more than their citizenship to ensure human rights protections within the European nations that they can only partially claim to belong to through the watered-down vision of inclusion that European citizenship offers.

The most recent and clearest example of this is the November 2014 decision by the European Court of Justice in a preliminary ruling regarding two Romanian nationals living in Germany, who applied for various social assis-tance payments. The Court ruled that Germany was not obligated to extend social assistance payments that people had not "earned" to non-nationals without permanent resident status. In other words, the "right of citizens of the Union to move and reside freely within the territory of the Member states" is subject to financial constraints. Both the language of the ruling, and its outcome, send powerful messages about the content of European citizenship.[3]

Two central concepts anchor the substance of the ruling: "economically active" and "special non-contributory cash benefits." "Economically active" individuals include workers, people looking for work, and people who are self-employed, as well as their family members. It also becomes clear as the ruling progresses that this category includes people who have no need to earn money in the local economy – the rich. This sleight of hand equating the idle rich with the economically active is necessary because the objective is to "prevent … persons from becoming an unreasonable burden on the social assistance system of the host Member State."[4] The phrase "special non-contributory benefits" repeats throughout the judgment because an earlier case had determined that when someone has contributed to a state-managed benefits scheme, such as unemployment insurance or a state pension, they are entitled to receive payments from it no matter where in the Union they reside. So the focus of the 2014 ruling is squarely on people without money or work who have not "earned" the money they seek to claim; in the words of the popular press, "benefit tourists." This discourse is a far cry from the robust notion of substantive citizenship. The Court was adamant that this be made plain:

> A Member State must therefore have the possibility... of refusing to grant social benefits to economically inactive Union citizens who exercise their right to freedom of movement solely in order to obtain another Member State's social assistance *although they do not have sufficient resources to claim a right of residence.*[5]

The ruling was warmly welcomed by many European politicians, particularly by the Cameron government in the United Kingdom. Further, it was hardly a surprising outcome given the strict wording of the 2004 Directive on benefits entitlements.

It is not the case that this ruling diminished European citizenship. Rather, it confirmed that European citizenship is not and never was about identity and robust social participation: it is about migrating for the purposes of economic activity and its limits are drawn by an inquiry about "sufficient resources." The rest of the world can only hope that this nasty and narrow version of citizenship remains firmly within European borders.

European citizenship is, therefore, the first feature of the contemporary European immigration landscape. A second crucial change bringing about a Europeanization of immigration rules has been the gradual removal of formal post-colonial immigration rules and the borrowing of New World immigration regulation patterns. These shifts have taken several decades to achieve but are now close to complete. Indeed, as Europe itself has grown through successive rounds of expansion, much immigration simply disappears. This happens in two ways. First, much movement that was previously considered to be immigration no longer fits in that category, and second, the perceived state need for temporary foreign workers, which is presently such an animating factor in the post-settler states, is minimized within Europe because nationals of the newer and poorer expansion states are available to fill many low-skilled and otherwise unappealing jobs. This is reflected in the post-2008 decline in immigration into the EU as a whole.[6] As a result, official European immigration programs now typically look very much like settler society immigration traditions: a focus on people coming from afar to settle permanently; rather than migration built around kinship ties, the earlier European patterns of colonial relationships, and geographic proximity.

The shift in migration rules is a slowly developing story. As the European powers withdrew from their roles as colonial rulers, one trace of that role that often remained was a right of nationals of the former colony to enter and remain in the European nation from which they had recently gained independence. This pattern of post-colonial linkage has been central to immigration patterns in Europe in the second half of the twentieth century, the era of decolonization. It has brought South Asians and Jamaicans to the United Kingdom, Algerians to France, Indonesians and Surinamers to the Netherlands, and Angolans to Portugal. The pattern of migration from South America to Spain was not quite as direct, but was still possible. Gradually, these pathways have been closed, and are now almost completely eliminated. The United Kingdom began this process with its 1971 *Immigration Act*, and completed it with the changes that made it impossible for overseas citizens in Hong Kong to return to the United Kingdom when the colony was returned to the People's Republic of China in 1997. In France, which has a longer history of significant immigration than most former colonial powers, the violent end of colonial rule in Algeria has strongly marked its immigration patterns and politics. Preferential rights for former colonial nationals are now closed, but there are numerous far-flung French territories that confuse the issue considerably. The Netherlands has ended this kind of preferencing, but only after the migration flows themselves diminished. In Spain, where preferentially colonial migration was never as significant as elsewhere, immigration privilege has finished, but there is still a shorter trajectory toward Spanish citizenship for many citizens of former colonies.[7]

Germany is somewhat of an outlier in this landscape. Without a colonial history, twentieth-century migration preferences to Germany were based on ethnic German connections. It was also the site of the most extensive and problematic guest worker programs of the 1970s and 1980s, and has been Europe's leading asylum host. It was not until 2001 that Germany had, for the first time, a formal permanent migration program organized around economic preferences.

As this colonial story was wound down, mainly through the 1970s and 1980s, these states shifted toward developing migration programs that look more like the settler society model. Family reunion principles ensure that colonial patterns continue in the absence of formal legal preferences. In part because the contemporary European approach to migration did not develop until the global asylum crisis was already in train, asylum-as-migration has been highly significant. Economic migration has now become a central feature of organized migration programs in most European countries. A number of countries have introduced very recently a "points system" for economic migration modeled on that pioneered in Canada (for example, Austria, Denmark, Sweden, and the United Kingdom) and others (Germany, France) have discussed the idea in various ways. This classic settler society innovation seems to be one of Europe's most current borrowings.

In the final decades of the twentieth century, European states were statistically transformed into nations of immigration.[8] This shift took place at differing times in different states, but by the end of the twentieth century, data
demonstrate that immigration outweighs emigration generally in Western
European states, with the most recent accession states, Bulgaria and
Romania, standing out as significant exceptions. The cultural shift that follows
the statistical pattern is equally important. The settler society pattern was built
on the idea that European states sent migrants and settler states received them.
Part of the present metamorphosis is the end of a vision of Europe as the
world's primary collection of sending states. This shift is implicated in our
vision of who migrates and why. In parallel, it affects our understanding of
what counts as "opportunity" in the twenty-first century, and deploys immigration's classic dividing line between "us" and "them" as yet another division
between the global South and the global North, as migrant flows are now
predominantly in one direction from South to North.

Finally, the transfiguration that is taking the longest is the harmonization of
a European regime for asylum and immigration. The first steps toward harmonizing asylum were taken as early as 1990, when the first Dublin
Convention was signed, and culminated in the strong wording of Article 79
of the Treaty on the Functioning of the European Union.[9] But in practical
terms, harmonization is not yet fully achieved. Crucially, harmonizing asylum
is the center of pan-European migration regulation. It is the only domain
where European states have harmonized the legal framework that operates at
external borders. Harmonization for immigrant entry policies has developed
more haltingly. The contrast between asylum and immigration harmonization
trajectories reveals the political tensions that underlie these conjoined policy
arenas, and that contribute to the contemporary political climate.

Harmonization of the asylum regime across Europe has two main features:
ensuring similar standards for determining refugee status, and deploying
similar procedural rights for those seeking that status. At first blush, these
two features appear unnecessary because all EU states are parties to the
Refugee Convention: in matters of asylum, they are all applying the same
international law. But the international law provides no procedural specifica-
tions at all, and, through fifty years of experience in interpretation of its
substantive provisions, significant disagreements have emerged. As a consequence, the aim of harmonizing both standards and procedures is surprisingly
meaningful. These goals are reflected in the Qualification Directive and the
Procedures Directive respectively.[10]

The unique objective of harmonization, however, has not been strengthening refugee law and, concomitantly, refugee protection. The impetus

for harmonization was primarily limiting state responsibility and controlling the movement of asylum seekers. The center-piece of the harmonization initiative is the Dublin Convention. This Convention requires that those seeking asylum must make a claim in the first Dublin Convention state that they reach and that the state of first arrival must take responsibility for determining that claim (subject to a few exceptions for family ties, unaccompanied minors, and states choosing to take on a case). If an asylum seeker leaves the state of first arrival and travels to another state participating in the Convention, that second state has a right to return her to the first state. The original Dublin Convention was amended in 2003 and then again in 2013, with each alteration integrating the principles more deeply into the core of EU law. Participating in the Dublin system was a requirement for accession states joining the EU in 2004 and 2007.

The Dublin rules ensure, of course, that states along the outer perimeter of the EU are responsible for many more asylum seekers than states that do not share a border with "the world beyond." One might say that this is "unfair," but there are so many things about international refugee law that are "unfair" in this ordinary sense, that this idea gets no political traction. It does, however, spur on harmonization in the following way: establishing European standards in matters of both procedure and interpretation allows European states to believe that the Dublin system appropriately protects the vital human rights at the core of refugee law. In other words, harmonization allows states to participate without feelings of guilt about passing their human rights protection obligations off to others. In this way, the Dublin system is both the reason for harmonization and the impetus behind giving harmonization the kind of teeth that the Qualification and Procedures Directives are designed to have.

The unevenness of this framework generates frictions. In 2011, the European Court of Justice ruled that conditions for asylum seekers in Greece, where approximately 90 percent of all asylum seekers arriving in Europe first land, were in breach of European human rights standards, and that the Greek refugee determination system put people at risk of being returned to face persecution and thus also breached requirements of the Refugee Convention. These findings led the Court to conclude that both Greece and Belgium were in breach of the European Human Rights Convention's Article 3 prohibition against "inhuman or degrading treatment" and were also in breach of the Article 13 requirement for effective access to legal remedies. Belgium was implicated because it had followed the common asylum system's enumerated procedures and returned an asylum seeker to Greece, where he was then detained in horrific conditions and later released to live on the street without food or shelter. In a follow-up ruling later that same year, the Court examined two cases concerning people that Ireland and the United Kingdom wanted to return to Greece for asylum determinations. In this ruling the Court was more explicit. It ruled that despite the "presumption" in the European Union that member states meet human rights standards, transfer of asylum seekers is prohibited where a state "cannot be unaware of" systematic deficiencies in meeting these standards. These rulings put a significant brake on the move toward a common asylum system by looking behind the façade of the common legal framework.[11] Fully aware of the far-reaching import of its decision, the Court in the second ruling stated, "At issue here is the raison d'être of the European Union and the creation of an area of freedom, security and justice and, in particular, the Common European Asylum System."[12] In other words, the comfortable human rights mythology of the Dublin Convention has serious cracks.

Another consequence of the harmonization rules is that EU citizens can no longer get refugee protection within Europe. The Qualification Directive states that refugee protection is available for third-country nationals only. There is a small and lingering irony that Europeans, the group for whom contemporary refugee law was first designed, are now barred from this status. While this is a formal rule within the EU, it reverberates worldwide. The largest group to be affected by this bar is the Roma. Roma populations, which are largest in Romania, Bulgaria, Spain, Hungary, and the Czech Republic, have faced a long history of discrimination that has often been recognized as reaching the level of persecution that attracts the protection of the international community. As EU citizens, Roma cannot seek refugee protection within other parts of the EU. However, as a historically disadvantaged group, which typically has lower health, education, and income indicators than the rest of the population, Roma face considerable barriers to moving to other countries and resettling simply on the basis of their EU citizenship. If they cannot successfully join the labor force, their EU citizenship is not enough to provide social inclusion. It is certainly not a coincidence that the "special non-contributory benefits" litigation originated with a Roma family.

Beyond the borders of Europe, EU expansion has made it difficult for Roma to claim refugee protection because decision makers have treated EU citizenship, and a right to cross internal borders, as a proxy for full human rights protections. While there is often evidence that this is not the case, it has been a difficult argument to make nonetheless. Decision makers in Canada and Australia have been slow to accept the paucity of EU citizenship; decision makers within Europe no longer need to attempt this reasoning.

For these reasons it is evident that asylum harmonization is yet incomplete. The legal framework looks comprehensive, but from a human perspective there remains considerable unevenness. Furthermore, harmonization, which is potentially desirable from a state perspective (especially if that state is far from the EU's southern and eastern borders), serves to make conditions worse for those seeking protection. In contravention of international rules, harmonization deprives individuals of the right to choose where to seek protection, and thus reduces their options in very real terms. It also makes refugees within Europe "disappear," in a more nefarious way than immigrants within the EU have disappeared. Asylum harmonization sends political sparks in many directions, as the Lampedusa example below shows.

Notwithstanding this incompleteness, asylum harmonization is considerably further advanced than its immigration parallel. Despite a stated intention for harmonization that dates from the Treaty of Amsterdam in 1999, the halting progress demonstrates that the hardest areas for states to relinquish control over are decisions about which foreigners to admit on a long-term basis. In the years immediately following Amsterdam, agreements were reached on the status of third-country nationals who were long-term residents, on the family reunification rights of these residents, and on integration policies and goals.[13] None of these agreements address *how* one comes to be a long-term resident; they concern the consequences of that status, however it may be acquired under national law. More recent agreements have moved progressively closer to the core of who gets admitted, with agreement about a common application process for work permits and an EU Blue Card providing highly qualified high earners with a right to residency throughout the EU after eighteen months of work in the state where they first applied. The Blue Card lasts for four years, and can be renewed. In 2013, a proposal regarding the admission of students, researchers, and volunteers was developed.

Notably, none of these provisions directly address avenues for admission to a permanent residency status. The EU has signaled an intention to move in this direction, but has had trouble doing so. Indeed, the report on the first full year of the Blue Card noted that the co-existing national schemes for highly qualified workers negatively affected its success, suggesting that states are not fully committed to the Blue Card initiative yet and are, instead, still actively competing for the best-qualified migrants.[14] Moving permanently to some other place used to be the core meaning of immigration. It is still the core idea behind many immigration statistics, as well as settlement and integration policy. The EU's slow progression to harmonizing this factor is partially about preserving the right of ultimate immigrant admission at the nation state level, and partially about redefining what immigration means.

One important result of the discourse of coordinated asylum and immigration in Europe is that the distinction between the two is fading.

The European Commission reports annually on asylum and immigration in a report that opens with concerns about international protection, and then considers migratory pressures and border management, before reaching what has over the past five years been its smallest section: EU rules about legal migration. Following the influx of people to Europe during the Arab Spring of 2011, the Commission presented a "Communication on Migration" aimed at establishing a "comprehensive European migration policy" that was triggered by an asylum crisis, and that focused heavily on security measures and proposed protecting the internal free movement principle by providing for reintroduction of visas for third-country nationals in times of crisis or when a member state was not meeting its obligations with respect to external borders. Very little was said in this document about legal migration.[15] Under the "comprehensive migration policy" banner, security and asylum clearly come first. Much of the rhetoric about immigration in Europe these days is in a technical sense about asylum seeking. All the more reason that nothing more precisely illustrates the present condition of European immigration than the island of Lampedusa.

LOCATING LAMPEDUSA

If maps could be freed of politics, tiny Lampedusa would not even be European. A mere twenty square kilometers, Lampedusa is closer to Tunisia than to Sicily, and much further again from the Italian mainland. Since the beginning of the twenty-first century, Lampedusa has been the scene of at least three distinct asylum crises, each of which reverberates through immigration politics more generally.

Italy joined the colonizers' club late because it did not emerge into its contemporary and united form until near the end of the nineteenth century. Between 1886 and the end of World War II, Italy colonized parts of East and North Africa, including Libya, Eritrea, and Somalia (as well as a wee bit of China and much of Albania). During that War, it occupied Tunisia for a time. The Lampedusa migration story is, therefore, sharply part of the post-colonial tale: a story that would have been averted had the colonizing impulse not been so strong, or had it been more completely relinquished. The recurring crises on Lampedusa happen because of its proximity to Tunisia and Libya, and because it is Italian sovereign territory. In her analysis of how various islands around the world are provocative sites for immigration politics, Alison Mountz argues that sovereignty is fragmented on such islands and this fragmentation is fertile ground for the immigration effects we see in these places.[16] But the law is too blunt an instrument to appreciate this nuance. Rather, from a legal point of view, Lampedusa is simply Italian. And this is the source of all of the problems.

The first round of crisis culminated in 2005, when a group of thirteen NGOs filed a complaint against the Italian government alleging that it was violating the right to claim asylum, as well as other human rights, of migrants on Lampedusa. The principal source of this complaint was an agreement between Italy and Libya that allowed for the mass expulsion to Libya of Libyan citizens and others who had reached Lampedusa after departing Libyan territory, prior to considering applications for asylum. In addition to readmission to Libya, the agreement provided for Italian-funded construction of detention centers for unauthorized migrants in Libya, for the International Organization for Migration to open an office in Tripoli, and for deportations to states in West Africa. Between October 2004 and March 2005, more than 1500 people were returned from Lampedusa to Libya. In total more than 4000 people were returned prior to the 2006 change of government in Rome, after which the practice was stopped. All of this took place at a time when Libya was still considered a "rogue" state in a global political sense, and when it was still keeping foreign medical personnel in prison for the alleged crime of infecting Libyan children with HIV. The European Commission declined to address the complaint, holding that commenting on Italian policy would exceed its competence. Despite the end of mass deportations, a new agreement between Italy and Libya in 2007 saw Italian ships patrolling the coastline in Libyan waters and returning migrants intercepted there to Libya, as well as efforts by the Libyan government to prevent people embarking in the first place.[17]

The second crisis was brought about by the Arab Spring of 2011, which brought with it the downfall of governments in both Tunisia and Libya and, accordingly, the demise of both state capacity and state desire to continue the agreements with Italy. Within a few weeks in early 2011, more than 45,000 people streamed out of these two northern African states toward Lampedusa, seeking protection, jobs, a better life, or even, simply, a way home. The volume of arrivals made the influx of the first decade of the century paltry in comparison. Most of those arriving sought asylum, and in the tumultuous circumstances, many could expect to receive it. Those arriving included not only Tunisians and Libyans, but also many people from other African states who had been laboring, legally and extra-legally, especially in the Libyan oil patch, and who alleged they had been poorly treated there.[18]

Lampedusa was quickly overwhelmed by this influx. The Italian government devised a plan to distribute asylum seekers throughout Italy and by April had announced a humanitarian amnesty policy that would allow people who had arrived between January 1st and April 5th to remain in Italy. Once on mainland Italy, some of the Lampedusa arrivees sought to move on to other European states, through Europe's open internal borders. This onward movement provoked France to close its border, in breach of EU regulations, in April 2011.[19]

Just as the second crisis grew out of the first, so the third emerged from the second. Following the Arab spring, new governments in Tunisia and especially in Libya did not resume the border control agreements of the previous decade. As a result the flow of migrant-laden boats traveling to Lampedusa returned to the pre-agreement levels. The mix of migrants on the boats has shifted since 2011, reflecting the politics of the region. The Syrian civil war that marked the tortured end of the Arab Spring has led to an almost unprecedented flow of refugees, some of whom have made their way to Lampedusa. The third distinct "crisis" involving Lampedusa was the sinking in October 2013 of a ship carrying 518 migrants. More than 366 died.[20]

Fighting in Iraq and Syria against the forces of the Islamic State raised the stakes for Lampedusa even further. The idea of refugee law as perpetual crisis, discussed in Chapter 3, resonates strongly here. As I worked to finalize this manuscript early in 2015, another series of boat sinkings en route to Lampedusa hit front pages around the globe with up to 300 people confirmed dead or missing in within a week.[21] By the time I was completing final revisions, 2015 had become the date of a full-blown fourth crisis, as the month of April saw more than 800 people die attempting to reach Lampedusa. This led to the unprecedented idea the EU might launch a military operation aimed at stopping boat crossings.[22] As I reviewed copy-edits in September 2015,the situation was escalating so rapidly that I wrote a Preface to the book reflecting on it.

The perpetual crisis of twenty-first century Lampedusa is a microcosm of all the tensions in the past and future of European immigration regulation. Lampedusa is the current crossroads. The enormous trouble that Lampedusa has been, and will continue to be for the foreseeable future, illustrates the sharp end of contemporary migration politics in Europe by showing how an integrated migration zone and a harmonized asylum policy are both working and not working, both real and not real. Italy, the last European power to join the colony stakes, is also proving the last to wrest its migration patterns away from a postcolonial imprint. Lampedusa illustrates all the reasons why European states are so keen to move their immigration policy away from former colonial ties. But for colonization, Lampedusa would not be European. On the map, Lampedusa appears as a tiny European finger reaching down into Africa. The last outpost of Europe – the frontier for the construction of a transformed empire. It is undoubtedly not deliberate that the rescue mission for asylum seekers in the Mediterranean that Italy conducted for a year following the 2013 drownings was named *Mare Nostrum*. This is the same moniker that Mussolini gave to his Mediterranean strategy. The contemporary *Mare Nostrum* initiative has been widely congratulated. This makes it politically uncomfortable to recall that humanitarian gestures are also constitutive of national, or possibly imperial, identities. *Noblesse oblige.*

One aspect of the Lampedusa microcosm is tension over human rights. The failure of the European Commission to consider a complaint about human rights protections on Lampedusa shows the weakness of human rights within Europe as far as non-nationals are concerned. It may well be that the Commission would take a different position in 2015, as I write this text, given that the harmonized asylum system has evolved considerably since 2005 and both the Court of Justice of the European Union and the European Court of Human Rights have taken up several cases related to the European asylum system. But there is no guarantee, especially as stories of egregious human rights breaches in Lampedusa's migrant holding facilities continue to emerge from time to time.[23] It seems, however, that subsequent crisis moments may have pushed crisis number one out of the spotlight. But the point here for the migration politics of Europe is that Lampedusa serves as an illustration of Europe's failure to take the human rights of migrants seriously in a general sense. This cuts against the human rights halo that Europe wears on many other occasions.

The successive waves of crisis starkly illustrate the tensions over Europe's open internal borders. Since the opening of borders began in 1995, 2011 marked the first time that the French had unilaterally closed their border with Italy, in breach of the Schengen principles that are now part of the core EU legal system. This signals that open borders have limits, and that a commitment to them is not unshakable. While the closure did not last long, and its effect was more symbolic than effective, politics is often a symbolic realm. In order for Europe to function as a whole, the commitment to open borders must be sacrosanct. Without this openness, the ability to "be European" and, indeed, the primary function of European citizenship, is deeply undermined. The innovation of a united Europe is expressed most completely in the freedom of movement that the open borders represent. Without this freedom, the European Union of the twenty-first century becomes much more like its predecessor the European Community, and much more like any free trade zone where goods and capital flow, but labor does not.

The Lampedusa microcosm also tells us two things about the way that harmonized asylum in Europe really works. For the most part, asylum seekers and other migrants arriving on Lampedusa are treated by other states as Italy's problem. This is the case even when, at a rhetorical level, the European Commission knows that this is wrong, although clearly not illegal. Consider this excerpt from the statement by Commissioner Cecilia Malmström on the first anniversary of the 2013 Lampedusa disaster:

> Let me be very clear – when it comes to accepting refugees, solidarity between EU member states is still largely non-existent. This is quite possibly our biggest challenge for the future. While some EU members are taking responsibility, providing refuge for thousands of refugees, several EU countries are accepting almost no-one. In some countries, the number of yearly refugees barely exceeds a few handfuls. Last year, six whole countries of the EU accepted less than 250 refugees between them. All this, while the world around us is in flames. These EU countries could quite easily face up to reality by accepting resettled refugees through the UN system, but despite our persistent demands they are largely refusing. This is nothing short of a disgrace.
>
> If all the promises after the Lampedusa tragedy are to mean anything, solidarity between EU countries must become reality. For this to happen, we must in the coming years develop a responsibility-sharing mechanism between all EU states. This is of course nothing that can be forced upon Member States. However, I believe it is an absolute necessity if the EU is to live up to its ideals.[24]

This language tells us both that Europe must respond as a whole to these arrivals if it is to truly act as one in migration matters, and that European states are divided as to whether or not to do this. The events of mid-2015 make this point ever more evident.

A closely related second element of the Lampedusa lesson about asylum harmonization is a thorny bit of its politics of unfairness. Even during this most recent decade of crisis, Italy has received fewer asylum seekers than the EU's big asylum players Greece and Germany. Indeed the total asylum flows into Italy have been more in line with the number received by Britain and France, each of which have substantially larger populations. Harmonized asylum in Europe is as much about exerting control and limiting asylum flows, and consequently curtailing asylum seeker rights, as it is about burden sharing and human rights standards. European states face very uneven asylum "burdens" and the harmonization initiative does little to shift that.[25]

Indeed, even as Lampedusa illustrates this unevenness, it also functions as an exception to the rule. On November 1, 2014, Italy's *Mare Nostrum* initiative was wrapped up and replaced by an EU-coordinated effort known as *Triton*, led by the border agency Frontex. *Triton* is unevenly supported by wealthy EU states, but it has still managed to come into existence, suggesting somehow that Lampedusa belongs to Europe, as much as to Italy. This distinguishes it from the EU's generally muted response to the continuing high number of asylum arrivals in Greece. As an island outpost, more geographically African than European, the symbolism of Lampedusa is more powerful than any number of Greek islands not quite so isolated. There were concerns at the outset that *Triton* was less ambitious than *Mare Nostrum*, and these concerns were echoed following the February 2015 drownings.

Returning to Alison Mountz's observation about fragmented sovereignty, it may be that the pressures on Lampedusa lie under legal sovereignty as volcanic gases, with a potential for destruction. The law is not well tooled for nuanced answers; it specializes, rather, in producing stark binaries. In the view of the law, sovereignty that is fragmented is destroyed. This is why the Italian state keeps Lampedusa as its own, and why giving it away to Tunisia or Libya, where an imaginary apolitical map would locate it, is never an option on the table. The lessons of Lampedusa engage the idea of sovereignty directly, and with it the question of whether and how sovereignty can belong to "Europe" as a whole.

THE EMPIRE'S NEW CLOTHES

The close of the post-colonial era of European immigration has two important ripple effects that undergird the new politics of immigration. The first is reframing what immigration means. The second is positioning immigration as a vital aspect of a new vision of Europe – a new empire.

The emergence of a pan-European migration framework generates both of these consequences. EU citizenship, relinquishing colonial ties, and the harmonizing initiative, each contributes a piece of the puzzle. Not only have most European countries become "nations of immigration," but the shape of their immigration programs has become more closely aligned, both through deliberate policy developments, such as the harmonization of asylum policy and adherence to the European Convention on Human Rights, and through coincidental initiatives, such as the development of points systems, and the general competition to attract the best and the brightest from around the world. The departure from historic immigration patterns in Europe has led to European nations becoming "late joiners and early rejecters" of the multiculturalism paradigm.

In joining the ranks of liberal democracies that are attractive destination states, European nations have subtly altered the meaning of immigration.

With the invention of European citizenship as an immigration category, intra-European immigration has rhetorically disappeared. When someone moves from Poland to work in London or from Berlin to marry a Spaniard, they are no longer immigrating. Some hurdles do remain, but an engagement with immigration law does not. New ways of conceptualizing this kind of movement are starting, but we are still in the testing phase. In this way, our conception of immigration is challenged, because moves that were once immigration, no matter where they occurred in the world, are no longer defined as such when they take place within the ever-expanding space of Europe. Permanent movement away from one's state of origin can, in the EU, be accomplished without the personal, economic, and family dislocation that are part and parcel of migration mythology.

Europeans also emerge as "non-immigrants" in another way, as these states are no longer the primary sending states for global migratory flows. The result is a reconfigured understanding of migration as a flow that is directed primarily from poor nations to richer ones. In this altered universe, desirable destinations are not wide-open frontiers where individuals can make their mark, but sophisticated economies where individuals can fit into pre-defined roles.

In a parallel development, the long-term resident who does not have European citizenship finds herself with a lesser status than previously. The pan-European immigration paradigm reinforces the "us–them" line that is at the core of all immigration politics. But it does so in a new way. In the new, open-bordered, Europe, the "us" group is all Europeans; third country nationals stand on the other side of the line. This means that long-term residents without a European citizenship have fewer rights than those who arrived yesterday from elsewhere in Europe. This shift is an indicator of one of the most important changes that emerges from pan-European immigration. The idea that long-term residents, by virtue of their "settlement" in a new state, acquire a kind of near-membership is undermined by the vast number of EU citizens who are almost full members, with no "settlement" factor at all. This transition severs the link between "settlement" and "belonging" that previously defined the immigrant experience. The definition, of course, derived from the settler society experience.

The transformation of how immigration is conceptualized happens in a third way as well. By closing the immigration pathways that formerly brought many colonial subjects from the global South to Europe, these states have further hardened the line between "us" and "them." The privileged "us" group is now more economically and culturally homogenous: it is defined by European citizenship. Formerly, the "us" group defined by immigration privilege within Europe had irregular boundaries, including groups of poor people from non-European cultures. This final severing of colonial responsibility and connection also serves to move immigration into a new era. The peak of colonial development coincided with the first historical peak of global immigration – the setting in which settler societies were created, and the mythology of immigration was established.

As a global community, we have yet to confront the way these shifts change immigration. Public and political attachment to an older vision of immigration contributes strongly to contemporary politics, as the final two chapters explore in detail. But before reaching that point, there is another significant conclusion to draw from the contemporary European immigration landscape: a new understanding of empire is emerging – with immigration at its core.

The evolution of the European Union to its contemporary state has been unfolding for almost half a century. As the transformation has deepened, its pace has accelerated. A bellwether in its evolution has been the Union's posture toward immigration. The present rise of Europe as a united whole, a challenge to the early twenty-first century's other powerhouses the United States, China, and Russia, owes a great deal to the decision to finally bring matters of immigration into the center of EU politics.

When six European states first joined together to form the European Economic Community in 1957, matters of immigration were not on the horizon. The innovation of European citizenship thirty-five years later was largely symbolic when first articulated, and only began to accrue meaning as the gradual expansion of the Schengen accords gave some meaning to the idea of having a European passport. The Tampere Agreement of 1999 brought matters of immigration, asylum, and crime to the center of EU competencies and introduced the idea of harmonizing asylum. Standards for integration of non-European outsiders became a focus of attention in the first decade of the twenty-first century. Along with this progression, decisions in the European Court of Human Rights and the Court of Justice of the European Union have given form to pan-European commitments regarding family unity, refugee protection, and deportation, creating further standards through judicial pronouncement.

What is evident in this trajectory is that immigration has been one of the very last areas of competence to become truly Europeanized. The Europeanization agenda has approached the nub of immigration policy slowly and circuitously, nearing the center but still not quite there. Within the EU, nation states remain free to choose which third-country nationals to invite in on an economic basis. Given that most Western liberal democracies have over the most recent decades turned to prioritize economic migrants, this "exception" is a major one. On the other hand, in the areas that have become more politically contentious, such as asylum, family reunification, and deportation, nations within the EU now face a range of compulsory constraints in the realm of migration policy. In all cases, when there is constraint, it takes the form of both politics and law, which is instructive in considering the new politics of immigration from a lawyer's point of view, an insight to which I return in the final chapter. My point for the moment is that I believe economic migration is the last unregulated arena because of the strong belief that migration can be harnessed directly to national need, and that this need can presently be understood in economic terms. This reflects an inaccurate and old-fashioned understanding of immigration (as well as pretty crude economics). I also believe, considering the EU's trajectory over the past three decades, that over time, the EU will emerge as a true immigration union.

It is no coincidence that immigration is currently highly politicized in many EU states. This was true well before 2015. In part this politicization demonstrates why immigration, despite its obvious "outward-facing" aspects, has been so slow in its shift to becoming a central competence of the EU. Immigration can scarcely be considered a primarily "internal" matter – it involves outsiders crossing the border. The contemporary politicization of immigration in Europe pulls both ways in terms of harmonization. On the one hand, the EU itself serves as an in-built scapegoat when national governments are unable to assert their will in migration matters. On the other hand, being able to have control over admission of (some) third-country nationals allows nations to continue to put a (limited) stamp of national identity on immigration policy, even as they are required to open their borders to non-nationals from the newer EU member states. The diminishing area of national control that remains is one of the few "outward facing" aspects in the EU that provides an avenue for such traditional expressions of state-level sovereignty as selecting immigrants. This in part accounts for the stridency of immigration politics.

Pan-European immigration policy, however, is a vital aspect of the new Europe. It is for this reason that these national-level politics are increasingly coordinated, and for this reason that the remaining distinctions are poised to decline over time. Europe is emerging as a new "empire" for the twenty-first century. A pre-requisite for a new reading of empire is a firm and final end to the old version of empire. The old version had colonies, sent migrants to the ends of the earth, and spawned settler societies. A new posture toward migration is both a way of removing these markers of the old, and a method for defining a new imperial era.

To call Europe an empire at this point in its history is partially straightforward and partially ironic. I use the epithet somewhat loosely, in the sense of a major power center of the globe. A place that leads world politics and is identified by a certain "style" of civilization. A hegemon. The tinge of irony comes from deploying empire against its orthodoxy of rule by monarchal power characterized by an appetite for expansion. Today's new Europe is decidedly set against its monarchal history, but it is expanding like no other contemporary political unit. Indeed, dis-aggregation is more typical these days – as the world continues to come to grips with the post-colonial consequences of the previous iterations of European powers. European expansion at present is not the hostile takeover of the colonial era. It rolls forward in the name of the advance of human rights and freedom. This claim is stated directly in the title of the final movement that brought immigration to the center of EU competence: the Area of Freedom, Security, and Justice. A capacity to be unselfconscious about expansion is another signifier that Europe is moving beyond its post-colonial phase.

The empire label works in three ways. First, in a contemporary echo of the colonial empire of old, it explains the current sovereignty dilemma. There has been considerable angst about the fate of national sovereignty under EU arrangements, and a myriad of answers to the question of whether EU arrangements transform the nature of sovereignty, or simply transfer it to a supra-state. The governance form of empire emerged as a power-sharing formula, where many powers were held by the colonial center, but some matters were governed locally within the colonies. This arrangement, although arising from differing forces and directions, can be fitted onto the EU arrangements with surprisingly little adjustment. We now understand the colonial area as exploitive and oppressive, whereas the new European Empire is benevolent and beneficial. But the sovereign arrangements are similar, and the story on the ground is certainly more complicated, as any nation "benefitting" from an EU bailout will certainly understand.

Second, the EU currently seeks, deliberately, to act as "one" in many arenas of global and internal affairs. The areas of European engagement are diverse, ranging from debt management, to negotiations with Russia over hostilities in Ukraine, to trade pacts with countries beyond its borders. As the *Triton* initiative in the Mediterranean demonstrates, the commitment of various states within the EU to these European "acts" often differs markedly. But this does not detract from the existence and political importance of the emergence of a European presence in global affairs, including external affairs, and extending well beyond the economic terrain that has been the frontier of globalization. With each "European" action, Europe itself becomes increasingly visible as a power center.

The third way in which the empire label is meaningful is that "European" identity is more cohesive than at any earlier point in history. This shift is closely linked to the second, but translates more directly into matters of immigration. This final development is both part of the foundation for pan-European immigration policy, and, in turn, strengthened by each move toward immigration harmonization. Immigration regulation has always been a key component of the "us–them" line that makes national identity meaningful. As migration control shifts outward from the borders of individual nations, to the borders of Europe itself, it is not only sovereignty that shifts, but also identity. The lived experience of individuals draws substance from the bare bones of the regulatory structure people live within. There is now a generation of adults in Europe who have grown up as EU "citizens," with open access to all of the EU as they plan their education and career prospects. A lived sense of being European, which is becoming more broadly shared, particularly among elites, serves as a basis for further harmonization of immigration policy. It also serves to further entrench the divide between Europeans and non-Europeans, and thus open a gap between citizens and long-term residents who are third-country nationals, which had previously diminished considerably.

The most powerful lesson to be drawn from the imagery of empire is that Europe has moved on from its colonial past. This is not to say that this is right, true, or even possible, but it is assuredly political and aspirational. The departure from the colonial past serves to distance European states from the responsibilities of former colonial masters and from the accompanying liberal guilt of post-colonial politics. However closely the post-colonial turn continues to follow Europe, the new empire is turning its back on this past. New Europe is engaged in a debate about how to be "post-national" rather than how to be responsibly post-colonial. The fashioning of Europe as a new empire also establishes new Europe as a global power in the post-Cold War era. Only by acting as a united whole can Europe continue as a major international actor in a "post-superpower" world. By relinquishing the old form of power, Europe continues powerful.

All of this changes Europe's relationship with migration. Europe is no longer the world's principal "source" of migrants. Rather, as the world's Empire of Human Rights, it attracts migrants from around the globe. In its effort to build a post-superpower economy, it is reducing the inclusive and symbolic power of citizenship by tying it to economic logic. These transmutations within Europe pave the way for the global migration convergence that we are currently witnessing. They play a role in ending the settler society paradigm and the immigration worldview that accompanied it. In today's

Europe, immigration is as politicized as in the former settler societies for which immigration was foundational. Maybe even more so. A great deal of the turmoil of the new politics of immigration grows out of the tension between how the meaning of immigration has shifted and the traditional picture of immigration in our collective memories.

Notes

1. The Preface adds important comments about the new politics of immigration in Europe. The place of guilt in this new politics is important, as the contrast in Germany's choices most recently signals.

2. T.H. Marshall, "Citizenship and Social Class" in Gershon Shafir, ed., *Citizenship Debates: A Reader* (Minneapolis: University of Minnesota Press, 1998); T.H. Marshall, *Class, Citizenship, and Social Development* (Garden City, NY: Doubleday & Company, 1964).

3. *Dano v. Leipzig*, C-333/13, [2014] ECR I-2358 [*Dano*]. The principal legal document interpreted in the case was a 2004 Directive. See EC, *Directive 2004/38/EC of the European Parliament and of the Council of 29 April 2004 on the right of citizens of the Union and their family members to move and reside freely within the territory of the Member States*, [2004] OJ, L 158/77.

4. *Dano*, *supra* note 3 at para 71 (although people are referred to as a "burden" repeatedly).

5. *Ibid.* at para 78 [emphasis added].

6. For details regarding intra-European immigration, see Appendix 8.

7. Klaus F. Zimmermann, ed., *European Migration: What Do We Know?* (Oxford: Oxford University Press, 2005); Paul Scheffer, *Immigrant Nations*, translated by Liz Waters (Cambridge, UK: Polity Press, 2011); Randall Hansen, "Migration to Europe since 1945: Its History and its Lessons" (2003) 74:1 *Political Q* 25.

8. See Appendix 8.

9. *Consolidated Version of the Treaty on the Functioning of the European Union*, [2012] OJ, C 326/01. The current version, and new name, of this treaty are the result of changes in the EU constitutional documents brought about by the *Treaty of Lisbon amending the Treaty on European Union and the Treaty Establishing the European Community*, [2007] OJ, C 306/01. Article 79 goes so far as to commit member states to adopting common measures regarding conditions of entry and residence of long-term residents (art 79(2)(a)), but also explicitly preserves the right of member states to determine the volume of third-country nationals to be admitted as workers (art 79(5)).

10. The principal legal devices for standards in these two areas are the (recast in 2011, originally issued in 2004) Qualification Directive (EC, *Directive*

2011/95/EU of the European Parliament and of the Council of 13 December 2011 on standards for the qualification of third-country nationals or stateless persons as beneficiaries of international protection, for a uniform status for refugees or for persons eligible for subsidiary protection, and for the content of the protection granted, [2011] OJ, L 337/9) and the Procedures Directive (EC, Council Directive 2005/85/EC of 1 December 2005 on minimum standards on procedures in member states for granting and withdrawing refugee status, [2005] OJ, L 326/13). The former deals with legal standards for asylum, the latter with procedures and conditions for those awaiting a decision and those already within the process.

11. The first case is MSS v. *Belgium and Greece*, No 30696/09, [2011] ECHR 108. The second is NS v. *Secretary of State for the Home Department of the UK and ME and others v. Refugee Applications Commissioner, Minister for Justice, Equality and Law Reform*, C-411/10 and C-493/10, [2011] ECR I-13905.

12. NS, *supra* note 11 at paragraph 83 of the judgment.

13. EC, *Council Directive 2003/109/EC of 25 November 2003 concerning the status of third-country nationals who are long-term residents*, [2004] OJ, L 16/44.

14. EC, Commission, *5th Annual Report on Immigration and Asylum 2013* (Brussels: EC, 2014) at 13.

15. EC, Commission, *Communication from the Commission to the European Parliament, the Council, the Economic and Social Committee and the Committee of the Regions: Communication on Migration* (Brussels: EC, 2011).

16. Alison Mountz, "The Enforcement Archipelago: Detention, Haunting, and Asylum on Islands" (2011) 30:3 *Political Geography* 118.

17. Silja Klepp, "A Contested Asylum System: The European Union Between Refugee Protection and Border Control in the Mediterranean Sea" (2010) 12:1 *Eur J Migr & L* 1 at 4–5; Rutvica Andrijasevic, "Deported: The Right to Asylum at EU's External Border of Italy and Libya" (2010) 48:1 *Intl Migration* 148 at 153–5. See also Elcano Royal Institute, *Recent Arrivals of Migrants and Asylum Seekers by Sea to Italy: Problems and Reactions*, by Paola Monzini, ARI 75/2011 (Spain: Elcano Royal Institute, April 13, 2011) at 1; Mountz, *supra* note 16; Helene Gacon et al., "Complaint against the Italian Government for Violation of European Community Law" (January 20, 2005) (signed by representatives of 10 NGOs based in Italy, France, and Spain), online: www.gisti.org/doc/act ions/2005/italie/complaint20-01-2005.pdf. Regarding the NGO complaint, see the European Parliament Committee on Civil Liberties, Justice and Home Affairs, *Report from the LIBE Committee Delegation on the Visit to the Temporary Holding Centre in Lampedusa (Report\581203)* (Brussels: EC, 2005).

18. Carlo Brusa and Davide Papotti, "Contemporary Italy Between Stable Immigration and Migratory Emergencies" (Lecture delivered at the Annual International Conference 2011 of the Royal Geographical Society, London, September 2, 2011).

19. Rachel Brown, "French Stop Asylum Seekers at Italian Border," *ABC News* (April 17, 2011), online: ABC Radio Australia www.abc.net.au/news/2011–04-18/french-stop-asylum-seekers-at-italian-border/2610830. Also, Brusa and Papoth, supra note 18. Border closing with the EU was unprecedented in 2011 but was used repeatedly as the 2015 crisis mounted; see Preface.

20. Lizzy Davies, "Lampedusa Boat Tragedy Is 'Slaughter of Innocents' Says Italian President," *The Guardian* (October 3, 2013), online: www.theguardian.com/world/2013/oct/03/lampedusa-boat-tragedy-italy-migrants; Iosto Ibba and Barbara Molinaro, "Eritrean Survivor of Lampedusa Tragedy Returns to Honour the Dead, Meet Pope Francis," *UNHCR News Stories* (October 2, 2014), online: www.unhcr.org/542doece5.html (note that the UNHCR numbers are higher than the news media sources: 523 people on board and 368 people dead); Jim Yardley and Elisabetta Povoledo, "Migrants Die as Burning Boat Capsizes Off Italy," (October 3, 2013), online: www.nytimes.com/2013/10/04/world/europe/scores-die-in-ship wreck-off-sicily.html.

21. Alessandra Bonomolo and Stephanie Kirchgaessner, "Migrant Boat Captain Arrested as Survivors of Sinking Reach Italy," *The Guardian* (April 21, 2015), online: www.theguardian.com/world/2015/apr/21/survi vors-800-migrant-boat-disaster-reach-italy-catania; Eric Reguly, "Latest Shipwreck Claims up to 700 Migrants on the Mediterranean," *The Globe and Mail* (April 19, 2015), online: www.theglobeandmail.com/news/world/hundreds-feared-dead-after-migrant-boat-capsizes-in-mediter ranean/article24018773/.

22. United Nations High Commissioner for Refugees, Press Release, "UNHCR urges Europe to create a robust search and rescue operation on the Mediterranean, as Operation Triton lacks resources and mandate needed for saving lives" (February 12, 2015), online: www.unhcr.org/54d c80f89.html.

23. Nick Squires, "Italy's 'Appalling' Treatment of Migrants Revealed in Lampedusa Footage," *The Telegraph* (December 18, 2013), online: www.telegraph.co.uk/news/worldnews/europe/italy/10525222/Italys-appalling-tre atment-of-migrants-revealed-in-Lampedusa-footage.html.

24. European Commission, Press Release, "Commissioner Cecilia Malmström commemorates the Lampedusa tragedy" (October 2, 2014), online: europa.eu/rapid/press-release_STATEMENT-14–296_en.htm.

25. See Appendix 3 for a summary of asylum arrivals in various European states over the past decade.

9

Contours and consequences of a new politics

The demise of settler society values and the departure from twentieth-century patterns in Europe together ground the new politics of immigration and point to its future directions. This politics is front and center in prosperous Western liberal democracies, filling the headlines and parliaments. But its effects reach every corner of the globe as these states dominate the global policy arena by virtue of being both the world's most sought after migration destinations and the traditional terrain of migration mythology.

The transformation in the values that former settler states and former colonial masters are now pursuing in immigration leads to the competitive migration convergence that has been evident for at least a decade. Increasingly, the immigration laws and policies enacted by Western liberal democracies look alike. This is true whether those states were once settler societies or whether they are among the new nations of immigration in Europe. This truth in and of itself is a challenge to our immigration imagination – to conclude that immigration operates socially and politically the same way in the United Kingdom or Germany as it does in Australia or the United States is significant as it has never been true in any earlier era. The convergence is competitive – all of these states want to attract the same highly skilled workers, and the same agile economic actors, as permanent migrants. All of these states want to keep asylum seekers at arm's length, and to impose limits on family reunification. These goals are broadly shared, even if they are pursued with differing tactics, or alongside some diminishing vestiges of ethnic kinship preferences.

In part, the competitive convergence results from taking a "non-discriminatory" posture toward immigrants. The emergence of points systems as the preferred model for economic immigrant selection in Western liberal democracies demonstrates a commitment to ignore cultural, ethnic, and even racial values, and to instead embrace a quasi-scientific or at least "neutral" selection method. This method ensures that the same individuals will end up being top choice immigrants across a range of states. Points systems were invented by settler states seeking to break with their racialized immigration histories. The systems, however, do not remove discrimination, they simply deploy it differently. People who come out at the top of points systems are well educated, multi-lingual, economically successful, and young. Accordingly, they are very likely to be wealthy, and to come from wealthy families. A preference for the rich is hardly non-discriminatory, but Western legal systems have struggled to recognize and remedy discrimination against either the rich or the poor. These groups do not fit liberal analysis of discrimination well because of the embedded assumption that wealth or poverty can be chalked up to individual choices and efforts. Selecting immigrants on the basis of economic values discriminates; it simply does so in a way that we are comfortable with because we feel, at some level, that this discrimination is deserved. After all, the point of selecting migrants is to discriminate between applicants. Accordingly, the turn toward "neutral" immigrant selection accelerates a type of discrimination that is invisible to legal liberalism.[1]

This preference for the wealthy turns the traditional logic of immigration on its head. These days, people cannot migrate in search of a better life; they migrate because they *have* a better life. A capacity to migrate is a marker of privilege in our globalized era. One feature of the competitive migration convergence going on at present is a simmering but frequently ignored concern about global brain drain. The idea that societal leaders, the best and brightest, are being lured from the global South to the wealthy states of the North surfaces from time to time, but is generally muted by the more powerful ideas that Northern states have a "right" to choose the migrants they want, and that individual actors can make their own choices about migration (within, of course, the parameters set for them by wealthy states).

The nation-building phase of global immigration has concluded. It was in this phase that migration regulation was invented and developed. Migration law across settler societies was a highly discretionary terrain, where states inscribed visions of themselves, their national identities and policy priorities. The strong tie between immigration law and national identity made sense when nations, and national populations, were being constructed through immigrant selection. The framework of immigration laws was constructed to substantiate this vision. This is no longer the case. Instead, in the early twenty-first century, immigration is locked into a nation-sustaining mode: its goals are to fill in gaps that emerge in national labor markets or to ensure demographic stability as national birth rates decline. These altered goals are, of course, still tied to national policy priorities, but in a new way. One change that we see here is simply the maturing of the settler societies: as these states are now well established, and have their own "cultures," the way that the "us–them" line is maintained begins to resemble how that line has always worked in Old World states. That is, even though it is European states that have become nations of immigration, transformation does not flow only one way. Both sides are grappling with convergence. Borrowings move in both directions also; for example, the immigration-based concern about forced marriage and the citizenship testing agenda began in European states and moved several years later to the former settler societies.

As states no longer need people, but rather widgets, the rise of "trial" migration follows logically. The past few years have brought dramatic increases in opportunities for both international students and temporary labor migrants to shift into permanent statuses. From the perspective of individuals, these programs present themselves as genuine opportunities. From a state perspective, such programs have a dual role. First, they allow states to "pre-test" potential permanent migrants, and to ensure that many of the costs and concerns of "settlement" are borne privately by the individual (or by the university) prior to the time when the state takes any moral responsibility for the immigrants by giving them formal permanent membership. Second, these programs have become a feature of the competition for the globe's most desired migrants: states now compete by offering better, quicker, easier options for ultimately remaining permanently. In the case of international students, a path toward permanent residency is a classic double-dip by the state. Allowing a foreign student to remain permanently means that the state benefits from foreign student tuition payments, and through the presence of people who spend money to live within the economy but who typically have a sharply limited right to work, and then, by converting that individual into a permanent member, the state retains the benefit of the education it has supported.

Treating temporary migration as a path to permanence also reflects the demise of "settlement" of migrants as a public value. One of the former distinctions between permanent and temporary migration was that the state was expected to invest in permanent migrants and support their trajectory toward full membership. This meant funding settlement services such as language education and labor market orientation assistance. Temporary migrants, on the other hand, were expected to leave and thus the state did not invest in them in the same way, and was not expected to do so. In Canada and Australia, for example, children of temporary residents can be charged fees to attend public schools which citizens and permanent residents attend for free. But, when a person arrives in a new country and spends the first three or four years as a temporary resident prior to attaining permanent status, much of the "work" of settlement will be done prior to receiving that status. Indeed, it is on the basis of already being "settled" that permanent residency is offered. This transmutation ensures that settlement services formerly provided by the state are not needed, not paid for, and not valued. There is, of course, a chicken and egg argument here, but in a rapidly shifting policy environment, withdrawing settlement services and attracting more temporary migrants probably both come first in an intertwined spiral. The rise of temporariness as a value lessens the bounds of attachment, and thus convergence extends as well to a haste to deport more people, more efficiently, and for a wider range of reasons.

The competitive migration convergence that currently prevails among Western liberal democracies is a vital clue to the new and mean-spirited politics of immigration that undergirds it. This chapter turns first to describing this politics based on the work of the previous two chapters and then to considering its consequences for immigration regulation.

CONTOURS OF A NEW POLITICS

The new politics of immigration is thrust to the surface by the clash between our intuitive, mythological understanding of immigration and a relatively rapid change in values about immigration. To recall the arc of my argument thus far, the three factors generating this value change are the asylum crisis, the fear of fundamental Islam, and the demise of multiculturalism. Each of these factors intersects with the others, heightening their intensity and sharpening their edges. While the shifting patterns of migration have taken some time to change, these three factors are conceptual and contribute to immigration values rather than statistics. The transformation of values generates the new politics.

One vital feature of this politics is that immigration is understood – and contested – in the same terms across Western liberal democracies. This follows from the transformation of European states into nations of migration and from the end of the nation-building phase, but it reaches well beyond. All Western liberal democracies now understand themselves as desirable destination states, entitled to "select" immigrants from the world at large and to provide humanitarian assistance from time to time, or not at all. The sense of entitlement is no different in states that were built from immigration than in those that emerged in their present configuration by sending migrants to the far corners of the earth.

This entitlement grows from the now well-anchored idea that states have a sovereign right to control entry. Control over immigration as a matter of sovereign identity grew out of the settler society paradigm. As a world-ordering idea, it came of age in the early twentieth century at the time that the paradigmatic settler societies were establishing their independence as nations. Settler societies needed this idea as a corollary of independence in a way that Old World nations did not. And, of course, the idea of control over entry is inimical to the model of colonial power, which depended upon ignoring borders set up by less powerful peoples. In other words, the idea that states have sovereign power over immigration, and, moreover, that under the late twentieth-century pressures of globalization this has become a defining feature of sovereignty, was never linked to the emergence of nation states, but rather to the emergence of settler societies as independent states. This idea has now been imbedded into our understanding of how Western liberal states regulate immigration.

As the distinction between Old and New World migration politics disappeared, one of the features of the new political landscape is that the "us–them" line, the distinction between insiders and outsiders, has taken on a new form. Immigration politics both needs and creates this line. Without a capacity to exclude, and a group to therefore be excluded, immigration regulation is meaningless. Migration policy convergence in the twenty-first century means that the globe can be divided into so-called sending states that migrants wish to leave, and prosperous industrial states that are desired migration destinations. Certainly many citizens of these prosperous states do migrate, but this movement is hardly visible. Mirroring the way skilled migration has disappeared in Europe, migration politics is not built up by taking positions on whether Australians should be able to migrate to Canada. It is consumed by a focus on the new "us–them" line that separates the global South from the global North. Indeed, immigration politics bears a key responsibility for the existence of these two symbolic geographies. Australians can, of course, immigrate to Canada, and vice versa, but migration among the "insider states" is not the source of contestation, and thus it does not drive forward the policy agenda.

What is new about the "us–them" line is its global aspect. Affinities between particular people and particular cultures have vanished. The idea that some receiving states would need or "prefer" different migrants to others has ended. People who qualify as immigrants to New Zealand or Sweden almost certainly could also choose Belgium or Australia. The logic of asylum law is similar. It should be equally possible to find protection in any of the 148 countries that participate in international refugee law. That this logic does not hold in practice does little to weaken the idea that the world can be divided into states that produce refugees and those that protect them. The issue is not that the dividing line does not exist; rather it is that the framework of refugee law does not fit neatly onto it. The global aspect of the "us–them" line means that it is more accurate than ever before to describe the divide as a separation between the rich and the poor. Particularity, culture, and tradition are washed away by the economic hegemony of this new understanding of immigration.

Fear has a new role in the transformed politics of immigration as well. In the old narrative, immigration meant fear of contagion or cultural dilution. In the new politics, the terrain of fear is existential. Western liberal democracies are relatively unconcerned about the old version of cultural dilution (a "privilege" of settler society maturity) and the dynamics of contagion are now hinged to travel, rather than migration. But migration fears have heightened to the extent of traditional securitization. We are afraid of the immigrant as terrorist – as the person who seeks to destroy our society entirely, not to alter or to imitate it. This fear picks up the traditional Western angst of Islamophobia and thrives on the unintelligibility with which liberalism meets Islam. Fear frees liberal immigration politics from basic liberal commitments.

Shifting fear into this dimension aligns with the other transformations that rob migration of a human face. The prototypical terrorist is literally masked. Devaluing the ideas of settlement and society makes it easier for this fear to take hold. Without these values we know less, and care less, about the new-comer other.

There is another dimension of existential threat that informs at least some aspects of the new politics, and that festers along the newly drawn divide between "us" and "them." This is the fear that without strict vigilance about migration prosperous Western states will be so overwhelmed by an influx of migrants that their cultures will not simply be diluted or altered but comple-tely overwhelmed and thus destroyed. This fear is fostered by the line drawn between global South and global North, and the belief that in a world of open borders, enormous populations would move whole scale into prosperous states. We have no idea whether this fear is in any way realistic. At present, 97 percent of people in the world live in the country where they were born. This figure simultaneously suggests two disparate facts; first, that few people actually want to move, and second, that even a small shift of 1 or 2 percent would be a huge number of people. And in the mythologies of migration, dueling narratives assert both that most people do not want to move, and that migration is a quintessentially human act. There is little hard data, but what matters is what people, especially opinion leaders and policy makers, believe. People's views about what would happen in an utterly fanciful borderless world strongly inform their political views about immigration. This is such an important underpinning to discourse that Gallup began polling on this question in 2007, asking people whether they would like to move, permanently or temporarily, to another country, and if so, where. The first data were released by Gallup in 2009 and polling continues on a rolling basis. In 2011,

Gallup stated that more than 630 million people, or about 14 percent of the world's adults, responded "yes" to the question about whether they would like to leave their home country permanently. Predictably, the data show that it is primarily those in the global South who want to move, and their preferred destinations are generally in the global North.[2]

But here again, the results must be regarded as at least somewhat fanciful – depending strongly on how individual survey respondents imagine that a fantasy future world would take shape, and relying on respondents to fill in the blank about what is required for migration to be possible in their own lives. Whatever we think of the survey methodology or results, there is no doubt that the unknowable answer to this question is a principal ingredient of the new politics of immigration.

Without the old stories of migration and nation or migration and empire, what is left is migration and money. This story operates at all levels. There is heightened competition for the best and brightest migrants. There is increased policy focus on tying migration more closely, more effectively, more nimbly, to increasingly anachronistic national economies. There is increasing concern about "mere economic migrants" slipping into the asylum system. There is a growing mass of illegal migrants that are understood as a now-nearly-necessary resource for the economies of Western democracies.

All this means that it is tempting to say that the new politics of immigration is only about economics. This is not true. Or at least it is not accurate to say that economics explains what is going on with immigration politics, or helps us predict what will happen next in terms of policy innovation. It is absolutely accurate that contemporary discourses about immigration are dominated by economic values and concerns, but economics stops short of having explanatory value for three reasons. Each of which says something about current politics. The first is that the "politics" of immigration matters more than at any previous point in time. This means that popular, public, and political discourses matter enormously. These discourses have picked up a lot of economic language, but are not strongly informed by nuanced economics and, vitally, have not relinquished earlier ideas about what matters in immigration. It is also in these discourses that fear of Islamophobia and the demise of multiculturalism are most strongly rooted, neither of which fits an economic logic.

The second reason that economic analysis cannot provide all the answers is that national-level control remains a central tenet of immigration analysis, even as national economies are becoming more permeable, and therefore less relevant as policy sites. Immigration discourse idealizes the national economy, even as all other forces make that notion increasingly nonsensical. The desire to micro-manage the insertion of foreign workers into available jobs is increasingly evident but very hard to achieve. This is one reason why the open borders of the EU have probably done a better job of meeting market demand than all the intricate policy shifting that has taken place in Canada, Australia, New Zealand, and the United States. Indeed the United States' model, which is far better established than the other three, has fostered the development of a massive "illegal" population that can fill labor market gaps more efficiently even than workers from the Eastern borders of the EU.

The final reason that economic analysis cannot carry the day is that, after all this time, workers are still human beings. Even when conforming to every regulation applied to them, immigrant workers continue to change their minds about the future, evaluate changes in the economy around them on an individual basis, have families, fall in love, learn new things, and develop new ideals.

These factors leave us with an immigration politics that pays a great deal of attention to economics, but where this feature of the politics leaves important blind spots. Immigration economists know this, and can assess and account for these gaps. But this politics is not an expert politics.

In this new configuration, immigration is more highly politicized than at any previous point in time. Throughout Western liberal democracies, it has become a key election issue for the twenty-first century. Where even in the paradigmatic settler states ministers for immigration were formerly supporting players, they are now key figures in any government. Australia's Phillip Ruddock and Canada's Jason Kenney both used immigration portfolios to rise to political prominence. In the United States, immigration reform has, finally, taken center stage in the final years of the Obama presidency. In France, the astonishing rise in popularity of the National Front is intertwined with a shift that means its anti-immigrant agenda can now play a part in mainstream politics. German Chancellor Merkel and British Prime Minister Cameron regularly comment on immigration. All of this was true in the decade prior to 2015, which ratcheted this politicization up even further.

This move toward center stage owes something to the predominance of economic discourse and something to the rise of existential fear and the securitization that has accompanied it. It is indebted to the globalizing forces that have reduced national control in so many areas that immigration policy has become a central repository of sovereign ambitions. It also grows in part from international policy convergence that it fuels: the sense that if it is important for other countries to control migration, it must be important for us too.

The contemporary politics of immigration is surprisingly resistant to partisan analysis. Or at least partisan politics does not fit squarely into the landscape. In the United States, it was the Clinton administration that began the fortification of the US–Mexico border, and deportation rates have risen on the same trajectory under the Obama administration as during the Bush years. In Canada, the Conservative government has led the complete restructuring of immigration policy, but with surprisingly little resistance from other parties, and with little confidence that a change of government will lead to a return to previous policies. In Australia, the relentless public pressure to halt asylum seekers has led successive governments to roll out new control measures, regardless of their partisan stripes (and Prime Minister Kevin Rudd paid a high political price, being ousted by his own party, in part for bucking this trend). In New Zealand, the far-right anti-immigration platform of Winston Peter's New Zealand First party has garnered some support and a lot of media attention but it has not forced the three major parties (National, Labour, and the Greens) to abandon their support for ongoing immigration.[3]

Heightened attention to immigration politics, combined with the strong contribution of securitization and economics, mean that rapid policy shifts are a prominent feature. Several factors contribute to this result. The increased scrutiny of immigration policies and the political mileage that can therefore be made by demonstrating action within this sector are a powerful incentive for change. The erosion of the nation-building ethos means that immigration policy is no longer a bedrock element of the political landscape, and thus tamper-resistant. Heightened economic discourses generate incentives to shift policy as economic indicators shift. The competitive policy convergence among Western industrialized states also contributes to the pace of change, as policy innovation in one state is often quickly imitated elsewhere. This occurs both in competition for talented workers and thinkers, and in the competition to fortify borders. Securitization of migration adds its own elements to the shifting policy arena. With each new terror-related event, many states respond with new crack-down provisions, which inevitably these days include migration-related provisions. For example, within months of a thwarted attack on the Canadian Parliament by a (Muslim) Canadian citizen, an anti-terror bill including provisions aimed at increasing the powers of border guards was introduced; within weeks of the *Charlie Hebdo* attacks in France in 2015, legal changes were introduced in Italy requiring additional scrutiny prior to mosques being built.[4]

The new politics of immigration is a nasty terrain. With its markers of shared and competitive goals throughout Western liberal democracies, a strong sense of sovereign entitlement, high stakes, resistance to traditional left–right partisanship, fear and securitization, a predominance of economic discourses, and a rapidly shifting policy arena, it is little wonder that contemporary immigration policies are mean-spirited and self-centered. The old settler society ideal that immigration policy was designed to further and reflect national identity has been transmogrified into an ugly echo of its former self. Immigration policy is now designed to further and reflect ever-shorter-term national goals, robbing it of its former breadth, which was at least occasionally aspirational and other-regarding.

In this new political configuration it has become impossible to say what states expect from immigrants. The former idea that immigrants would stay permanently and become members, that they would aspire to integration in a way that made integration and assimilation closely related, that they would provide cultural enrichment but not cultural challenge, that they would be hard-working, self-sacrificing, fiercely independent, and oriented toward the next generation, has faded away in the face of policies that make it impossible to recruit people who fit this model. Indeed, current policy frameworks make this ideal impossible to achieve, regardless of who is actually recruited. We cannot recruit people willing to make enormous personal sacrifices in order to secure a better future for their children when we are selecting wealthy well-educated people who are already comfortably middle class. These people know it is unfair to refuse to recognize their credentials, unreasonable to require their children to relinquish cultural traditions, and impossible to compel them to relinquish ties to a former home. We cannot expect people to integrate socially and culturally in the same ways as a quarter century earlier, when we have rolled back or eliminated settlement services programs and language education, and instead require that immigrants arrive ready to fit into economies, even as such a fit is less and less hinged to national borders. Current policies often prefer immigrants who arrive with no social, political, or economic need to integrate. It is hardly surprising that the meaning of integration is altered.

But in place of the old vision of the good immigrant, no new immigrant ideal has yet emerged. Reading from the contours of the new politics, it appears that what states most want from new migrants is that they behave and appear as "non-migrants". This is impossible. New migrants cannot be other than migrants. And thus we have reached a point where migrants can never live up to their idealized form. Political contestation follows inevitably from this. It will not be resolved until Western societies take these changes seriously. We are not yet at the stage where we can see any inclination to even begin to do so. And thus, the consequences of this new politics continue to unfold with remarkable intransigence.

CONSEQUENCES OF THIS POLITICS

Understanding the new terrain of migration politics makes visible the connections between current trends and allows us to read these trends as consequences of this new politics and the transformed understanding of immigration that they draw upon. We have reached a point where we can analyze the linkages between the "crimmigration" trend, the rise in deportation, the rollback of permanent migration programs, the drop in priority for family reunification, the rapidly climbing illegal migration statistics, and the failure to attend to global brain drain. These factors are all part and parcel of the new politics of immigration. They emerge from the constellation of values this politics presents, and in varying degrees can be read as consequences of this new politics.

The first of these factors began to emerge in the final decade of the twentieth century. In this sense, they are all newish, not completely novel. But what is now obvious, and more important, is that they are here to stay. The firm end of the settler society era, and the understanding of immigration fostered by it, mean that these features of immigration policy cannot be read as a passing political trend, which could be rolled back after a new series of elections, or modified in the face of new economic indicators. The combined effects of the asylum crisis, the fear of fundamental Islam, and the demise of multiculturalism have redrawn the frame for immigration policy, and each of these current policy features is captured in this frame in a way that gives it added resonance.

One consequence of this new politics is that immigration involves more "hard" law than was formerly the case. This is the direct consequence of constructing harsher immigration regimes throughout the prosperous West. Harshness is communicated through law because these states embrace a rule of law ethos: the state acts through law. In one sense, this is a logical continuation of the progression of immigration regulation over the past century. At the time of the last great wave of human migration, the 1880s to the 1920s, migration regulation was just being invented. During this current wave, there are new legal provisions promulgated every day. This shifts the relationship between immigration and the state, because throughout the twentieth-century immigration policy in Western liberal democracies was marked by extensive discretionary powers.[5] High levels of discretion mean that immigration statutes were often written as legislative frameworks, within which the details that gave the law meaning could be developed outside of the glare of democratic scrutiny and quickly altered without the burden of democratic processes. High levels of discretion were, thus, a marker of the strong link between migration control and sovereignty.

Nothing about this link has changed, but the transformation of discretion is palpable. Immigration laws are changing more frequently, with more and more details being spelled out in legislation itself, rather than left for regulations or guidelines that will follow. Australia was a leader in this trend, with more than twenty-five legislative amendments to its *Migration Act* between 1990 and 2000 (and just as many in the following decade). This was, at the time, out of step with similarly situated countries such as Canada, New Zealand, the United Kingdom, or even the United States. Now, it is more the norm. In Canada, the *Immigration and Refugee Protection Act* has been amended on thirteen separate occasions in the past five years (with two more proposed amendments in bill form as this book goes to press), including by three separate budget bills, which provide a vehicle for quick amendment with minimal scrutiny because the focus of the legislation is elsewhere. In the United Kingdom, the tribunal structure for immigration review has gone through two major alterations in the past eight years, and in the United States immigration reforms are being drafted and redrafted, with the pace of change slowed only by the drag weight of partisan politics.

No one involved in this frenzy of law reform is seeking primarily to reduce executive discretion. In fact, many of these changes *grant* discretion to executive decision makers. But they do so in ways that reduce it nonetheless, by putting increasing amounts of text into the hands of the courts. This is a perverse result of the controlling impulse. So when the Australian legislature seeks to define "significant harm" for the purposes of refugee decision making, the result is a text which ties the hands of executive decision makers, and gives courts an additional basis for scrutinizing government action. When the Canadian Parliament replaces a one-sentence-long discretion-granting provision with three pages of legislative text aimed at determining how that discretion will be used, to what ends, and for whom, the result is less discretion.[6] Part of the current immigration reform battle in the United States is pushed forward by a desire to enact new law so that the option of partial reform via presidential discretionary action is not the only means of achieving results. This trend leads inexorably to a more law "full" policy terrain. Having more law is not inherently a good thing or a bad thing, not does it align with left or right politics; within a liberal democracy, it is amenable to either. What is certain is that it is a marked change from how immigration regulation has henceforth taken shape in Western states. The import of which no one has started to care about yet. One thing is clear, this much law is not simply going to disappear. Law as mode of action accounts in part for the permanence of the current politics.

One of the clearest reflections of more law is more unauthorized migration. Unauthorized migration fits with the loss of inclusion and integration story of

Chapter 7. As Chapter 3 discussed, the reduction in migration possibilities for people with few skills and little education also puts enormous pressure on asylum systems, exceeding the already enormous pressure on those systems that comes from having anywhere from 10 to 15 million refugees in the world who need, somehow, to find protection. It is for all these reasons that I have assented to talking about "illegal" migration rather than unauthorized, undocumented, irregular, or otherwise euphemistic migration. The law is responsible, directly and indirectly, for illegal migration. Without migration law, it would not exist.

There is no doubt that illegal migration is an overwhelming and persistent feature of the current landscape of global migration. Nor is there any doubt that it is a necessary result of the contemporary political landscape of migration. The number of illegal migrants worldwide has grown to the extent that it may now be as much as one-quarter to one-third of all migrants globally. No agency is attempting to make this estimate, but it is a reasonable guess, based on comparing available state-level estimates to the overall UN migration figures. Illegal migration is a profound challenge to any attempt to regulate migration. It also contributes directly to weakening both economic analyses and the power of human rights. The effect on economic analysis is straightforward: migrants operating clandestinely defy calculation and prediction. We understand that illegal migrants comprise an even more flexible and disposable workforce than temporary foreign workers, but state policy cannot be built upon the idea that economic needs will be met by illegal immigrants. At least not state policy in liberal democracies. Because immigration politics these days is largely about control, admitting to the economic utility of illegal migration is officially impossible, and thus leaves a logic gap in any economic analysis that aspires to meaning in the political arena. The effect of rising rates of illegal migration on human rights arguments is more complicated, and I return to it presently.

The rise of illegal migration also connects to another consequence of the current politics – the emergence of what has been coined "crimmigration" and a rapid uptick in deportation rates. Juliet Stumpf coined the term "crimmigration" in 2006 in the United States to refer to the intertwining of criminal and immigration law agendas. This phenomenon is by no means limited to the United States, although the United States was a leader in the rise in deportation rates, and it built this policy success through focusing on immigrants who had committed crimes.[7]

Several ideas are intertwined here, and they reflect and refract varying aspects of the new politics. The core idea of "crimmigration" is that we have focused so much attention on the criminal activities of immigrants that it almost amounts to criminalizing immigration. As such, it turns the old narrative of immigration upside down. In this new narrative, immigration is inherently bad, something to be suspect, rather than an unqualified good that is essential to constructing the nation.

Most liberal states have long had provisions for deporting non-citizens who are convicted of crimes. What has changed is the extent of these provisions, the way these provisions are enforced, and how they are imagined in popular culture. In Canadian law, the number of crimes for which a person can be deported has steadily expanded since the mid-1990s. In 2013 the *Faster Removal of Foreign Criminals Act* became the most recent step in this now long-term progression. This legislation reduced appeal rights for permanent residents convicted of crimes, reduced Ministerial discretion to carve out exceptions to criminal inadmissibility provisions, and lowered the threshold for crimes to be considered "serious." In the United States the Obama administration has deported more people annually than the George W. Bush administration, the greatest number of whom are deported on the basis of immigration "crimes" and 91 percent of whom are men.[8]

The objective of extending the criminality provisions within immigration law is directly linked to the desire to deport more people.[9] The legal framework creates deportability; actual deportation requires a further injection of political will. It is typical of liberal democratic states that the number of people who could technically be removed from the country under immigration law provisions far exceeds the number who are actually deported. Deportation presents a direct challenge to liberal democracies – at its sharp end it requires near-draconian deployment of state resources against individuals. Deportation is resource intensive, and it typically cannot be accomplished unilaterally; it requires another state's cooperation. For decades, it was accepted wisdom that deportability would far outstrip actual deportations because liberal states lacked the will to enforce their laws in this area. At its most extreme, deportation has involved forcing shackled and hooded people onto airplanes, sometimes drugging them to keep them quiet. A number of people have died while being deported, including several being flown on regular commercial flights. These examples are statistically rare, and most deportations are not dramatic in these ways. But the willingness to effect deportation at even this extreme is what stands behind all current deportation policy.[10]

That deportation is no longer abhorrent for liberal democracies is a direct consequence of the new politics of immigration. It is now often the opposite – many governments are anxious to demonstrate their will to deport. The UK government endured scandal in 2006 for failing to effectively deport non-citizens who had spent time in jail.[11] Deportation statistics have risen sharply across the former settler societies, especially since the start of the twenty-first century. In the United States, this trend began under the Clinton administration, and has continued its steady rise to the present, regardless of who was in power.

In the United Kingdom and in Canada, the deportation impulse has reached its nadir with new provisions allowing for the deportation of citizens. Both of these states have introduced laws that permit the government to strip dual citizens of their UK or Canadian citizenship on the basis of particular criminal activities. The removal of citizenship for criminal activity renders citizens deportable. A marker of the politics of our times is that this does not sound nearly as unusual as it would have been a decade or two ago. Citizenship stripping is extraordinary – the contemporary equivalent of the medieval punishment of banishment. Removal of citizenship has previously been almost unheard of in Western liberal democracies – reserved for cases of fraud and for instances of treason. For the moment, only dual citizens can be stripped of their citizenship, although the Canadian government initially introduced a bill that would have extended to all citizens. The practical side of the matter, however, is that without some remaining citizenship, there would be no destination state for such putative deportees. In both the UK and Canada, the provisions apply to "born" as well as naturalized citizens. By February 2014, the UK has deported thirty-seven citizens under these provisions. Canada has yet to use its new law.[12]

A more far-reaching change has accompanied the expansion of immigration consequences of crime and the rise in deportation rates – the idea that immigration itself is criminalized. In the mid-1990s, when I was first learning about immigration law, transgressions of immigration provisions were understood as mere regulatory offences, not true crimes. This seems so unimaginable now that it is hard to believe it was only twenty years ago. Immigration law breaches are now *hyper*-criminalized, such that people who have overstayed their visas, worked beyond the provisions of their permits, or crossed the border without permission are understood as inherently "illegal", in one large undifferentiated category. The intertwining of immigration and crime is so thoroughly accomplished by this point that Aas and Bosworth, with strong support from others, have introduced the concept of a "criminology of mobility." In their words, "[T]he criminology of mobility is . . . a study of the contested and precarious nature of membership in a deeply divided global order, and the practices of policing of its (physical and symbolic) boundaries."[13] This conceptualization brings to the fore the symbolic exclusionary force of the criminalization trend.

Like the expansion of illegal migration, criminalization of migration and a rise in deportation rates each involve growth of immigration law. The rule of law tradition of Western liberal democracies means that these types of provisions, rules that reduce individual rights, are written down and passed by legislatures. There are several reasons for this, which reflect strongly on the place of law in our societies and the way immigration law is altered by the new politics. The traditions of criminal law have, at the very broadest level, been the opposite of those of immigration law. Criminal law, since as long ago as the *Magna Carta*, has paid attention to the rights of the accused and to the unequal balance between the power of the state and that of the individual whose liberty is at risk. Even while the argument that this paradigm is honored in the breach is strong, pillars of criminal law such as "innocent until proven guilty," the right to counsel, and the array of fair trial provisions (such as rights to silence, to confront one's accuser, to cross-examine) reflect this ideal. With this framework comes the idea that the law must be knowable (because ignorance of it will not excuse) and that it cannot be retrospective. Within this framework, discretion has a narrow role at best. Immigration provisions have traditionally been the opposite. Although they feature the same individual versus state power imbalance, the stock story is about the state having rights (to exclude, to select) and the individual migrant having mere privileges. This meant, until the end of the twentieth century, that immigration law was a terrain of vast discretion. The criminalization of immigration has not only expanded the texts of immigration law, it has also brought the trends of criminal law into those texts. This introduction creates tensions that are now being played out in our courts, of which the security cases discussed in Chapter 4 provide an array of examples. More litigation in turn leads to more law – especially in the common law systems of the former settler states.

The illegal migration, criminalization, and deportation stories closely reflect the end of settler society values. Deportation emphatically breaks the connection between the nation and the immigrant, and a rise in its occurrence and political palatability reflects a demise of settlement and integration values. This demise is also demonstrated by the expansion of criminal exclusion provisions, where it is now routine that long-term, legal permanent residents can and will be deported because of criminal convictions (predominantly convictions that have nothing to do with terrorism or national security). This extension of the deportation's reach, and the general acceptance that this trend is appropriate, undermines the idea that permanent residents are nearly equivalent to "full" members and further bolsters the idea that the early twenty-first century is marked by a resurgence of citizenship rights. In this framework, migrants are considered as conditionally admitted to a state, no matter how long ago that admission took place. The political trajectory of illegal migration presents a more subtle erosion of the old immigrant paradigm. "Illegality" creates pockets of exclusion within the borders of the nation, and operates both rhetorically and legally to ensure that long-term, law-abiding residents do not accrue membership attachments. These consequences of the new politics simultaneously bolster its continuance.

The rapidly shifting, economically dominated, high-stakes contemporary setting for immigration policy also has consequences that are not so directly tied to the growth of law and expansion of exclusionary devices. Declining attention to family reunion provisions in the migration frameworks of Canada, Australia, and New Zealand (where parent migration sponsorships are now "tiered" according to income) are examples of this, as is the widespread turn to temporary migration as a step toward permanence. The lack of interest in global brain drain also follows this logic. For a time, in the final decades of the twentieth century, Western policy makers and scholars had begun to attend to the inequities of migration policies that drew talented and educated citizens of the global South into permanent lives in the industrialized North.[14] Thinking along these lines has now almost completely disappeared, pushed aside by the ever-stronger embrace of economic values, the core commitments of liberal legalism, and the urgent need for migration scholars to attend to the security turn and the concomitant rise of Islamophobia.

Paying attention to brain drain has fallen from attention, even as Western states intensify their competition for international students and in consequence extend recruitment efforts more resolutely to the global South. Foreign students are ideal migrants for the new politics because they arrive with temporary permission, requisite bank balances, and restricted work rights. Their integration is privatized – a concern for their campus communities, but not for national governments. They are a vital part of financial plans for private and public institutions alike, throughout Western liberal democracies these days. The question of brain drain is rarely, if ever, raised in this context. Meanwhile, Western governments benefit from a classic double-dip: their institutions of higher education benefit from collecting high international tuition fees, and then the states benefit from retaining (directly and indirectly) students that have local credentials, ready made for professional regulatory bodies, and "pre-integrated." The complicated discomfort of brain drain analysis is rarely introduced into discussions of the many benefits of international students. International students are, by definition, wealthy, capable, and on the way to being well educated. Those who do not succeed academically can be "returned." In a politics dominated by economic rhetoric, there is no space for a discussion of concerns about global equality and contemporary post-colonial plunder that once lurked at the edges of this analysis.

Not all types of law are flourishing in the new political configuration. Human rights for non-citizens have experienced significant setbacks. The most important is the failure of the International Convention on the Protection of the Rights of All Migrant Workers and Members of Their Families to emerge as a significant instrument. This Convention must now be read as an emblem of the new politics. In the latter years of the twentieth century the story that human rights were developing significant heft in protecting non-citizens was well propagated, and supported by persuasive evidence. Participation in the drafting of a new Convention for migrant workers included most prosperous Western states that were primarily migrant-receiving countries. The drafting history of the Convention was unremarkable; the working group was established in 1980 and by 1990 the Convention was opened for ratification. It was at this point, just as the 1980s spike in asylum numbers was transforming into a perpetual crisis, that the story derailed.

It took thirteen years for the so-called Migrant Workers Convention to attract enough ratifications to come into force, which it finally did on July 1, 2003. By this time, the transformation of the political landscape was well in train. None of the prosperous Western states that had participated in drafting had ratified by that time, and to date only forty-seven states are parties to the Convention, even following a global campaign to promote ratification. Most states parties are migrant-sending states of the global South. Mexico and Turkey stand out on the list as states that are also significant migrant hosts. To date, the individual complaints procedure set out in the Convention is not in force because fewer than ten states have agreed to participate. The Migrant Workers Convention has almost the lowest ratification rate among the ten treaties that the United Nations Office of the High Commissioner for Human Rights lists as the world's core human rights commitments. Considering the two more recent treaties on this list makes an interesting comparison. The Convention on the Rights of Persons with Disabilities has 153 states parties and was opened for ratification in December 2006 and brought into force by the twentieth ratification in May 2008. The International Convention for the Protection of All Persons from Enforced Disappearance was opened for ratification in December 2006 but did not come into force until December 2010. It currently has forty-six states parties, just slightly fewer than the Migrant Workers Convention that is sixteen years older and has potential application to many more people.[15]

The explanation for this pronounced lack of enthusiasm is in part a simple story of states getting cold feet. The chill was generated by the shift in prevailing political winds. Part of the problem is undoubtedly that the Convention contains some genuine innovations. Most prominently, it extends human rights protection, explicitly, to migrant workers who are, in the Convention's words "non-documented or in an irregular situation."[16] The potential of this innovation is only partially realized even within the text of the Convention because the rights for unauthorized migrants are fewer than for those with legal authority, and the Convention also requires states to commit to working to eliminate extra-legal migration. But it is still significant. The Convention seeks to address what by 1990 was already emerging as a significant human rights challenge – migrants without status were denied even very basic protections on the basis of procedural exclusion arguments. Strikingly, the Migrant Workers Convention provisions for "non-documented" migrants do not go any further than basic provisions contained in other, already established, human rights instruments (some of the core rights provisions echoed here include a right to life; a right to be free from torture and cruel, inhuman, or degrading treatment; freedom from slavery), but in the new Convention these are explicitly extended to "irregular" migrant workers, bringing them within the "human" category to which human rights ought extend.

The Convention is emblematic of the new politics for all of these reasons: the very slow uptake; the fact that Western migrant-receiving states are not participating; the paucity of rights for non-documented workers; and the commitment to eliminating irregular migration. Perhaps most importantly, the Convention is anchored in an economic discourse, extending its protection to "workers" (and work seekers), not to "migrants." All of this is not to say that this Convention is not valuable, or that states ought not ratify it. Broad participation in the Migrant Workers Convention has the potential to alter the rights landscape for many migrants. The campaign to extend participation is valuable and should be continued. As legal tools go, this is one of the best we are likely to see for some time to come. Indeed, that is probably the most important point: in the new politics of immigration, even the very best and most innovative rights-based advocacy has sharp limits. The Migrant Workers Convention makes this crystal clear.

Luckily (or profoundly unluckily) legal protections for migrants are often so weak that rights-based arguments can be very useful despite their sharp limits. Furthermore, clever and courageous lawyers and judges have deployed legal doctrines other than human rights in pursuit of better outcomes for migrants. Some examples that come to mind here are rule of law arguments in English

courts on behalf of destitute asylum seekers, habeas corpus and other administrative law remedies that had some success in Australia, and some features of
the litigation trail emanating from Guantanamo Bay.[17] What is more, one of
the most optimistic features of the law is its hermeneutic nature: interpretations can change. In addition to the immediate potential of any new rights
protections (like those of the Migrant Workers Convention) there is the
potential that five or ten or fifty years from now, lawyers and judges will be
able to invest existing rights with different meanings. This is hardly satisfying
to anyone standing before a court in 2015, but in the long game of migrant
advocacy, it is a source of some distant optimism.

Understanding the new politics of immigration helps in the quest to
understand how human rights arguments are currently positioned. We have
long been able to observe that human rights for migrants do not seem able to
accomplish much. Even when rights protections exist, such as labor law
provisions that protect migrant workers, they are often not used because of
other problems that are familiar to the law: lack of resources, fear of repercus-
sions, jurisdictional problems, or a simple inability to stay in the country to see
a complaint through. All of these problems are exacerbated by the pressures of
the new politics, which ensure that rights to remain are increasingly temporary
and better enforced, that an economic logic prevails which subtracts the
"human" and thus "human rights" elements, and that policies change rapidly
and thus potential rights protections are often short-lived. Migrants are less
likely than ever before to be seen as members of the community, and the
bundle of "citizen-like" rights to which they are entitled is diminished. These
features of the new politics are snugly embedded in the old politics of
immigration regulation – the key feature of which is that when the talk turns
to rights, the state's right to enforce its borders is the strongest of all rights. The
ultimate trump.

NAMING A NEW POLITICS

The most important reason for naming this politics as "new" and detailing its
contours and consequences is to begin to grapple with this contemporary
framework for immigration law and policy. Accepting and then analyzing
the new parameters has been difficult to achieve and is, by now, overdue.

The resistance to embracing this new framework comes from its ugliness
and its inconvenience. For politicians and policy leaders who are at the
forefront of this shift in values, there is a sleight-of-hand maneuver at play.
Even as these actors implement the consequences of the new politics, the
older, kinder image of immigration does them good service in two ways. First,

the settler society paradigm tied immigration closely to national identity as well as political sovereignty; this remains vitally important and provides a continuing justification for much contemporary activity. Second, the older picture of successful immigration yields a now impossible immigrant ideal, which is politically valuable because it fuels the persistent narrative that today's immigrants are failing. Centering sovereignty and the idea that contemporary migrants are somehow not as good, or as successful, as their predecessors, are both vital to current politics. Both ideas are supported by adherence to an outdated vision.

On the advocacy side, the reason to embrace the settler society ideal is that it offers a so much more promising account of the value of immigration and the humanity of immigrants than does the new politics. In the pursuit of better outcomes and better protections for immigrants, the old story is better than the new, and seeking to continue its relevance and resonances makes sense.

The problem, however, is that immigration politics is now stuck. Something new has supplanted the old ideas, but the new politics is both unappealing and misunderstood, sometimes deliberately. The most compelling evidence of this predicament is the almost complete failure of policy innovation, even as advocates, migrants, and states recognize new ideas are desperately needed. The clearest example of this policy paralysis is the massive effort of the Global Commission on International Migration.

The Global Commission on International Migration was tooled for innovation. Launched in 2003 by then Secretary General of the United Nations Kofi Annan, it was the largest ever effort to confront migration as a truly international issue. Not since the early twentieth century had there been such an extensive effort to tackle migration on the international plane. Kofi Annan had identified migration as a priority issue for the international community in his agenda for strengthening the United Nations. The idea of a global commission was originally championed by Sweden, Switzerland, Brazil, Morocco, and the Philippines – a handful of key states from the South and North – and was eventually guided by a Core Group of States comprised of participants from around the world and led by nineteen Commissioners from leadership positions in government and international organizations. The Commission was sufficiently well-funded to commission dozens of research reports from scholars all over the world and its explicit mandate was to generate new ideas. The Commission's research directorate both produced analysis and commissioned work from leaders in the field and, deliberately, from junior scholars potentially more likely to promote original ideas. The two-year-long trajectory of work included regional consultations around the globe.[18] This extensive promise was largely unrealized because, among the thirty-three recommendations, there are scarcely any new ideas. This included no new specific suggestions for international-level migration management. Among a series of suggestions that can be summarized as a recommendation to "strengthen existing ideas" there is a smattering of best practice examples, and a suggestion that the international conversation launched by the Commission be continued, but without any specific policy mandate.

What can account for the innovation failure of such a powerful and well-resourced initiative? One might cynically suggest that the interests of powerful states loomed large. But this is, at the very best, a partial answer. In addition to spreading the net of research and analysis far wider than formal governmental players, there was increasing evidence available to the Commission that many states are at least somewhat interested in innovation. Indeed one factor behind the now rapidly shifting policy terrain is state dissatisfaction with the status quo. It is not so much that states are not willing to make changes, but that changes that are politically feasible are near impossible to conceive. The toxic mix that is the new politics of immigration explains this. Immigration policy must these days be generated and implemented in an environment dominated by economic rhetoric, existential fear, a narrow spectrum for debate because of partisan allegiances, heightened public scrutiny, and a marked desire for instant outcomes. The principal tools for addressing the power dynamic created by strong assertions of state power – human rights – have been deeply shaken by the loss of the older, more holistic, and thus "human" vision of migration. It is difficult to design rights to fit "widgets" when the whole weight of new policy rhetoric is aimed at reducing elements of "human"-ity.

Two United Nations High-Level Dialogues on Migration and Development have, in some sense, been follow-ons from the work of the Global Commission. The first was held in 2006 and the second in 2013. The themes of these dialogues have been very similar to those of the Global Commission, focusing strongly on human rights and costs of migration. Two results of the first dialogue were the establishment of the Global Forum on Migration and Development, a state-led dialogue initiative, and of the Global Migration Group, to foster cooperation among international agencies. The second dialogue involved significant outreach to civil society groups but, in the assessment of those groups, "no firm commitments."[19] The high-level dialogues are interesting because they represent the first efforts at the international level since the early twentieth century, when the emergence of the group of settler societies as independent nations spurred dialogue. At this point, it is hard to say, however, whether these initiatives have the potential to shift discourse beyond the constrained parameters of the new politics. They have not yet done so.

The new politics of immigration casts human rights and economics as antagonists. As neither discourse is yielding the results its advocates seek, the tendency is to ratchet up the demands. This posturing contributes strongly to the current policy paralysis as economic values are seen to undermine human rights arguments and vice versa. There is no space at present for the necessary conclusion that neither economic rationale nor human rights arguments can move us beyond the impasse of the new politics. The ideas that formerly anchored long-term state aspirations in this area – settlement, integration, and multiculturalism – have disappeared. Without taking all of this into account, it is impossible to generate new ideas. Taking all of this into account requires confronting new ideas that are sobering or pessimistic.

Notes

1. A points system operates by scoring potential immigrants according to a fixed scale on the basis of a list of criteria that the state determines in advance to be of interest or value to it. Typically points are awarded for factors such as education, work experience, and language skills. There is no limit to how a points system can be constructed. Additional factors such as age, previous experience in a country, education in the host country, whether one has a partner who is similarly educated or experienced, or whether one has family members in the host state, are all ideas that have been used. Accordingly, any points system enshrines a particular set of values. In this sense it is not neutral, but it has a strong air of neutrality.

2. See Neli Esipova, Julie Ray, and Anita Pugliese, *Gallup World Poll: The Many Faces of Global Migration* (Geneva: IOM Migration Research Series, 2011), online: International Organization for Migration publications.iom.int/bookstore/free/MRS43.pdf.

3. See John Armstrong, "Resurgent Peters Out to Rally the Regions," *The New Zealand Herald* (April 4, 2015), online: <www.nzherald.co.nz/nz/news/article.cfm?c_id=1&objectid=11427538>; Richard Bedford, "New Zealand: The Politicization of Immigration" (January 1, 2003), online: Migration Policy Institute www.migrationpolicy.org/article/new-zeal and-politicization-immigration; Simon Collins, "Tighten Visa Control, Says OECD Report," *The New Zealand Herald* (July 10, 2014), online: www.nzherald.co.nz/business/news/article.cfm?c_id=3& objectid=11290777; Shabnam Dastgheib, "A Simmering Melting Pot," *The Sunday Star-Times* (April 12, 2015) A12, online: www.pressreader .com/new-zealand/sunday-star-times/20150412/282746290289856/TextView; Isaac Davidson, "Fast Visas and Longer Job Stays for Chinese," *The*

New Zealand Herald (November 22, 2014), online: www.nzherald.co
.nz/nz/news/article.cfm?c_id=1&objectid=11362683; Patrice Dougan,
"Religious Affiliation Fades as New Zealand Bucks Trend,"
The New Zealand Herald (April 10, 2015), online: www.nzherald.co
.nz/nz/news/article.cfm?c_id=1&objectid=11430295; Brian Fallow,
"Kiwis Quitting Australia Fuel Immigration Surge," *The New
Zealand Herald* (July 22, 2014), online: www.nzherald.co.nz/busi
ness/news/article.cfm?c_id=3&objectid=11296969; David Fisher,
"David Fisher: The Kim Dotcom Wrecking Ball Rolls On," *The
New Zealand Herald* (July 25, 2015), online: www.nzherald.co.nz/nz/
news/article.cfm?c_id=1&objectid=11299179; Brian Gaynor, "Brian
Gaynor: Record Migration Population Game-Changer," *The New
Zealand Herald* (February 7, 2015), online: www.nzherald.co.nz/busi
ness/news/article.cfm?c_id=3&objectid=11397805; Kim Gillespie,
"Editorial: Spy Claims – More Needed from Both Sides," *Rotorua
Daily Post* (September 17, 2014): online: www.nzherald.co.nz/rotorua-
daily-post/opinion/news/article.cfm?c_id=1503435&objectid=11326285;
Angela Gregory, "Migrants Quitting NZ in Bigger Numbers," *The New
Zealand Herald* (June 22, 2006); Bernard Hickey, "Bernard
Hickey: Budget Buries Migration Bomb," *The New Zealand
Herald* (May 18, 2014), online: www.nzherald.co.nz/business/news/article
.cfm?c_id=3&objectid=11256878; "Migration Hits New Record in
February," *The New Zealand Herald* (March 20, 2015), online: www
.nzherald.co.nz/business/news/article.cfm?c_id=3&objectid=11420424;
"Rapper Tyler, the Creator Pens Song about NZ Ban," *The New
Zealand Herald* (April 14, 2015), online: www.nzherald.co.nz/enter
tainment/news/article.cfm?c_id=1501119&objectid=1143255; Lincoln
Tan, "Asian Auckland: How Our City Has Changed – Explore
Our Interactive," *The New Zealand Herald* (March 10, 2015),
online: www.nzherald.co.nz/nz/news/article.cfm?c_id=1&objec
tid=11414457; Lincoln Tan, "Immigration Policies on Debate
Agenda," *The New Zealand Herald* (August 29, 2014), online: www.nzher
ald.co.nz/nz/news/article.cfm?c_id=1&objectid=11316011; Lincoln Tan,
"Inside Auckland's Fake-Monk Scam: Beggars Recruited in
China," *The New Zealand Herald* (January 20, 2015), online www.nzher
ald.co.nz/nz/news/article.cfm?c_id=1&objectid=11388879; John Weekes,
"NZ's First Human Trafficking Trial," NZME (November 27, 2014),
online: www.nzherald.co.nz/nz/news/article.cfm?c_id=1&objec
tid=11365531; "Winston Peters Criticises Foreign Student Numbers,"
NZME (January 27, 2015), online: www.nzherald.co.nz/nz/news/arti
cle.cfm?c_id=1&objectid=11392652; "Woman Jailed over Immigration
Offences," *The New Zealand Herald* (April 14, 2015), online: www
.nzherald.co.nz/nz/news/article.cfm?c_id=1&objectid=11432571.

4. Bill C-51, *Anti-Terrorism Act*, 2015, 2nd Sess, 41st Parl, 2015 (Committee Reporting the Bill with Amendments April 2, 2015); Josephine Engreitz, "European Muslims Face New Challenges Post-Charlie Hebdo," *Cornell Chronicle* (February 18, 2015), online: www.news.cornell.edu/stories/2015/02/european-muslims-face-new-challenges.

5. This has been analyzed from several perspectives, with the common theme that discretion was linked to both the nation-building agenda and the assertion of strong sovereignty. See T. Alexander Aleinikoff, *Semblances of Sovereignty: The Constitution, the State and American Citizenship* (Cambridge, MA: Harvard University Press, 2002); Stephen H. Legmosky, *Immigration and the Judiciary: Law and Politics in Britain and America* (Oxford: Oxford University Press, 1987); Catherine Dauvergne, *Humanitarianism, Identity, and Nation* (Vancouver: UBC Press, 2005).

6. *Migration Act 1958* (Cth), s 36; *Immigration and Refugee Protection Act*, SC 2001, c 27, s 25.

7. Juliet P. Stumpf, "The Crimmigration Crisis: Immigrants, Crime, and Sovereign Power" (2006) 56:2 *Am U L Rev* 367; Juliet P. Stumpf, "Doing Time: Crimmigration Law and the Perils of Haste" (2011) 58:6 *UCLA L Rev* 1705. See also Daniel Kanstroom, *Deportation Nation: Outsiders in American History* (Cambridge, MA: Harvard University Press, 2010); Antje Ellermann, *States Against Migrants: Deportation in Germany and the United States* (Cambridge: Cambridge University Press, 2009).

8. *Faster Removal of Foreign Criminals Act*, SC 2013, c 16. Regarding the United States, see Marc R. Rosenblum and Kristen McCabe, *Deportation and Discretion: Reviewing the Record and Options for Change* (Washington, DC: Migration Policy Institute, 2014).

9. See Appendix 9 for an overview of deportation statistics.

10. After a series of deaths on Lufthansa flights, NGOs began the very well-publicized 'Deportation Air' campaign (www.noborder.org/archive/www.deportation-class.com/). Lufthansa subsequently withdrew from deportation for a time. See Matthew J. Gibney and Randall Hansen, "Deportation and the Liberal State: the Forcible Return of Asylum Seekers and Unlawful Migrants in Canada, Germany and the United Kingdom" (2003) UNHCR Working Paper No 77.

11. Mary Bosworth, "Deportation, Detention and Foreign-National Prisoners in England and Wales" (2011) 15:5 *Citizenship Studies* 583 at 586. This scandal repeated itself in 2014. See UK, Comptroller & Auditor General, *Managing and Removing Foreign National Offenders* (London: National Audit Office, 2014).

12. Matthew Gibney, "Don't Trust the Government's Citizenship-Stripping Policy" (2 February 2014), *The Conversation* (blog), online: theconversa tion.com/dont-trust-the-governments-citizenship-stripping-policy-22601. For further analysis of these provisions, see Matthew Gibney, "'A Very Transcendental Power': Denaturalisation and the Liberalisation of Citizenship in the United Kingdom" (2013) 61:3 *Political Studies* 637; Matthew Gibney, "Should Citizenship Be Conditional? The Ethics of Denationalization" (2013) 75:3 *J Politics* 646.

13. Mary Bosworth and Katja Franko Aas, *The Borders of Punishment* (Oxford: Oxford University Press, 2014) at viii.

14. A Google Scholar search for articles analyzing immigration-related brain drain shows that among the first 100 most relevant articles, more than 60 percent were published between 1998 and 2006, and only one has been published since 2009.

15. *International Convention on the Protection of the Rights of All Migrant Workers and Members of their Families*, 18 December 1990, 2220 UNTS 3 (entered into force July 1, 2003) [*Migrant Workers Convention*]. Ratification data are reported on the United Nations Treaty Collection website at: treaties.un.org (ratification data reported as of April 17, 2015). The Office of the High Commissioner for Human Rights lists the core international human rights instruments at: www.ohchr.org/EN/Professi onalInterest/Pages/CoreInstruments.aspx. This listing could be contested. In my view, the *Convention Relating to the Status of Refugees*, 28 July 1951, 189 UNTS 150 (entered into force April 22, 1954) is an obvious oversight. For more about the history of the *Migrant Workers Convention*, see Paul de Guchteneire, Antoine Pecoud, and Ryszard Cholewinski, eds., *Migration and Human Rights: the United Nations Convention on Migrant Workers' Rights* (Cambridge: Cambridge University Press, 2009).

16. *Migrant Workers Convention, supra* note 15, art 5.

17. See, for example, *Hamdan v. Rumsfeld*, 548 US 577 (2006); *Hamdi v. Rumsfeld*, 542 US 507 (2004); *Rasul v. Bush*, 542 US 466 (2004).

18. Global Commission on International Migration, *Migration in an Interconnected World: New Directions for Action* (Geneva: Global Commission on International Migration, 2005), online: International Organization for Migration www.iom.int/jahia/webdav/site/myjahiasite/ shared/shared/mainsite/policy_and_research/gcim/GCIM_Report_Com plete.pdf.

19. Global Forum on Migration and Development Civil Society, "Second UN High-Level Dialogue Results in Convergence" (January 23, 2014), online: gfmdcivilsociety.org/second-un-high-level-dialogue-results-in-convergence/. In regard to the high-level dialogues generally, see General Assembly of the United Nations, "High-Level

Meetings of the 68th Session of the General Assembly" (October 3–4, 2013), online: www.un.org/en/ga/68/meetings/migration/about.shtml; United Nations Department of Economic and Social Affairs, Population Division, "High-Level Dialogue on International Migration and Development" (September 14–15, 2013), online: www .un.org/esa/population/migration/hld/.

10

Imagining immigration without a past – stories for the future

The challenge of identifying the contours and consequences of the new politics of immigration is to use this diagnosis to say something about the future. This trajectory is typical of what we might call the narrative arc of academic non-fiction: identify the problem, at some considerable length, and then outline a solution, often frustratingly briefly. The momentum of the concluding movement impels one toward the view that there must surely be a way out of this dilemma, the possibility of a resolution.

There is almost nothing about contemporary migration politics, however, that suggests optimism. Furthermore, over the past twenty years, the reasons for pessimism have multiplied. There are millions and millions of people who want, or need, or have a right to, a better place to live. We also are beginning to understand that a considerable number of these people actually see migration as a desirable option in their lives. The prosperous Western states that set the terms for global migration regulation are more powerful than ever, and are taking ever more steps to ensure that their borders are harder and harder to cross. States of the global South are emulating them. The global population is expanding so quickly that migratory pressures mount considerably even when the percentage of people migrating shifts only slightly. The population of the global South far outstrips that of the global North, and thus population growth is centered in precisely the places that people seek to leave rather than enter. There is no moral basis to migration privilege. Prosperous states are desirable migration locations because of their histories, their economies, and their societal structures. But the right to exclude others that these states now possess arises from the power to do so. There is no way to address the biggest of migration questions with a theory of justice, because the origins of the current politics cannot be accounted for within the terms that justice demands.

Given all of this it would be fanciful and naïve to conclude with a few broad brush-stokes gesturing toward some resolution – however difficult to achieve – of a world where the politics of immigration are less mean-spirited and despondent. One conclusion from the emergence of this new politics is that things could certainly get worse. Or, rather, that if things do not get better the path that we have embarked upon will lead to things becoming worse. Equilibrium is not an option. Stasis is impossible in matters of contemporary migratory flows.

This conclusion, therefore, does two things. It looks forward both optimistically and pessimistically. Optimistically, because the point of any thoroughgoing analysis such as this book is to build the groundwork for something better. Pessimistically, because the new politics of immigration is deeply pessimistic and there is no way at this point to return to the kinder, gentler, settler society era. Traversing this terrain involves outlining what makes human rights arguments about migration succeed or fail; gathering up the glimmers of something different that are hidden within the story of the new politics; assessing the transformative potential for the concept of state sovereignty; and revisiting the human rights–economics dyad. In the end, the pessimistic story is the more persuasive, because the new politics of immigration is so strongly weighted in that direction, and is so resolutely turned to neglecting the lessons that we could draw from the immigration mythology of the past, the stories that made immigration such an inherently optimistic idea during our settler society past.

WHEN HUMAN RIGHTS WORK

Human rights for migrants are puzzling. On the one hand, the whole history of the twentieth century in prosperous Western states can be read as a progress narrative of the robust flourishing of human rights. Increasing waves of inclusion and identity politics have resulted in successive expansions of human rights protections, and the quality of these protections have been strengthened considerably over this time, gaining more legal "teeth" in many national and international settings. The trajectory is certainly, not linear, and with the expansion of rights protections we have become increasingly able to discern the limits and pitfalls of rights. But even in the face of an increasingly sophisticated critique, the progress narrative remains cogent.

For migrants, however, the rights story is more complex. Each of the factors that mark the end of settler societies has an intricate relationship with human rights. The asylum crisis has intensified enormously, while at the same time the underlying legal right to be granted asylum has strengthened, and while the core of refugee law has come to rely increasingly on human rights principles. Human rights in the asylum setting spur on state resistance to asylum, because they are stronger, and more law-like, than ever before. In confronting the fear of fundamental Islam, human rights have been the basis for some important legal victories, but have also been the principal tool for papering over the unintelligibility with which the West encounters Islam, and have been an integral part of Western states' willingness to accept more openly than ever before the illiberalism of their immigration laws. In the demise of multiculturalism, human rights reveal their limits in addressing the needs of both "groups" and "culture." In this setting rights are both inadequate and plainly not to the point: in the national arena that is the setting for multi-culturalism, citizenship rights are the endgame. All of this has occurred at the same time as the international community has reached the limit of its will-ingness to fashion and accept new rights for migrants. The Convention on the Rights of All Migrant Workers and Their Families has stalled quite dramati-cally, and initiatives surrounding ideas such as rights for internally displaced persons or those displaced by climate degradation have failed to get off the ground.

This is not to say that rights arguments are not useful for migrants. In a policy domain that is increasingly legalized, rights are indispensable tools. They are the language of the law. This tells us two important things. First, that the politics of immigration is so dire these days that the limitations of rights arguments are not especially relevant. There is much to be gained in rights terms, even if rights arguments are not well-positioned to deliver a robust version of equality or inclusion. The situation of temporary migrant workers is an excellent example of this. Second, the rights dilemma points us in the direction of the limits of the law. Because this policy domain is now dominated by law, it is difficult or impossible to find solutions that are not legalistic. Law has a binary structure; it draws bright lines such as the line between "us" and "them" that motives migration regulation. It is woefully bad at nuance. This problem cannot be sheeted home to law – it cannot be other than what it is – but it must be tallied up somehow, somewhere. Many of the problems of migration derive from the binary thinking about inclusion and exclusion (or South and North, skilled and unskilled, deserving and undeserving ... the list could go on) that instantiates the contemporary politics. Legal solutions will simply not help to shift this. Furthermore, it is vital to recall that once a migration issue is framed in rights terms, the right of sovereign states to exclude people looms large, even when it is framed as a right to protect their citizens or defend their borders.

Much of the story of the new politics demonstrates when human rights arguments fail. But the challenge of fostering optimism requires looking more closely at the nuance of when rights are succeeding. Asylum is emerging as one of the most valuable human rights protections in the world, and the jurisprudence of asylum has grown with the interpretive reach of human rights. Every effort to strengthen asylum is doubly effective because it leverages the very best of human rights. The overlap of citizenship rights and human rights is also important and instructive. The capacity for immigrants to naturalize and to engage in the political process is extraordinarily meaningful. Working to protect and, against the odds, expand naturalization and to encourage those who can naturalize to do so, remain a key advocacy terrain. This is even important in the European Union, where the fight ought also to include resistance against the hollowing out of the very idea of citizenship that has come with changing citizenship into a migration right. (To repeat: migration rights are not strong.) Finally, there is increasing evidence that while rights for "migrant" workers have stalled, labor rights have some considerable potential. Progress has been made by labor unions embracing both "regular" and "irregular" migrant workers.

It is instructive that human rights arguments on behalf of migrants have been more successful in the Old World than in the former settler societies. One reason for this is the influence of Europe-wide, binding human rights standards. The role of not-quite-international legal standards has had some genuine influence in matters of migration, both within asylum law and beyond. This is genuinely instructive because it reveals the potential that comes from injecting something other than the state into the "states versus migrants" standoff that rights discourses provoke. That is, once one enters the terrain of rights discourses, the state's right to exclude becomes constructed as a trump. The influence of European law, both its Convention on Human Rights and the capacity of the Court of Justice of the European Union to enforce pan-European standards related to asylum and migration harmonization, has added something new and important to the terrain. European states have moved faster and farther in terms of family reunion rights for migrants, and in terms of protections against indefinite detention and deportation to face torture. These shifts are all related to European law. This signals the potential for other international legal developments, and also shows why states resist them so strongly and will inevitably continue to do so.

But there is probably something more to the story as well. The former settler societies have been slower than the Old World sending nations to conceptualize issues such as forced marriage in human rights terms (for better *and* worse), and this turn has had nothing to do with legal capacity at the

European level. European nations led the turn away from multiculturalism, including the extent to which this turn focuses more squarely on individual rather than group rights. These shifts, and their human rights effects, have more to do with differences in how migration and the difference it brings "home" are conceptualized within individual nations. Here it would be fair to conclude the European states have been leaders in re-imagining immigration. Part of this re-imagination may offer some basis for human rights optimism. But it is a long and circuitous road.

One of the most important avenues for optimism in terms of human rights is that the law is hermeneutic and thus unpredictable. Even if human rights arguments have often been unsuccessful for non-citizens, the possibility of a significant legal victory at some time in the future is at each moment embedded within the law. The existence of rights arguments is important for the future because of this potentiality. Despite law's dominant conservatism, its interpretive methodology means that it does evolve. Law's conservatism is dominant, not exclusive. Furthermore, the optimism here is genuine. This is largely because outside the realm of asylum, human rights have not done terribly much for migrants up to this point. This means that the ever-possible unpredictability of the law does not present much risk because there is little to be lost here. Everything is to be gained.

Alongside the legal space they occupy, human rights also occupy a political space. In the new politics of immigration, human rights are currently less robust, even, than in the binary "win or lose" context of the courts. Everything about contemporary politics leaves very little rhetorical space for thinking of migrants as holders of robust human rights entitlements. Even in terms of asylum, where the law is increasingly firm and where the human rights needs are stark, politics are hostile. This hostility amounts to a failure to imagine migrants as truly, fully "human." In legal terms, the "rights" part of human rights predominates, but in political discourses, it is the "humanity" that matters. The subtle reconceptualization of immigrants – who they are and what they do – which has accompanied the end of settler societies is damaging to our capacities to see migrants as human. Figuring out how to counter this, and to tell new stories for the new era, has to be part of any advocacy strategy that builds on the lessons of the new politics.

THE ECONOMICS–HUMAN RIGHTS DYAD

It is easy to locate the tension between economics and human rights that is embedded in the new politics of immigration. It is much harder to offer an account of where this dyad originates and whether it can be displaced.

As the settler society fades into the background, no compelling account of states' interests in immigration has emerged that is not economic. The old understanding of immigration offered alternative perspectives, and called on nations to imagine themselves as humanitarian, and as beneficent repositories of culture. These alternatives are no longer compelling. The end of settler societies demonstrates why this is so. Furthermore, the intense and mounting migratory pressures are creating a sense of urgency that narrows options. The only possible way out of this tunnel vision is to foster a new immigration narrative. For obvious reasons, in an increasingly legalized terrain advocates have turned to human rights arguments for resistance on a variety of fronts. But as the discourse about immigration narrows, the odds of these arguments succeeding are reduced. In many ways, these two factors sum up much of what we see in global immigration in the first two decades of the twenty-first century.

The economics–human rights dyad is a principal source of policy gridlock because each half of the equation contains a totalizing claim. From an economic (especially a political-rhetorical economic) perspective, it is diffi-cult or impossible to assign human rights of non-members enough "value" for them to matter at all. Like national identity, culture, and humanitarianism, they don't add up. On the human rights side of the equation, economic indicators do not generate any "rights," and it is impossible to conduct a balancing act that puts human rights and life chances on one side and economic value on the other side. These two discourses contribute to the disconnect because they are incommensurate. Countering economic arguments with human rights arguments, and vice versa, will sometimes work for incremental gains, but it cannot shift the terrain. The proverbial "win-win-win" policy analysis of temporary foreign work is illusory because it fails to understand that in the new politics of immigration the foundation stone of both economics and human rights has shifted: the national framework does not operate as it used to, and states clinging to it will not change that. The state no longer controls its own economic destiny, and its rights claims are stronger than those of any individuals. Economics and human rights stand in the new politics of immigration as a rock and a hard place.

The pessimistic version of this conclusion must certainly be that there is nothing on the near horizon that is poised to alter this positioning. Every incremental change of the past decade, especially in the former settler socie-ties, has been about trying to get more economic value out of immigration programs, both permanent and temporary. Every rights victory has been partial, and has come at a cost. A future trajectory that fails to alter this standoff will lead to a sharper economic-political calculus that limits options for immigrants, fosters narrow definitions of "skilling," and fails to perceive non-economic actors as migrants in any way. On the human rights side of the coin, the pessimistic – and likely – trajectory is that some rights victories will emerge in courts, from time to time, but that each victory is likely to provoke a political retrenchment of some sort. As a result, while some migrants will "win," the predictable state response will be to curtail the number of people that benefits from each win. As long as state "rights" are stronger than "human" rights, this vicious circle is a near certainty.

The optimistic version of this conclusion has to pursue dislodging this dyad. Vitally, the dyad depends on a strong and old-fashioned understanding of both state sovereignty and economics. One way out of the dilemma, therefore, is to pursue the argument that these old understandings are no longer accurate. Economies are no longer nationally bounded in any meaningful way. A shift in the global price of oil, or in Chinese production rates, may have as much effect on Western industrialized economies as any national policy adjustment. The idea that state rights ought to trump human rights is out of step with the theoretical underpinnings of the human rights revolution, and therefore must eventually fall away. Neither of these arguments is new. Migration advocates, and others, have been pursuing them for decades. Progress is slow. Or non-existent. There are two reasons for this. The first is that state sovereignty is a remarkably powerful anchor for the international system, and political power is concentrated and organized at the national level. The second reason is that both of these arguments remain focused on the economics–human rights dyad that they are posited against.

Moving forward more optimistically would require a concerted effort addressing both of these factors. Organizing and advocating in ways that decenter the state is vital to shifting migration politics. Efforts at the civil society level, as well as at the international level, are important to pursue. Fully decentering the human rights and economics dyad has, however, even more potential. Strategies that delink or bypass these concepts are crucial. It is here that we enter the terrain of re-imagining immigration, by concluding that the path to optimism lies in arguments that deploy rhetorical tools other than economics and human rights. What might this look like? It must include valuing immigration for reasons that are not economic, and advocating on the basis of reasons that are not rights. This is, in fact, how immigration was conceptualized in the nation-building stage of the settler society era. Immigration provided community, culture, and identity, in addition to labor. People migrated because of need, or family, or adventure, or simply in search of a better life – an idea that was never solely economic. The older story was much more robust. A return to the past is not possible, the end of settler societies ensures that, but any future optimism has to include similarly robust stories that look toward the future.

What fragments are visible in the new politics of immigration that contain some glimmer of optimistic possibility for changing the future trajectory? Or, casting the question a different way, what is visible on the horizon that does not fit squarely into the human rights–economics dyad and the ensuing policy paralysis, and how might the awkward fits be jostled and irritated in order to spring them loose completely? These are difficult questions, but well worth risking an answer.

One glimmer might be found in the trend toward legalization and, especially, crimmigration. To recapitulate for a moment, crimmigration is the term Juliet Stumpf coined as a label for seepage into immigration law of criminal law trends and doctrines. It is a firm feature of the new politics, and Stumpf's analysis highlights how crimmigration draws on membership theory and its strong account of exclusion based on a "lack of desert." "Crimmigration" was coined to explain the myriad negative effects that are driving up detention and deportation rates, and fostering the view that immigrants are tinged with criminality. Despite all of this, there is a tiny sliver of potential embedded in the closer relationship with criminal law. Criminal law is the classic terrain where the individual is pitted against the state, and where liberty itself is at risk. Against this setting, strong protections for the individual have developed within both common law and civil law traditions, from the *Magna Carta* onward. Crimmigration brings this strong tradition into proximity with immigration law, and raises the possibility that some of the best of criminal law will also seep into the immigration realm.

A clear example of how this might work is the 2015 Canadian constitutional challenge to the existing human smuggling law. The main concern with the law as written from a migrant advocate's point of view is its intersection with asylum. Under the very broad existing provisions, anyone helping someone to enter the country without permission faces significant criminal penalties. The law has been used to exclude people from refugee protection on the basis that they had assisted others on boats crossing the Pacific by giving out medicines, working in the kitchen, or repairing the engines after crew members had abandoned the voyage. It has also been used, of course, to charge individuals who organized such voyages and collected thousands of dollars, or more, from every migrant on board. The case that reached the Supreme Court in 2015 brought together the constitutional arguments made by a number of refugee claimants who had been excluded, as well as the criminal case against the four individuals who had been criminally charged as ringleaders for one boat. Of the five cases that were joined, the only one where the constitutional argument had been successful in any of the courts below, was the criminal matter. That is, the case involving the least sympathetic individuals. This success was possible because of the distinct way that the issue was framed in a court concerned with criminality and with rights protections in that context. This became the basis for a more robust evidentiary record, and for distinct and novel legal reasoning, to be put before the Supreme Court of Canada. As this book goes to press, that Court is still considering the matter.[1]

Another interesting fragment to pursue is contained within European Union citizenship. As is the case with crimmigration, there are many downsides that arise from hollowing out the concept of citizenship in this way and turning it into an immigration category. The glimmer of possibility comes from the way that European Union citizenship brings with it voting rights at the local level. This right in and of itself is unlikely to alter many electoral outcomes, and was undoubtedly initially included because it appears utterly unthreatening. But it has the provocative effect of bypassing the national level, and of attaching immigrants directly to the communities where they live. The imperative to bypass the nation is vital to dislodging the new politics of immigration. It is important not to overstate what is happening here. Nothing subversive of national policy has yet taken place. But there is an untapped potential in the idea of meaningful political participation, especially for non-nationals, being wrested away from the nation-state arena. If we are to truly think beyond the state, we must look below it as well as above and beside. Cities are vitally important in global migration patterns; often more so than nations themselves – save for the fact that it is nations that set the rules. Thus migration reality fits well with a turn to political engagement at the local level.

We can locate another glimmer in the evolving role of the massive "illegal" population of the United States. In this case, it is almost as if the sheer enormity of the numbers involved is initiating some transformations. One part of this narrative is, just like in the EU, that local variations are important. Some states, such as California, have begun granting drivers' licenses in the absence of formal migration status, as an alternative to having hundreds of thousands of unlicensed drivers on the road.[2] But the local is not always better for migrants. The recent raft of Arizona anti-immigrant legislation is good evidence of how smaller-scale decision making can also be negative, and a powerful reminder that a move away from the national level is not a guarantee of any particular outcome. What is truly most interesting about migration in the contemporary United States is that the size of the illegal population has fostered a discourse about legitimacy that extends beyond the narrow binary of whether or not one has migration status. DREAM Act activists reveal this discourse, as does the idea of the DREAM legislation itself because it aims deliberately to look beyond, behind, the "legal–illegal" binary, and it enshrines a vision of membership and belonging that defies these categorizations. It is also in the United States that the labor movement has come full circle in its approach to undocumented labor, and where some significant advances have been made for illegal laborer inclusion through the work of the unions.

In a different vein, it is instructive to consider the evolving conversation surrounding "climate refugees." Early this century, environmental scientists demonstrated conclusively that people would be displaced by climate degradation, including displacements that will arise because, within my lifetime, rising sea levels will submerge some sovereign states. Initially, this information was met with calls to accommodate these individuals within refugee law. Most analysts and advocates have now moved on from this idea because climate-displaced people do not fit the refugee law framework, and, for all the reasons that the asylum crisis has become permanent, that framework is too fragile to risk changing. But the reality of people being displaced remains. Two things are obvious: places such as Kiribati are going to disappear by the middle of this century; and, as an international community, we are not going to allow the people living in these states to simply perish. There will be a resolution. The open questions are what will it be, and how will it be achieved. In this scenario, legal innovation is inevitable. The rejection of refugee law as a potential solution to climate displacement has ensured that these displacements will lead to other forms of legal innovation. It may well be that the innovations will not emerge until the very last moment, but they are coming nonetheless. Under the umbrella of the Nansen Initiative, states of the global North are working toward change. In the South Pacific itself, some states are negotiating bilateral migration plans.[3]

What these glimmers of something different have in common is that they can each be read, in part, as an unintended consequence. Each of these possible new avenues for innovation has arisen in spite of state policies. Most have arisen in the absence of high-level consultations or international efforts. The potentiality of criminal law emerges at the core of a very damaging trend; the promise of local voting was initially envisioned as having little impact. In the case of responses to the illegal population of the United States, or to climate-displaced persons, responses are being generated because the reality of the situation has, finally, grown to the extent that it penetrates the prevailing discursive framework that would deny its very existence. In other words, it tells a new story.

Any optimistic conclusion must draw on these new stories.

There are other fragments that can be shored up against the oppressive weight of the new politics. Some of these I have mentioned earlier in the book. For example, the UN's High-Level Dialogues on International Migration and Development are an innovation to pay close attention to. As of yet, they have not succeeded in shifting policy paralysis, but they are new, in form and process, and have begun to move beyond the aftermath of the Global Commission on International Migration from which they emerged. Also, the prominence of legalization in the new politics of immigration contains with it the transformative potential of the law. This is often unrealized, but always worth fostering because of the immense power of the law as a social ordering mechanism. Because law is endlessly reinterpreted and reapplied, it is perpetually possible that instruments such as the Migrant Workers Convention will be deeply transformed at some unforeseeable future point. For all of these more predictable avenues of migrant advocacy, understanding the new politics and striving to dislodge it with counter narrative are indispensable tools.

FOSTERING FUTURE UNCERTAINTY

The most likely future directions of the new politics of immigration are negative ones. Simply repeating, and ratcheting up, existing policies cannot address the deeply embedded dilemmas of contemporary migration. In the final weeks of drafting this manuscript, the boat arrivals crisis surrounding Lampedusa hit yet another new low, with hundreds more lives lost and a death rate higher than any previous year. One of the responses suggested in the early days following this renewal of crisis was that the EU mount a military operation aimed at stopping the boats.[4] A clearer expression of the new politics is hardly imaginable: bar asylum at all costs; spare no expense; border integrity is somehow portrayed as a solution to a humanitarian catastrophe. While these events were unfolding in the Mediterranean, Thailand and Malaysia made global headlines by denying landing rights to migrants adrift in the Bay of Bengal. Both states eventually relented, after two weeks of constant media attention. Neither has the global heft of the EU. In the midst of both these crises, the Australian Minister of Immigration and Border Protection announced that he would like to pursue legislation to give Australia the same citizenship-stripping powers that Canada and the United Kingdom have arrogated to themselves.[5]

The new mean-spirited politics of immigration will generate endless variations on these stories unless or until some of their core components change.

My principal objective in this book has been to demonstrate how and why this is so. Changing the core components of this politics is enormously difficult. The contemporary politics of immigration is deeply entrenched. It has lost the connections to the past that made immigration discourses more robust and varied. More optimistic. And the absence of the past turns the future into tunnel vision. Astonishingly, the straightforward notion of telling better stories, of addressing immigration at a conceptual, even imaginary, plane is vital to disrupting the route forward that is presently visible.

How we imagine immigration affects how we regulate it, measure it, and theorize it, and how we relate to migrants themselves. The idea of a settler society depended upon a particular vision of migration that became the world's vision, the underlying logic of immigration. The changes to our political landscape at the outset of the twenty-first century make it impossible to return to a previous time when immigration, and immigrants themselves, fit these patterns. The current politics is propelled forward by ignoring the past, and by willful blindness about how migration used to make sense.

It is time to begin a new narrative of migration. This new narrative will have elements of human rights and economics, but if it is to make inroads into the present mess, it must go well beyond this. A very different human rights story would emerge, for example, if the starting point were that people have rights and states do not. That is, from emphasizing the "human" element of the phrase, rather than the rights. From such a perspective, one might ask how a temporary foreign worker program could be designed to ensure that workers will be able to return home by making coming back and forth straightforward, making family reunification seamless, and by ensuring taxation rules foster movement. In the realm of asylum, one could dramatically turn the tables by shifting the positions of asylum and resettlement. If it were realistic for millions of people to be resettled by prosperous Western states every year, millions fewer would be on boats in the Mediterranean, the Bay of Bengal, or the Gulf of Aden. If we were to begin by a deep understanding that cultural difference takes us, inevitably, to the threshold of unintelligibility and even beyond, we could begin to return to a rich account of multiculturalism that moves beyond liberal diversity.

There is no straightforward path toward any of these objectives. The worst of the new politics of immigration is that we are not yet even able to fully imagine how the world could be differently ordered. This is surely the first order of business – to launch into the enterprise of uncertainty, aiming to disrupt what is otherwise a desperate trajectory. Hoping to discover among the fragments of unintended consequences opportunities and imperatives that will alter the route.

Notes

1. *Francis Anthonimuthu Appulonappa et al.* v. *Her Majesty the Queen et al.*, 2014 BCCA 163, leave to appeal to SCC granted, 35958 (October 9, 2014); *B010* v. *Minister of Citizenship and Immigration*, 2013 FCA 87, leave to appeal to SCC granted, 35388 (July 17, 2014); *JP et al.* v. *Minister of Public Safety and Emergency Preparedness*, 2013 FCA 262, leave to appeal to SCC granted, 35688 (April 17, 2014); *B306* v. *Minister of Public Safety and Emergency Preparedness*, 2013 FCA 262, leave to appeal to SCC granted, 35685 (April 17, 2014); *Jesus Rodriquez Hernandez* v. *Minister of Public Safety and Emergency Preparedness*, 2013 FCA 262, leave to appeal to SCC granted, 35677 (April 17, 2014). The Supreme Court of Canada heard these five cases together on February 16–17, 2015, with judgment reserved at the time of copy-editing. On November 27,2015, the SCC handed down its ruling: a victory for humanitarian advocates.

2. In California, an Assembly Bill (AB 60) was passed obligating the DMV to issue a driver's license to any applicant unable to provide proof of legal status in the United States but otherwise able to meet all the other requirements for a license. This program was implemented in January 2015. See: http://apps.dmv.ca.gov/ab60/index.html.

3. For a thoughtful discussion of the environmental refugee debate, see Jane McAdam's work in Jane McAdam, *Climate Change, Forced Migration, and International Law* (Oxford: Oxford University Press, 2012); Jane McAdam, ed., *Climate Change and Displacement: Multidisciplinary Perspectives* (Oxford: Hart, 2010). For a thorough overview of the current international law that can potentially address this situation, see Kerstin Walter, *Mind the Gap: Exposing the Protection Gaps in International Law for Environmentally Displaced Citizens of Small Island States* (LLM Thesis, University of British Columbia Faculty of Law, 2012).

4. See Bernd Riegert, "EU to Take Military Action against Human Traffickers," *Deutsche Welle* (May 19, 2015), online: www.dw.de/eu-to-take-military-action-against-human-traffickers/a-18462321; Ian Traynor, "EU Draws Up Plans for Military Attacks on Libya to Stop Migrant Boats," *The Guardian* (May 10, 2015), online: www.theguardian.com/world/2015/may/10/eu-considers-military-attacks-on-targets-in-libya-to-stop-migrant-boats. See the Preface regarding developments later in 2015.

5. See "Australia to Strip Citizenship of Australian-Born Jihadis with Immigrant Parents," *CBC News* (May 21, 2015), online: www.cbc.ca/news/world/australia-to-strip-citizenship-of-australian-born-jihadis-with-immigrant-parents-1.3081688.

Census questions about ethnicity

Canada	The 2011 NHS ethnic origin question asked: "What were the ethnic or cultural origins of this person's ancestors?"	Provided 28 examples: Canadian, English, French, Chinese, East Indian, Italian, German, Scottish, Irish, Cree, Mi'kmaq, Salish, Métis, Inuit, Filipino, Dutch, Ukrainian, Polish, Portuguese, Greek, Korean, Vietnamese, Jamaican, Jewish, Lebanese, Salvadorean, Somali, and Colombian
United States	The 2010 Census form asked two questions about race and ethnicity. First, people were asked whether they are of Hispanic, Latino, or Spanish origin. Then they were asked to choose one or more of 15 options that make up five race categories – white, black, American Indian/Alaska Native, Asian, or Native Hawaiian/Other Pacific Islander.	Provided the following examples: White Black American Indian or Alaska Native Asian Indian Chinese Filipino Other Asian Japanese Korean Vietnamese Native Hawaiian Guamanian Samoan Other Pacific Islander Some other Race
New Zealand	Ethnicity is the ethnic group or groups a person identifies with or has a sense of belonging to. It is a measure of cultural affiliation (in contrast to race,	European Maori Pacific Peoples Asian

(continued)

	ancestry, nationality, or citizenship). Ethnicity is self-perceived and a person can belong to more than one ethnic group.	Middle Eastern/Latin American/ African (several sub-groups included) Other Ethnicity
Australia	What is the Person's ancestry? (provide 2 maximum) Options are:	English Irish Italian German Chinese Scottish Australian Other (examples: Greek, Vietnamese, Hmong, Dutch, Kurdish, Maori, Lebanese, South Sea Islander)

Refugee resettlement

UNHCR resettlement departures 2009–2013

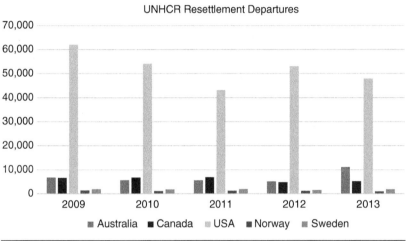

UNHCR Resettlement Departures

Australia ■ Canada ▨ USA ■ Norway ▨ Sweden

	2009	2010	2011	2012	2013
Austral.	6,720	5,636	5,597	5,079	11,117
Canada	6,582	6,706	6,827	4,755	5,140
NZ	675	535	477	719	682
USA	62,011	54,077	43,215	53,053	47,875
UK**	969	695	424	989	750
Norway	1,367	1,088	1,258	1,137	941
Sweden	1,880	1,789	1,896	1,483	1,832
Germany*	2,064	457	22	323	1,092

Source: UNHCR, *UNHCR Global Resettlement Statistical Report 2013* (Geneva: UNHCR, 2015) at 61, online: www.unhcr.org/52693bd09.html.
* Started accepting cases through the Humanitarian Admission Programme (HAP) since 2013.
** Started accepting cases through the Humanitarian Admission Programme (HAP) since 2014.

Information about asylum seeking

Asylum applications

Country	Applications 1980	Applications 1990	Applications 2000	Applications 2010	Applications 2013
USA	26,512	73,637	91,595	42,971	68,135
Germany	107,818	193,063	117,648	48,589	126,907
Canada	1,000	36,735	n/a	22,543	10,299
United Kingdom	2,352	26,205	128,425	40,536	38,593
Netherlands	1,350	21,208	43,895	15,148	17,040
France	19,912	54,813	20,124	80,207	100,682
Switzerland	3,020	35,836	32,434	15,567	27,875
Sweden	n/a	29,420	16,303	45,114	68,739
Australia	n/a	12,128	19,579	10,955	15,821

Source:
1980, 1990:
UNHCR, *UNHCR Asylum Applications in Industrialized Countries: 1980–1999*
(Geneva: UNHCR, 2001) at Table I.1 for 1980, Table III.1 for 1990,
online: www.unhcr.org/3c3eb4of4.pdf.
2000, 2010, 2013:
UNHCR, *UNHCR Statistical Online Population Database*, online: www.unhcr.org/pages/4a013
eb06.html.
2014 figures were 45% higher overall, and were released after this manuscript was substantially
completed.

Refugee population by country of asylum

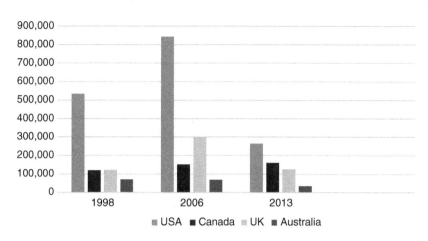

	1996	1997	1998	2004	2005	2006	2011	2012	2013
USA	607,024	563,837	533,969	420,854	379,340	843,498	264,763	262,023	263,662
Canada	138,435	125,184	119,371	141,398	147,171	151,827	164,883	163,758	160,349
UK	98,577	107,933	121,716	298,844	303,181	301,556	193,510	149,799	126,055
Austral.	67,313	66,074	69,745	63,476	64,984	68,948	23,434	30,083	34,503
NZ	3,788	3,646	4,097	5,350	5,307	4,906	1,934	1,517	1,403

Source:
UNHCR, *UNHCR Statistical Online Population Database*, online: www.unhcr.org/pages/4a013
cb06.html.
   Notes from the UNCHR concerning the data (UNHCR Statistical Online Population
Database: Sources, Methods and Data Considerations, online: www.unhcr.org/45c06c662.html):
In UNHCR statistics, refugees include individuals recognized under the 1951 Convention relating to
the Status of Refugees; its 1967 Protocol; the 1969 OAU Convention Governing the Specific Aspects
of Refugee Problems in Africa; those recognized in accordance with the UNHCR Statute;
individuals granted complementary forms of protection; or, those enjoying "temporary protection."
The 2007–2013 refugee population category also includes people in a refugee-like situation, most
of who were previously included in the Others of concern group. This sub-category is descriptive
in nature and includes groups of persons who are outside their country or territory of origin and
who face protection risks similar to those of refugees, but for whom refugee status has, for practical
or other reasons, not been ascertained. . ..
Most industrialized countries lack a refugee register and are thus not in a position to provide
accurate information on the number of refugees residing in their country. Up to and including
2006, to ensure that the refugee population in these countries is reflected in the global statistics, the
number of refugees was estimated by UNHCR based on the arrival of refugees through
resettlement programmes and the individual recognition of refugees over a 10-year (Europe and,
since 2006, the United States) or 5-year (the United States before 2006, Canada and Oceania)
period. Starting with the 2007 data, the cut-off period has been harmonized and now covers a
10-year period for Europe and non-European countries. Resettled refugees, however, are excluded
from the refugee estimates in all countries. . .

Information about Muslim immigration

There are a variety of methods for assembling information about Muslim migration patterns. One method is to consider migration by nationals of predominantly Muslim states, which probably over-counts migration by Muslims. The first set of charts presents this data. The second set of charts, reproduced and/or reassembled from the Pew Research Center's *Future of the Global Muslim Population* report, consider trends looking forward (with similar estimation issues).

International migration flow to Canada for selected countries

	Afghanistan	Iraq	Iran	Indonesia	Pakistan	Bangladesh	Somalia
1996	2010	1839	5833	221	7761	2448	1198
1997	2115	1919	7486	159	11239	2929	946
1998	1583	1395	6775	157	8089	1948	1304
1999	2111	1396	5909	534	9303	1825	1499
2000	2845	1384	5617	1155	14201	2715	1361
2001	3182	1597	5746	930	15354	3,393	988
2002	2971	1365	7889	712	14173	2616	598
2003	3010	969	5651	498	12351	1896	799
2004	2527	1140	6063	509	12793	2374	1172
2005	2908	1316	5502	598	13575	3940	980
2006	2552	977	7073	585	12329	3838	896
2007	2262	1601	6663	624	9545	2735	982
2008	1811	2570	6010	685	8051	2716	750
2009	1507	4567	6064	499	6213	1854	988

(*continued*)

	Afghanistan	Iraq	Iran	Indonesia	Pakistan	Bangladesh	Somalia
2010	1549	4545	6815	731	4986	4364	1194
2011	1978	4698	6840	368	6074	2449	1256
2012	2154	2124	6463	376	9931	2449	1129

Source:
OECD, StatExtracts, *International Migration Database*, online:
stats.oecd.org/Index.aspx?lang=en&SubSessionId=3774ae46-b849-4cfd-a7bc-891d2b485009&the
metreeid=-200.

International migration flow to the United States of America for selected countries

	Afghanistan	Iraq	Iran	Indonesia	Pakistan	Bangladesh	Somalia
1996	..	5479	11084	..	12516	8221	..
1997	1127	3243	9635	905	12959	8680	4004
1998	830	2217	7873	1017	13083	8616	2623
1999	877	3360	7176	1186	13485	6038	1690
2000	1011	5087	8487	1767	14504	7,204	2393
2001	1202	4965	10425	2525	16393	7,152	3007
2002	1759	5174	12960	2418	13694	5483	4535
2003	1252	2450	7230	1805	9415	4616	2444
2004	2137	3494	10434	2419	12086	8061	3929
2005	4749	4077	13887	3924	14926	11487	5829
2006	3417	4337	13947	4868	17418	14644	9462
2007	1753	3765	10460	3716	13492	12074	6251
2008	2813	4795	13852	3606	19719	11753	10745
2009	3165	12110	18553	3679	21555	16651	13390
2010	2017	19855	14182	3032	18258	14819	4558
2011	1648	21133	14822	2856	15546	16707	4451

Source:
OECD, StatExtracts, *International Migration Database*, online: stats.oecd.org/Index.aspx?lang=
en&SubSessionId=3774ae46-b849-4cfd-a7bc-891d2b485009&themetreeid=-200.

International migration flow to New Zealand for selected countries

	Afghanistan	Iraq	Iran	Indonesia	Pakistan	Bangladesh	Somalia
1996	..	1086	208	97	..	159	151
1997	..	744	208	79	..	69	491
1998	..	276	121	166	..	85	481
1999	..	420	189	702	..	231	320
2000	341	600	258	672	217	254	343
2001	341	734	355	614	398	160	285
2002	403	903	299	362	323	128	191
2003	76	409	272	404	289	137	247
2004	726	204	198	232	159	86	178
2005	95	141	305	207	146	77	104
2006	204	72	122	239	120	86	67
2007	107	216	137	161	124	64	57
2008	122	304	101	164	148	71	78
2009	129	187	208	171	155	68	46
2010	138	176	127	172	193	82	55
2011	94	153	144	160	202	84	52

Source:
OECD, StatExtracts, *International Migration Database*, online: stats.oecd.org/Index.aspx?lang=
en&SubSessionId=3774ae46-b849-4cfd-a7bc-891d2b485009&themetreeid=-200.

International migration flow to Australia for selected countries

	Afghanistan	Iraq	Iran	Indonesia	Pakistan	Bangladesh	Somalia
1997	368	2114	1061	2149	793	577	537
1998	620	2055	804	2369	588	312	811
1999	852	1782	638	3051	755	371	608
2000	887	2000	878	3367	865	310	286
2001	456	1333	847	4493	1124	348	298
2002	660	1340	632	5794	1124	644	281
2003	1015	2903	780	4678	1030	768	231
2004	1340	1841	761	4381	1419	1075	217
2005	3463	3310	987	3841	1714	1444	183
2006	3465	5065	931	3311	1577	1714	233
2007	2560	2522	977	3152	1809	2355	334
2008	2033	2566	1153	3162	1881	2805	155
2009	2009	4417	2214	2930	2145	2239	434

(continued)

	Afghanistan	Iraq	Iran	Indonesia	Pakistan	Bangladesh	Somalia
2010	3171	2852	2107	2449	2019	2114	671
2011	3427	3298	3254	2932	2068	2307	374
2012	3644	2459	..		..	..	360

Source:
OECD, StatExtracts, *International Migration Database,* online: stats.oecd.org/Index.aspx?lang=
en&SubSessionId=3774ae46-b849-4cfd-a7bc-891d2b485009&themetreeid=−200.

World Muslim population by region and country, 1990–2030

	1990 Estimated Muslim Population	2010 Estimated Muslim Population	2030 Projected Muslim Population
Australia	154,000	399,000	714,000
New Zealand	7,000	41,000	101,000
United States	1,529,000	2,595,000	6,216,000
Canada	313,000	940,000	2,661,000
United Kingdom	1,172,000	2,869,000	5,567,000
France	568,000*	4,704,000	6,860,000
Germany	2,506,000	4,119,000	5,545,000
Italy	858,000	1,583,000	3,199,000

Source:
Pew Research Center, Forum on Religion & Public Life, *The Future of the Global Muslim
Population: Projections for 2010–2030* (Washington, DC: Pew Research Center, 2011) at 158, www
.pewforum.org/files/2011/01/FutureGlobalMuslimPopulation-WebPDF-Feb10.pdf.
* Flagged as an undercount by PEW

AMERICAS

Countries with the Largest Projected **Increase** in **Number of Muslims,** 2010-2030

Countries	ESTIMATED MUSLIM POPULATION 2010	PROJECTED MUSLIM POPULATION 2030	PROJECTED NUMERICAL INCREASE 2010-2030
United States	2,595,000	6,216,000	3,621,000
Canada	940,000	2,661,000	1,721,000
Argentina	1,000,000	1,233,000	233,000
Venezuela	95,000	121,000	26,000
Brazil	204,000	227,000	23,000
Mexico	111,000	126,000	16,000
Suriname	84,000	96,000	12,000
Panama	25,000	32,000	7,000
Honduras	11,000	15,000	4,000
Colombia	14,000	17,000	3,000

Population estimates are rounded to thousands.
Figures may not add exactly due to rounding.

Pew Research Center's Forum on Religion & Public Life
The Future of the Global Muslim Population, January 2011
Reprinted with permission

AMERICAS

Countries with the Largest Projected **Percentage Increase in Number of Muslims, 2010-2030**

Countries	ESTIMATED MUSLIM POPULATION 2010	PROJECTED MUSLIM POPULATION 2030	PROJECTED PERCENTAGE INCREASE 2010-2030
Canada	940,000	2,661,000	183.1 %
United States	2,595,000	6,216,000	139.5
Honduras	11,000	15,000	37.8
Panama	25,000	32,000	27.9
Venezuela	95,000	121,000	27.9
Colombia	14,000	17,000	23.7
Argentina	1,000,000	1,233,000	23.3
Suriname	84,000	96,000	14.9
Mexico	111,000	126,000	14.3
Brazil	204,000	227,000	11.1

Population estimates are rounded to thousands. Percentages are calculated from unrounded numbers. Rankings are determined by undrounded numbers; some countries may appear to be tied due to rounding.
Note: Countries with fewer than 5,000 Muslims are exluded.

Pew Research Center's Forum on Religion & Public Life
The Future of the Global Muslim Population, January 2011
Reprinted with permission

AMERICAS

Countries with the Largest Projected **Increase** in Share of Population that is Muslim, 2010-2030

Countries	ESTIMATED PERCENTAGE OF POPULATION THAT IS MUSLIM 2010	PROJECTED PERCENTAGE OF POPULATION THAT IS MUSLIM 2030	PROJECTED POINT CHANGE 2010-2030
Canada	2.8%	6.6%	3.9 pts
United States	0.8	1.7	0.9
Argentina	2.5	2.6	0.2

Figures are calculated from unrounded numbers and may not add exactly due to rounding.

Pew Research Center's Forum on Religion & Public Life
The Future of the Global Muslim Population, January 2011
Reprinted with permission

Top 10 Destination Countries

For Muslim migrants

❶	Saudi Arabia	5,620,000
❷	Russia	4,030,000
❸	Germany	3,230,000
❹	France	3,040,000
❺	Jordan	2,830,000
❻	Pakistan	2,460,000
❼	United States	2,130,000
❽	Iran	2,100,000
❾	United Arab Emirates	2,090,000
❿	Syria	1,970,000

Population estimates are rounded to ten thousands.

Pew Research Center's Forum on Religion & Public Life • Global Religion and Migration Database 2010
Reprinted with permission

Regional Origins
of Muslim Migrants

*Percentage and estimated number of Muslim migrants who have **come from** each region*

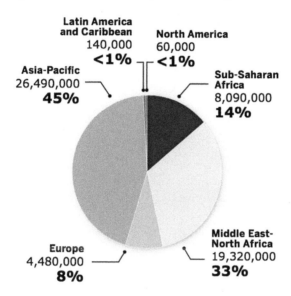

Latin America and Caribbean
140,000
<1%

North America
60,000
<1%

Asia-Pacific
26,490,000
45%

Sub-Saharan Africa
8,090,000
14%

Europe
4,480,000
8%

Middle East-North Africa
19,320,000
33%

Population estimates are rounded to ten thousands.
Percentages are calculated from unrounded numbers
and may not add to 100 due to rounding.

Pew Research Center's Forum on Religion & Public Life
Global Religion and Migration Database 2010
Reprinted with permission

Regional Destinations
of Muslim Migrants

*Percentage and estimated number of Muslim migrants who have **gone to** each region*

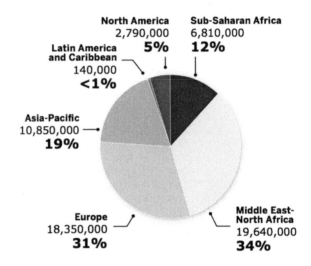

Population estimates are rounded to ten thousands. Percentages are calculated from unrounded numbers and may not add to 100 due to rounding.

Pew Research Center's Forum on Religion & Public Life
Global Religion and Migration Database 2010
Reprinted with permission

ASIA-PACIFIC

Countries with the Largest Projected **Percentage Increase in Number of Muslims,** 2010-2030

Countries	ESTIMATED MUSLIM POPULATION 2010	PROJECTED MUSLIM POPULATION 2030	PROJECTED PERCENTAGE INCREASE 2010-2030
New Zealand	41,000	101,000	146.9%
Australia	399,000	714,000	78.9
Afghanistan*	29,047,000	50,527,000	73.9
Philippines	4,737,000	7,094,000	49.8
Pakistan*	178,097,000	256,117,000	43.8
Nepal	1,253,000	1,705,000	36.2
Tajikistan*	7,006,000	9,525,000	35.9
Brunei*	211,000	284,000	34.4
Cambodia	240,000	320,000	33.5
India	177,286,000	236,182,000	33.2

* Muslim-majority country
Population estimates are rounded to thousands. Percentages are calculated from unrounded numbers. Note: Countries with fewer than 5,000 Muslims not shown.

Pew Research Center's Forum on Religion & Public Life
The Future of the Global Muslim Population, January 2011
Reprinted with permission

Source:
Pew Research Center, Forum on Religion & Public Life, *Faith on the Move: The Religious Affiliation of International Migrants* (Washington, DC: Pew Research Center, 2012), online: www.pewforum.org/files/2012/03/Faithonthemove.pdf.

Pew Research Center, Forum on Religion & Public Life, *The Future of the Global Muslim Population: Projections for 2010–2030* (Washington, DC: Pew Research Center, 2011), online: www.pewforum.org/files/2011/01/FutureGlobal MuslimPopulation-WebPDF-Feb10.pdf.

With respect to the make-up of the Asia-Pacific region, Pew indicates the following:

The Pacific includes 24 countries and territories: American Samoa, Australia, Cook Islands, Federated States of Micronesia, Fiji, French Polynesia, Guam, Kiribati, Marshall Islands, Nauru, New Caledonia, New Zealand, Niue, Northern Mariana Islands, Palau, Papua New Guinea, Pitcairn Islands, Samoa, Solomon Islands, Tokelau, Tonga, Tuvalu, Vanuatu, and Wallis and Futuna.

(See Pew Research Center, Forum on Religion & Public Life, *The Future of the Global Muslim Population: Projections for 2010–2030* [Washington, DC: Pew Research Center, 2011] at 73 n 23, online: www.pewforum.org/files/2011/01/Future GlobalMuslimPopulation-WebPDF-Feb10.pdf)

Overall migration to the paradigmatic settler states
(and selected comparators)

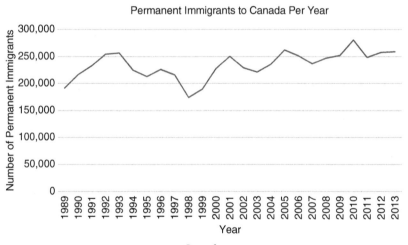

Canada

Source:
Citizenship and Immigration Canada, *Facts and Figures 2013 – Immigration Overview: Permanent Residents*, "Canada – Permanent Residents by Gender and Category, 1989 to 2013", online: www.cic.gc.ca/english/resources/statistics/fact s2013/permanent/01.asp.

Totals consist of sum of economic immigrants, family class, refugees, and other immigrants.

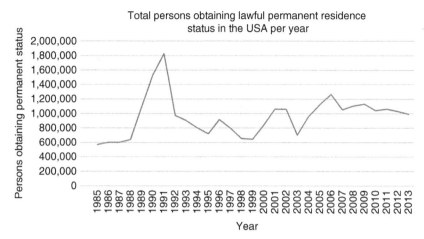

United States of America

Source:
US, Department of Homeland Security, *Yearbook of Immigration Statistics: 2013*
(Washington, DC: Department of Homeland Security, Office of Immigration
Statistics, 2014) at 5, online: www.dhs.gov/sites/default/files/publications/ois_
yb_2013_0.pdf.

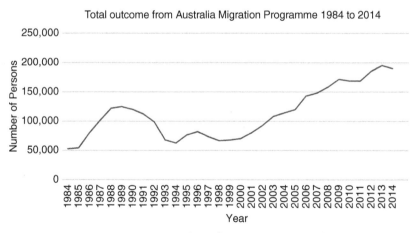

Australia

Source:
The numbers include migrants in the family, skilled, and special eligibility
streams.

Australia, Department of Immigration and Border Protection, "Historical
Migration Statistics", online: www.immi.gov.au/media/statistics/historical-migra
tion-stats.htm.

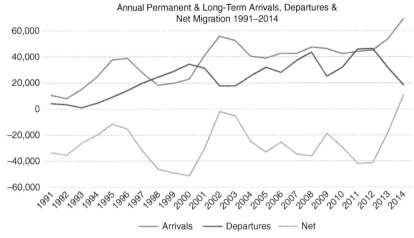

Annual Permanent & Long-Term Arrivals, Departures &
Net Migration 1991–2014

——— Arrivals   ——— Departures   ——— Net

Permanent and Long-Term Migration to New Zealand

Source:
NZ, Statistics New Zealand, Infoshare, online: www.stats.govt.nz/infoshare/View
Table.aspx?pxID=9233b4d8-bc8b-429b-bf89-97b31cbde286.
Numbers represent annual rates calculated in December.
Notes from the Statistics New Zealand site:
Permanent and long-term arrivals include overseas migrants who arrive in New
Zealand intending to stay for a period of 12 months or more (or permanently), plus
New Zealand residents returning after an absence of 12 months or more.
Permanent and long-term departures include New Zealand residents departing
for an intended period of 12 months or more (or permanently), plus overseas
visitors departing New Zealand after a stay of 12 months or more.

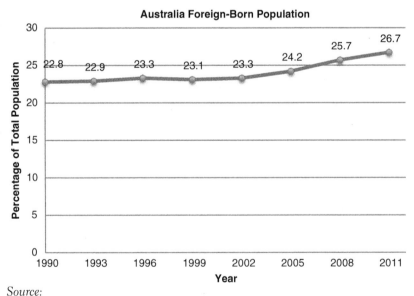

Australia Foreign-Born Population

Source:
OECD, *Migration*, "Foreign-Born Population," online: https://data.oecd.org/mig
ration/foreign-born-population.htm. Figures include people born abroad as
nationals of Australia.

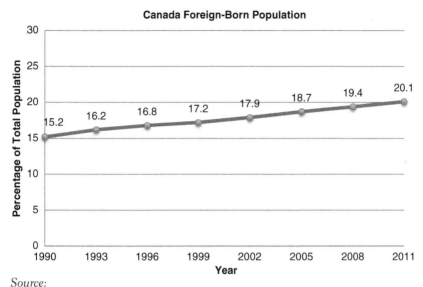

Source:
OECD, *Migration*, "Foreign-Born Population," online: https://data.oecd.org/mig ration/foreign-born-population.htm. Figures include people born abroad as nationals of Canada.

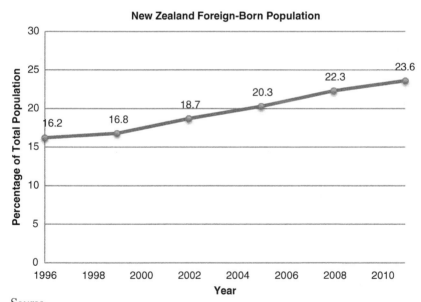

Source:
OECD, *Migration*, "Foreign-Born Population," online: https://data.oecd.org/mig ration/foreign-born-population.htm. Figures include people born abroad as nationals of New Zealand.

United States Foreign-Born Population

Source:
OECD, *Migration*, "Foreign-Born Population," online: https://data.oecd.org/mig ration/foreign-born-population.htm. Figures include people born abroad as nationals of the United States.

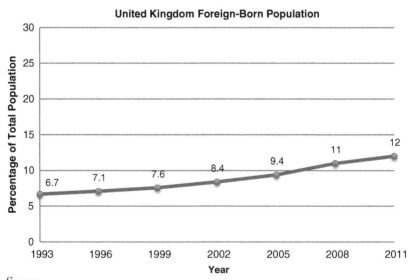

United Kingdom Foreign-Born Population

Source:
OECD, *Migration*, "Foreign-Born Population," online: https://data.oecd.org/mig ration/foreign-born-population.htm. Figures include people born abroad as nationals of the United Kingdom.

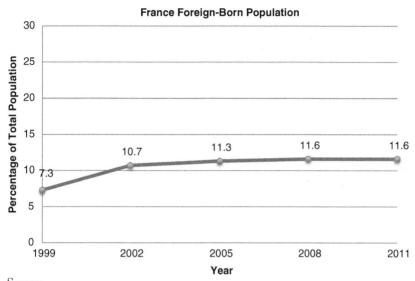

Source:
OECD, *Migration*, "Foreign-Born Population," online: https://data.oecd.org/mig
ration/foreign-born-population.htm. Figures include people born abroad as
nationals of France.

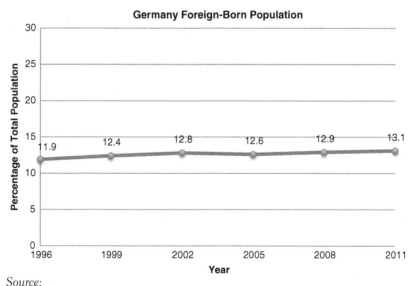

Source:
OECD, *Migration*, "Foreign-Born Population," online: https://data.oecd.org/mig
ration/foreign-born-population.htm. Figures include people born abroad as
nationals of Germany.

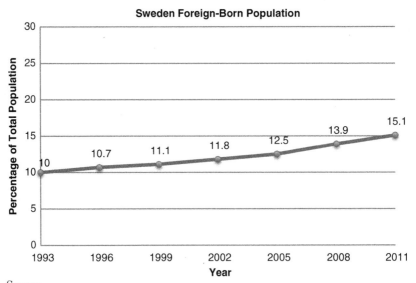

Source:
OECD, *Migration,* "Foreign-Born Population," online: https://data.oecd.org/mig
ration/foreign-born-population.htm. Figures include people born abroad as
nationals of Sweden.

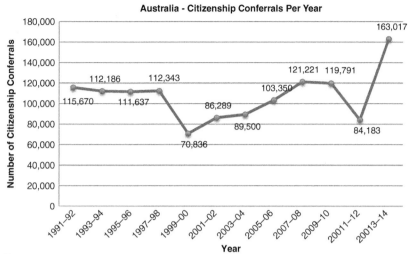

Source:

1991–1992 to 1999–2000:
Australia, Department of Immigration and Multicultural and Indigenous Affairs, Statistics Section, *Australian Immigration Consolidated Statistics* (Canberra, ACT: Department of Immigration and Multicultural and Indigenous Affairs, 2002).

2001–2002:
Australia, Department of Immigration and Multicultural and Indigenous Affairs, *Population Flows: Immigration Aspects*, 2002–03 edn. (Belconnen, ACT: Department of Immigration and Multicultural and Indigenous Affairs, 2004) ch 7.

2003–2004:
Australia, Department of Immigration and Multicultural and Indigenous Affairs, *Population Flows: Immigration Aspects*, 2004–05 edn. (Belconnen, ACT: Department of Immigration and Multicultural and Indigenous Affairs, 2005) ch 7.

2005–2006:
Australia, Department of Immigration and Multicultural Affairs, *Population Flows: Immigration Aspects*, 2005–06 edn. (Belconnen, ACT: Department of Immigration and Multicultural Affairs, 2007) ch 7.

2007–2008:
Australia, Department of Immigration and Citizenship, *Population Flows: Immigration Aspects*, 2007–08 edn. (Belconnen, ACT: Department of Immigration and Citizenship, 2009) ch 1.

2009–2010:
Australia, Department of Immigration and Citizenship, *Population Flows: Immigration Aspects*, 2009–10 edn. (Belconnen, ACT: Department of Immigration and Citizenship, 2011) ch 7.

2011–2012:
Australia, Department of Immigration and Citizenship, *Australia's Migration Trends 2011–12* (Belconnen, ACT: Department of Immigration and Citizenship, 2013) ch 8.

2013–14:
Australia, Department of Immigration and Border Protection, "Facts and Statistics," online: www.citizenship.gov.au/learn/facts-and-stats/.

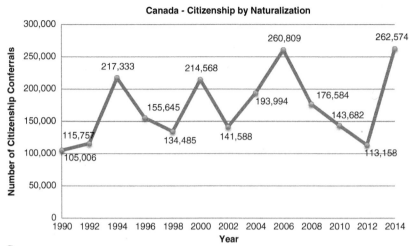

Canada - Citizenship by Naturalization

Source:
1990–2008:
Citizenship and Immigration Canada, Citizenship Registration System Database (1990–2003) as of May 2015.

Citizenship and Immigration Canada, Global Case Management System (2004–2008) as of May 2015.

2009–2014:
Citizenship and Immigration Canada, *CIC Operational Databases, 4th Quarter 2014* cited in "Quarterly Administrative Data Release," online: www.cic.gc.ca/english/resources/statistics/data-release/2014-Q4/index.asp (updated June 5, 2015).

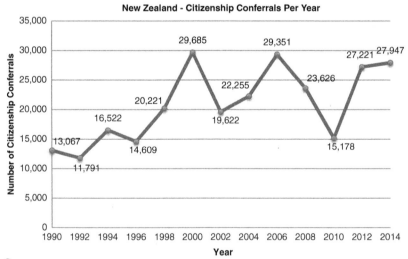

New Zealand - Citizenship Conferrals Per Year

Source:
NZ, Department of Internal Affairs, "Citizenship Statistics", online: www.dia.govt.nz/diawebsite.nsf/wpg_URL/Services-Citizenship-Citizenship-Statistics.

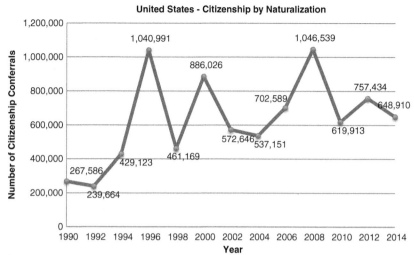

Source:

1990–2012:
US, Department of Homeland Security. *Yearbook of Immigration Statistics: 2013* (Washington, DC: Department of Homeland Security, Office of Immigration Statistics, 2014), online: www.dhs.gov/sites/default/files/publications/ois_yb_2013_0.pdf.

2014: This figure represents the number of naturalization applications approved, compiled from quarterly reports:
US, Department of Homeland Security, US Citizenship and Immigration Services, "Data Set: Form N-400 Application for Naturalization," online: www.uscis.gov/tools/reports-studies/immigration-forms-data/data-set-form-n-400-application-naturalization.

APPENDIX 6

Temporary worker migration

These data compare temporary worker admissions and permanent admissions to the United States, Canada, Australia, New Zealand, and the United Kingdom. There are significant variations in the way states report this information, so the data are not identical across the nations, but they are broadly comparable. The data represented in the tables here have been compiled from publicly available government data in each country.

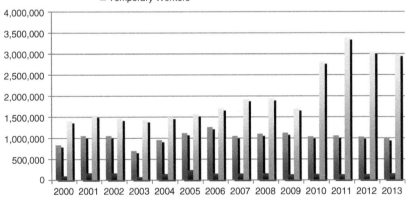

FIGURE 1 Permanent and Temporary Migration to the United States
(Admissions, Including Family Members)

Source:
US, Department of Homeland Security, *Yearbook of Immigration Statistics: 2013* (Washington, DC: Department of Homeland Security, Office of Immigration Statistics, 2014) at 5, online: www.dhs.gov/sites/default/files/publications/ois_yb_2013_0.pdf.

CAPTION FOR FIGURE 1 (cont.)

US, Department of Homeland Security, *Annual Flow Report: U.S. Lawful Permanent Residents: 2013* (Washington, DC: Department of Homeland Security, Office of Immigration Statistics, 2014), online: www.dhs.gov/sites/default/files/publications/ois_lpr_fr_2013.pdf.

US, Department of Homeland Security, *Annual Flow Report: Nonimmigrant Admissions to the United States: 2013* (Washington, DC: Department of Homeland Security, Office of Immigration Statistics, 2014), online: www.dhs.gov/sites/default/files/publications/ois_ni_fr_2013.pdf.

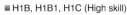
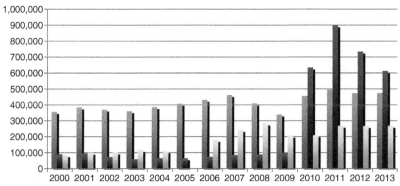

FIGURE 2 Temporary Labor Migration to the United States by Skill Classification (Admissions, Not Including Family Members)

Source:
US, Department of Homeland Security, *Annual Flow Report: Nonimmigrant Admissions to the United States: 2013* (Washington, DC: Department of Homeland Security, Office of Immigration Statistics, 2014), online: www.dhs.gov/sites/default/files/publications/ois_ni_fr_2013.pdf.

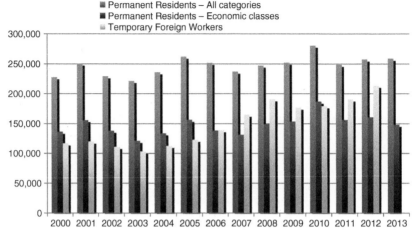

FIGURE 3 Permanent and Temporary Migration to Canada (Admissions)
Source:
Citizenship and Immigration Canada website.

2013 Permanent Residents – All categories:
Citizenship and Immigration Canada, *Facts and Figures 2013 – Immigration Overview: Permanent Residents*, "Canada – Permanent Residents, 1860 to 2013," online: www.cic.gc.ca/ENGLISH/resources/statistics/facts2013/permanent/index .asp#figure1.

2013 Permanent Residents – Economic classes:
Citizenship and Immigration Canada, *Facts and Figures 2013 – Immigration Overview: Permanent Residents*, "Canada – Permanent Residents by Category," online: www.cic.gc.ca/ENGLISH/resources/statistics/facts2013/permanent/02.asp.

* 2013 Temporary Foreign Workers numbers are not available as of June 2015.

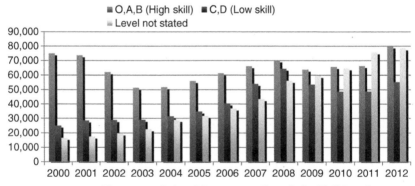

FIGURE 4 Temporary Labor Migration to Canada by Skill Level
Source:
Citizenship and Immigration Canada, *Facts and Figures 2013 – Immigration Overview: Permanent Residents*, online: www.cic.gc.ca/ENGLISH/resources/ statistics/facts2013/.

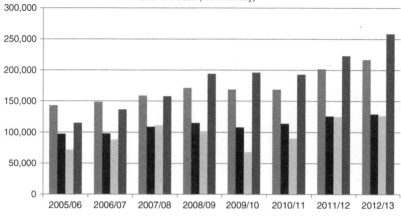

FIGURE 5 Temporary and Permanent Migration to Australia

Source:
Australia, Department of Immigration and Citizenship, *Trends in Migration: Australia 2010–11* (Belconnen, ACT: Department of Immigration and Citizenship, 2012), online: www.immi.gov.au/media/publications/statistics/trends-in-migration/trends-in-migration-2010–11.pdf.

Australia, Department of Immigration and Border Protection, *Australia's Migration Trends 2012–13* (Belconnen, ACT: Department of Immigration and Border Protection, 2014), online: www.immi.gov.au/pub-res/Pages/statistics/migration-trends-2012–13.aspx.

*From November 2012, the Business (Long Stay) (subclass 457) visa was renamed the Temporary Work (Skilled) (subclass 457) visa.

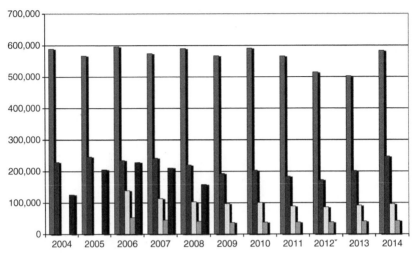

FIGURE 6 Temporary and Permanent Migration to the UK

Source:
Net Permanent Migration and Work Related:
UK, Office for National Statistics, *Migration Statistics Quarterly Report, February 2013* (Newport, Wales: Office for National Statistics, 2013), online: www.ons.gov .uk/ons/dcp171778_300382.pdf.

Worker Registration Scheme, 2009 and 2010:
UK, Office for National Statistics, *Migration Statistics Quarterly Report: No 7: November 2010* (Newport, Wales: Office for National Statistics, 2010) at 15, online: www.ons.gov.uk/ons/rel/migration1/migration-statistics-quarterly-report/ november-2010/index.html.
The Worker Registration Scheme category closed in 2011.

2013:
UK, Office for National Statistics, *Migration Statistics Quarterly Report, November 2013* (Newport, Wales: Office for National Statistics, 2013), online: www.ons.gov .uk/ons/rel/migration1/migration-statistics-quarterly-report/november-2013/msqr .html.
   UK, Home Office, *Immigration Statistics, October to December 2013* (London, UK: Home Office, 2014), online: www.gov.uk/government/publications/immigra tion-statistics-october-to-december-2013/immigration-statistics-october-to-decem ber-2013.

2014:
UK, Office for National Statistics, *Migration Statistics Quarterly Report, November 2014* (Newport, Wales: Office for National Statistics, 2014), online: www.ons.gov .uk/ons/rel/migration1/migration-statistics-quarterly-report/november-2014/stb-msqr- nov-2014.html.

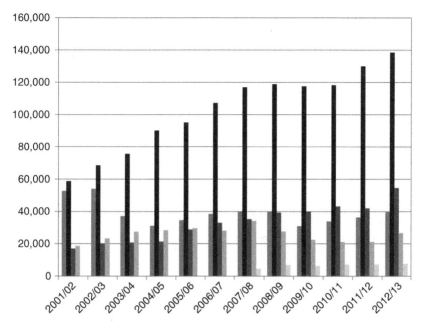

■ Net permanent and long-term migration non-New Zealand citizens

■ Temporary worker migration

■ Working holidaymaker visas

▨ Essential skills visas

▨ Recognised seasonal employer visa

FIGURE 7 Temporary and Permanent Migration to New Zealand
Source:
NZ, Ministry of Business, Innovation and Employment, "Migration Trends and Outlook", online: www.dol.govt.nz/research/migration/monthly-migration-trends/annual.asp.

New Zealand data:
Migrants with temporary work visas:
NZ, Ministry of Business, Innovation and Employment, "Migration Trends and Outlook 2010–2011: Migration Flows," online: www.dol.govt.nz/publications/research/migration-trends-1011/data.asp?id=fig3-6.

NZ, Ministry of Business, Innovation and Employment, *Migration Trends and Outlook 2012/2013* (Wellington: Ministry of Business, Innovation and Employment, 2013), online: www.dol.govt.nz/publications/research/migration-trends-1213/MigrationTrend-and-Outlook-12–13.pdf.

Number of work visa approvals
NZ, Ministry of Business, Innovation and Employment, *Migration Trends and Outlook 2012/2013* (Wellington: Ministry of Business, Innovation and Employment, 2013), online: www.dol.govt.nz/publications/research/migration-trends-1213/MigrationTrend-and-Outlook-12–13.pdf.

CAPTION FOR FIGURE 7 (cont.)

Working holidaymaker visa
NZ, Ministry of Business, Innovation and Employment, "Migration Trends and Outlook 2010–2011: Temporary Migration," online: www.dol.govt.nz/publications/research/migration-trends-1011/data.asp?id=fig4-7.

Skill shortage work permits
NZ, Department of Labour, *Migration Trends 2003/2004* (Wellington: Department of Labour, 2004), online: www.dol.govt.nz/research/migration/pdfs/MigrationTrends200304.pdf.

Comparison chart: NZ, Ministry of Business, Innovation and Employment, "Migration Trends & Outlook 2008/09: Temporary Migration," online: www.dol.govt.nz/publications/research/migration-outlook-200809/mto-08 09-fig42-large.asp.

(2004, 2005) NZ, Department of Labour, *Migration Trends 2005/06* (Wellington: Department of Labour, 2006), online: www.dol.govt.nz/publica tions/research/migration-trends/MigrationTrends-2005–06.pdf.

(2009–2014) NZ, Ministry of Business, Innovation and Employment, *Migration Trends: Key Indicators Report June 2014* (Wellington: Ministry of Business, Innovation and Employment, 2014), online: www.dol.govt.nz/research/migration/monthly-migration-trends/14jun/MigrationTrendsKeyIndicatorsReport June-2014.pdf.

APPENDIX 7

Illegal migration

This appendix represents a best attempt at making the estimates of so-called "illegal" immigrants from various countries and regions comparable. The reporting methods of the estimates vary and unauthorized immigrants are not categorized in a consistent manner across countries and organizations. In each case, the relevant year is the most recent available. Notes contain precise dates.

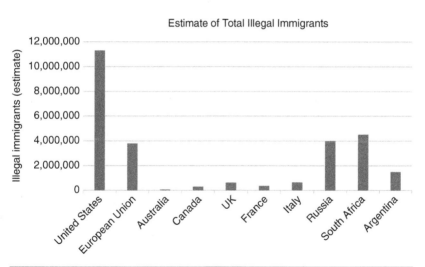

Estimate of Total Illegal Immigrants

Country	Estimate of total illegal immigrants (irregular or undocumented)
United States	11.3 Million[1]
European Union	1.9 million to 3.8 million[2]
Australia	58,400[3]

(continued)

Country	Estimate of total illegal immigrants (irregular or undocumented)
Canada	80,000 to 500,000[4]
United Kingdom	618,000[5]
France	300,000 to 400,000[6]
New Zealand	14,044[7]
Austria	36,252[8]
Italy	651,000[9]
Germany	400,000[10]
Russia	4 million[11]
South Africa	3 million to 6 million[12]
Argentina	1.5 million[13]

[1] Estimate for 2013: Jeffrey S Passel et al., As Growth Stalls Unauthorized Immigrant Population Becomes More Settled (Washington, DC: Pew Research Center's Hispanic Trends Project, 2014), online: www.pewhispanic.org/2014/09/03/as-growth-stalls-unauthorized-immigrant-population-becomes-more-settled/.

[2] Estimate for 2008: Eurostat, Statistics Explained, "Statistiques sur la migration et la population migrante," online: ec.europa.eu/eurostat/statistics-explained/index.php/Migration_and_migrant_population_statistics/fr; European Commission 2010, Kovacheva and Vogel 2009.

[3] Estimate for 2011: Figures obtained by *The Advertiser* from the Immigration Department and under the Freedom of Information Act. See Miles Kemp & Peter Mickelburough, "58,000 Illegal Immigrants in Australia Have Arrived by Plane," *The Advertiser* (November 21, 2011), online: www.adelaidenow.com.au/news/illegal-immigrants-arrive-by-plane/story-e6frea6u-1226200568050.

[4] Estimate for 2008: Les Linklater, *Committee Evidence*, Meeting No 13 (February 25, 2008) at 15:50, online: www.parl.gc.ca/HousePublications/Publication.aspx?DocId=3866154&Language=E&Mode=1&Parl=40&Ses=2&File=138, cited in House of Commons, Standing Committee on Citizenship and Immigration, Temporary Foreign Workers and Non-status Workers (May 2009) (Chair: David Tilson) at n 124, online: www.parl.gc.ca/HousePublications/Publication.aspx?DocId=3866154&Language=E&Mode=1&Parl=40&Ses=2.

[5] Estimate for 2008: Clandestino Database on Irregular Migration, "Stocks of Irregular Migrants: Estimates for United Kingdom" (November 2009), online: www.irregular-migration.net/typo3_upload/groups/31/3.Database_on_IrregMig/3.2.Stock_Tables/UnitedKingdom_Estimates_IrregularMigration_Nov09.pdf. Estimate for 2005 by the UK Home Office was 430,000. The Home Office noted that its best estimate was 430,000 but that the number could be between 310,000 and 570,000. The Home Office estimate does not include asylum seekers whose claims are being processed, or who are appealing against a refusal. See Jo Woodbridge, Sizing the Unauthorised (Illegal) Migrant Population in the United Kingdom in 2001 (UK: Home Office, 2005).

[6] Estimate for 2012: Elise Vincent, "Immigration : les régularisations ont bondi de 50 % en 2013," *Le Monde* (10 April 2014), online: www.lemonde.fr/societe/article/2014/04/10/immigration-les-regularisations-ont-bondi-de-50-en-2013_4398953_3224.html#rUZXsfEKhoj7p13u.99.

7   Estimate for 2012: Immigration Minister in testimony to Parliament. See NZ, *Hansard*, Questions To Ministers: Immigration, Illegal—Statistics and Costs (No 8) 17 October 2013 (Michael Woodhouse).

8   Estimate for 2008: Clandestino Database on Irregular Migration, "Stocks of Irregular Migrants: Estimates for Austria" (October 2009), online: www.irregular-migration.net/typo3_upload/ groups/31/3.Database_on_IrregMig/3.2.Stock_Tables/Austria_Estimates_IrregularMigration_ Oct09.pdf.

9   Estimate for 2008: Clandestino Database on Irregular Migration, "Stocks of Irregular Migrants: Estimates for Italy" (October 2009), online: www.irregular-migration.net/typo3_upload/groups/ 31/3.Database_on_IrregMig/3.2.Stock_Tables/Italy_Estimates_IrregularMigration_Oct09.pdf; Gian Carlo Blangiardo, "The Centre Sampling Technique in Surveys on Foreign Migrants. The Balance of a Multi-year Experience" (2008) United Nations Economic Commission for Europe and Eurostat Working Paper No 12, online: <www.unece.org/fileadmin/DAM/stats/ documents/ece/ces/ge.10/2008/wp.12.e.pdf>.

10 Estimate for 2010: Clandestino Database on Irregular Migration, "Stocks of Irregular Migrants: Estimates for Germany" (July 2012), online: www.irregular-migration.net/fileadmin/irregular-migration/dateien/3.Database_on_IrregMig/3.2.Stock_Tables/Germany_Estimates_Irregular Migration_Jul12.pdf; Dita Vogel, Update Report Germany: Estimate of Irregular Foreign Residents in Germany (2010) (Clandestino Database on Irregular Migration, 2012), online: irregular-migration.net/index.php?id=229.

11 Estimate for 2008: ProCon.org, "Illegal Immigration around the World: 13 Countries Compared to the United States," online: immigration.procon.org/view.resource.php? resourceID=005235#Germany; Alin Chindea et al, Migration in the Russian Federation (Geneva: International Organization for Migration, 2008) at 55, online: publications.iom.int/ bookstore/free/Russia_Profile2008.pdf.

12 Estimate for 2008: The SA Police Services (SAPS) in its latest (2008/09) annual report. See "South Africa: How Many Undocumented Migrants? Pick a Number," *Irin* (November 13, 2009), online: www.irinnews.org/report/87032/south-africa-how-many-undocumented-migrants-pick-a-number.

13 2010 Argentine Census. See James A Baer, "Documenting the Undocumented within Latin America" (November 18, 2014), online: Council on Hemispheric Affairs www.coha.org/docu menting-the-undocumented-within-latin-america.

APPENDIX 8

European migration

Migration within the EU and from non-member countries in 2012

Country	Total Immigrants 2012	Citizens of Other EU States	Citizens of Non-Member Countries
Belgium	147,387	64,900	64,800
Bulgaria	14,103	4,100	5,000
Czech Republic	34,337	12,100	15,500
Denmark	54,409	19,800	16,000
Germany	592,175	298,500	205,100
Estonia	2,639	100	1,000
Ireland	54,439	22,300	15,600
Greece	110,139	24,800	42,700
Spain	304,053	100,300	172,200
France	327,431	90,800	120,900
Croatia	8,959	1,300	3,400
Italy	350,772	104,100	217,200
Cyprus	17,476	10,200	6,000
Latvia	13,303	500	3,100
Lithuania	19,843	700	1,700
Luxembourg	20,478	15,600	3,800
Hungary	33,702	10,400	10,000
Malta	7,111	2,500	2,900
Netherlands	124,566	51,200	31,800
Austria	91,557	51,900	31,400
Poland	217,546	24,400	57,100
Portugal	14,606	1,300	3,900
Romania	167,266	3,500	8,200

(continued)

Country	Total Immigrants 2012	Citizens of Other EU States	Citizens of Non-Member Countries
Slovenia	15,022	2,200	10,100
Slovakia	5,419	2,400	500
Finland	31,278	10,300	12,600
Sweden	103,059	25,300	56,900
United Kingdom	498,040	157,600	260,300

Source:
Eurostat, Statistics Explained, "Immigration by Citizenship, 2012," online: ec.europa.eu/eurostat/
statistics-explained/index.php/File:Immigration_by_citizenship,_2012_YB14_II.png.

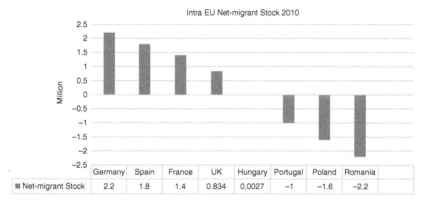

Net Migrant Stock within the EU for Selected EU Countries 2010
Source:
Figures are from the World Bank, 2010, and were represented in The Migration
Observatory's Briefing. See Carlos Vargas-Silva, "EU Migrants in Other EU
Countries: An Analysis of Bilateral Migrant Stocks," Oxford: COMPAS, University
of Oxford, 2012), online: The Migration Observatory www.migrationobservatory
.ox.ac.uk/sites/files/migobs/EU%20migrant%20stocks.pdf.

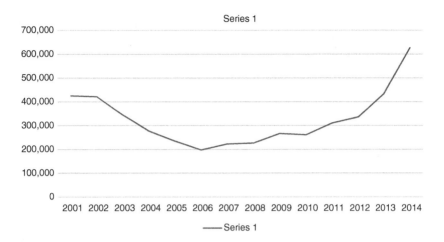

Asylum Applications in EU States, 2001–2014

Source:

1998–2007:
Eurostat, "Asylum Applicants by Citizenship till 2007: Annual Data," online:
appsso.eurostat.ec.europa.eu/nui/show.do?dataset=migr_asyctz&lang=en.

2008–2014:
Eurostat, "Asylum and First Time Asylum Applicants by Citizenship, Age and Sex:
Annual Aggregated Data," online: appsso.eurostat.ec.europa.eu/nui/show.do?
dataset=migr_asyappctza&lang=en.

Selected Years of Net Migration for EU Countries

Country	Population Jan 1 2014	Net Migration 2005	Net Migration 2009	Net Migration 2013
Belgium	11,203,992	49,186	64,136	26,078
Bulgaria	7,245,677	−16,903	−18,241	−1,108
Czech Republic	10,512,419	30,449	25,378	−1,297
Denmark	5,627,235	6,734	15,341	21,204
Germany	80,767,463	81,578	−10,681	455,473
Estonia	1,315,819	−5,184	−2,132	−2,642
Ireland	4,605,501	63,372	−19,068	−25,106
Greece	10,903,704	35,946	−16,755	−70,036
Spain	46,512,199	633,878	136,838	−251,531
France	65,835,579	187,185	31,755	31,880
Croatia	4,246,809	10,924	888	−4,884
Italy	60,782,668	202,743	212,363	1,183,877
Cyprus	858,000	8,128	17,784	−12,078
Latvia	2,001,468	−10,952	−34,477	−14,262
Lithuania	2,943,472	−51,096	−32,013	−16,807
Luxembourg	549,680	6,106	6,583	10,348
Hungary	9,877,365	17,268	17,321	5,720
Malta	425,384	1,605	2,293	3,224
Netherlands	16,829,289	−22,824	38,522	19,618
Austria	8,506,889	49,938	17,677	55,225
Poland	38,017,856	−12,878	−1,196	−26,943
Portugal	10,427,301	15,381	15,408	−36,232
Romania	19,947,311	−84,257	−110,782	−8,109
Slovenia	2,061,085	6,436	11,508	487
Slovakia	5,415,949	−712	−295	2,379
Finland	5,451,270	9,152	14,566	17,934
Sweden	9,644,864	26,724	62,614	65,780
United Kingdom	64,308,261	298,425	237,267	200,619

Source:
Eurostat, "Population Change – Demographic Balance and Crude Rates at National Level,"
online: appsso.eurostat.ec.europa.eu/nui/show.do.

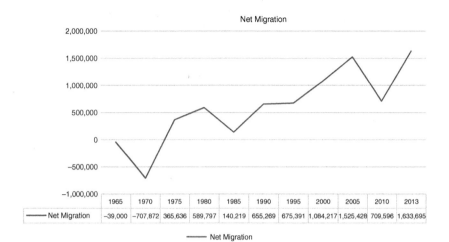

	1965	1970	1975	1980	1985	1990	1995	2000	2005	2010	2013
Net Migration	−39,000	−707,872	365,636	589,797	140,219	655,269	675,391	1,084,217	1,525,428	709,596	1,633,695

Net Migration

European States as Nations of Immigration

Source:
Eurostat, "Population Change – Demographic Balance and Crude Rates at
National Level," online appsso.eurostat.ec.europa.eu/nui/show.do?
dataset=demo_gind&lang=en.

Deportation

Significant efforts were made to include data from the 1990s, including access to information requests and the examination of annual reports from various government departments. The years presented on the graphs are the result of best attempts at including reliable data for as many years as possible over the past quarter century.

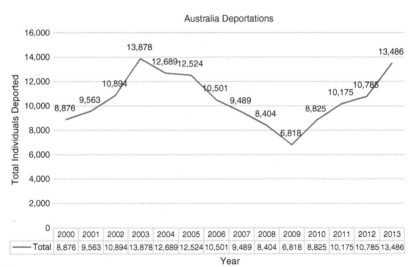

Australia Deportations

	2000	2001	2002	2003	2004	2005	2006	2007	2008	2009	2010	2011	2012	2013
Total	8,876	9,563	10,894	13,878	12,689	12,524	10,501	9,489	8,404	6,818	8,825	10,175	10,785	13,486

Year

Source:
Figures are from the Australian Department of Immigration and Citizenship Annual Reports and can normally be found in the *Departures* folder. Occasionally they are reported in the *Compliance* section or can be found in the *Year at a Glance* section as in the 2011–2012 report (page 2): Australia, Department of Immigration and Citizenship, *Annual Report 2011–12* (Belconnen, ACT: Department of Immigration and Citizenship, 2012), online: www.immi.gov.au/about/reports/annual/2011–12/pdf/2011–12-diac-annual-report.pdf.

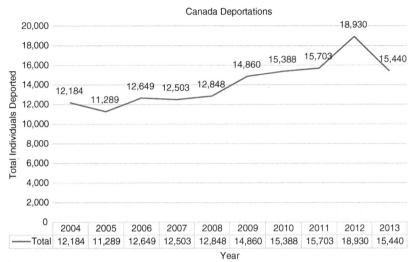

Source:
Figures are from Canadian Border Services Agency, provided pursuant to an
access to information request, CIC DWS – Enforcement – Removals, July 18, 2014.

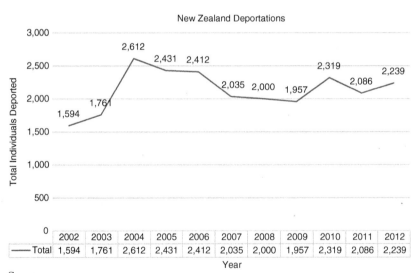

Source:
The data for this table were collected and shared by Rebecca Powell, Managing
Director of the Border Crossing Observatory, as part of the institute's research into
deportation trends: Border Crossing Observatory, "Researching Deportation Trends
around the World" (November 25, 2013), online: artsonline.monash.edu.au/thebor
dercrossingobservatory/researching-deportation-trends-around-the-world/.

CAPTION (cont.)

The numbers were taken from the New Zealand Department of Labour Annual Reports. The reports define Total Deportations and Removals as follows:

2001–2002: investigations and removals, deportations, section 35A permits and voluntary departure

2002–2003: investigations and removals, deportations, section 35A permits and voluntary departures

2003–2004: investigations and removals, deportations, section 35A permits and voluntary departures

2004–2005: investigations and removals, deportations, Section 35A permits, special directions, and voluntary departures

2005–2006: investigations and removals, deportations, Section 35A permits, special directions, and voluntary departures took place

2006–2007: investigations and removals, deportations, section 35A permits and voluntary departures

2007–2008: no reporting on the number of total removals and deportations in this year's annual report

2008–2009: investigations and removals, deportations, section 35A permit referrals and voluntary departures

2009–2010: investigations and removals, deportations, section 35A permit referrals and voluntary departures

2010–2011: number of people who will be removed, deported, depart voluntarily, be referred to a branch to apply for a Section 35A permit, or be granted a special direction or Ministerial direction

2011–2012: number of people deported, departed voluntarily, referred to a branch to apply for a Section 61 visa, or granted a special direction or Ministerial direction

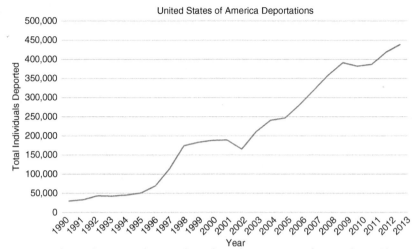

United States of America Deportations

* Removals are the compulsory and confirmed movement of an inadmissible or deportable alien out of the United States based on an order of removal. An alien who is removed has administrative or criminal consequences placed on subsequent re-entry owing to the fact of the removal.
Source:
US, Department of Homeland Security, ENFORCE Alien Removal Module (EARM), January 2014.
   US, Department of Homeland Security, Enforcement Integrated Database (EID), November 2013.

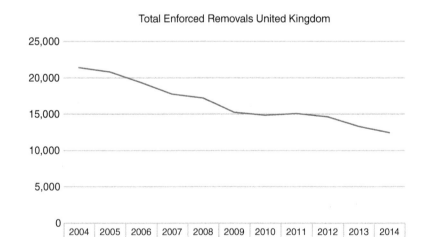

Total Enforced Removals United Kingdom

	2004	2005	2006	2007	2008	2009	2010	2011	2012	2013	2014
Total	21,425	20,808	19,372	17,770	17,239	15,252	14,854	15,063	14,647	13,311	12,460

Source:
UK, Home Office, "Immigration Statistics: Removals and Voluntary Departures," online: data.gov.uk/dataset/immigration-statistics-removals.

Bibliography

BOOKS AND ARTICLES

Acer, Eleanor. "Refuge in an Insecure Time: Seeking Asylum in the Post 9/11 United States" (2004) 28:5 *Fordham Intl L J* 1361.

Aleinikoff, T. Alexander. *Semblances of Sovereignty: The Constitution, the State and American Citizenship* (Cambridge, MA: Harvard University Press, 2002).

Allen, Chris. *Islamophobia* (Surrey, UK: Ashgate, 2010).

Anderson, Benedict R. O'G. *Imagined Communities: Reflections on the Origin and Spread of Nationalism* (London, UK: Verso Editions, 1983).

Andrijasevic, Rutvica. "Deported: The Right to Asylum at EU's External Border of Italy and Libya" (2010) 48:1 *Intl Migration* 148.

Anker, Deborah E. and Michael H. Posner. "The Forty Year Crisis: A Legislative History of the Refugee Act of 1980" (1981–82) 19:1 *San Diego L Rev* 9.

Arbel, Efrat. "Gendered Border Crossings" in Efrat Arbel et al., eds., *Gender in Refugee Law: From the Margins to the Centre* (London, UK: Routledge, 2014) 243.

Awan, Muhammed Safeer. "Global Terror and the Rise of Xenophobia/Islamophobia: An Analysis of American Cultural Production since September 11" (2010) 49:4 *Islamic Studies* 521.

Barron, Elisha. "The Development, Relief and Education for Alien Minors (DREAM) Act" (2011) 48:2 *Harv J on Legis* 623.

Basch, Linda, Nina Glick Schiller, and Cristina Szanton Blanc. *Nations Unbound: Transnational Projects, Postcolonial Predicaments, and Deterritorialized Nation-States* (Langhorne, PA: Gordon and Breach, 1994).

Bauböck, Rainer. *Migration and Citizenship* (Amsterdam: Amsterdam University Press, 2007).

Bauder, Harald. *Immigration Dialectic: Imagining Community, Economy and Nation* (Toronto: University of Toronto Press, 2011).

Bennett, Colin J. "Unsafe at Any Altitude: The Comparative Politics of No-Fly Lists in the United States and Canada" in Mark B. Salter, ed., *Politics at the Airport* (Minneapolis: University of Minnesota Press, 2008) 51.

Bennett, Sarah-Jane and Meghan Tait. "The Australian Citizenship Test" (2008) 1:2 *Queensland L Student Rev* 75.

Bigo, Didier and Anastassia Tsoukala, eds. *Terror, Insecurity and Liberty: Illiberal Practices of Liberal Regimes after 9/11* (New York: Routledge, 2008).

Bloemraad, Irene. *Becoming a Citizen: Incorporating Immigrants and Refugees in the United States and Canada* (Berkeley: University of California Press, 2006).

"Unity in Diversity: Bridging Models of Multiculturalism and Immigrant Integration" (2007) 4:2 *Du Bois Rev* 317.

Borjas, George J. *Immigration Economics* (Cambridge, MA: Harvard University Press, 2014).

Bosworth, Mary. "Deportation, Detention and Foreign-National Prisoners in England and Wales" (2011) 15:5 *Citizenship Studies* 583.

Bosworth, Mary and Katja Franko Aas. *The Borders of Punishment* (Oxford: Oxford University Press, 2014).

Branco, Manuel Court. *Economics Versus Human Rights* (New York: Routledge, 2009).

Brawley, Sean. *White Peril: Foreign Relations and Asian Immigration to Australasia and North America, 1919–1978* (Sydney: University of New South Wales Press, 1995).

Carens, Joseph. *Immigrants and the Right to Stay* (Cambridge, MA: MIT Press, 2010).

Castles, Stephen. "Guestworkers in Europe: A Resurrection?" (2006) 40:4 *Intl Migration Rev* 741.

Castles, Stephen and Mark Miller. *The Age of Migration: International Population Movements in the Modern World* (New York: Guilford Press, 2003).

Cole, David. *Enemy Aliens: Double Standards and Constitutional Freedoms in the War on Terror* (New York: New Press, 2003).

Cole, David and Jules Lobel. *Less Safe, Less Free: Why America is Losing the War on Terror* (New York: New Press, 2007).

Coombes, Annie E., ed. *Rethinking Settler Colonialism: History and Memory in Australia, Canada, New Zealand and South Africa* (Manchester: Manchester University Press, 2006).

Dauvergne, Catherine. "Citizenship, Migration Laws and Women: Gendering Permanent Residency Statistics" (2000) 24:2 *Melbourne UL Rev* 280.

"Globalizing Fragmentation – New Pressures on the Women Caught in the Immigration Law – Citizenship Law Dichotomy" in Seyla Benhabib and Judith Resnick, eds., *Migration and Mobilities: Citizenship, Borders and Gender* (New York: New York University Press, 2009) 333.

"How the *Charter* Has Failed Non-citizens in Canada: Reviewing Thirty Years of Supreme Court of Canada Jurisprudence" (2013) 58:3 *McGill LJ* 663.

Humanitarianism, Identity, and Nation (Vancouver: UBC Press, 2005).

Making People Illegal: What Globalization Means for Migration and Law (Cambridge: Cambridge University Press, 2008).

"Refugee Law as Perpetual Crisis" in Satvinder Singh Juss and Colin Harvey, eds., *Contemporary Issues in Refugee Law* (Cheltenham, UK: Edward Elgar, 2013) 13.

Dauvergne, Catherine and Sarah Marsden. "Beyond Numbers Versus Rights: Shifting the Parameters of Debate on Temporary Labour Migration" (2014) 15:3 *J Intl Migration & Integration* 525.

"The Ideology of Temporary Labour Migration in the Post-Global Era" (2014) 18:2 *Citizenship Studies* 224.

Dauvergne, Catherine and Jenni Millbank. "Forced Marriage as a Harm in Domestic and International Law" (2010) 73:1 *Mod L Rev* 57.

Dummett, Ann and Andrew Nicol. *Subjects, Citizens, Aliens and Others: Nationality and Immigration Law* (London, UK: Weidenfeld and Nicolson, 1990).

Duncan, Howard. "The Pragmatism of the Global Commission on International Migration" (2009) 22:1 *Center for Migration Studies Special Issue* 36.

Ellermann, Antje. *States Against Migrants: Deportation in Germany and the United States* (Cambridge: Cambridge University Press, 2009).

Elver, Hilal. "Racializing Islam Before and After 9/11: From Melting Pot to Islamophobia" (2012) 21:2 *Transnat'l L & Contemp Probs* 119.

Fitzpatrick, Peter. *Modernism and the Grounds of Law* (Cambridge: Cambridge University Press, 2001).

Foster, Michelle. "The Implications of the Failed 'Malaysia Solution': The Australian High Court and Refugee Responsibility Sharing at International Law" (2012) 12:1 *Melbourne J Intl L* 395.

Fourcade, Marion. *Economists and Societies: Discipline and Profession in the United States, Britain and France* (Princeton, NJ: Princeton University Press, 2009).

Freeman, Gary P. "Can Liberal States Control Unwanted Migration?" (1994) 534:1 *Annals American Academy Political & Social Sciences* 17.

"The Decline of Sovereignty? Politics and Immigration Restriction in Liberal States" in Christian Joppke, ed., *Challenge to the Nation-State: Immigration in Western Europe and the United States* (Oxford: Oxford University Press, 1998) 86.

Gibney, Matthew. "Should Citizenship Be Conditional? The Ethics of Denationalization" (2013) 75:3 *J Politics* 646.

"'A Very Transcendental Power': Denaturalisation and the Liberalisation of Citizenship in the United Kingdom" (2013) 61:3 *Political Studies* 637.

Goodwin-Gill, Guy S. and Jane McAdams. *The Refugee in International Law*, 3rd edn. (Oxford: Oxford University Press, 2007).

Green, David A. and Christopher Worswick. "Immigrant Earnings Profiles in the Presence of Human Capital Investment: Measuring Cohort and Macro Effects" (2012) 19:2 *Labour Economics* 241.

Guchteneire, Paul de; Antoine Pecoud, and Ryszard Cholewinski, eds. *Migration and Human Rights: the United Nations Convention on Migrant Workers' Rights* (Cambridge: Cambridge University Press, 2009).

Gunew, Sneja. *Haunted Nations: The Colonial Dimensions of Multiculturalisms* (London, UK: Routledge, 2004).

Hackell, Melissa. "Taxpayer Citizenship and Neoliberal Hegemony in New Zealand" (2013) *J Political Ideologies* 129.

Haddad, Emma. *The Refugee in International Society: Between Sovereigns* (Cambridge: Cambridge University Press, 2008).

Hage, Ghassan. *White Nation: Fantasies of White Supremacy in a Multicultural Society* (New York: Routledge, 2000).

Hansen, Randall A. "Migration to Europe since 1945: Its History and Its Lessons" (2003) 74 *Political Quarterly* 25.

"A New Citizenship Bargain for an Age of Mobility: Citizenship Requirements in Europe and North America" (Washington, DC: Migration Policy Institute, 2008).

Hathaway, James C. *The Rights of Refugees under International Law* (Cambridge: Cambridge University Press, 2005).

Hathaway, James C. and Michelle Foster. *The Law of Refugee Status*, 2nd edn. (Cambridge: Cambridge University Press, 2014).

Held, David et al. *Global Transformations: Politics, Economics and Culture* (Cambridge, UK: Polity Press, 1999).

Hollinger, David. *Postethnic America: Beyond Multiculturalism*, 2nd edn. (New York: Basic Books, 2000).

Humpage, Louise. "Talking About Citizenship in New Zealand" (2008) 3 *Kōtuitui* 121.

Huntington, Samuel P. *The Clash of Civilizations and the Remaking of World Order* (New York: Simon & Schuster, 1996).

Hyndman, Jennifer and Margaret Walton-Roberts. "Interrogating Borders: A Transnational Approach to Refugee Research in Vancouver" (2000) 44:3 *Canadian Geographer* 244.

Ip, Manying. "Chinese Immigrants and Transnationals in New Zealand: A Fortress Opened" in Laurence J.C. Ma and Carolyn Cartier, eds., *The Chinese Diaspora: Space, Place, Mobility and Identity* (Lanham, MD: Rowman and Littlefield, 2003) 339.

Jacobson, David. *Rights Across Borders: Immigration and the Decline of Citizenship* (Baltimore: Johns Hopkins University Press, 1996).

Jacobson, David and Galya Benarieh Ruffer. "Courts Across Borders: The Implications of Judicial Agency for Human Rights and Democracy" (2003) 25:1 *Hum Rts Q* 74.

Johnson, Kevin B. "Racial Profiling After September 11: The Department of Justice's 2003 Guidelines" (2004) 50:1 *Loy L Rev* 67.

Jones, Nicky. "Religious Freedom in a Secular Society: The Case of the Islamic Headscarf in France" in Paul Babie and Neville Rochow, eds., *Freedom of Religion under Bills of Rights* (Adelaide: University of Adelaide Press, 2012) 216.

Joppke, Christian. *Citizenship and Immigration* (Cambridge, UK: Polity Press, 2010).

Selecting by Origin: Ethnic Migration in the Liberal State (Cambridge, MA: Harvard University Press, 2005).

"Through the European Looking Glass: Citizenship Tests in the USA, Australia and Canada" (2013) 17:1 *Citizenship Studies* 1.

Jupp, James. *From White Australia to Woomera: The Story of Australian Immigration* (Cambridge: Cambridge University Press, 2001).

Kanstroom, Daniel. *Deportation Nation: Outsiders in American History* (Cambridge, MA: Harvard University Press, 2010).

Kaushal, Asha. *The Jurisdiction of Difference: Groups and the Law* (PhD Thesis, University of British Columbia Faculty of Law, 2013) [unpublished].

Kerwin, Donald. "Counterterrorism and Immigrant Rights Two Years Later" (October 13, 2013) 80:39 *Interpreter Releases* 1401.

Klepp, Silja. "A Contested Asylum System: The European Union Between Refugee Protection and Border Control in the Mediterranean Sea" (2010) 12:1 *Eur J Migr & L* 1.

Kritz, Mary M. "Improving International Migration Governance" (2009) 2291 *Center for Migration Studies Special Issue* 56.

Kymlicka, Will. *Multicultural Citizenship: A Liberal Theory of Minority Rights* (Oxford: Oxford University Press, 1995).

"Multicultural Citizenship Within Multination States" (2011) 11:3 *Ethnicities* 281.

Multicultural Odysseys: Navigating the New International Politics of Diversity (Oxford: Oxford University Press, 2007).

Labman, Shauna. "Resettlement's Renaissance: A Cautionary Advocacy" (2007) 24:2 *Refuge* 35.

Latapi, Agustin Escobar. "The Economy, Development, and Work in the Final Report of the GCIM" (2006) 44:4 *Intl Migration* 15.

Law, Anna O. "The Diversity Visa Lottery: A Cycle of Unintended Consequences in United States Immigration Policy" (2002) 21:4 *J American Ethnic History* 3.

Legmosky, Stephen H. *Immigration and the Judiciary: Law and Politics in Britain and America* (Oxford: Oxford University Press, 1987).

Lesaffer, Randall. "Argument from Roman Law in Current International Law: Occupation and Acquisitive Prescription" (2005) 16:1 *Eur J Intl Law* 25.

Levey, Geoffrey Brahm. "Liberal Nationalism and the Australian Citizenship Tests" (2014) 18:2 *Citizenship Studies* 175.

Ley, David. *Millionaire Migrants: Trans-Pacific Life Lines* (Malden, MA: Wiley-Blackwell, 2010).

Li, Wei. *Ethnoburb: The New Ethnic Community in Urban America* (Honolulu: University of Hawai'i Press, 2009).

(ed.) *From Urban Enclave to Ethnic Suburb: New Asian Communities in Pacific Rim Countries* (Honolulu: University of Hawai'i Press, 2006).

MacDermott, Therese and Brian Opeskin. "Regulating Pacific Seasonal Labour in Australia" (2010) 83:2 *Pacific Affairs* 283.

Marshall, T.H. "Citizenship and Social Class" in Gershon Shafir, ed., *Citizenship Debates: A Reader* (Minneapolis: University of Minnesota Press, 1998) 93.

Class, Citizenship, and Social Development (Garden City: Doubleday & Company, 1964).

Martin, Philip; Manolo Abella, and Christiane Kuptsch. *Managing Labor Migration in the Twenty-First Century* (New Haven, CT: Yale University Press, 2006).

McAdam, Jane, ed. *Climate Change and Displacement: Multidisciplinary Perspectives* (Oxford: Hart, 2010).

Climate Change, Forced Migration, and International Law (Oxford: Oxford University Press, 2012).

McAdam, Jane and Fiona Chong. *Why Seeking Asylum is Legal and Australia's Policies Are Not* (Sydney: University of New South Wales Press, 2014).

Michalowski, Ines. "Required to Assimilate? The Content of Citizenship Tests in Five Countries" (2011) 15:6–7 *Citizenship Studies* 749.

Millbank, Jenni and Catherine Dauvergne. "Forced Marriage and the Exoticization of Gendered Harms in United States Asylum Laws" (2011) 19:3 *Colum J Gender & L* 898.

Modood, Tariq. *Multiculturalism: A Civic Idea*, 2nd edn. (Cambridge, UK: Polity Press, 2013).

Multicultural Politics: Race, Ethnicity, and Muslims in Britain (Minneapolis: University of Minnesota Press, 2005).

Morey, Peter and Amina Yaqin, eds. *Framing Muslims: Stereotyping and Representation After 9/11* (Cambridge, MA: Harvard University Press, 2011).

Mountz, Alison. "The Enforcement Archipelago: Detention, Haunting, and Asylum on Island" (2011) 30:3 *Political Geography* 118.

Olivas, Michael A. "The Political Economy of the DREAM Act and the Legislative Process: A Case Study of Comprehensive Immigration Reform" (2009) 55:4 *Wayne L Rev* 1757.

Ongley, Patrick and David Pearson. "Post-1945 International Migration: New Zealand, Australia and Canada Compared" (1995) 29:3 *Intl Migration Rev* 765.

Parekh, Bhikhu. *Rethinking Multiculturalism: Cultural Diversity and Political Theory*, 2nd edn. (Basingstoke, UK: Palgrave Macmillan, 2006).

Pearson, David. *The Politics of Ethnicity in Settler Societies: States of Unease* (New York: Palgrave, 2001).

Piatti-Crocker, Adriana and Laman Tasch. "Unveiling the Veil Ban Dilemma: Turkey and Beyond" (2012) 13:3 *J Intl Women's Studies* 17.

Pickering, Sharon. *Women, Borders and Violence: Current Issues in Asylum, Forced Migration, and Trafficking* (New York: Springer, 2010).

Pickus, Noah. "Laissez-Faire and Its Discontents: US Naturalization and Integration Policy in Comparative Perspective" (2014) 18:2 *Citizenship Studies* 160.

Purvis, Trevor and Alan Hunt. "Discourse, Ideology, Discourse, Ideology, Discourse, Ideology..." (1993) 44:3 *British J Sociology* 473.

Qadeer, Mohammad and Sandeep Kumar. "Ethnic Enclaves and Social Cohesion" (2006) 15:2 *Canadian J Urban Research* 1.

Radhakrishnan, Priyanca. *Unholy Matrimony: Forced Marriage in New Zealand* (MA Thesis, Victoria University of Wellington, 2012) [unpublished].

Ramirez, Deborah A., Jennifer Hoopes, and Tara Lai Quinlan. "Defining Racial Profiling in a Post- September 11 World" (2003) 40:3 *Am Crim L Rev* 1195.

Rana, Junaid. "The Story of Islamophobia" (2007) 9:2 *Souls: Critical J Black Politics, Culture, & Society* 148.

Razack, Sherene H., ed. *Race, Space and the Law: Unmapping a White Settler Society* (Toronto: Between the Lines, 2002).

Regan, Paulette. *Unsettling the Settler Within: Indian Residential Schools, Truth Telling, and Reconciliation in Canada* (Vancouver: UBC Press, 2010).

Roach, Kent. *The 9/11 Effect: Comparative Counter Terrorism* (Cambridge: Cambridge University Press, 2011).

Robinson, W. Courtland. *Terms of Refuge: The Indochinese Exodus and the International Response* (London, UK: Zed Books, 1998).

Rosewarne, Stuart. "Globalisation and the Commodification of Labour: Temporary Labour Migration" (2010) 20:2 *Economic & Labour Relations Review* 99.

Rubenstein, Kim. "Citizenship in a Borderless World" in Antony Anghie and Garry Sturgess, eds, *Legal Visions of the 21st Century: Essays in Honour of Judge Christopher Weeramantry* (The Hague: Kluwer Law International, 1998) 183.

Rubenstein, Kim and Daniel Adler. "International Citizenship: the Future of Nationality in a Globalized World" (2000) 7:2 *Ind J Global Leg Stud* 519.

Russell, Peter H. *Constitutional Odyssey* (Toronto: University of Toronto Press, 2004).

Ryder, Bruce. "Racism and the Constitution: The Constitutional Fate of British Columbia Anti-Asian Immigration Legislation, 1884–1909" (1991) 29:3 *Osgoode Hall LJ* 619.

Sarfaty, Galit A. *Values in Translation: Human Rights and the Culture of the World Bank* (Stanford: Stanford University Press, 2012).

Sassen, Saskia. *Losing Control? Sovereignty in an Age of Globalization* (New York: Columbia University Press, 1996).

Saunders, Doug. *The Myth of the Muslim Tide* (Toronto: Knopf Canada, 2012).

Scheffer, Paul. *Immigrant Nations*, translated by Liz Waters (Cambridge, UK: Polity Press, 2011).

Schlesinger, Arthur M. *The Disuniting of America: Reflections on a Multicultural Society*, revised ed (New York: WW Norton & Company, 1998).

Schuck, Peter H., Karin D. Martin, and Jack Glaser. "Racial Profiling" in Judith Gans, Elaine M. Replogle, and Daniel J. Tichenor, eds., *Debates on U.S. Immigration* (Thousand Oaks, CA: SAGE Publications, 2012) 491.

Scott, Joan Wallach. *The Politics of the Veil* (Princeton, NJ: Princeton University Press, 2007).

Seuffert, Nan. *Jurisprudence of National Identity: Kaleidoscopes of Imperialism and Globalisation from Aotearoa New Zealand* (Aldershot, UK: Ashgate, 2006).

Shachar, Ayelet. *Multicultural Jurisdictions: Cultural Differences and Women's Rights* (Cambridge: Cambridge University Press, 2001).

Siddiqui, Hannana. "There Is No 'Honour' in Domestic Violence, Only Shame!: Women's Struggles Against 'Honour' Crimes in the UK" in Lynn Welchman and Sara Hossain, eds., *"Honour": Crimes, Paradigms and Violence Against Women* (London, UK: Zed Books, 2005) 263.

Simmons, Frances and Jennifer Burn. "Without Consent: Forced Marriage in Australia" (2013) 36:3 *Melbourne UL Rev* 970.

Singham, Mervin. "Multiculturalism in New Zealand – the Need for a New Paradigm" (2006) 1:1 *Aotearoa Ethnic Network J* 33.

Smith, Anthony D. *The Ethnic Origins of Nations* (New York: Blackwell, 1986).

National Identity (Reno: University of Nevada Press, 1991).

Stasiulis, Davia and Nira Yuval-Davis, eds. *Unsettling Settler Societies: Articulations of Gender, Race, Ethnicity and Class* (London, UK: SAGE Publications, 1995).

Stumpf, Juliet P. "Doing Time: Crimmigration Law and the Perils of Haste" (2011) 58:6 *UCLA L Rev* 1705.

"The Crimmigration Crisis: Immigrants, Crime, and Sovereign Power" (2006) 56:2 *Am U L Rev* 367.

Sweetman, Arthur. "Spotlight on the Economic Effects of Immigration: A North American Perspective" in Christiane Kuptsch, ed., *The Internationalization of Labour Markets* (Geneva: International Institute for Labour Studies, 2010) 15.

Takaki, Ronald. *A Different Mirror: A History of Multicultural America* (Boston: Little, Brown & Company, 2008).

Taylor, Charles. *Multiculturalism: Examining the Politics of Recognition*, ed. by Amy Gutmann (Princeton, NJ: Princeton University Press: 1994).

Transatlantic Council on Migration. *Talent, Competitiveness and Migration*, ed. by Bertelsmann Stiftung and Migration Policy Institutes (Gütersloh, Germany: Bertelsmann Stiftung, 2010).

Trebilcock, Michael. "The Law and Economics of Immigration Policy" (2003) 5:2 *Am L & Econ Rev* 271.

Torpey, John. *The Invention of the Passport: Surveillance, Citizenship and the State* (Cambridge: Cambridge University Press, 2000).

Varady, David P., ed. *Desegregating the City: Ghettos, Enclaves, and Inequality* (Albany, NY: State University of New York Press, 2005).

Veracini, Lorenzo. *Settler Colonialism: A Theoretical Overview* (New York: Palgrave MacMillan, 2010).

Walks, R. Alan and Larry S. Bourne. "Ghettos in Canada's Cities? Racial Segregation, Ethnic Enclaves and Poverty Concentration in Canadian Urban Areas" (2006) 50:3 *Canadian Geographer* 273.

Walter, Kerstin. *Mind the Gap: Exposing the Protection Gaps in International Law for Environmentally Displaced Citizens of Small Island States* (LLM Thesis, University of British Columbia Faculty of Law, 2012). [unpublished].

Weil, Patrick. *The Sovereign Citizen: Denaturalization and the Origins of the American Republic* (Philadelphia: University of Pennsylvania Press, 2012).

Weitzer, Ronald. *Transforming Settler States: Communal Conflict and Internal Security in Northern Ireland and Zimbabwe* (Berkeley: University of California Press, 1990).

Young, Iris Marion. *Justice and the Politics of Difference* (Princeton, NJ: Princeton University Press, 1990).

Zhang, Kevin Honglin and Shunfeng Song. "Rural-Urban Migration and Urbanization in China: Evidence from Time-Series and Cross-section Analyses" (2003) 14:4 *China Economic Rev* 386.

Zimmerman, Klaus F., ed. *European Migration: What Do We Know?* (Oxford; New York: Oxford University Press, 2005).

Reports and Papers

Anis, Maryum, Shalini Konanur, and Deepa Mattoo. *Who – If – When to Marry: The Incidence of Forced Marriage in Ontario* (Toronto: South Asian Legal Clinic of Ontario, 2013).

Arbel, Efrat and Alletta Brenner. *Bordering on Failure: Canada-U.S. Border Policy and the Politics of Refugee Exclusion* (Cambridge, MA: Harvard Immigration and Refugee Clinical Law Program, 2013).

Australia, Attorney-General's Department, Criminal Justice Division. *Discussion Paper: Forced and Servile Marriage* (Barton, ACT: Attorney-General's Department, 2010).

Australia, Department of Immigration and Border Protection. *Australia's Migration Trends 2012–13* (Belconnen, ACT: Department of Immigration and Border Protection, 2014), online: www.immi.gov.au/pub-res/pages/statistics/migration-trends-2012–13.aspx.

Australia, Department of Immigration and Border Protection. *Proposal Paper: Simplification of the Skilled Migration and Temporary Activity Visa Programmes* (Belconnen, ACT: Department of Immigration and Border Protection, 2014).

Australia, Department of Immigration and Citizenship. *Annual Report 2011–12* (Belconnen, ACT: Department of Immigration and Citizenship, 2012), online: www.immi.gov.au/about/reports/annual/2011–12/pdf/2011–12-diac-annual-report.pdf.

Australia, Department of Immigration and Citizenship. *Australia's Migration Trends 2011–12* (Belconnen, ACT: Department of Immigration and Citizenship, 2013).

Australia, Department of Immigration and Citizenship. *Population Flows: Immigration Aspects*, 2009–10 edn. (Belconnen, ACT: Department of Immigration and Citizenship, 2011).

Australia, Department of Immigration and Citizenship. *Population Flows: Immigration Aspects*, 2007–08 edn. (Belconnen, ACT: Department of Immigration and Citizenship, 2009).

Australia, Department of Immigration and Citizenship. *Simpler Visas: Implementing a Simpler Framework for Temporary Residence Work Visas* (Belconnen, ACT: Department of Immigration and Citizenship, 2010).

Australia, Department of Immigration and Citizenship. *Trends in Migration: Australia 2010–11* (Belconnen, ACT: Department of Immigration and Citizenship, 2012), online: www.immi.gov.au/media/publications/statistics/trends-in-migration/trends-in-migration-2010–11.pdf.

Australia, Department of Immigration and Multicultural Affairs. *Population Flows: Immigration Aspects*, 2005–06 edn. (Belconnen, ACT: Department of Immigration and Multicultural Affairs, 2007).

Australia, Department of Immigration and Multicultural and Indigenous Affairs. *Population Flows: Immigration Aspects*, 2004–05 edn. (Belconnen, ACT: Department of Immigration and Multicultural and Indigenous Affairs, 2005).

Australia, Department of Immigration and Multicultural and Indigenous Affairs. *Population Flows: Immigration Aspects*, 2002–03 edn. (Belconnen, ACT: Department of Immigration and Multicultural and Indigenous Affairs, 2004).

Australia, Department of Immigration and Multicultural and Indigenous Affairs. Statistics Section, *Australian Immigration Consolidated Statistics* (Canberra, ACT: Department of Immigration and Multicultural and Indigenous Affairs, 2002).

Australia. *Strategic Review of the Student Visa Program 2011* (June 30, 2011) (Hon. Michael Knight).

Bauböck, Rainer and Christian Joppke, eds. "How Liberal Are Citizenship Tests" (2010) European University Institute Working Paper No RSCAS/2010/41.

BC Civil Liberties Association. *Racial Profiling: A Special BCCLA Report on Racial Profiling in Canada* (Vancouver: BC Civil Liberties Association, 2010).

Bertocchi, Graziella and Chiara Strozzi. "Citizenship Laws and International Migration in Historical Perspective" (2004) Centre for Economic Policy Research Discussion Paper No 4737.

Blangiardo, Gian Carlo. "The Centre Sampling Technique in Surveys on Foreign Migrants. The Balance of a Multi-year Experience" (2008) United Nations Economic Commission for Europe and Eurostat Working Paper No 12, online: www.unece.org/fileadmin/dam/stats/documents/ece/ces/ge.10/2008/wp.12.e.pdf.

Canada, Department of Justice. *Report on the Practice of Forced Marriage in Canada: Interviews with Frontline Workers*, by Naïma Bendriss (Ottawa: Department of Justice, 2008).

Chindea, Alin et al. *Migration in the Russian Federation* (Geneva: International Organization for Migration, 2008), online: publications.iom.int/bookstore/free/russia_profile2008.pdf.

Citizenship and Immigration Canada. *Exploring Minority Enclave Areas in Montréal,* *Toronto, and Vancouver,* by Daniel Hiebert (Ottawa: Citizenship and Immigration Canada, 2009), online: www.cic.gc.ca/english/resources/research/ minority-enclave.asp.

Commission of Inquiry into the Actions of Canadian Officials in Relation to Maher Arar. *Report of the Events Relating to Maher Arar* (Ottawa: Public Works and Government Services Canada, 2006).

Connor, Phillip, D'Vera Cohn, and Ana Gonzalez-Barrera. *Changing Patterns of* *Global Migration and Remittances* (Washington, DC: Pew Research Center, 2013).

EC, Commission, *Annual Report on Immigration and Asylum (2010)* (Brussels: EC, 2011).

EC, Commission, *5th Annual Report on Immigration and Asylum (2013)* (Brussels: EC, 2014).

EC, Commission, *First Annual Report on Immigration and Asylum (2009)* (Brussels: EC, 2010).

EC, Commission, *4th Annual Report on Immigration and Asylum (2012)* (Brussels: EC, 2013).

EC, Commission, *3rd Annual Report on Immigration and Asylum (2011)* (Brussels: EC, 2012).

Elcano Royal Institute. *Recent Arrivals of Migrants and Asylum Seekers by Sea to Italy:* *Problems and Reactions,* by Paola Monzini, ARI 75/2011 (Spain: Elcano Royal Institute, April 13, 2011).

Esipova, Neli, Julie Ray, and Anita Pugliese. *Gallup World Poll: The Many Faces of* *Global Migration* (Geneva: IOM Migration Research Series, 2011), online: International Organization for Migration publications.iom.int/bookstore/free /mrs43.pdf.

European Parliament Committee on Civil Liberties, Justice and Home Affairs. *Report* *from the LIBE Committee Delegation on the Visit to the Temporary Holding Centre* *in Lampedusa (Report\581203)* (Brussels: EC, 2005).

Gibney, Matthew J. and Randall Hansen. "Deportation and the Liberal State: the Forcible Return of Asylum Seekers and Unlawful Migrants in Canada, Germany and the United Kingdom" (2003) UNHCR Working Paper No 77.

Global Commission on International Migration. *Migration in an Interconnected* *World: New Directions for Action* (Geneva: Global Commission on International Migration, 2005), online: International Organization for Migration www.iom.int/jahia/webdav/site/myjahiasite/shared/shared/mainsite/policy_ and_research/gcim/gcim_report_complete.pdf.

Heiman, Heather and Jeanne Smoot. *Forced Marriage in Immigrant Communities in* *the United States: 2011 National Survey Results* (Falls Church, VA: Tahirih Justice Center, 2011), online: www.tahirih.org.

Migration Policy Institute. *MPI Updates National and State-Level Estimates of* *Potential DREAM Act Beneficiaries* (December 2010), cited in *We Cannot* *Afford Not to Pass the DREAM Act: A Plea from America's Scholars,* online: www.immigrationpolicy.org/sites/default/files/docs/scholar%20sign-on%20 dream.pdf.

NZ, Department of Labour. *Migration Trends 2003/2004* (Wellington: Department of Labour, 2004), online: www.dol.govt.nz/research/migration/pdfs/MigrationTrends 200304.pdf.

NZ, Ministry of Business, Innovation and Employment. "Migration Trends and Outlook," online: www.dol.govt.nz/research/migration/monthly-migration-trends/ annual.asp.

NZ, Ministry of Business, Innovation and Employment. *Migration Trends and Outlook 2012/2013* (Wellington: Ministry of Business, Innovation and Employment, 2013), online: www.dol.govt.nz/publications/research/migration-trends-1213/migration trend-and-outlook-12–13.pdf.

NZ, Ministry of Business, Innovation and Employment. *Migration Trends: Key Indicators Report June 2014* (Wellington: Ministry of Business, Innovation and Employment, 2014), online: www.dol.govt.nz/research/migration/monthly-migra tion-trends/14jun/migrationtrendskeyindicatorsreportjune-2014.pdf.

NZ, Department of Labour. *Migration Trends 2005/06* (Wellington: Department of Labour, 2006), online: www.dol.govt.nz/publications/research/migration-trends/ migrationtrends-2005–06.pdf.

Passel, Jeffrey S. et al. *As Growth Stalls Unauthorized Immigrant Population Becomes More Settled* (Washington, DC: Pew Research Center's Hispanic Trends Project, 2014), online: www.pewhispanic.org/2014/09/03/as-growth-stalls-unauthorized-im migrant-population-becomes-more-settled/.

Pew Research Center. *Changing Patterns of Global Migration and Remittances: More Migrants in U.S. and Other Wealthy Countries; More Money to Middle-Income Countries* (Washington, DC: Pew Research Center, 2013), online: www.pewsocial trends.org/files/2013/12/global-migration-final_12–2013.pdf.

Pew Research Center, Forum on Religion & Public Life. *Faith on the Move: The Religious Affiliation of International Migrants* (Washington, DC: Pew Research Center, 2012), online: www.pewforum.org/files/2012/03/Faithonthemove.pdf.

Pew Research Center, Forum on Religion & Public Life. *The Future of the Global Muslim Population: Projections for 2010–2030* (Washington, DC: Pew Research Center, 2011), online: www.pewforum.org/files/2011/01/futureglobalmuslimpopula tion-webpdf-feb10.pdf.

Pew Research Center, Forum on Religion & Public Life. *Mapping the Global Muslim Population: A Report on the Size and Distribution of the World's Muslim Population* (Washington, DC: Pew Research Center, 2009), online: www.pew forum.org/files/2009/10/muslimpopulation.pdf.

Report of the Extraordinary Meeting of 8 December 2009 of the Sixty-First Session of the Executive Committee of the Programme of the United Nations High Commissioner for Refugees, UNGAOR, 2009, UN Doc A/AC.96/1080.

Rosenblum Marc R. and Kristen McCabe. *Deportation and Discretion: Reviewing the Record and Options for Change* (Washington, DC: Migration Policy Institute, 2014).

Statistics Canada. *Recent Immigration and the Formation of Visible Minority Neighbourhoods in Canada's Large Cities*, by Feng Hou (Ottawa: Statistics Canada, Business and Labour Market Analysis Division, 2004).

UK, Comptroller & Auditor General. *Managing and Removing Foreign National Offenders* (London: National Audit Office, 2014).

UK, Home Office. *Immigration Statistics, October to December 2013* (London, UK: Home Office, 2014), online: https://www.gov.uk/government/publications/immi gration-statistics-october-to-december-2013/immigration-statistics-october-to-december-2013.

UK, Office for National Statistics. *Migration Statistics Quarterly Report, February 2013* (Newport, Wales: Office for National Statistics, 2013), online: www.ons.gov.uk /ons/dcp171778_300382.pdf.

UK, Office for National Statistics. *Migration Statistics Quarterly Report: No 7: November 2010* (Newport, Wales: Office for National Statistics, 2010) at 15, online: www.ons.gov.uk/ons/rel/migration1/migration-statistics-quarterly-report /november-2010/index.html.

UK, Office for National Statistics. *Migration Statistics Quarterly Report, November 2014* (Newport, Wales: Office for National Statistics, 2014), online: www.ons.gov.uk /ons/rel/migration1/migration-statistics-quarterly-report/november-2014/stb-msqr-nov-2014.html.

UK, Office for National Statistics. *Migration Statistics Quarterly Report, November 2013* (Newport, Wales: Office for National Statistics, 2013), online: www.ons.gov .uk/ons/rel/migration1/migration-statistics-quarterly-report/november-2013/msqr .html.

UNDESA, Population Division. *International Migration Report 2013*, UNDESA, 2013, ST/ESA/SER.A/346.

UNDESA, Population Division. *United Nations Expert Group Meeting on Population Distribution, Urbanization, Internal Migration and Development: New York, 21–23 January 2008*, UNDESA, 2008, ESA/P/WP.206.

UNDESA, Population Division & OECD. World Migration in Figures: A Joint Contribution to UN High-Level Dialogue on Migration and Development, October 3–4, 2013, online: www.oecd.org/els/mig/World-Migration-in-Figures.pdf.

UNHCR. *Asylum Applications in Industrialized Countries: 1980–1999* (Geneva: UNHCR, 2001), online: www.unhcr.org/3c3eb40f4.pdf.

UNHCR. *Global Trends 2013: War's Human Cost* (Geneva: UNHCR, 2014).

UNHCR. *UNHCR Global Resettlement Statistical Report 2013* (Geneva: UNHCR, 2015), online: www.unhcr.org/52693bd09.html.

UNICEF. *Committing to Child Survival: A Promise Renewed* (New York: UNICEF Division of Policy and Strategy, 2012), online: www.unicef.org/ethiopia/apr_pro gress_report_2012_final.pdf.

United Nations Global Commission on International Migration. *Migration in an Interconnected World: New Directions for Action* (Geneva: Global Commission on International Migration, 2005), online: www.refworld.org/publisher, gcim,,,435f81814,0.html.

US, Department of Homeland Security. *Annual Flow Report: Nonimmigrant Admissions to the United States: 2013* (Washington, DC: Department of Homeland Security, Office of Immigration Statistics, 2014), online: www.dhs .gov/sites/default/files/publications/ois_ni_fr_2013.pdf.

US, Department of Homeland Security. *Annual Flow Report: U.S. Lawful Permanent Residents: 2013* (Washington, DC: Department of Homeland Security, Office of Immigration Statistics, 2014), online: www.dhs.gov/sites/default/files/publications/ ois_lpr_fr_2013.pdf.

US, Department of Homeland Security. *Yearbook of Immigration Statistics: 2013* (Washington, DC: Department of Homeland Security, Office of Immigration Statistics, 2014), online: www.dhs.gov/sites/default/files/publications/ois_yb_2013_0.pdf.

Vargas-Silva, Carlos. "EU Migrants in Other EU Countries: An Analysis of Bilateral Migrant Stocks" (Oxford: COMPAS, University of Oxford, 2012), online: The Migration Observatory www.migrationobservatory.ox.ac.uk/sites/files/migobs/eu%20migrant%20stocks.pdf.

Vertovec, Steven. "Is Circular Migration the Way Forward in Global Policy?" (2006) International Migration Institute Working Paper.

Vogel, Dita. *Update Report Germany: Estimate of Irregular Foreign Residents in Germany (2010)* (Clandestino Database on Irregular Migration, 2012), online: irregular-migration.net/index.php?id=229.

Woodbridge, Jo. *Sizing the Unauthorised (Illegal) Migrant Population in the United Kingdom in 2001* (UK: Home Office, 2005).

Media

Armstrong, John. "Resurgent Peters Out to Rally the Regions," *The New Zealand Herald* (April 4, 2015), online: www.nzherald.co.nz/nz/news/article.cfm?c_id=1&objectid=11427538.

"Australia to Strip Citizenship of Australian-Born Jihadis with Immigrant Parents," *CBC News* (May 21, 2015), online: www.cbc.ca/news/world/australia-to-strip-citizenship-of-australian-born-jihadis-with-immigrant-parents-1.3081688.

"Australia to Take 4,400 Refugees From Syria and Iraq, Scott Morrison Says," *ABC News* (August 17, 2014), online: www.abc.net.au/news/2014-08-17/stopping-boats-frees-up-places-for-iraq-syria-refugees-morrison/5676608.

Beeby, Dean. "Massive Failure Rates Follow New, Tougher Canadian Citizenship Tests," The Toronto Star (November 29, 2010), online: www.thestar.com/news/canada/2010/11/29/massive_failure_rates_follow_new_tougher_canadian_citizenship_tests.html.

Bedford, Richard. "New Zealand: The Politicization of Immigration" (January 1, 2003), online: Migration Policy Institute www.migrationpolicy.org/article/new-zealand-politicization-immigration.

Blatchford, Christie. "So-Called Via Rail Pair Left Little Doubt They Were a Public Menace," *The National Post* (March 20, 2015), online: news.nationalpost.com/full-comment/christie-blatchford-so-called-via-rail-pair-left-little-doubt-they-were-a-public-menace.

Bonomolo, Alessandra and Stephanie Kirchgaessner. "Migrant Boat Captain Arrested as Survivors of Sinking Reach Italy," *The Guardian* (April 21, 2015), online: www.theguardian.com/world/2015/apr/21/survivors-800-migrant-boat-disaster-reach-italy-catania.

Bowcott, Owen and Jenny Percival. "Bangladeshi 'Forced Marriage' GP Due Back in Britain Tomorrow," *The Guardian* (December 15, 2008), online: www.theguardian.com/uk/2008/dec/15/gp-bangladesh-forced-marriage.

Brown, Rachel. "French Stop Asylum Seekers at Italian Border," *ABC News* (April 17, 2011), online: ABC Radio Australia www.abc.net.au/news/2011-04-18/french-stop-asylum-seekers-at-italian-border/2610830.

Burns, John F. "Cameron Criticizes 'Multiculturalism' in Britain," *The New York Times* (February 5, 2011), online: www.nytimes.com/2011/02/06/world/europe/06 britain.html?_r=0.

Citizenship and Immigration Canada. News Release, "Canada to Resettle 1,300 Syrian Refugees by end of 2014" (July 3, 2013), online: news.gc.ca/web/article-en.do?crtr .sj1D=&crtr.mnthndVl=12&mthd=advSrch&crtr.dpt1D=6664&nid=754739&c rtr.lc1D=&crtr.tp1D=1&crtr.yrStrtVl=2002&crtr.kw=&crtr.dyStrtVl=1&crtr.au d1D=&crtr.mnthStrtVl=1&crtr.page=4&crtr.yrndVl=2013&crtr.dyndVl=31.

Citizenship and Immigration Canada. News Release, "Government of Canada to help gay and lesbian refugees fleeing persecution" (March 24, 2011).

Cohen, Tobi. "New Rules Will Allow Free Do Over for Applicants Who Fail Canadian Citizenship Test," *The National Post* (June 2, 2013), online: news.nationalpost .com/news/canada/canadian-politics/new-rules-will-allow-free-do-over-for-appli cants-who-fail-canadian-citizenship-test#__federated=1.

Collins, Simon. "Tighten Visa Control, Says OECD Report," *The New Zealand Herald* (July 10, 2014), online: www.nzherald.co.nz/business/news/article.cfm? c_id=3&objectid=11290777.

Coorey, Phillip. "Gillard, Lowy Defend Multiculturalism," *The Sydney Morning Herald* (September 20, 2012), online: www.smh.com.au/federal-politics/political-news/gillard-lowy-defend-multiculturalism-20120919-26710.html.

D'Aliesio, Renata and Joe Friesen. "Temporary Foreign Workers Hired in Area with High Aboriginal Unemployment," *The Globe and Mail* (October 14, 2014), online: www.theglobeandmail.com/news/national/first-nations-coming-second-to-tem porary-foreign-workers/article21084696/.

Dastgheib, Shabnam. "A Simmering Melting Pot," *The Sunday Star-Times* (April 12, 2015) A12, online: www.pressreader.com/new-zealand/sunday-star-times/20150412/ 282746290289856/textview.

Davidson, Isaac. "Fast Visas and Longer Job Stays for Chinese," *The New Zealand Herald* (November 22, 2014), online: www.nzherald.co.nz/nz/news/article.cfm? c_id=1&objectid=11362683.

"Migrant Worker Abuse Crackdown," *The New Zealand Herald* (February 25, 2014), online: www.nzherald.co.nz/nz/news/article.cfm?c_id=1&objectid=11209212.

Davies, Lizzy. "Lampedusa Boat Tragedy Is 'Slaughter of Innocents' Says Italian President," *The Guardian* (October 3, 2013), online: www.theguardian.com/world/ 2013/oct/03/lampedusa-boat-tragedy-italy-migrants.

Dougan, Patrice. "Religious Affiliation Fades as New Zealand Bucks Trend," *The New Zealand Herald* (April 10, 2015), online: www.nzherald.co.nz/nz/news/article.cf m?c_id=1&objectid=11430295.

Engreitz, Josephine. "European Muslims Face New Challenges Post-Charlie Hebdo," *Cornell Chronicle* (February 18, 2015), online: www.news.cornell.edu/stories/2015/ 02/european-muslims-face-new-challenges.

European Commission. Press Release, "Commissioner Cecilia Malmström commemorates the Lampedusa tragedy" (October 2, 2014), online: europa.eu /rapid/press-release_statement-14-296_en.htm.

Falloon, Matt. "Multiculturalism Has Failed in Britain, PM Cameron Says," *The Globe and Mail* (February 5, 2011), online: www.theglobeandmail.com/news/world/multiculturalism-has-failed-in-britain-pm-cameron-says/article565157/.

Fallow, Brian. "Kiwis Quitting Australia Fuel Immigration Surge," *The New Zealand Herald* (July 22, 2014), online: www.nzherald.co.nz/business/news/article.cfm?c_id=3&objectid=11296969.

Field, Michael. "Ethnic Rights Advice Stuns Communities," *Sunday Star Times* (February 12, 2012), online: www.stuff.co.nz/national/6403952/ethnic-rights-advice-stuns-communities.

Fisher, David. "David Fisher: The Kim Dotcom Wrecking Ball Rolls On," *The New Zealand Herald* (July 25, 2015), online: www.nzherald.co.nz/nz/news/article.cfm?c_id=1&objectid=11299179.

Gaynor, Brian. "Brian Gaynor: Record Migration Population Game-Changer," *The New Zealand Herald* (February 7, 2015), online: www.nzherald.co.nz/business/news/article.cfm?c_id=3&objectid=11397805.

Gillespie, Kim. "Editorial: Spy Claims – More Needed from Both Sides," *Rotorua Daily Post* (September 17, 2014): online: www.nzherald.co.nz/rotorua-daily-post/opinion/news/article.cfm?c_id=1503435&objectid=11326285.

Goodspeed, Peter. "Canada Slow to Respond to Syrian Refugee Crisis," *Toronto Star* (September 19, 2014), online: www.thestar.com/news/atkinsonseries/2014/09/22/canada_slow_to_respond_to_syrian_refugee_crisis.html.

Gregory, Angela. "Migrants Quitting NZ in Bigger Numbers," *The New Zealand Herald* (June 22, 2006).

Hechtkopf, Kevin. "Tom Tancredo Tea Party Speech Slams 'Cult of Multiculturalism,'" *CBS News* (February 5, 2010), online: www.cbsnews.com/news/tom-tancredo-tea-party-speech-slams-cult-of-multiculturalism/.

Hickey, Bernard. "Bernard Hickey: Budget Buries Migration Bomb", *The New Zealand Herald* (May 18, 2014), online: www.nzherald.co.nz/business/news/article.cfm?c_id=3&objectid=11256878.

Ibba, Iosto and Barbara Molinaro. "Eritrean Survivor of Lampedusa Tragedy Returns to Honour the Dead, Meet Pope Francis," *UNHCR News Stories* (October 2, 2014), online: www.unhcr.org/542d0ece5.html.

Jolly, David. "For Americans Abroad, Taxes Just Got More Complicated," *The New York Times* (April 15, 2012), online: www.nytimes.com/2012/04/16/business/global/for-americans-abroad-taxes-just-got-more-complicated.html?_r=0.

Kemp, Miles and Peter Mickelburough. "58,000 Illegal Immigrants in Australia Have Arrived by Plane," *The Advertiser* (November 21, 2011), online: www.adelaidenow.com.au/news/illegal-immigrants-arrive-by-plane/story-e6frea6u-1226200568050.

Knaup, Horand et al. "Risky Deterrence: Europe Prepares Plan to Fight Human Traffickers," *Spiegel Online International* (May 12, 2015), online: www.spiegel.de/international/europe/eu-plans-military-action-to-stem-tide-of-illegal-migrants-a-1033388.html.

Leblanc, Daniel. "Marois Blasts Multiculturalism in Defence of 'Values' Charter," *The Globe and Mail* (September 6, 2013), online: www.theglobeandmail.com/news/politics/marois-blasts-multiculturalism-promises-gradual-phase-in-of-quebec-secular-values-charter/article14158590/.

Levitz, Stephanie. "Canada Finally Fills 2013 Syrian Refugee Promise, Says Work Is Underway on Next One," *The Globe and Mail* (March 26, 2015), online: www .theglobeandmail.com/news/politics/canada-finally-fills-2013-syrian-refugee-pro mise-says-work-underway-on-next-one/article23628469/.

Lynch, Laura. "457 Syrian Refugees Resettled in Canada, but Pledge Was for 1,300," *CBC News* (December 4, 2014), online: www.cbc.ca/news/politics/457-syrian-refu gees-resettled-in-canada-but-pledge-was-for-1-300-1.2860721.

"Man Who Brought Pipe Bomb to Edmonton Airport Blasted by Judge," *Toronto Star* (January 16, 2014), online: www.thestar.com/news/canada/2014/01/16/edmonto n_airport_staff_let_go_teen_found_with_explosive.html.

Mas, Susana. "Canada to Resettle 10,000 More Syrian Refugees over 3 Years," *CBC News* (January 7, 2015), online: www.cbc.ca/news/politics/canada-to-resettle-10–0 00-more-syrian-refugees-over-3-years-1.2892652.

"Mediterranean Migrants: Hundreds Feared Dead after Boat Capsizes," *BBC News* (April 19, 2015), online: <www.bbc.com/news/world-europe-32371348>.

"Merkel Says German Multicultural Society Has Failed," *BBC News* (October 17, 2010), online: www.bbc.com/news/world-europe-11559451.

"Migration Hits New Record in February", *The New Zealand Herald* (March 20, 2015), online: www.nzherald.co.nz/business/news/article.cfm?c_id=3&objectid=114 20424.

"Nicholas Sarkozy Declares Multiculturalism Had Failed," *The Telegraph* (February 11, 2011), online: www.telegraph.co.uk/news/worldnews/europe/france/8317497 /Nicolas-Sarkozy-declares-multiculturalism-had-failed.html.

O'Neil, Peter. "BC Coal Mine's Temporary Workers Will Be Here for Years, Maybe Decades," *The Vancouver Sun* (January 7, 2013), online: www.vancouversun.com/ coal+mine+temporary+workers+from+China+will+here+years+maybe+dec ades/7388916/story.html.

Politi, James et al. "Italy Arrests Trafficking Suspects after Hundreds Drown off Libya," *Financial Times* (April 21, 2015), online: www.ft.com/cms/s/0/2e61fc44-e761-11e4-a01 c-00144feab7de.html#slideo.

"Rapper Tyler, the Creator Pens Song about NZ Ban," *The New Zealand Herald* (April 14, 2015), online: www.nzherald.co.nz/entertainment/news/article.cfm? c_id=1501119&objectid=1143255.

Reguly, Eric. "EU Tables Plan to Fight Human Traffickers as Tragedies Mount," *The Globe and Mail* (April 20, 2015), online: www.theglobeandmail.com/news/world/ eu-rallies-to-combat-migrant-crisis-as-more-die-in-mediterranean/arti cle24025901/.

"Latest Shipwreck Claims up to 700 Migrants on the Mediterranean," *The Globe and Mail* (April 19, 2015), online: www.theglobeandmail.com/news/world/hun dreds-feared-dead-after-migrant-boat-capsizes-in-mediterranean/article24018773/.

Reilly, Mollie. "Judge Blocks Obama Administration from Detaining Asylum-Seekers as Immigration Deterrent," *Huffington Post* (February 2, 2015), online: www.huf fingtonpost.com/2015/02/20/immigration-detention-injunction_n_6724662.html.

Riegert, Bernd. "EU to Take Military Action against Human Traffickers," *Deutsche Welle* (May 19, 2015), online: www.dw.de/eu-to-take-military-action-against-hum an-traffickers/a-18462321.

"Sarkozy Calls Multiculturalism a 'Failure,'" *Maclean's* (February 11, 2011), online: www.macleans.ca/general/sarkozy-calls-multiculturalism-a-failure/.

"South Africa: How Many Undocumented Migrants? Pick a Number," *Irin* (November 13, 2009), online: www.irinnews.org/report/87032/south-africa-how-many-undocumented-migrants-pick-a-number.

Squires, Nick. "Italy's 'Appalling' Treatment of Migrants Revealed in Lampedusa Footage," *The Telegraph* (December 18, 2013), online: www.telegraph.co.uk/news/worldnews/europe/italy/10525222/italys-appalling-treatment-of-migrants-revealed-in-lampedusa-footage.html.

"Migrants Severely Burned in Latest Human Trafficking Horror," *The Telegraph* (April 17, 2015), online: www.telegraph.co.uk/news/worldnews/europe/italy/11546105/migrants-severely-burned-in-latest-human-trafficking-horror.html.

"Statement from Humayra Abedin," *The Guardian* (December 19, 2009), online: www.theguardian.com/world/2008/dec/19/statement-nhs-doctor-abedin-forced-marriage.

Tan, Lincoln. "Asian Auckland: How Our City Has Changed – Explore Our Interactive," *The New Zealand Herald* (March 10, 2015), online: www.nzherald.co.nz/nz/news/article.cfm?c_id=1&objectid=11414457.

"Immigration Policies on Debate Agenda," *The New Zealand Herald* (August 29, 2014), online: www.nzherald.co.nz/nz/news/article.cfm?c_id=1&objectid=11316011.

"Inside Auckland's Fake-Monk Scam: Beggars Recruited in China," *The New Zealand Herald* (January 20, 2015), online www.nzherald.co.nz/nz/news/article.cfm?c_id=1&objectid=11138879.

"Temporary Foreign Worker Program Misuse Sanctioned by Harper Government, Union Says," *CBC News* (August 15, 2014) online: www.cbc.ca/news/canada/calgary/temporary-foreign-worker-program-misuse-sanctioned-by-harper-government-union-says-1.2737422.

Traynor, Ian. "EU Draws Up Plans for Military Attacks on Libya to Stop Migrant Boats," *The Guardian* (May 10, 2015), online: www.theguardian.com/world/2015/may/10/eu-considers-military-attacks-on-targets-in-libya-to-stop-migrant-boats.

UNHCR. Press Release, "UNHCR urges Europe to create a robust search and rescue operation on the Mediterranean, as Operation Triton lacks resources and mandate needed for saving lives" (February 12, 2015), online: www.unhcr.org/54dc80f89.html.

Vincent, Elise. "Immigration: les régularisations ont bondi de 50 % en 2013," *Le Monde* (April 10, 2014), online: www.lemonde.fr/societe/article/2014/04/10/immigration-les-regularisations-ont-bondi-de-50-en-2013_4398953_3224.html#ruzxsfekhoj7p13 u.99.

Walker, Peter. "NHS Doctor Saved from Forced Marriage Gets Court Safeguards," *The Guardian* (December 19, 2008), online: www.theguardian.com/world/2008/dec/19/humayra-abedin-forced-marriage.

Weaver, Matthew. "Angela Merkel: German Multiculturalism Has 'Utterly Failed,'" *The Guardian* (October 17, 2010), online: www.theguardian.com/world/2010/oct/17/angela-merkel-german-multiculturalism-failed.

Weekes, John. "NZ's First Human Trafficking Trial," *The New Zealand Herald* (November 27, 2014), online: www.nzherald.co.nz/nz/news/article.cfm? c_id=1&objectid=11365531.

"Winston Peters Criticises Foreign Student Numbers," *The New Zealand Herald* (January 27, 2015), online: www.nzherald.co.nz/nz/news/article.cfm? c_id=1&objectid=11392652.

"Woman Jailed over Immigration Offences," *The New Zealand Herald* (April 14, 2015), online: www.nzherald.co.nz/nz/news/article.cfm?c_id=1&objectid=11432571.

Wordsworth, Araminta. "American Expats Feeling Less Free As Draconian Tax Law Kicks In," *The National Post* (September 27, 2013), online: fullcomment.national post.com/2013/09/27/american-expats-feeling-less-free-as-draconian-tax-law-kicks-in/.

Yardley, Jim and Elisabetta Povoledo. "Migrants Die as Burning Boat Capsizes Off Italy" (October 3, 2013), online: www.nytimes.com/2013/10/04/world/europe/scores-die-in-shipwreck-off-sicily.html.

Case Law

A (FC) and others (FC) (Appellants) v. Secretary of State for the Home Department (Respondent); X (FC) and another (FC) (Appellants) v. Secretary of State for the Home Department (Respondent), [2004] UKHL 56.

Al-Kateb v. Godwin, [2004] HCA 37.

Bruker v. Marcovitz, [2007] 3 SCR 407.

B306 v. Minister of Public Safety and Emergency Preparedness, 2013 FCA 262, leave to appeal to SCC granted, 35685 (17 April 2014).

B010 v. Minister of Citizenship and Immigration, 2013 FCA 87, leave to appeal to SCC granted, 35388 (17 July 2014).

Charkaoui v. Canada (Citizenship and Immigration), [2007] 1 SCR 350.

Dano v. Leipzig, C-333/13, [2014] ECR I–2358.

Delgamuukw v. British Columbia, [1997] 3 SCR 1010.

Dred Scott v. Sandford, 60 US 393 (1857).

Francis Anthonimuthu Appulonappa et al. v. Her Majesty the Queen et al., 2014 BCCA 163, leave to appeal to SCC granted, 35958 (October 9, 2014).

Hamdan v. Rumsfeld, 548 US 577 (2006).

Hamdi v. Rumsfeld, 542 US 507 (2004).

Jesus Rodriquez Hernandez v. Minister of Public Safety and Emergency Preparedness, 2013 FCA 262, leave to appeal to SCC granted, 35677 (April 17, 2014).

JP et al. v. Minister of Public Safety and Emergency Preparedness, 2013 FCA 262, leave to appeal to SCC granted, 35688 (April 17, 2014).

Mabo and Others v. Queensland (No 2), [1992] HCA 23; 175 CLR 1.

Mouvement laïque québécois v. Saguenay (City), 2015 SCC 16.

MSS v. Belgium and Greece, No 30696/09, [2011] ECHR 108.

Multani v. Commission scolaire Marguerite-Bourgeoys, [2006] 1 SCR 256.

NS v. Secretary of State for the Home Department of the UK and ME and others v Refugee Applications Commissioner, Minister for Justice, Equality and Law Reform, C-411/10 and C-493/10, [2011] ECR I–13905.

Plaintiff M70/2011 v. Minister for Immigration and Citizenship, [2011] HCA 32, 280 ALR 18.

Rasul v. Bush, 542 US 466 (2004).

R I L-R, et al. v. Jeh Charles Johnson, et al., Memorandum Opinion, Civil Action No 15–11 (JEB) (DC Cir 2015).

R v. NS, [2012] 3 SCR 726.

Zaoui v. Attorney-General, [2005] 1 NZLR 577 (CA).

Treaties and Legislation

An Act to amend the Citizenship Act, SC 2008, c 14.

An Act to amend the Citizenship Act and make consequential amendments to other Acts, SC 2014, c 22.

Anti-social Behaviour, Crime and Policing Act 2014 (UK), c 12.

Australia Act 1986 (UK), 1986 c 2.

Australian Citizenship Act 2007 (Cth).

Balanced Refugee Reform Act, SC 2010, c 8.

Bill C-51, *Anti-Terrorism Act, 2015*, 2nd Sess, 41st Parl, 2015 (Committee Reporting the Bill with Amendments April 2, 2015).

Bill 156–2, *Immigration Amendment Bill No. 2*, (NZ), 2013, 50–51 Parl (In Committee March 31, 2015).

Bill 60, *Charter affirming the values of State secularism and religious neutrality and of equality between women and men, and providing a framework for accommodation requests*, 1st Sess, 40th Leg, Quebec, 2013.

Bill S-7, *Zero Tolerance for Barbaric Cultural Practices Act*, 2nd Sess, 41st Parl, 2015 (second reading March 23, 2015).

British North America Act (UK), 1867, 30–31 Vict, c 3.

Canada Act 1982 (UK), 1982, c 11.

Canadian Charter of Rights and Freedoms, Part I of the Constitution Act, 1982, being Schedule B to the Canada Act 1982 (UK), 1982, c 11.

Canadian Multiculturalism Act, RSC 1985, c 24 (4th Supp).

Chinese Exclusion Act (An act to inaugurate certain treaty stipulations relating to Chinese), c 126, 22 Stat 58 (1882).

Convention against Torture and Other Cruel, Inhuman or Degrading Treatment or Punishment, 10 December 1984, 1465 UNTS 85 (entered into force June 26, 1987).

Convention on Consent to Marriage, Minimum Age for Marriage and Registration of Marriages, 7 November 1962, 521 UNTS 231 (entered into force December 9, 1964).

Convention on the Elimination of All Forms of Discrimination Against Women, 18 December 1979, 1249 UNTS 13 (entered into force September 3, 1981).

Convention relating to the Status of Refugees, 28 Jul 1951, 189 UNTS 150 (entered into force April 22, 1954).

Crimes Legislation Amendment (Slavery, Slavery-like Conditions and People Trafficking) Act 2013 (Cth), amending *Criminal Code Act 1995* (Cth).

EC, *Commission Implementing Regulation (EU) No 118/2014 of 30 January 2014 amending Regulation (EC) No 1560/2003 laying down detailed rules for the application of Council Regulation (EC) No 343/2003 establishing the criteria and mechanisms for determining the Member State responsible for examining an asylum application lodged in one of the Member States by a third-country national*, [2014] OJ, L 39/1.

EC, *Commission Regulation (EC) 1560/2003 of 2 September 2003 laying down detailed rules for the application of Council Regulation (EC) No 343/2003 establishing the criteria and mechanisms for determining the Member State responsible for examining an asylum application lodged in one of the Member States by a third-country national*, [2003] OJ, L 222/3.

EC, *Consolidated Version of the Treaty on the Functioning of the European Union*, [2012] OJ, C 326/01.

EC, *Convention determining the State responsible for examining applications for asylum lodged in one of the Member States of the European Communities*, [1997],OJ, C 254/1.

EC, Commission, *Communication from the Commission to the European Parliament, the Council, the Economic and Social Committee and the Committee of the Regions: Communication on Migration* (Brussels: EC, 2011).

EC, *Council Directive 2005/85/EC of 1 December 2005 on minimum standards on procedures in member states for granting and withdrawing refugee status*, [2005] OJ, L 326/13.

EC, *Council Directive 2004/83/EC of 29 April 2004 on minimum standards for the qualification and status of third country nationals or stateless persons as refugees or as persons who otherwise need international protection and the content of the protection granted*, [2004] OJ, L 304/12.

EC, *Council Directive 2003/109/EC of 25 November 2003 concerning the status of third-country nationals who are long-term residents*, [2004] OJ, L 16/44.

EC, *Directive 2011/95/EU of the European Parliament and of the Council of 13 December 2011 on standards for the qualification of third-country nationals or stateless persons as beneficiaries of international protection, for a uniform status for refugees or for persons eligible for subsidiary protection, and for the content of the protection granted*, [2011] OJ, L 337/9.

EC, *Directive 2004/38/EC of the European Parliament and of the Council of 29 April 2004 on the right of citizens of the Union and their family members to move and reside freely within the territory of the Member States*, [2004] OJ, L 158/77.

EC, *Regulation (EU) No 604/2013 of the European Parliament and of the Council of 26 June 2013 establishing the criteria and mechanisms for determining the Member State responsible for examining an application for international protection lodged in one of the Member States by a third-country national or a stateless person (recast)*, [2013] OJ, L 180/31.

EC, *Regulation (EU) No 603/2013 of the European Parliament and of the Council of 26 June 2013 on the establishment of 'Eurodac' for the comparison of fingerprints for the effective application of Regulation (EU) No 604/2013 establishing the criteria and mechanisms for determining the Member State responsible for examining an application for international protection lodged in one of the Member States by a third-country national or a stateless person and on requests for the comparison with Eurodac data by Member States' law enforcement authorities and Europol for law enforcement purposes, and emending Regulation (EU) No 1077/2011 establishing a European Agency for the operational management of large-scale IT systems in the area of freedom, security and justice (recast),* [2013] OJ, L 180/1.

EC, *Treaty of Lisbon amending the Treaty on European Union and the Treaty establishing the European Community,* [2007] OJ, C 306/01.

European Convention for the Protection of Human Rights and Fundamental Freedoms, 4 November 1950, 213 UNTS 221 (entered into force September 3, 1953).

Faster Removal of Foreign Criminals Act, SC 2013, c 16.

Immigration and Refugee Protection Act, SC 2001, c 27.

International Convention on the Protection of the Rights of All Migrant Workers and Members of their Families, 18 December 1990, 2220 UNTS 3 (entered into force July 1, 2003).

International Covenant on Civil and Political Rights, 19 December 1966, 999 UNTS 171 (entered into force March 23, 1976).

International Covenant on Economic, Social and Cultural Rights, 16 December 1966, 993 UNTS 3 (entered into force January 3, 1976).

Migration Act 1958 (Cth).

North American Free Trade Agreement Between the Government of Canada, the Government of Mexico and the Government of the United States, 12 December 1992, Can TS 1994 No 2 (entered into force January 1, 1994).

Protocol relating to the Status of Refugees, 16 December 1966, 606 UNTS 267 (entered into force October 4, 1967).

Refugee Act of 1980, Pub L No 96–212, 94 Stat 104 (codified as amended at 8 USC §§ 1157–1159 (1980)).

Universal Declaration of Human Rights, GA Res 217A (III), UNGAOR, 3rd Sess, Supp No 13, UN Doc A/810 (1948).

US, Bill S 744, *Border Security, Economic Opportunity, and Immigration Modernization Act,* 113th Congress, 2013 (Committee on the Judiciary December 10, 2014).

US, Bill S 952, *DREAM Act of 2011,* 112th Cong, 2011.

US Const amend XIX.

Other

Australia, Department of Employment. "Pacific Seasonal Worker Pilot Scheme," online: employment.gov.au/pacific-seasonal-worker-pilot-scheme.

Australia, Department of Employment. "Seasonal Worker Program," online: employment.gov.au/seasonal-worker-program.

Australia, Department of Immigration and Border Protection, online: www.immi.gov.au.

Australia, Department of Immigration and Border Protection. "Facts and Statistics," online: www.citizenship.gov.au/learn/facts-and-stats/.

Australia, Department of Immigration and Border Protection. "Historical Migration Statistics," online: https://www.immi.gov.au/media/statistics/historical-migration-stats.htm.

Australia, Department of Immigration and Border Protection. "The Special Humanitarian Programme (SHP)," online: https://www.immi.gov.au/visas/huma nitarian/offshore/shp.htm.

Australia, Department of Immigration and Citizenship. *The People of Australia: Australia's Multicultural Policy* (Belconnen, ACT: Department of Immigration and Citizenship, 2011).

Baer, James A. "Documenting the Undocumented within Latin America" (November 18, 2014), online: Council on Hemispheric Affairs www.coha.org/documen ting-the-undocumented-within-latin-america.

Border Crossing Observatory. "Researching Deportation Trends around the World" (November 25, 2013), online: artsonline.monash.edu.au/thebordercrossingobserva tory/researching-deportation-trends-around-the-world/.

Brusa, Carlo and Davide Papotti. "Contemporary Italy Between Stable Immigration and Migratory Emergencies" (Lecture delivered at the Annual International Conference 2011 of the Royal Geographical Society, London, September 2, 2011).

Canadian Border Services Agency, CIC DWS – Enforcement – Removals, July 18, 2014.

Citizenship and Immigration Canada, online: www.cic.gc.ca.

Citizenship and Immigration Canada, CIC Operational Databases, 4th Quarter 2014 cited in "Quarterly Administrative Data Release," online: www.cic.gc.ca/english/ resources/statistics/data-release/2014-q4/index.asp (updated June 5, 2015).

Citizenship and Immigration Canada, Citizenship Registration System Database (1990–2003) as of May 2015.

Citizenship and Immigration Canada, Global Case Management System (2004–2008) as of May 2015.

Citizenship and Immigration Canada. *Discover Canada: The Rights and Responsibilities of Citizenship* (Ottawa: Citizenship and Immigration Canada, 2012) at 9, online: www.cic.gc.ca/english/pdf/pub/discover.pdf.

Citizenship and Immigration Canada. *Facts and Figures 2013 – Immigration Overview: Permanent Residents*, online: www.cic.gc.ca/english/resources/statistics/facts2013/.

Citizenship and Immigration Canada. *Facts and Figures 2013 – Immigration Overview: Permanent Residents*, "Canada – Permanent Residents, 1860 to 2013," online: www.cic.gc.ca/english/resources/statistics/facts2013/permanent/index.asp#figure1.

Citizenship and Immigration Canada. *Facts and Figures 2013 – Immigration Overview: Permanent Residents*, "Canada – Permanent Residents by Category," online: www.cic.gc.ca/english/resources/statistics/facts2013/permanent/02.asp.

Citizenship and Immigration Canada. *Facts and Figures 2013 – Immigration Overview: Permanent Residents*, "Canada – Permanent Residents by Gender and Category, 1989 to 2013," online: www.cic.gc.ca/english/resources/statistics/facts2013/perma nent/01.asp.

Citizenship and Immigration Canada. "Urgent Protection Program (UPP)," online: www.cic.gc.ca/english/refugees/outside/resettle-gov.asp.

Clandestino Database on Irregular Migration. "Stocks of Irregular Migrants: Estimates for Austria" (October 2009), online: www.irregular-migration.net/typo3_upload/

groups/31/3.database_on_irregmig/3.2.stock_tables/austria_estimates_irregularmi
gration_octo9.pdf.

Clandestino Database on Irregular Migration. "Stocks of Irregular Migrants: Estimates
for Germany" (July 2012), online: www.irregular-migration.net/fileadmin/irregular-
migration/dateien/3.database_on_irregmig/3.2.stock_tables/germany_estimates_
irregularmigration_jul12.pdf.

Clandestino Database on Irregular Migration. "Stocks of Irregular Migrants: Estimates
for Italy" (October 2009), online: www.irregular-migration.net/typo3_
upload/groups/31/3.database_on_irregmig/3.2.stock_tables/italy_estimates_irregu
larmigration_octo9.pdf.

Clandestino Database on Irregular Migration. "Stocks of Irregular Migrants:
Estimates for United Kingdom" (November 2009), online: www.irregular-migra
tion.net/typo3_upload/groups/31/3.database_on_irregmig/3.2.stock_tables/united
kingdom_estimates_irregularmigration_novo9.pdf.

Eurostat. "Asylum and First Time Asylum Applicants by Citizenship, Age and Sex:
Annual Aggregated Data", online: appsso.eurostat.ec.europa.eu/nui/show.do?
dataset=migr_asyappctza&lang=en.

Eurostat. "Asylum Applications by Citizenship till 2007: Annual Data," online: appsso
.eurostat.ec.europa.eu/nui/show.do?dataset=migr_asyctz&lang=en.

Eurostat. "Population Change – Demographic Balance and Crude Rates at
National Level," online: appsso.eurostat.ec.europa.eu/nui/show.do?
dataset=demo_gind&lang=en.

Eurostat. "Population Grows in Twenty EU Member States," by Monica
Marcu (Luxembourg: European Union, 2011), online: ec.europa.eu/eurostat/
documents/3433488/5579248/ks-sf-11-038-en.pdf/26acc7be-a712-4181-8fc1-
88aaf94c208e.

Eurostat, Statistics Explained. "Foreign and Foreign-Born Population by Group of
Citizenship and Country of Birth 2012," online: ec.europa.eu/eurostat/statistics-e
xplained/index.php/file:foreign_and_foreign-born_population_by_group_of_citi
zenship_and_country_of_birth_2012.png.

Eurostat, Statistics Explained. "Immigration by Citizenship, 2012," online: ec.europa
.eu/eurostat/statistics-explained/index.php/file:immigration_by_citizenship,_2012
_yb14_ii.png.

Eurostat, Statistics Explained. "Statistiques sur la migration et la population migrante,"
online: ec.europa.eu/eurostat/statistics-explained/index.php/migration_and_mi
grant_population_statistics/fr.

Foreign Affairs, Trade & Development Canada. "Forced Marriage," online: travel.gc
.ca/assistance/emergency-info/forced-marriage.

Frontex. "Budget 2015," online: frontex.europa.eu/assets/about_frontex/governance_
documents/budget/budget_2015.pdf.

Gacon, Helene et al. "Complaint against the Italian Government for Violation of
European Community Law" (January 20, 2005) (signed by representatives of 10
NGOs based in Italy, France and Spain), online: www.gisti.org/doc/actions/2005/
italie/complaint20-01–2005.pdf.

Gibney, Matthew. "Don't Trust the Government's Citizenship-Stripping Policy" (February 2, 2014), *The Conversation* (blog), online: theconversation.com/dont-trust-the-governments-citizenship-stripping-policy-22601.

Global Forum on Migration and Development Civil Society. "Second UN High-Level Dialogue Results in Convergence" (January 23, 2014), online: gfmdcivilsociety .org/second-un-high-level-dialogue-results-in-convergence/.

Linklater, Les. *Committee Evidence*, Meeting No 13 (February 25, 2008) at 15:50, online: www.parl.gc.ca/housepublications/publication.aspx?doci d=3866154&language=e&mode=1&parl=40&ses=2&file=138, cited in House of Commons, Standing Committee on Citizenship and Immigration, *Temporary Foreign Workers and Non-status Workers* (May 2009) (Chair: David Tilson) at n 124, online: www.parl.gc.ca/housepublications/publica tion.aspx?docid=3866154&language=e&mode=1&parl=40&ses=2.

Memorandum from Janet Napolitano, Secretary, Department of Homeland Security, to David V Aguilar, Acting Commissioner, US Customs and Border Protection, et al (June 15, 2012) re Exercising Prosecutorial Discretion with Respect to Individuals Who Came to the United States as Children, online: www.dhs.gov/ xlibrary/assets/s1-exercising-prosecutorial-discretion-individuals-who-came-to-us -as-children.pdf.

Migration Observatory at the University of Oxford, online: www.migrationobservatory .ox.ac.uk/about-us.

Minister of Citizenship and Immigration Canada & Minister of Public Safety, *Ministerial Instruction regarding the Parent and Grandparent Super Visa* (November 30, 2011), online: www.cic.gc.ca/english/department/mi/super visa.asp.

NZ, *Hansard*, Questions To Ministers: Immigration, Illegal—Statistics and Costs (No 8) October 17, 2013 (Michael Woodhouse).

NZ, Department of Internal Affairs. "Citizenship Statistics," online: www.dia.govt.nz/ diawebsite.nsf/wpg_url/services-citizenship-citizenship-statistics.

NZ, Ministry of Business, Innovation and Employment, online: www.dol.govt.nz.

NZ, Ministry of Business, Innovation and Employment. "Migration Trends & Outlook 2008/09: Temporary Migration," online: www.dol.govt.nz/publications/research/ migration-outlook-200809/mto-0809-fig42-large.asp.

NZ, Ministry of Business, Innovation and Employment. "Migration Trends and Outlook 2010–2011: Migration Flows," online: www.dol.govt.nz/publications/rese arch/migration-trends-1011/data.asp?id=fig3-6.

NZ, Ministry of Business, Innovation and Employment. "Migration Trends and Outlook 2010–2011: Temporary Migration," online: www.dol.govt.nz/publica tions/research/migration-trends-1011/data.asp?id=fig4-7.

NZ, Statistics New Zealand. Infoshare, online: www.stats.govt.nz/infoshare/viewtable .aspx?pxid=9233b4d8-bc8b-429b-bf89-97b31cbde286.

OECD. *Migration*, "Foreign-Born Population," online: https://data.oecd.org/migra tion/foreign-born-population.htm.

OECD. StatExtracts. *International Migration Database*, online: stats.oecd.org.

ProCon.org, "Illegal Immigration around the World: 13 Countries Compared to the United States," online: immigration.procon.org/view.resource.php?resourceid=005235#germany.

Queen's University. *Multiculturalism Policy Index*, online: www.queensu.ca/mcp/index.html.

Ray, Julie and Neli Esipova. "World's Potential Migrants Are Often Young, Educated, Well-Off: But Most Likely to Be Underemployed" (July 5, 2011), online: www.gallup.com/poll/148376/world-potential-migrants-often-young-educated-off.aspx.

Suzuki, David. *The Global Eco-Crisis: Diversity, Resilience and Adaptability* (2014 Milton K Wong Lecture delivered at the University of British Columbia, May 14, 2014), online: www.alumni.ubc.ca/2014/events/2014-milton-k-wong-lecture/.

Thibos, Cameron and Sara Bonfanti. "Worldwide Protracted Refugee and IDP Populations" (December 10, 2014), online: Migration Policy Centre www.migrationpolicycentre.eu/worldwide-protracted-refugee-idp-populations/.

UK, Foreign and Commonwealth Office & Home Office, Forced Marriage Unit, online: www.gov.uk/forced-marriage.

UK, Foreign and Commonwealth Office & Home Office, Forced Marriage Unit. *The Right to Choose: Multi-agency Statutory Guidance for Dealing with Forced Marriage* (London: Cabinet Office, 2014) at 1, online: www.gov.uk/government/uploads/system/uploads/attachment_data/file/322310/hmg_statutory_guidance_publication_180614_final.pdf.

UK, Home Office. "Immigration Statistics: Removals and Voluntary Departures," online: data.gov.uk/dataset/immigration-statistics-removals.

UK, Office for National Statistics, online: www.ons.gov.uk.

UNDESA, Population Division. "High-Level Dialogue on International Migration and Development" (September 14–15, 2013), online: www.un.org/esa/population/migration/hld/.

UN General Assembly. "High-Level Meetings of the 68th Session of the General Assembly" (October 3–4, 2013), online: www.un.org/en/ga/68/meetings/migration/about.shtml.

UNHCR. *UNHCR Statistical Online Population Database*, online: www.unhcr.org/pages/4a013eb06.html.

UNHCR. "Syria Emergency: Operational Data Portal" (last updated May 7, 2015), online: data.unhcr.org/syrianrefugees/regional.php#_ga=1.12899249.745513563.1429299991".

UNHCR. *UNHCR Historical Refugee Data*, online: data.unhcr.org/dataviz/.

USAID, "Child, Early, and Forced Marriage: United States Government's Response" (Washington, DC: USAID, 2014), online: www.usaid.gov/news-information/fact-sheets/child-early-and-forced-marriage-usg-response.

US, Department of Homeland Security, online: www.dhs.gov.

US, Department of Homeland Security, ENFORCE Alien Removal Module (EARM), January 2014.

US, Department of Homeland Security, Enforcement Integrated Database (EID), November 2013.

US, Department of Homeland Security, US Citizenship and Immigration Services. "Data Set: Form N-400 Application for Naturalization," online: www.uscis.gov/ tools/reports-studies/immigration-forms-data/data-set-form-n-400-application-naturalization.

US, Department of Homeland Security, US Citizenship and Immigration Services. "Green Card Through the Diversity Immigrant Visa Program," online: www.uscis.gov/green-card/other-ways-get-green-card/green-card-through-diversity-immigration-visa-program/green-card-through-diversity-immigrant-visa-program.

Index

9/11 (terrorist attacks), 48, 63–4, 65, 67, 69–70, 72, 77, 79, 81, 92

Aas, Katja Franko, 188
Abu-Ghraib, 63
Algeria's National People's Assembly, 68
Almrei, Hassan. *See Charkaoui* case
American Civil War, 11
American War of Independence, 11, 23
anchor baby, 20
Anderson, Benedict, 14
Annan, Kofi, 194
anti-immigrant legislation, 209
Arab Spring, 160, 161, 162
Arar, Mahar, 65
Arendt, Hannah, 138
Asian immigration, 19
asylum
    and human rights, 23, 36, 45, 53, 54, 57
    Australia, 56
    Canada, 56
    extra-legal migration, 44–7, 50, 55, 118, 135, 137, 192
    illegal migration, 120, 126, 132, 134–6, 138, 140, 141, 184, 186, 189, 190
    Indochinese boat crisis, 56
    United States–Canada Safe Third Country Agreement, 44, 48
asylum crisis
    "bogus refugee," 49, 50, 56
    "queue jumper," 49, 50, 56
    Lampedusa, 4, 151, 159, 160–5, 172, 173, 211, 272, 273, 275
    Mare Nostrum, 163, 164, 165
    MV *Tampa*, 43
    Rio Grande, 4
    roots of, 39, 43
    Triton, 165, 169
asylum seekers, 39, 41–4, 45, 46, 47–52, 56, 157, 161, 163, 164, 174, 182, 193, 248

Balkan crisis, 57
Bauder, Harold, 26
Belmarsh case, 69–70, 71, 81
Bloemraad, Irene, 96
Bosworth, Mary, 188
Brennan, Justice Gerard (Australia), 24
British North America Act, 21
Bush administration, 182, 187

Cameron, Prime Minister David, 1, 96, 181
Charkaoui case, 70–1, 72
Charkaoui, Adil. *See Charkaoui* case
Charlie Hebdo attacks, 182
Charter of Rights and Freedoms (Canada), 71, 107, 108
Chinese Exclusion Act of 1882, 19
citizenship
    birthright, 20, 21, 103
    dual, 20, 104, 188
    European, 8, 151–4, 163, 166, 167
    jus sanguinis, 20, 105
    jus soli, 20, 105
    lack of test, New Zealand, 103, 107
    law, Canada, 103, 104
    law, New Zealand, 103
    lost Canadians, 104
    stripping, 104, 188, 211
    testing, 100–5
    testing, Australia, 101, 102

citizenship (cont.)
  testing, Canada, 101–2
  testing, Europe, 100–1, 176
  testing, United States, 102
Clinton administration, 182, 188
Cold War, 39, 55
colonization, 5, 11, 24, 150, 160
Convention Against Torture. *See* Torture
  Convention
Convention on the Rights of Persons with
  Disabilities, 191
Convention relating to the Status of Refugees.
  See Refugee Convention
crimmigration, 184, 186, 208–9
Crusades, 63, 64
cultural mosaic, 17, 80

Dano case, 153–4
decolonization, 5, 11, 23, 24, 91, 155
deportation, 45, 68, 69, 85, 127, 137, 147, 161,
  167, 168, 182, 184, 186, 187–9, 204, 208,
  256, 257
detention, 43, 44, 59, 67–9, 70, 71, 72, 73, 82, 121,
  161, 204, 208, 274
DREAM Act (US), 12, 136–7, 210
Dred Scott v. *Sandford*, 20
Dublin Convention, 48, 156, 157–8

economics, 8, 117–19, 121–2, 143, 180–1, 182,
  195–6, 202, 205–8, 212
ethnic enclaves, 124, 134–5, 138–41, 143
ethnic immigration, 26
ethnicity, 13, 94, 143
ethnoburb, 138–40, 148
EU Blue Card, 159
European Commission, 160, 161, 163, 164, 173,
  248, 272
European Convention on Human Rights, 21,
  22, 23, 69, 70, 71, 72, 157, 165
European Court of Human Rights, 52, 71,
  163, 167
European Court of Justice, 153, 154, 157, 158,
  163, 167, 204

Faster Removal of Foreign Criminals Act
  (Canada), 187
forced marriage, 62, 67, 73–9, 82, 121, 176, 204
  Australia, 74
  Canada, 74, 75, 102
  Europe, 73, 78
  Forced Marriage Unit (UK), 74, 77
  New Zealand, 74

United Kingdom, 74, 79
United States, 74, 76
Fourteenth Amendment, 20
Freeman, Gary, 120
Frontex, 44, 165

Gillard, Prime Minister Julia, 50, 96, 108
Global Commission on International
  Migration, 25, 194, 195, 211
globalization, 125–6, 134, 169, 178
green card lottery, 12
Guantanamo Bay, 36, 63, 67, 193
guestworker programs, 127, 155
guestworkers, 136

Hage, Ghassan, 92, 93
Harkat, Mohamed. *See Charkaoui* case
Harper, Prime Minister Stephen, 50, 108
Held, David, 12
High Court of Australia, 24, 43
Hollinger, David, 98
House of Lords (UK), 69, 70, 71
Howard, Prime Minister John, 101, 108
human rights, 52–5, 67, 70, 71, 72, 73, 75, 76,
  77–8, 79, 81, 82–3, 91, 94, 106, 107, 108, 117,
  119–22, 127, 128, 133, 137, 143, 153, 157–8,
  161, 163, 164, 169, 170, 186, 191, 192, 193, 195,
  196, 202–8, 212
Hunt, Alan, 93
Huntington, Samuel, 63

Imagined Communities, 14
immigrant identity, 13, 16, 17
immigrant nation. *See* nations of immigration
Immigrant Nations, 26
Immigration Act (UK), 155
Immigration and Refugee Board (Canada), 43
Immigration and Refugee Protection Act
  (Canada), 70, 185
Immigration Dialectic, 26
immigration mythology, 11, 19, 142, 202
immigration regulation, 5, 7, 18, 21, 27, 28, 36,
  62, 151, 152, 154, 162, 177, 178, 184, 185, 193
indigenous
  cultures, 91, 94
  First Nations, 14
  justice, 13
  land claims, 24
  peoples, 12, 13, 14, 95, 98
  populations, 11, 12, 17, 18, 24
  societies, 5
  unemployment, 130

International Convention for the
Protection of All Persons from
Enforced Disappearance,
191
International Convention on the Protection of
the Rights of All Migrant Workers and
Members of their Families, 23, 120, 191–2,
193, 203, 211
international law, 18, 21, 23, 29, 40, 52, 54,
156, 213
International Organization for Migration, 161
Islam, 63, 64, 66, 179, 203
headscarf controversy, 77, 81
unintelligibility, 62, 64, 73, 77, 79, 80, 81, 83,
98, 108, 121, 179, 203
Islamic Salvation Front, 68
Islamophobia, 57, 62, 63–4, 65–7, 73, 74, 78, 79,
98, 120, 121, 134, 179, 180, 190
and 9/11, 64
and forced marriage, 74
and immigration policy, 66
history of, 63

Jacobson, David, 120, 153
Joppke, Christian, 26, 101, 120
jus cogens, 54

Kenney, Minister Jason, 50, 97, 181
Kymlicka, Will, 92, 96

Lamer, Chief Justice Antonio (Canada), 24
League of Nations, 18
Li, Wei, 138, 139, 140

Maastricht Treaty, 152
Mabo case, 24
Magna Carta, 189, 208
Making People Illegal, 46
Malmström, Cecilia, 164
Maori, 11, 98
Marois, Pauline, 96
Marsden, Sarah, 133
Marshall, T.H., 153
melting pot, 17, 80
Merkel, Chancellor Angela, 1, 96, 181
Migrant Workers Convention. *See*
International Convention on the
Protection of the Rights of All
Migrant Workers and Members of their
Families
Migration Act (Australia), 185

migration patterns
chain, 124
circular, 26, 43, 117, 124
cyclical, 124
Modi, Prime Minister Narendra, 1
Modood, Tariq, 92, 93, 96, 99, 108, 109
Mountz, Alison, 160, 165
multiculturalism, 17, 36, 78, 83, 90–109, 142,
165, 196, 212
and asylum crisis, 91
and fear of Islamic fundamentalism, 91
and Islamophobia, 99, 108, 139
demise of, 7, 9, 35–6, 47, 51, 57, 90–2, 93,
99–100, 105–9, 121, 124, 134, 139, 177, 180,
184, 203

Nansen Initiative, 210
nation building, 11, 16, 18, 19, 20, 21, 23, 26, 51,
57, 83, 90, 99, 105, 106, 109, 119, 122, 125,
132, 133, 138, 139, 141, 142, 175, 177, 182, 198,
207
national identity, 11, 12, 14, 15, 17, 24, 57, 67, 98,
100, 103, 106, 168, 170, 175, 183, 194, 206
nations of immigration, 5, 13, 20, 28, 99, 125,
150, 151, 156, 165, 174, 176
Naz, Rushkana, 73
New World, 8, 9, 11, 13, 15, 16, 27, 55, 80, 96, 103,
108, 141, 144, 154, 178
No One Is Illegal movement, 135
non-refoulement, 21, 22, 54
North American Free Trade Agreement
(NAFTA), 134

Obama administration, 137, 181, 182, 187
Obama, President Barack, 1, 50
Office of the United Nations High
Commissioner for Human Rights
(OHCHR), 191
Old Country, 13, 17, 77, 91, 142
Old World, 8, 9, 13, 20, 27, 55, 78, 80, 82, 96, 99,
100, 103, 105, 107, 108, 109, 125, 135, 176,
178, 204

Pearson, David, 26
permanent residency, 22, 36, 106, 127, 153, 159,
176, 177
permanent resident admissions, 130
permanent residents, 71, 74, 106, 176,
187, 189
Peters, Winston, 182
Pickus, Noah, 102

points system, 19, 141, 155, 165, 174, 175
population displacement, 39, 57
Purvis, Trevor, 93

Quebec Charter of Values, 81

race-based immigration restrictions, 19, 132
refugee law
    1967 Protocol, 21, 40, 41
    and human rights law, 52–5
    constraints on state sovereignty, 52
    human rights core, 53, 54, 56, 203
    intersection with human rights law, 53
    Refugee Convention, 22, 39–41, 44, 46–7, 52, 53, 54, 55, 69, 71, 144, 156, 157
refugees. *See also* asylum
    "bogus refugee," 49, 50, 56
    "queue-jumper," 49, 50, 56
    climate refugees, 210
    Syrian, 56
Roma, 158
Rudd, Prime Minister Kevin, 50, 182
Ruddock, Minister Phillip, 14, 181
rule of law, 6, 7, 54, 55, 184, 189, 192

Sassen, Saskia, 120, 153
Saunders, Doug, 80
Schengen
    accord, 151, 167
    principles, 163
Schlesinger, Arthur, 92, 96
Second World War. *See* World War II
securitization, 7, 120, 179, 181, 182, 183
September 11. *See* 9/11 (terrorist attacks)
Sheffer, Paul, 26
Stasiulis, Davia, 26
Statute of Westminster, 23
Stumpf, Juliet, 186
Supreme Court of Canada, 70, 71, 72, 108, 208, 209
Supreme Court of New Zealand, 68, 69, 71
Suzuki, Dr. David, 95, 97, 109
Syria, 56, 65, 162

Tahirih Justice Center, 74
Takaki, Ronald, 96
Tampere Agreement, 167
temporary foreign workers, 127–34, 144, 154, 186, 212
terra nullius, 18
The Clash of Civilizations and the Remaking of World Order, 63
The Myth of the Muslim Tide, 80
Torture Convention, 22, 69
Treaty of Amsterdam, 159
Treaty on the Functioning of the European Union, 156
Turnbull, Prime Minister Malcolm, 1

United Nations, 53, 194
United Nations Department of Economic and Social Affairs (UN DESA), 25
United Nations High Commissioner for Refugees (UNHCR), 41, 44, 46, 48, 49
United Nations High-Level Dialogues on Migration and Development, 195
United Nations Human Rights Committee, 54
United Nations Torture Committee, 54
Universal Declaration of Human Rights, 73

Vietnam draft, 55

War on Terror, 63, 67
Western liberal democracies, 2, 4, 6, 8, 53, 56, 66, 67, 78, 92, 100, 105, 108, 125, 150, 167, 174, 177, 179, 181, 182, 184, 189, 190
World War I, 23
World War II, 16, 19, 36, 39, 40, 52, 91, 160

Yuval-Davis, Nira, 26

Zaoui case, 68–9, 71
Zaoui, Ahmed. *See Zaoui* case
Zero Tolerance for Barbaric Cultural Practices Act (Canada), 74